1,000 HATS

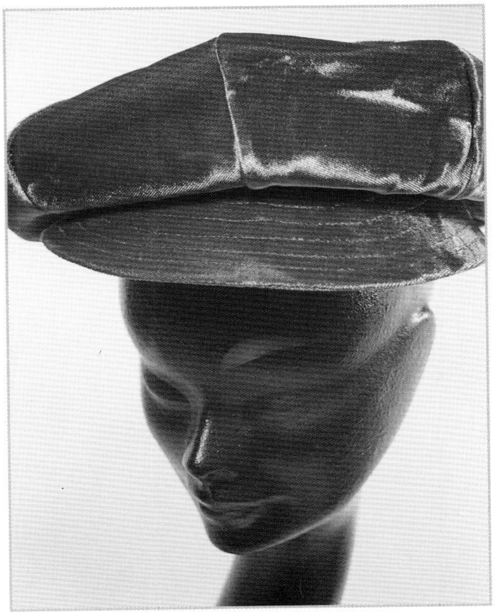

Text and photographs by Norma Shephard

Schiffer Publishing Ltd ®
4880 Lower Valley Road, Atglen, PA 19310 USA

Dedication

To my mother
who placed the purchase of a good hat
above many other considerations...
and rightly so!

Library of Congress Control Number: 2005937055

Designed by "Sue"
Type set in Zapf Chancery Bd BT/Zurich BT

ISBN: 0-7643-2403-9
Printed in China
1 2 3 4

Published by Schiffer Publishing Ltd.
4880 Lower Valley Road
Atglen, PA 19310
Phone: (610) 593-1777; Fax: (610) 593-2002
E-mail: Info@schifferbooks.com

For the largest selection of fine reference books on this and related subjects, please visit our web site at
www.schifferbooks.com
We are always looking for people to write books on new and related subjects. If you have an idea for a book please contact us at the above address.

This book may be purchased from the publisher.
Include $3.95 for shipping.
Please try your bookstore first.
You may write for a free catalog.

In Europe, Schiffer books are distributed by
Bushwood Books
6 Marksbury Ave.
Kew Gardens
Surrey TW9 4JF England
Phone: 44 (0) 20 8392-8585; Fax: 44 (0) 20 8392-9876
E-mail: info@bushwoodbooks.co.uk
Free postage in the U.K., Europe; air mail at cost.

Contents

Foreword by Patricia Boyle 4
Prologue: Where Did You Get That Hat? 5
Introduction: The Allure of Hats 6
Chapter I. Millinery Retrospective: 1790 - 1837 21
Chapter II. Victoriana: 1837 - 1901 30
Chapter III. Edwardian Grandeur: 1901 - 1920 54
Chapter IV. Flapper Fantasies: 1920 - 1930 77
Chapter V. Dignified Beauty: 1930 - 1940 86
Chapter VI. War and Postwar Ingenuity: 1940 - 1950 104
Chapter VII. Socialites, Church Ladies, and Debutantes: 1950 - 1960 125
Chapter VIII. The End of an Age: 1960 - 1970 142
Chapter IX. The Demise of Millinery: 1970 - 1980 171
Chapter X. The Return of Millinery: 1980 and Beyond 174
Chapter XI. The Sketch Pad 179
Chapter XII. Special Collections 183
- Aline Banting Collection 183
- Ascot Hats 212
- Christmas Hats 215
- Daisies 218
- Feathered Hats 220
- Furs, Hides, and Imitations 223
- Nursing Caps 235
- Philip Warde Collection 235
- Red Hats 245
- Wedding Hats 247

Acknowledgments 255
Bibliography 255
Index 256

Foreword

By Patricia Boyle, author of *The Hat Lady* (Volumes Publishing)

"Mothers told their daughters when the hats had been in style, men pointed out the ones their mothers and wives had sported, and the fingers of the women who had originally worn the pieces, inched shakily toward them, remembering."

— *Jenna Gibb, Museum clerk*

It is a pleasure for me to write the foreword to Norma Shephard's third book, *1,000 Hats*. In this volume, Canada's celebrity curator shares favorites from the more than 2,500 chapeaux in her museum, placing them in social and historical context.

Many of these treasures reveal labels from famous designers, some personally crafted in their own ateliers. Some have been created at pioneer kitchen tables, others in North American or European factories, still others are custom couture. Each was originally fashioned as an item of personal apparel and adornment, has graced the head of one or more women, and is now lovingly cared for in the *Mobile Millinery Museum* archives.

The *Mobile Millinery Museum* has intrigued me since its inception, in 1999, when Norma Shephard conceived the idea of taking portions of a major costume collection into the community, to present retrospective fashion shows and exhibits. I have watched audiences respond to, not only the collection, but also the dedication and joy of the museum's director, with excitement, curiosity, and delight.

Some months ago I began assisting Norma with her appearances in order to gather "behind the scenes" research for my biography of this interesting woman. What a time we have had, travelling from city to town, presenting in large halls, small dining rooms, air-conditioned facilities, hot, stuffy rooms, and one where the wonderful smell of farm animals mixed with the aroma of fresh coffee. Hat fanciers, collectors, retirees, long-term care residents, church members, and Red Hatters, lots of them, came and laughed and nodded and remembered and admired. Cameras flashed, hands applauded the models, questions flew from the floor, and Norma picked up many new anecdotes and jokes to share at future shows.

Organizers appreciate Shephard's unique approach to fashion history as well. Jennifer Dunkerson, Curator/Manager of the *Fieldcote Museum* in Ancaster, Ontario, sent her a thank you note that stated, "Your efforts in compiling such a large collection of hats is exemplary, for those of us in museum work, and your desire to share it with others, through programs like yours, is a great way to make material history fun."

In this, her latest book, Norma Shephard's love and passion for hats are obvious in each photograph and description. May your imagination take flight as you read and examine the pages of a historical journey down this millinery memory lane.

Prologue
Where Did You Get That Hat?

"The way you wear your hat, the way you sip your tea, the memory of all that, no, they can't take that away from me."

-- *Robbie Williams, singer/songwriter*

By its label, one would expect this charming felt topper to serve green tea. Reminiscent of Schiaparelli's shoe hat, this technically difficult, teapot hat was designed and created by theatrical milliner Nancy Hooper. *Private Collection*. $400-450.

I have never met a hat I didn't like. In fact, hats have always been a comforting part of my life. As a child in the fifties, I studied them at church. From an early age, standing on my seat at the front of the sanctuary, arms resting on the back of the pew, I faced the congregation during Sunday services. I memorized each feather, floral, or fur confection that entered the room. Some appeared only once, others were steady favorites, but most changed with the seasons.

I studied those beautiful hats in much the way I examine them now. How they did or didn't suit each face. The features they concealed or emphasized. I considered the colours and fabrication, the selection and placement of each trim. I drank them in and hurried to grow up so that I too could buy and wear such elegant chapeaux.

At home, when our black Persian wouldn't answer to "Kitty, Kitty," I would head for my parent's bedroom. There on a shelf in the closet, I'd have only to lift the lid on the big square box that housed my mother's brown velvet widebrim and, sure enough, I'd find a sleeping Tinkerbell, crushing the crown of that beautiful hat with his soft, warm body.

My mother purchased the hat on a vacation trip to Quebec City and despite a loaded car – the five of us plus a dog, the cat, and luggage – she had to have it. That summer, I rode home in the back of our Studebaker, with Mom's extravagant purchase on my lap.

When I was old enough for fashion hats myself, there was no such thing as a quick trip to the mall. I would linger in the millinery departments of *Eaton's*, *Simpson's*, and *Morgan's* department stores, trying on every confection that suited my fancy. I loved them all. People said that I had a "hat head" and sometimes even strangers stopped to admire me in the millinery temptations that I could not afford.

When I was sixteen, my husband proposed to me. He advised me to "keep it under my hat" until we were old enough to properly announce our engagement. By the time I married in 1973, hats were out of fashion. A few unisex, felt fedoras might be seen and the occasional poorboy cap left over from the sixties, but fur was a dirty word and florals were reserved for eccentric old ladies. Even my chosen profession betrayed me. When I entered the RN program at *Vanier College* in Montreal, I discovered, to my horror, that nurses had abandoned their caps. I was out of step with the culture.

In the eighties, I discovered a spirited millinery boutique on a business trip to Seattle, where I spent a good two hours trying on hats and snapping pictures. The owner, who admitted to having worn many of the pieces herself, did not seem to mind.

The nineties were different. As the decade ran out, a crazy old hat changed my life. It called to me from a thrift store bin and I had to have it. I refer to it as my green straw monstrosity and finding it unleashed a passion that eventually developed into the establishment of the *Mobile Millinery Museum*, a unique costume archive that travels to a wide range of community groups — museums, libraries, historical societies, schools, conventions, hospitals, retirement homes, churches, etc. — to teach, entertain, and assist with charitable fundraising.

Hat lovers from across Canada have begun donating their own treasured favourites to the cause. The museum now receives contributions from the United States and France. Many of the hats sent through the mail, or dropped on my doorstep, remind me of my first loves, the ones I enjoyed so much in church in the 1950s. Others, like Victorian bonnets and Edwardian finery, handed down from original owners, carry with them stories of another time. Tales like the ones my grandmother and great aunt told me about growing up in the 1890s and coming of age during la Belle Époque.

Auntie Ella had a room where she kept cherished keepsakes from that era. No living person was permitted to enter the cloister but her. A sort of magician's hat, it gave up its secrets, one at a time. Often, Auntie Ella would slip through the door, which did not fully open, and extract an unexpected treasure, to punctuate one of her stories, or serve as raw material for a sewing project we would share. The seen and unseen contents of that room sparked imaginings of Edwardian grandeur, mostly hats, and remain in my mind's eye to this day.

This green straw harlequin is secured when tilting forward by means of an elastic chignon strap. *Mobile Millinery Museum*. $200-250.

Introduction
The Allure of Hats
When a Hat is "All That"

Six little angels in identical "hats".

"Halos are just great big electric hats."

— *Nancy Hooper, theatrical milliner*

"A hat may have attitude but it holds no opinions."

— *Marie Minaker, Archivist*

"Her hat looked like a ship in full sail."

— *guest book comment referencing a hat worn by the author*

"A hat like that I could wear, but a sensible one would look terrible."

— Co*mment heard at a millinery fashion show, in reference to a hat worn by the author.*

Hats possess power. They enjoy the ability to shape the mood of the wearer and to influence the disposition of the viewer. A hat will speak to the beholder on a subconscious level, inviting us to make judgments about the individual togged up under it. These judgements – that one is snooty, sophisticated, wealthy, impoverished, intelligent, or simply *au courant* with the latest fashion — might be accurate or incorrect but they will be held until new information is given to replace them.

"I fell in love with a hat once, that was quite extravagant – in price as well as design – but I saved the money and purchased the hat, then wore it to church. A woman remarked, 'I really admire your hat.' I felt great until she added, 'Furthermore, I admire your courage to wear it.'"

— *Anonymous*

Hats and hat accessories (ribbons, feathers, and pins) have been used historically to identify professional and social status as well as to confer rank. During the Middle Ages, for example, licensed court jesters were recognized by a coxcomb, or strip of notched red fabric, worn in their caps. At times, even the absence of a hat has had the authority to grant or deny status. During the decline of millinery (1970 – 2000) women risked being thought of as eccentric if they dared wear hats in certain circles. Many hat fanciers, unable to resist the urge to purchase a beautiful headpiece, admit to having kept their treasures in the closet, unwilling to risk wearing them.

Hat Hunters

"She wore a raspberry beret, the kind you find in a second hand store."

— *Prince, singer/songwriter*

A pair of contemporary hats and their boxes. *Private Collection*.

Hat collecting is not new. The Emperor Charlemagne is said to have been so fond of berets that he collected over five hundred of them as a hobby. Hat collecting has become such a popular pastime in the last few years that the serious enthusiast will find considerable competition for the best pieces. Even children, recognizing the great dress-up potential of a beautifully designed hat, are getting into the act. I encounter young buyers regularly at thrift stores and flea markets.

Antique hats are unique treasures in the world of collecting in that they are intimately tied to social history, being fashioned and worn according to such variables as season, time of day, activity, social status, age, etc., and reflect up to the minute style changes, often based upon historical events. They can stand alone as beautiful, sculptural objects or be appreciated for the secrets they tell about the people who wore them and the times they reflect. It is easy to imagine how an original owner may have felt in her new chapeau and fun to speculate about where the hat might have taken her.

Antique hats are now available through estate sales, auctions, internet sites, antique stores, and charity shops. This was not always the case. As recently as a decade ago, antique dealers discarded many lovely vintage hats as they could find a market for their boxes and trims only. Many report that they harvested the feathers from old hats for resale to fly fishermen. Even mainstream museums turned away lovingly preserved antique hats, leaving theatre groups to benefit from donations.

Authenticating a Vintage Hat

When shopping for vintage millinery, a savvy collector will be able to distinguish between an authentic period piece and a reproduction. An original Victorian or Edwardian hat, though lavishly trimmed, for example, will possess an intangible air of softness. Reproductions on the other hand are often harsh and overdone – they are all that and more! Reproductions may also feel stiff, revealing no signs of having been previously worn. Well-loved hats of the 1950s and '60s may show traces of make-up on the inner band or appear new, having been purchased for a special occasion and worn only once.

Tangible clues to a hat's origins are to be found in the method of construction. Traces of glue are clues to late and careless, or factory, manufacture. Look for trims that are applied without tension if you desire a handmade "salon" hat, as trimmers were taught to employ a single, secure-but-slack stitch when adorning a hat with roses or other flowers. Stitching, unless decorative, should be visible only on the inside, if at all.

Assess the material content of fabric hats and crown linings. Early hats will betray their natural fibre content. But do not dismiss a fine hat if it seems anachronistic. Many hats have been altered over the years with updated trimmings and modifications.

Study labels and original price tags if fortunate enough to find them intact. Many old hats are preserved in their original box with bill of sale included. This information is particularly important if you are documenting your collection or plan to resell your millinery possessions.

Relying upon style alone to authenticate a hat can lead to mistakes in dating as through the years many styles have been revived or adapted to the current mode. Authentic looking pieces may also have been created for the theatre to mimic costume from an earlier period. Individuals who have found a particular style flattering may have worn variations of it for decades. As well, designers often hold a preference for the lines or feel of a certain fashion era. Consequently, elements of the favored period will appear in their work no matter what the current style. This is well evidenced in the work of Toronto's Philip Warde who created chapeaux reminiscent of the Belle Époque, well into the 1960s and beyond.

Late 1940s, feathered wide brim with flat, pink, velvet crown. Label: Flo-Raye. *Mobile Millinery Museum*. $250-300.

Price Guide

The price of a vintage hat varies widely and does not always reflect its historic importance. For the purposes of this book, hats shown are appraised according to their condition, workmanship, style, rarity, fabrication, wearability, designer, and provenance (if known). Added value is assigned to those pieces associated with extinct species of wildlife or trimmed with uncommon or exceptional pins, buttons, ribbons, or jewels. It is assumed that prices given apply to purchases made at the highest retail level and reflect the current marketplace.

Theatrical Millinery

"The hat is the last item of costume an actor dons before stepping on stage. The placement of the hat on the head, the adjustment, that last look in the mirror – that is the defining moment."

— *Nancy Hooper, Theatrical Milliner*

In theater, hats are used to instantly profile personality, conferring upon actors historical placement, professional ability, character traits, and eccentricities. Theatrical milliner Nancy Hooper explains that her role is to create a hat that pushes the character a little further. Costume and makeup begin the transformation but the hat is the final preparation for stepping into a borrowed persona.

Nowhere is this better illustrated than in *Harry Potter and the Philosopher's Stone* in which the Sorting Hat becomes an actual character, able to think, speak, and determine the residency of the students, thereby playing a role in their ultimate destiny.

This sequined feather headdress is the topper to a red taffeta, showgirl's costume. *Mobile Millinery Museum*. $250-300.

These reproduction bonnets are two of seven made in 1999 for the production of *Emily the Musical* at Charlottetown's Confederation Centre for the Arts. The brims are shaped of finely woven, willow wood. Theatrical milliner Nancy Hooper remembers crafting the hats to disguise the women's faces, designing the hats to give "the characters the feeling of vultures or crows."

Black feather aigrette designed to be worn in the hair. *Mobile Millinery Museum*. $50-60.

For an understanding of theatrical millinery magic, consider the witch's hat in its various incarnations. The black, shiny, spiky piece worn by the Wicked Witch of the West in the *Wizard of Oz* is in distinct contrast to those fashioned by Lindy Hemming for the Minerva character in *Harry Potter and the Chamber of Secrets*. With their textured fabrics, folds, softened peaks, and feather adornments, the chapeaux worn by Professor McGonigall, while still suggestive of a witch, are relaxed, collegiate, and alluring.

An assortment of feathers to be worn in the hair or on a hat. *Mobile Millinery Museum.* $25-50 each.

A Glossary of Styles and Millinery Terms

"The ugly bonnet had served well to keep her complexion fair; its indoors pallor had now a faint flush in it."

— from The Day of Their Wedding, by William Dean Howells, 1895

"As to Dolly, there she was again, the very pink and pattern of good looks, in a smart little cherry-coloured mantle, with a hood of the same drawn over her head, and upon the top of that hood, a little straw hat trimmed with cherry-coloured ribbons, and worn the merest trifle on one side - just enough in short to make it the wickedest and most provoking head-dress that ever a malicious milliner devised."

— from Barnaby Rudge, by Charles Dickens, 1841

Many styles (turban, pillbox, boater, cartwheel, etc.) are recognized as classics, reinterpreted over the decades and centuries with slight alterations and innovations. Others are of a time only – short-lived fads or trends. Some fashions carry several names, as milliners of the same period may have chosen to associate their design with a particular person, article, or trend.

Aigrette: A tuft of feathers or a spray of gems, worn on the head. Originally the term referred to feathers taken from the Egret.
Alpine: A soft, peaked cap with turned up brim.
Alsatian Bows: Large bows placed in the front of a hat, popular following the loss of Alsace Lorraine in the Franco-Prussian war, c.1870.

A frog-green felt, c.1870, greets the world with a double Alsatian bow in green and cream ribbon. Label: Lady Fashion. *Mobile Millinery Museum*. $200-250.

Apple Pie Hat: A narrowly brimmed, shallow-crowned hat, resembling its namesake.

Astrakhan: Soft, fur-like wool, from young or stillborn Astrakhan lambs.

Bandanna: Although the word bandanna can be traced to 1782 when it referred to a tie-dyed, silk handkerchief, it is more commonly associated with nineteenth century American cowboys who tied these printed, cotton squares around their brow to absorb perspiration. The bandanna, which is tie-dyed in one color, leaving white or yellow spots, was adopted by gangs in the late twentieth century and referred to as "colors" to denote club membership.

Bandeau: A narrow headdress, worn about the forehead or the crown.

Bangkok: Woven palm leaf, used in the construction of hats.

Baseball Cap: Also referred to as a "trucker's cap", this icon of the twentieth century is comprised of a sectioned cap of cotton or wool and a long, stiffened visor. It is sometimes fitted with a plastic or Velcro strap at the back of the crown to adjust for fit. The style, which originated as a functional head covering for baseball players, was favored by sports fans in the 1920s, blue-collar workers in the 1950s, college students in the '60s, and movie directors in the 1980s. The hat has been adopted by women, who can opt to pull long hair through the gap between the cap and adjuster strap at the back, and is a favorite of commercial advertisers who use it to sell products by displaying company logos on the crown.

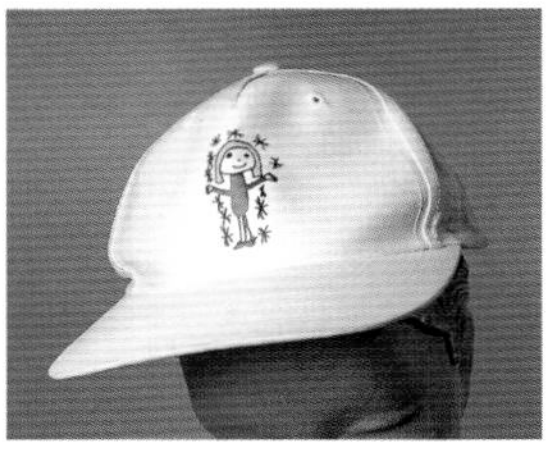

A souvenir baseball cap exhibits the logo from the musical *Aah-Pootee! That's Snow!* Label: 100% cotton. *Private Collection*. $40-80.

For certain gang members, the baseball cap represents a symbolic language, pertaining to the various angles at which it is worn. This is akin to the body language of the Victorian ladies fan.

Bavolet: A drape of fabric, often in lieu of a brim, which depends from the back of the crown to shade the neck.

Beach hat: A shade hat, popularized in the mid-twentieth century; a casual, widebrimmed hat, usually constructed of straw.

Beanie: A skullcap, made in four, six, or eight segments; historically one of the most basic head coverings.

Beaver: A word used since 1528 to describe a hat made of beaver fur, beaver felt, or an imitation.

A visored beanie in four segments proudly displays the colors of *Queen's University*, Kingston, Ontario. *Courtesy of Art Minaker*. $120-150.

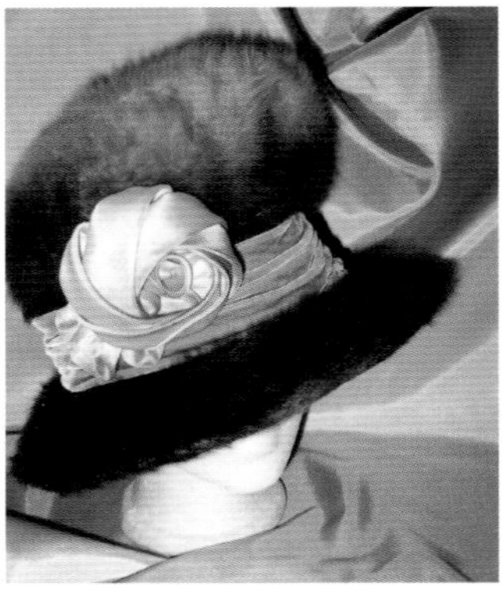

A stunning winter confection of shaded beaverette is bound with apricot velvet and finished with an exquisitely shaped, green silk rose. Label: Custom Made by Gotham, 175 King E., Hamilton. *Mobile Millinery Museum*. $450-500.

Beaverette: Plush felt of beaver or imitation.

Benjy: Slang for a widebrim, straw hat.

Beret: A flat, round cap first worn by the ancient Greeks. Roman women c.500 also favored a bejewelled version of the beret. More recently, the style was associated with the French, when it was adopted by Renaissance artists. This cap, usually fashioned of wool or felt, can be worn at several angles. In its basic form, the beret is a unisex style, adopted over the years by artists, Olympic teams, and the military.

A dressy beret of fuzzy, turquoise, mohair announces its arrival with a grosgrain cockade. Label: Jacoll, Made in England. *Mobile Millinery Museum*. $60-80.

Bergère: A flat, straw, summer hat adorned with ribbons and flowers.

Beretta: Draped beret.

Berretino: Name given to a cardinal's scull cap.

Bicorne: A hat with brim folded upwards in front and at back to give the appearance of having two corners.

Early twentieth century hat block of milliner Alma Hawke Nichols of Owen Sound, Ontario, who began her millinery apprenticeship at the age of 14. Nichols settled in Toronto in 1920 where she worked making hats for Joseph Milton. *Mobile Millinery Museum*. $200-250.

Bigeminal: Feathers, flowers, or other millinery trim arranged in pairs.

Biggin: A seventeenth century cap worn by children and revived in the 1940s to resemble a snood.

Biggonet: A knitted cap with ear flaps and chin ties.

Bird Cage: A stiffened, dome-shaped veil that encases the face.

Block: A wooden form used to shape felt, straw, and buckram hat frames.

Blue Bonnet: This derivative of the beret, also known as the Scotch Bonnet, was traditionally woven of blue wool. The addition of a ribbon cockade or feathers signified the wearer's position within his clan. For example, a feather trio traditionally graced the bonnet of a Scottish clan chieftain.

Boater: A hard straw hat with flat crown and brim, originally worn by men. When adopted by women in the late 1800s, the hat was trimmed with ribbons, bows, and/or flowers.

Bobby Dazzler: An elaborately trimmed hat, which epitomized the Edwardian effort to achieve distinction through one's headwear. A walking hat, the style sometimes weighed as much as five pounds.

Bodkin: A long, blunt pin or decorative lancet used by women to fasten the hair; first used c.1580.

Bonnet: Although this term referred to a head-dress for men and boys until the late eighteenth century, the word was used to describe a brimless, out-of-doors, woman's head covering as early as 1499.

Bonnet Board: A heavy, cardboard substance, patterned by machine, which was used in the construction of a bonnet.

Boudoir Cap: A nineteenth century, indoor cap that takes its name from the room where a lady would retire to be alone or to receive intimate friends. Also known as the lingerie cap.

Bourrelet: Originally a twisted, scarf-like turban, this close fitting, fabric hat with round, padded brim was popular in the 1940s.

Bow: A hair or hat adornment of looped ribbon, lace, straw, felt, fabric, or leather. Decorative hat bows are a respectful nod to tradition as the earliest hats were nothing more than a leather thong, tied in a bowknot and tightened about the forehead.

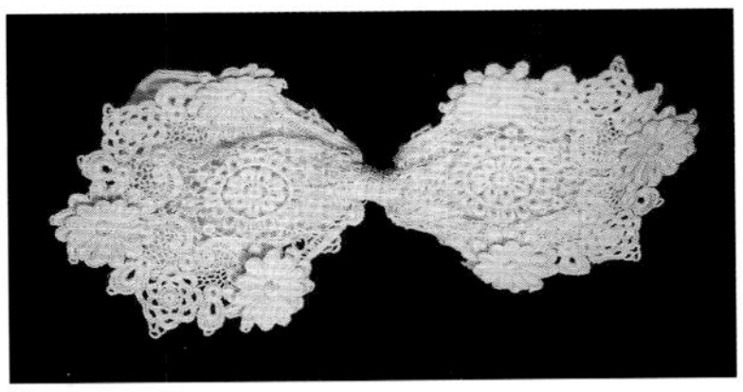

Lace bow-knot, c.1900. *Mobile Millinery Museum*. $125-150.

These Edwardian-era sisters pose for the camera in hairdos adorned with matching bow-knots.

A length of metallic braid is tied in a bow-knot to adorn a 1960s, tan-colored felt. *Mobile Millinery Museum*. $120-150.

Bowler: Named for the nineteenth century, London hat manufacturer, William Bowler, this gentleman's low-crowned, narrow-brimmed hat of stiff felt, has often been imitated by milliners for ladies wear.

Breton: This round, flat-crowned hat with a one-to-three-inch rolled brim originated centuries ago in Normandy. It is usually of felt or straw and banded with ribbon.

Male model Arthur Hillyer tops a pin stripe suit with a fashionable felt bowler, c. 1910. *Photo by Underwood and Underwood, Montreal. Hillyer Collection, Mobile Millinery Museum.*

Brezhnev: A Russian hat, usually of fur, also known as a papakha. This envelope style hat may be brimless or made with a brim, which folds back upon itself. The style was popularized in America in the 1960s after Leonoid Brezhnev presented President Johnson with one.

Brimmer: A broad brimmed hat.

Bucket Hat: Usually of canvas or soft fabric, this sport hat has a down-turned brim, which follows the lines of the crown.

Buckram: A coarse fabric, stiffened with gum or paste.

Bumper: Having a tubular brim.

Bunch: A grouping of floral, fruit, or foliage sprays, artistically arranged to trim a hat.

Vinyl bucket hat, purchased new in 2005 for $12.99. *Private Collection*.

A bunch of cloth-stemmed posies rest on velvet leaves as if recently picked from the garden. *Mobile Millinery Museum*. $50-75.

Busby: Usually of fabric or fur, this tall hat narrows at the center crown, like a pastry bag, to hang over the right side.

Button: Now mostly decorative, a button, placed at the top of a hat, originally served as a fastener for earflaps.

Cadogan bows: Ribbon bows worn at the back of the head, c.1870 - 1880.

Calash: A collapsible silk bonnet invented by the Duchess of Bedford in 1765. The fabric was supported by a series of hoops, made from reeds or whalebone, which formed accordion pleats. The device was also called a "bashful bonnet".

A pearl bead, set atop a tower of crystals, forms a decorative button for this coal black, woven straw. *Mobile Millinery Museum*. $225.

Calot: A sectional beanie.

Canotier: A sailor or boater.

Capulet: A Juliet cap with a cuff or split brim, named for the Shakespearian heroine, Juliet Capulet.

Cartwheel: A shallow-crowned, flat hat with a large, round, stiff brim. When seen from above, the hat resembles a wagon wheel.

Cap: A brimless headdress with many incarnations.

Canadian Air Force Cap of blue serge, lined with navy felt. Label: Principal Cap & Sportswear 1951, Montreal, Canada. A second label identifies the owner as Nagloren, C.M., 42710 – W. *Courtesy of Marie Minaker*.

Wren cap (Women's Royal Naval Service). *Courtesy of Kathryn Crowder.*

Mennonite prayer cap of white muslin. These were traditionally worn with black ribbon ties until a woman was married. *Private collection.*

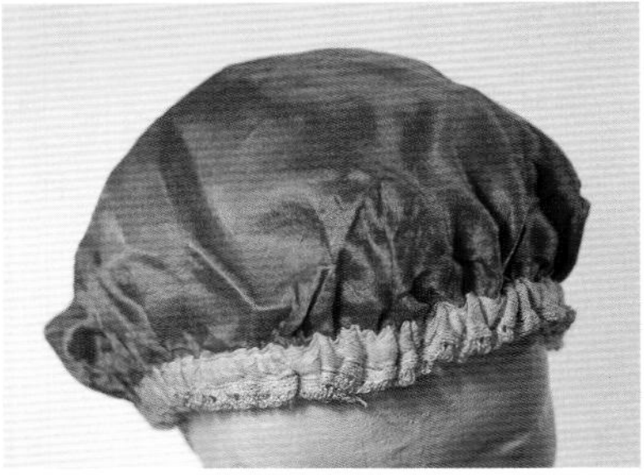

Dust cap of copper colored silk, edged in ecru lace. *Mobile Millinery Museum.* $125.

Postcard, c.1906, of a nineteenth century Blommer painting, in which a woman wears an informal indoor cap.

Capeline: A term used by milliners in the 1920s to describe a slope-brimmed hat with a skullcap crown. The term formerly referred to a loose-textured, woollen hood, worn by ladies, c.1868.

This satin-lined, black velvet, capeline is typical of styles from the 1920s. A green celluloid and bead hatpin secures a seventeen-inch plume. Lucy Maud Montgomery, author of *Anne of Green Gables*, wore a similarly shaped hat when she was presented to the Prince of Wales in 1927. *Mobile Millinery Museum.* $250-300.

Capote: A term used in 1812 to describe a woman's shaggy cloak or mantle and later (1880) assigned to a stiff brimmed bonnet, cut away in back.

Cartwheel: A shallow crowned, flat brimmed hat.

Casque: This style, resembling a helmet, takes many forms.

Casquette: A brimless, visored cap.

Cavalier: A high crowned, plumed hat with upturned brim.

Chapeaux bras: A small, folded hat carried under the arm by diplomats and naval officers. Canadian parliament opens each year with the arrival of the *Gentleman Usher of the Black Rod*. Dressed in black, this representative of the Governor General carries a folded bicorn, or chapeau bras, under his left arm.

Charlotte Corday: A mobcap with rosette and tricolor ribbon band, named for the famous French assassin.

Checkerboard Veiling: Medium gauge silk or rayon veiling with sporadically reinforced intersection points; traditionally available in 6-inch widths.

Chef's Hat: A proper chef's hat is a white tower constructed of 100 pleats, traditionally believed to denote the number of ways a master chef is able to prepare eggs.

Chicken Coop Veiling: Heavy gauge, square-patterned veiling, waxed at times; traditionally available in 12-inch widths.

Chignon Strap: A band attached to the back of the hat and slung beneath the hair. This device was used in the 1870s to hold a hat in place. Designers of the 1930s and '40s also employed this apparatus.

Chimney pot: An early, nineteenth century, gentleman's high hat, similar to a top hat, but brimless.

Chou: A millinery trim resembling a cabbage rose.

A millinery chou leans against a hat box, ready to adorn a hat. *Mobile Millinery Museum.* $30-40.

Chouquette: A hat of crocheted straw.

Cloche: A crown hugging, soft hat popularized in the 1920s to complement bobbed hair. The *Canadian Museum of Civilization* houses a fine collection of these, purchased from the unsold stock of over 500 hats created by a single milliner, Miss Katharine Newton.

A striking panama straw cloche of crisp white straw is banded cleanly with midnight blue grosgrain. A ribbon sleeve at the center back allows for the addition of trim. Label: Frank Olive for Bonwit Teller. *Mobile Millinery Museum.* $160-180.

Close Hat: A crown-hugging hat, often with small brim, popular in the 1950s. This style is now referred to as a Lucy hat for Lucille Ball's famous "I Love Lucy" character.

Cluster: A bouquet-like arrangement of millinery flowers.

Cockade: Usually refers to a disc of ribbon, which has been folded flat against itself, accordion fashion, then pressed flat. The term previously referred to any ribbon, knot of ribbons, or rosette worn on a gentleman's hat as a badge of office. In the eighteenth century any hat worn tilted to the side was referred to as a cockade.
Coif: A brimless cap that hugs the crown of the head. In Tudor and Elizabethan times this was made of elaborately embroidered, soft fabrics. Children wore the style in the eighteenth century as a protective head covering.
Coonskin: A winter hat of racoon skin with hanging tail.
Copatain: A hat with a high, pointed crown, similar to a sugar loaf.
Coronet: A mini-crown with vertical interest. Also refers to a wreath worn across the forehead, c.1590.
Cossack: A tall, brimless hat, usually of fur, which is wider at the crown than at the band.
Crepinier: A form of snood.
Cruise hat: Worn to shade the face and attract attention, this hat is named for where it is usually purchased and worn.
Day Cap: Also known as a bonnet cap: A nineteenth century linen or silk cap worn indoors or under a bonnet. These are often paired with lappets, which hang behind or are pinned to the crown of the cap. There are some early literary references to caps being worn over bonnets.
Deerstalker: A double visored, plaid hunting cap with earflaps, usually of wool or tweed; also known as a "Sherlock Holmes."

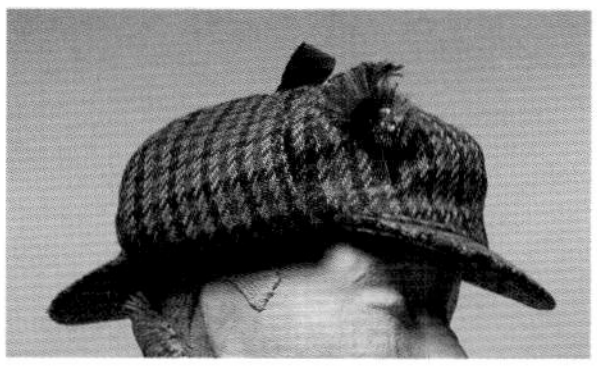

Deerstalker, c.1960. Made in Scotland. *Private Collection*.

Interior view.

Derby: A precursor to the bowler, this round crowned, narrow brimmed hat, named for the Earl of Derby, was originally an English riding hat. The term was adopted by American hat makers c.1888.
Diadem: A hairband-like headpiece associated with sovereignty; adopted for bridal wear by twentieth century milliners.
Diamond Dot Veiling: A double patterned, silk veiling, moderately reinforced at intersection points; traditionally available in 9-inch widths.
Dish hat: An innovation in millinery style by Christian Dior, c.1947, this hat style shows no distinction between the crown and the brim. Also known as the "platter" and "flying saucer" hat.
Disk: A flat, circular hat worn tilted over the forehead and secured by a chignon strap or snood.
Doll Hat: A small hat worn forward on the head The term was used in the nineteenth century but more commonly refers to the "tilt hats" of the early 1940s.
Dolly Varden Bonnet: A hat style popular during the 1870s and named for a character in *Barnaby Rudge* by Charles Dickens. A painting of Dolly by William Frith hangs in London's *Victoria and Albert Museum*.
Dormeuse: A late eighteenth century sleeping cap.
Double Hatting: The fashion of wearing one hat while carrying another. Fourteenth century gentlemen wearing fur-trimmed, felt hats, developed the custom of showing off a second hat by carrying it over the shoulder or balancing it on the tip of a walking stick. Nineteenth century women practiced double hatting when traveling by carriage to a social event. They would carry a small party hat while wearing a practical bonnet for the journey. Carrying a small hatbox became a status symbol.
Drawn Bonnet: A rigid bonnet with horizontal, reed or whalebone, brim supports.
Dutch Cap: A starched, pleated cap with the appearance of a folded towel. The style, which features a pointed crown, originated in Holland, where the process of starching was invented c.1560.
Eggshell: A brimless, crown-hugging hat from the 1950s with an irregular outline, resembling a cracked egg.

Eggshell hat of watermelon green, c.1950. *Mobile Millinery Museum*. $150-180.

Empress Eugenie: A style named for the wife of Napoleon III and popular c.1859. The small hat with narrow brim, curved up at the sides, tilts forward on the brow. In the 1930s, Molyneux used the name to describe a crown-hugging beige creation of his that tipped to the right and sprouted a cluster of matching coq feathers. A larger version of the Empress Eugenie was favored by Princess Diana in the 1980s and copied by bridal wear designers.
Faille: A ribbed fabric with a lustreless finish.
False Beaver: A wool felt, faced with long nap beaver, popular c.1815.
Fanchon Bonnet: A kerchief style, triangular bonnet, c.1860.
Fan Hat: A fan-like, collapsible sun hat.
Fascinator: A loosely knit, hooded scarf.
Fedora: A medium brimmed hat with a front-to-back creased crown, usually of felt.

The author's great uncle Will Hillyer looks dapper in a tweed fedora, c.1915. *Hillyer Collection, Mobile Millinery Museum.*

Fez: A flat topped, brimless cylinder, fitted with a tassel at the center of the crown.

Flocked Veiling: A round patterned veiling, usually of nylon, which is heavily reinforced in a random pattern.

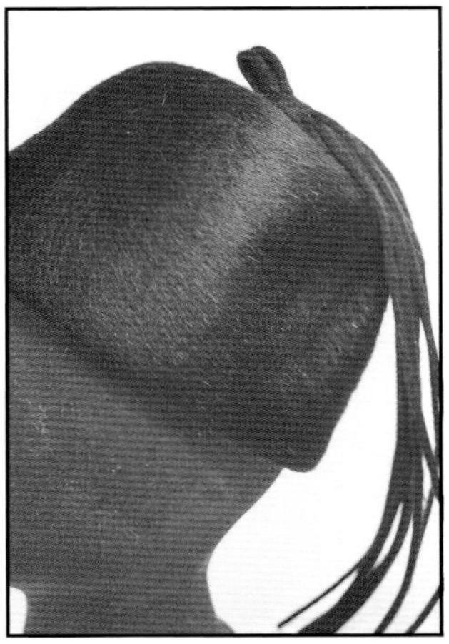

Borrowed from the men: A fashionable fez in long nap felt. *Mobile Millinery Museum*. $80-100.

Floppy Hat: A large brimmed hat cut to fall in soft folds.

Flower Pot: A hat shaped for its namesake; popular during the 1960s.

Fore and Aft Cap: A cap with a visor both in front and back.

Circa 1966: A young woman clowns in a stylish floppy hat. *Ella Philip Collection, Mobile Millinery Museum.*

Frames: Wire supports used in the making of a hat, particularly during the Victorian era.

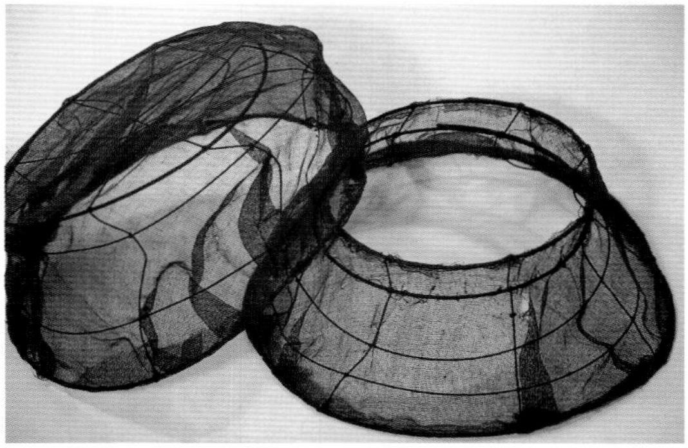

A pair of Victorian wire hat frames wrapped in silk gauze. *Mobile Millinery Museum*. Ensemble: $80-120 for the pair.

French Jet: Widely used during the Victorian era, these black glass, lead backed beads were wired together to form hats, veiling, or embroidery for cuffs, collars, bodices, hems, etc. Originally this was less costly than authentic jet.

Funnel Hat: A tapered, brimless hat of felt, fur, or fabric.

Gainsborough: Originally an enormous hat, worn at an angle over the towering wigs of the late eighteenth century. It was named for English portrait painter Thomas Gainsborough. Gainsborough is also the trade name for an early twentieth century hat maker.

Glengarry: A brimless, woollen cap with creased crown, originating in Glengarry, Scotland. The hat, which comes to a point in front, is usually trimmed with short ribbon streamers at the back.

A quartet of highland dancers top their Scottish costumes with Glengarry bonnets. Photo by Hayward Studios, Montreal, Quebec. *Laurabelle MacLean Collection, Mobile Millinery Museum.*

A young Victorian boy poses in a Glengarry cap with his sister. Photo by William Notman. *Hillyer Collection, Mobile Millinery Museum*.

A Glengarry cap completes the dress uniform of one Colonel Matheson.

Gondolier: A shallow crowned hat with wide, flat brim worn straight on the head. The gondolier is similar in appearance to the boater but is of different proportions. The term was also applied to a beaded net bag worn to enhance an evening coiffure, c.1859.

Gypsy Bonnet: A bonnet tied to the head with a handkerchief or scarf. The term also refers to a simple, broad brimmed hat.

Hairline Veiling: Finely meshed, silk veiling, traditionally available in six and nine-inch widths.

Half Hat: Introduced in the 1940s and popular throughout the 1950s, this crown-hugging hat partially covers the head.

Halo Hat: A hat with upturned brim worn in such a way as to form a halo for the face.

Harlequin: A cuffed hat with a decorative side extension or flare.

Hat Band: A decorative element applied at the crown/brim join of a hat, often of leather or ribbon. This is a nod to the evolution of hats, as the first hats were little more than a band of cloth, leather, or fur, tied about the forehead.

Hatbox: Originally termed a "band box," this box protects a hat when being stored or carried. Most hatboxes are made of heavy cardboard but can also be constructed of leather, vinyl, plastic, or wood. During the nineteenth century, hatboxes were decorated with wallpaper to celebrate special occasions or reflect individual taste. Twentieth century boxes were more often printed with graphics and used to advertise individual milliners or salons.

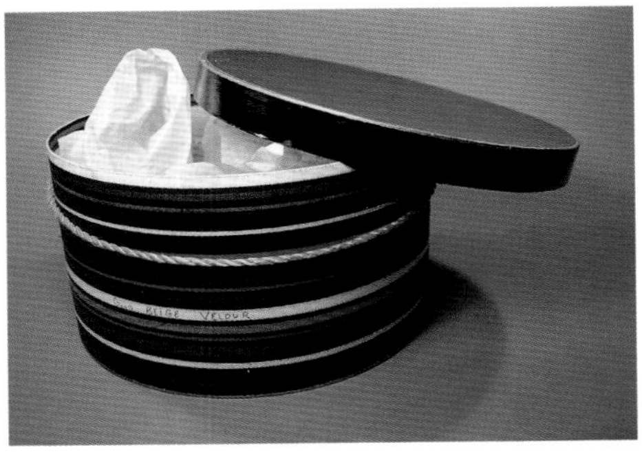

A mid-twentieth century cardboard hat box. *Mobile Millinery Museum*. $60-80.

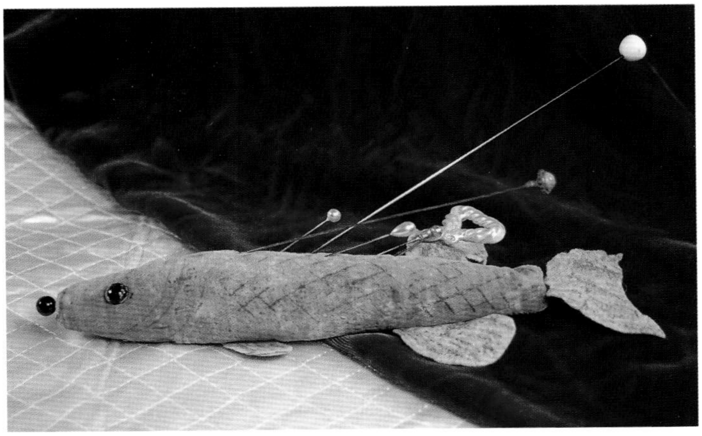

A velvet hatpin holder from the Victorian era is stuffed with sawdust. The nose of the fish sits on a removable, six inch hatpin. *Mobile Millinery Museum*. $150-200.

A pair of lengthy, rhinestone-capped, hatpins. *Philip Warde Collection, Mobile Millinery Museum*. $250-350 each.

A pair of hatpins from the Edwardian era. $120-150 each. *Mobile Millinery Museum*.

Hatpin: A hat adornment comprised of a length of metal, sharply pointed on one end and decorated on the other.

Headscarf: A length of material wound round the head or tied under the hair. This headdress remained primarily an element of ethnic costume until the Second World War when it became highly fashionable.

Helmet: A military inspired style shaped to protect the head.

Hennin: A fifteenth century, conical hat with trailing veil.

Henry II Toque: A large, ostrich feathered toque worn by gentlemen, c.1870 - 1880.

Pheasant tail feathers sweep majestically over the crown of this military inspired helmet in black velour. Twin Labels: Bonwit Teller/Adolpho Réalités, New York, Paris. *Mobile Millinery Museum*. $300-350.

A 1950s black felt homburg. Label: Battersby, London. Size 7 1/4. Brown leather inner band. *Mobile Millinery Museum*. $275-325.

Homburg: A gentleman's hat with a narrow, rolled brim and lengthwise, dented crown.

Hood: A soft, fabric covering for the head and neck, which may be attached to or separate from a garment.

Ice Cube Veiling: A hexagonal patterned veiling, traditionally available in nine-inch widths.

Jet: This lightweight, shiny, black/brown substance derived from fossilized driftwood was used to decorate hats and costume and carved into mourning jewellery during the Victorian era.

Jockey Cap: A widebrimmed cap with six-panelled crown.

Juliet Cap: Popular for bridal wear and originally of open mesh, this small brimless hat conforms to and sits at the back of the head.

Karakurl: The silky, coal black, fleece of the karakurl lamb, also known as the fur sheep.

Kerchief: An informal lacy headdress that originated in the early seventeenth century. It is placed on the head so that the edges fall free at either side. Also a name for headscarf.

Lace: Ornamental, openwork fabric.

Lampshade: A deep, stiff hat with flaring brim worn straight on the head to resemble a lampshade.

Langtry Bonnet: A small, close fitting bonnet.

Leghorn: A finely plaited straw from Livorno, Italy.

Lingerie hat: A washable hat or one of lace or embroidery.

Made Bird: A hat adornment resembling a bird, comprised of feathers, glued to a cork or fabric body.

Mantilla: A lace headscarf at times worn over a vertical comb.

Marquis: A woman's three-cornered hat.

Mary Stuart: A delicate, wired cap with a widow's peak at the center of the forehead.

Matador: A horizontal hat with rounded extensions to resemble bullhorn stubs, also known as a toreador.

Milkmaid: A garden or summer straw with drooping brim and chin ties.

Minaret: Tower or turret shaped millinery structure.

Mitre: A tall, ecclesiastical headdress, which tapers to a point at front and back.

Mephisto feathers, c.1911: A hat trimming of long narrow plumes arranged in pairs.

Merry Widow: A large, black picture hat, trimmed with feathers. Lucille designed the hat for an operetta, c.1907.

Midshipman, c.1870: a large straw boater, presenting double or triple Alsatian bows in front.

Milkmaid: An eighteenth century, country garden hat tied with ribbons under the chin.

Mobcap: A large, circular bonnet with deep lacy frills, inspired by the headgear of eighteenth century English market women.

Mongolian Lamb: The long, white, silky fur of a species by the same name.

Monte Cristi: A fine quality, panama straw made originally by hand in Monte Cristi from jipijapa leaves. These hats are so finely woven they are often marketed as being foldable or crushable.

Morion: This helmet, worn by the Swiss Guard, presents a pointed brim, turned up in back, and a red ostrich plume, which extends from back to front.

Mortarboard: An academic cap topped with a stiff, square crown. A silk tassel, attached at the center crown, is flipped from one side to the other upon receipt of the diploma at a graduation ceremony.

Newsboy Cap: A peaked cap with oversized, droopy crown. Sometimes known as a Gatsby or Jackie Cougan.

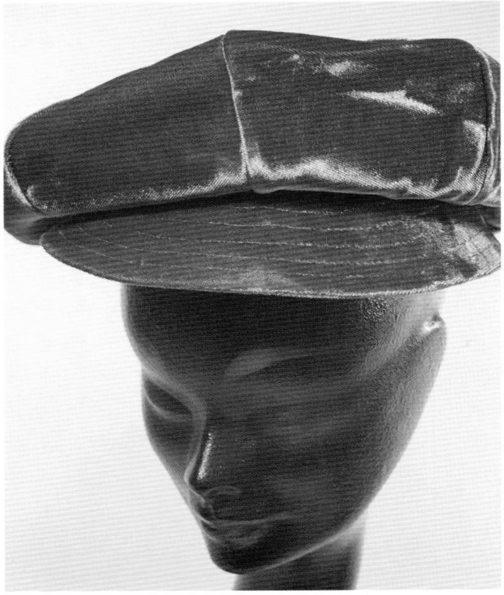

A 1980s version of the newsboy cap in purple velveteen. The six-sectioned crown is fitted with darts where it meets the band in order to provide exaggerated fullness. Label: Flemming by Fashion Hat, Toronto. *Mobile Millinery Museum*. $80-120.

The author's father sports a traditional mortarboard for his graduation from McGill University. *Courtesy of Iris Hillyer*.

Nightcap: A soft, fabric head covering for wearing in bed.

Three young men ham it up in early twentieth century ladies night caps. *Hillyer Collection, Mobile Millinery Museum.*

Claque or collapsible silk opera hat. Label: A. Casse, Made in France. *Mobile Millinery Museum*. $220-250.

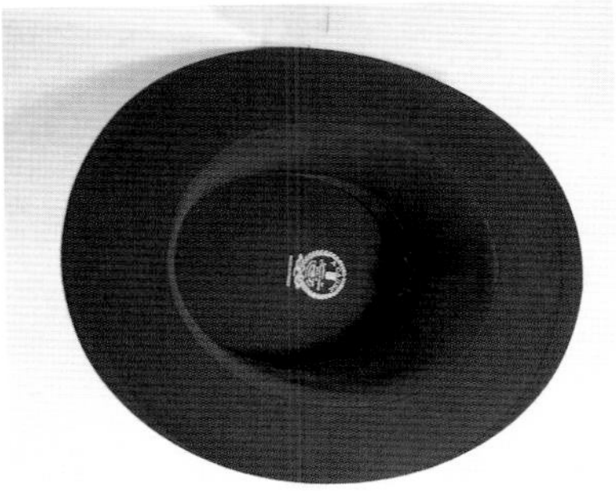

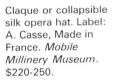

Opera hat, interior view.

Opera Hat: A collapsible, silk top hat, also known as a claque. The invention was conceived by Frenchman Antoine Gibus, in 1823. Top hats were so popular at the time that public cloakrooms were inadequate to store the large hats while patrons dined or enjoyed the theatre. Gibus's idea enabled the hat to be carried or stored flat when not being worn. Gibus acquired a patent for his mechanical device, which collapsed the hat on hidden, folding springs, in 1837.
Pagodine: A pyramid shaped hat.
Paillettes: Spangles.
Pamela Bonnet: A widebrimmed bonnet, often of straw.

Ladies panama hat is stamped "Equador" on the inner crown. Label: Eaton's Fashions. *Mobile Millinery Museum*. $250-300.

Panama Hat: A widebrimmed, high-crowned, tropical hat popularized by American sailors, c.1895.
Parson's hat: A flat, broad-brimmed felt adapted from the clergy.

Parson's hat, c.1910, trimmed with a silk and velvet chou in stripes of raspberry and emerald green. Label: Florette, size 23. *Mobile Millinery Museum*. $250-300.

Peach Basket: A large straw with tapered crown, popular during the Edwardian era.
Peau de Pêche: Having a peach-skin texture.
Peau de Souris: French for "mouse skin"; a soft, textured silk.
Petal Hat: Fashioned on a pillbox frame, this style is layered with felt or fabric petals, which may be lined or unlined. It can be worn back on the head or forward, depending upon facial contour.
Picot: Having an edge finished with small loops or projections, usually of ribbon or straw.
Picture Hat: This hat's flat, widebrim forms a frame for the face when worn at the back of the head.
Piecrust: A felt hat cut and shaped to resemble piecrust.
Pillbox: A flat, round, brimless hat.
Pith Helmet: A cloth covered, cork helmet, first worn by the British army in India.

A 1960s straw pith helmet. Chenille dotted veiling feminizes the brim. *Mobile Millinery Museum*. $200-250.

Pixie: Cone-shaped, brimless hat, which sits at the back of the head.
Pleureuse: Weeping willow ostrich plume.
Plumassier: A workshop for the creation of feather arrangements.
Poke Bonnet: An early nineteenth century bonnet with a small crown and wide, protruding brim, usually of straw. The hat was first called a poke bonnet (because of the brim style) and later the entire hat was referred to as a "poke". The term was shortened to "poke" in 1815.
Pompadour frame: A hat support device, first available c.1902, over which a woman's hair was built up. False hair and "combings" were added if needed. Also called a transformation.
Ponyskin: A name for calfskin.
Popcorn Veiling: Large gauge veiling, moderately reinforced at intersection points; traditionally available in 18-inch widths.
Pork Pie: A small round hat with bumper brim, resembling a pork pie.

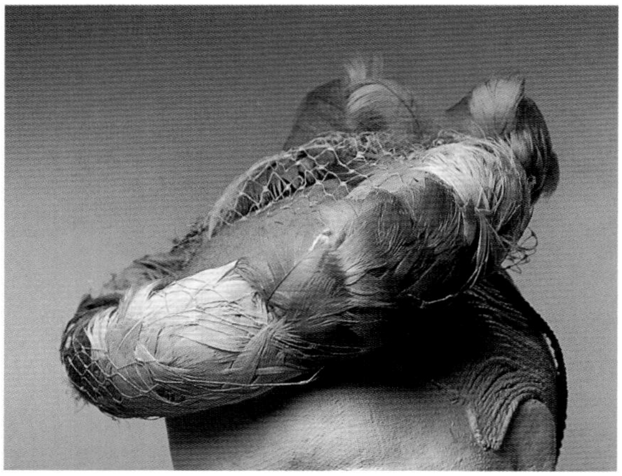

Feather-trimmed, pigeon-gray, felt pork pie, c.1880. Fine gray veiling wraps the brim at front. Label: Imperial Millinery, Montreal. *Mobile Millinery Museum*. $300-350.

Postillion: A high crowned hat with a narrow brim, which rolls upward at the sides.
Profile Hat: A brimmed hat tilted to the side to frame the wearer's face.
Puggree: A scarf wound around the crown of a hat.
Puritan: A broad brimmed hat with high, tapered crown. A ribbon band passes through a large buckle.
Quadricorn: A hat with four, upward pointing corners.
Red Hatters: Members of the *Red Hat Society*.
Roller: A small round hat, usually of felt with narrow, rolled up brim.
Russian Bonnet: A style popular in the 1870s and 1880s. This scarlet velvet hat demonstrated black feather trim.
Russian Veiling: A silk or rayon, square-patterned veiling, moderately reinforced at intersection points; traditionally available in 9-inch widths.
Sen Sen: A silk or rayon, square-patterned veiling, with finely reinforced intersection points; traditionally available in 9 and 18-inch widths.
Shako: A tall, cylindrical hat with military origins.
Short-Back Sailor: Boater style hat with a large, broad brim in front but no brim in back.
Slouch Hat: Northern and Southern officers wore this felt hat, with crushable brim, during the Civil War. Also known as the Garbo hat, the style was reinterpreted in the 1930s.
Snap Brim: A gentleman's hat with brim turned down in front and up in the back.
Snood: A loosely woven net to hold hair at the back of the neck.
Sou'wester: Originally a waterproof sailor's hat with a broad, back brim.

A Mexican sombrero in deep, peacock-blue, velvet. The under-brim is decorated in the same fashion as the upper brim with white stitching and large multicolored sequins Label: Sombrero Salazar, Mecho En Mexico. *Mobile Millinery Museum*. $150-200.

Sombrero: A Mexican, widebrim hat with high, conical crown.
Spray: A single sprig of floral, foliage, or fruit trimming.
Stetson: The Oxford paperback dictionary defines Stetson as a "slouch hat with a very widebrim and a high crown." The term is synonymous with cowboy hat and developed into common usage through the popularity of a western hat, designed by the *John B Stetson Co.* of Philadelphia. Stetson manufactured many styles of hats including fashion hats for women in the early years. The Stetson style was adopted as the official hat of Canada's *North West Mounted Police* (now the *Royal Canadian Mounted Police*) in 1901, after officers began wearing cowboy hats while on patrol.

Mid-twentieth century black felt Stetson with narrow, self-fabric band and ornamental metal buckle. Labels: Stetson/Paris Hatters, San Antonio Texas. *Courtesy of Kathryn Crowder*. $150-200.

Interior view.

The author's mother, Iris Hillyer, enjoys a bit of fishing on the lake in a practical sou'wester.

Storm Protector: A plastic hat cover. These were widely used by men in the 1950s and 1960s as rain guards for their fine felt fedoras, homburgs, and semi-homburgs. Storm protectors were manufactured for women's hats as well.

Stovepipe: Term for a tall top hat, the brim of which curls along the sides.

This silk-lined stovepipe, with a six inch crown, belonged to Edward Ramsay, who worked as a baggage man for the T, H, and B Railway, c.1880. Label: Pritchard & Company, 58 & 60 Stamford Street, London, England. *Bette Eccles Collection, Mobile Millinery Museum*. $300-350.

Strass: Lead glass, set in silver, invented in the eighteenth century to imitate diamonds. Used on buckles to trim hats.

Straw: Dried stalks of grain used in the manufacture of hats.

A spiraling crown of lemon and orange straw braid awaits the addition of a brim. *Mobile Millinery Museum*.

Stroller: A casual, tailored hat, usually of felt, worn with a suit or pants.

Sugarloaf: A hat with tapered, conical crown resembling the shape of sugar loaves, packed for merchandizing.

A Victorian sugar loaf in saffron colored straw is elegantly trimmed with a black leather band and bow. Posterior strap secures the hat beneath upswept hair. Label: Size 22. *Mobile Millinery Museum*. $250-350.

Sunbonnet: An informal, outdoor bonnet with widebrim and bavolet.

Sweater Hat: A wool hat with rolled brim.

Tambourine: Flat topped, round hat resembling a tambourine.

Tam O'shanter: A soft cap with a flat, circular crown, the circumference of which is twice that of the head. The crown is encased in a hatband and a pom pom usually marks the center crown. This hat is named for the hero of a Robert Burns poem.

Telescope crown: A crown, which narrows at the top and appears to be stacked in sections.

Tiara: A crescent shaped, jeweled, metal headpiece.

Tile: A nineteenth century term for hat, in use from 1823.

Top Hat: A tall, stiff, felt hat with a flat-topped, circular crown and narrow brim. The style originated as an English county gentleman's riding hat in the late eighteenth century. In 1790 when a Charing Cross hatter, named John Heatherington, wore a silk plush version of the hat in London, a near riot ensued. Heatherington was officially accused of "frightening timid people" and was required to put up a bond. The Englishman also achieved acclaim for inventing hatter's plush, a process that gives felt the appearance of silk.

Silk toppers were invented by a Frenchman named Betta. It is reported that while in China, Betta commissioned a hat maker to make him a silk hat using his tall beaver hat as a model. Upon his return to Paris, the design was widely copied.

The top hat in black, gray, or white continues to be worn with formal attire and is tied by tradition to many present-day rituals. In Canada, the first captain to enter the *St. Lawrence Seaway*, each spring, is awarded a ceremonial top hat.

A top hat by Tress & Co. This London firm was awarded gold medals at the Paris exhibition of 1878.The owner's initials "J.M." in gold paper are affixed to the watered silk crown lining. Inner band of camel colored leather. Label: Watson Prickard, 16, North John Street, Liverpool. *Mobile Millinery Museum*. $275-325.

Toque: A close-fitting brimless hat or bonnet.

Trapunto: Decorative surface stitching in evenly spaced rows.

Trotteau: A walking hat.

Tuque: A tapered, cylindrical, wool toque, worn by nineteenth century, French Canadian Habitants, and revived as a popular winter sport hat in Canada.

Tricorn: A cocked hat with the brim turned up on three sides. A popular hat for European men during the eighteenth century.

Trilby: A soft felt hat worn by men and named in 1895 for the heroine of Du Maurier's novel of the same name.

Tulle: A fine silk or cotton bobbin-net, first manufactured, c.1768, in Nottingham, England, and later produced in Tulle, France.

Turban: A brimless hat made by draping or wrapping fabric about the crown of the head. Originally called a tuliban, it is a headdress of Muslim origin.

Tyrolean: An alpine-inspired hat with a pointed crown and narrow, folded brim.

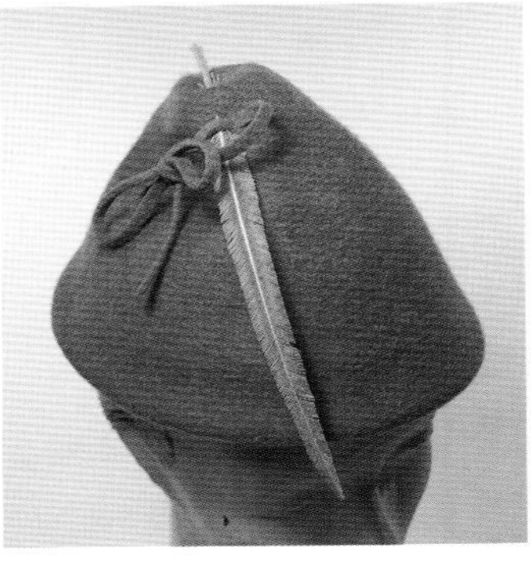

A clipped, ash-colored, feather pierces the crown of this felt Tyrolean in attractive antique brick. A narrow, self-fabric bow adds a touch of femininity. *Mobile Millinery Museum*. $150-250.

Ushanka: A brimless fur or faux fur hat with earflaps, worn by the Soviet military.

Ugly: A shade for the face projecting from a lady's bonnet. The term was used to describe a detachable shade but was later applied to any deep-brimmed bonnet.

Visor: A rigid projection along the front of a cap.

A pair of visored yachting caps. *Courtesy of Kathryn Crowder*.

Voilette: A small veil.

Widow's Weeds: A Victorian woman's mourning attire.

Velvet bonnet wreath, c.1860. *Mobile Millinery Museum*. $40-60.

Wimple Hat: Hat with attached veil, which drapes around the neck or under the chin.

Wreath: Millinery fruit, flowers, or foliage, wired together to encircle a crown or anchor a veil.

Yarmulke: A skullcap worn by observant Jewish males, also known as a kippah.

An empire bonnet, draped with black net and a lace-trimmed mantle; suitable mourning attire for a Victorian widow. *Mobile Millinery Museum*. Ensemble: $350-450.

Chapter I
Millinery Retrospective: 1790 - 1837

Charlotte Mann is photographed in a costume worn by her ancestor at the court of Queen Anne (1702 - 1714). The bonnet is held with what appears to be black velvet ribbon that fastens at the left and dangles to the waist. Shaded ostrich plumes adorn the right side and nod to the back.

"Three things a woman can make out of anything... a salad, a hat, and an argument."

— *John Barrymore*

The Great Age of Millinery

Millinery as a profession developed, c.1770, when women's hats became an integral element of a fashionable ensemble. In addition to making hats, capes, and hoods, early milliners were responsible for embellishing an entire costume by trimming it with laces, frills, ribbons, bows, buttons, and other adornments. Many of the trims and fine straws used at the outset of the millinery era were produced in Milan, hence the name applied to practitioners of the art.

Prior to the age of mass production, fashion originated with the upper classes and standards set for court dress in Britain and France trickled down to influence styles adopted by the masses.

Details of the current *mode* were disseminated by means of fashion plates – hand colored sketches of the Paris couture. The great designers also advertised their work through the sale of fashion dolls, often of wax. These miniatures were dressed in detailed ensembles, to replicate the *dernier cri* or latest fashion.

During the 1760s and 1770s the *Academie Française* published an encyclopedia of costume related trades that explored the arts of button making, weaving, embroidery, etc. and set the stage for early French fashion periodicals. By 1830, *Godey's* ladies book was published, providing season-by-season instruction on dressmaking and bonnet design to milliners and seamstresses in America. Collectors should keep in mind that this and other fashion magazines of the day depict an exaggerated version of what most people actually wore.

Fashion plates such as this were often hand colored. *Courtesy of David Tetrault*.

These millinery fashion plates grace the upstairs hall of a Niagara Falls bed and breakfast. *Courtesy of David Tetrault.*

Millinery Inspiration

As in any fashion era, milliners of the late eighteenth and early nineteenth century designed hats and headdresses with the hairstyles and costume of the day in mind. As tall, powdered wigs fell out of fashion and short styles emerged, the great age of the milliner was born. Turbans, capotes, visored cap, and helmet-style hats enclosed Grecian style hairdos and short wigs. The collapsible calash bonnet, made necessary by the towering hairstyles of the late eighteenth century, decreased in height and eventually gave way to the drawn bonnet.

The Beaver Trade

Social, economic, and political factors also influenced millinery designs and fabrication. In the fashion arena, the word 'beaver' has almost always been synonymous with hat. For centuries, hat makers have known that the thick, gray underfur of the beaver pelt lends itself most nicely to the felting process and so produces the finest quality felt hats as well as head coverings of piled fur.

Canadian pelts were highly prized from a very early date. It is recorded that Charles I of England was beheaded in 1648 wearing a hat made from Canadian beaver, proving my contention that there indeed exists a suitable hat for every occasion.

During the eighteenth century, European hat makers purchased over 200,000 beaver skins from North America per year. These were prepped for sale through the removal of their long, reddish guard hairs, leaving only the thick underfur, but the Canadians continued to wear the fur in its natural state into the first decade of the twentieth century.

After the harvest in 1625, a small number of Mayflower pilgrims set out up the Kennebec River and returned with seven hundred pounds of beaver. Three decades later, the British parliament prohibited the use of any other material in hat making and the search for these prized pelts increased in North America. The humble beaver was so instrumental in the settlement of what is now Canada that its image was chosen for the nation's five-cent coin.

Mad as a Hatter: The practice of applying heat to mercury treated fur, a felt making procedure introduced in 1720, caused serious nerve damage to hat makers.

Hats, Bonnets, and Hair Ornaments

Following the French Revolution, a trend for inexpensive jewelry caught on, with strass pins ornamenting costumes as well as hats. For evening, ladies worked hair ornaments such as combs, arrow-shaped hairpins, and dangling gold balls into elaborate hairstyles. Top knots worn with curls and even false curls prevailed and for a short time (1805-1810), hair was coiffed differently on either side of a center part. Jeweled ornaments, known as ferronieres, were strung across the forehead and delicate ropes of pearls or crystals dangled from fine chains, tucked into the hair.

Nineteenth century hair adornment of crystal beads on a fine metal chain. *Mobile Millinery Museum*. $150-200.

In North America, pioneer women embraced practical headgear, which could be easily made at home. Cotton, cambric, and gingham sunbonnets were worn daily, then patched or darned to preserve their usefulness.

The poke bonnet, or *invisible,* with its stiff projecting brim, provided protection from the sun for complexion-conscious ladies, but interfered with the wearer's ability to hear at times. Women and children relied upon the popular hat, in its various incarnations, trimming it and re-trimming it year round, to coordinate with assorted outfits.

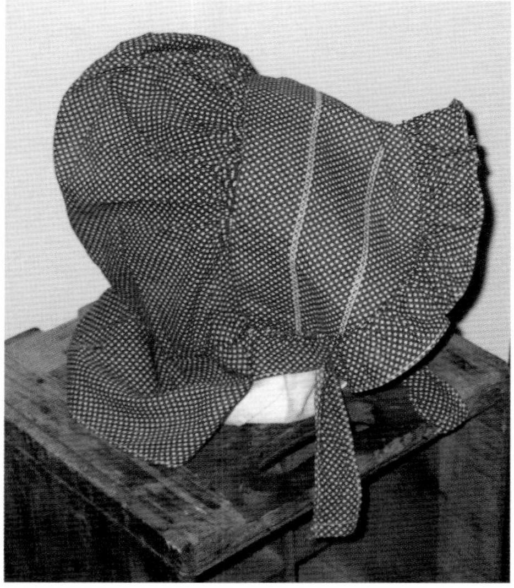

Red and white calico sunbonnet with self-fabric bavolet and chin ties.

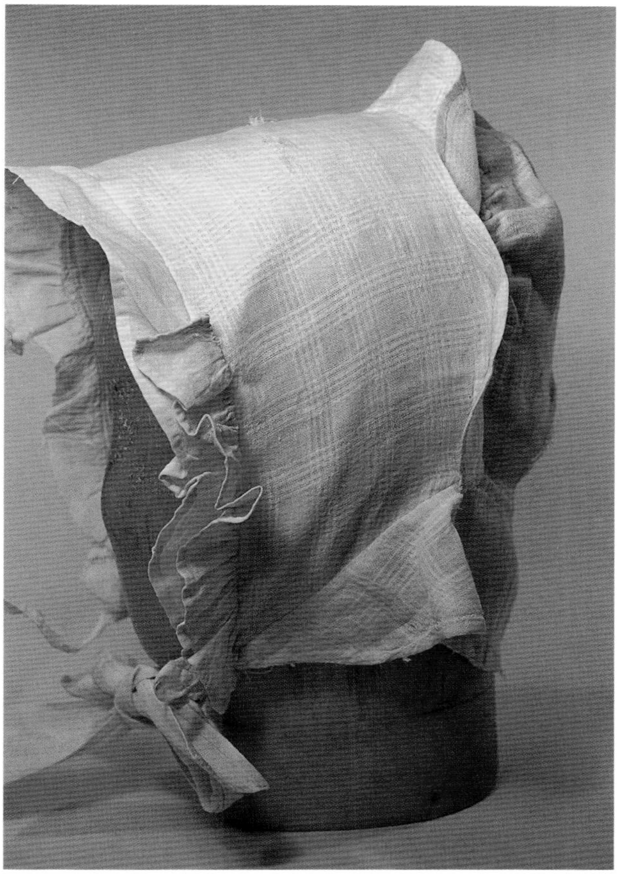

This fully lined, cambric, sunbonnet shows mended areas on the back of the crown. It's small size suggests it was worn by children. *Mobile Millinery Museum*. $200-250.

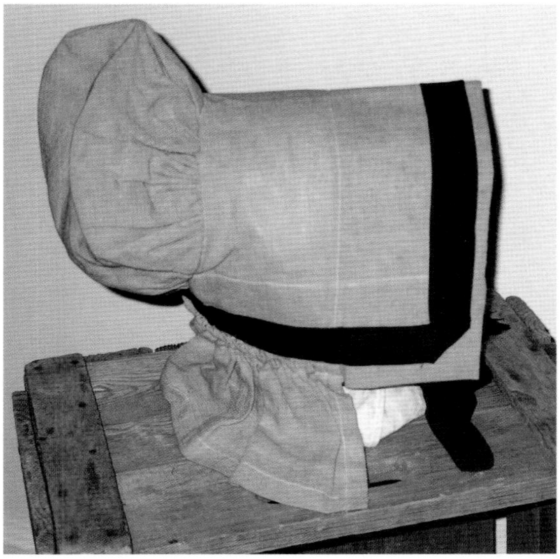

White sunbonnet with black border and ties, the brim of which is fashioned over paste board.

By 1820, French designers favored white when dressing evening hats with feathers and flowers, taking their inspiration from the white flag of the French restoration. Milliners combined the royal white with gold when fashioning fabric bonnets and used their talents to skillfully gild feathers and wheat stocks, as trim for hair and hats. A draped style, known as the desert turban, opened in the back to expose tumbles of hair.

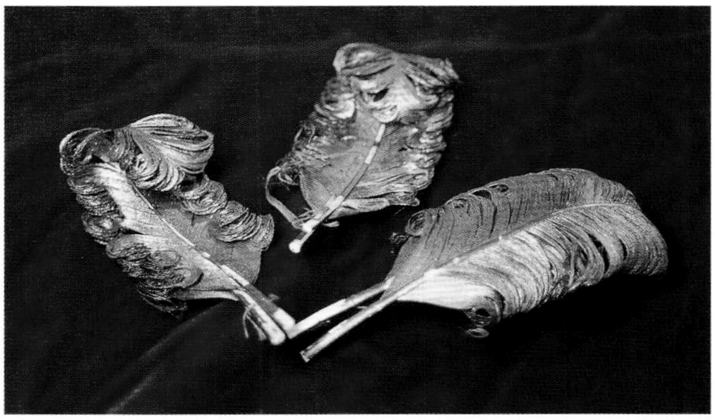

A trio of curled and gilded feathers for millinery use. *Mobile Millinery Museum*. $80-120.

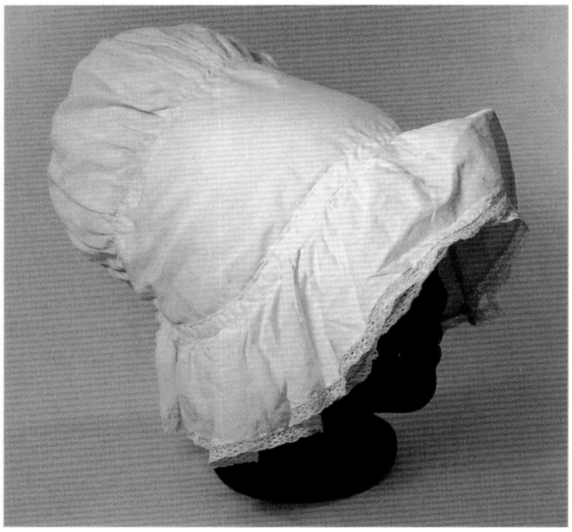

Cotton sunbonnet, threadbare in places due to multiple launderings. *Mobile Millinery Museum*. $200-250.

For daytime outings, women and children decorated white or light colored poke bonnets of straw, felt, or fabric with flowers, feathers, and ribbons or combinations of these. Green was especially popular with young women, while matrons preferred black bonnets and trim.

Optional bonnet veils hung from the front, the back, or draped across the brim of a bonnet. A drawstring, fed through a casing along the hemmed edge, secured the transparencies, which at times were worn in place of a hat.

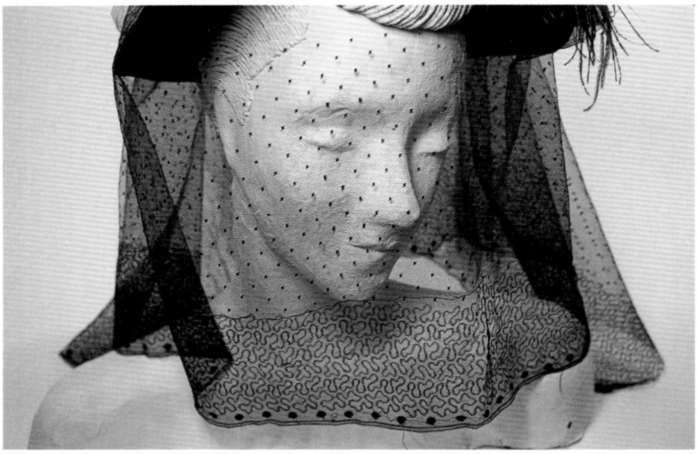

The hem of this Chantilly lace bonnet veil, c.1860, is punctuated with chenille dots. *Mobile Millinery Museum*. $1200-1500.

Most bonnets of the early 1800s were made of plaited straw, silk covered buckram, straw cloth, or bonnet board. Italian leghorn straw was highly valued for hat making but milliners also relied on Switzerland, Belgium, England, and China for less expensive raw materials. A buyer could expect to pay upwards of twenty dollars for an untrimmed, leghorn bonnet. She might re-trim her bonnet season by season, extending the value of her initial investment. Late eighteenth and early nineteenth century hat styles changed frequently. Examples from this period are unlined as they were worn atop day caps.

According to the *American Museum of Straw Art,* the first patent awarded a woman in America went to Sophia Woodhouse in 1806, for her method of weaving straw cloth. Other sources award the honor to Mary Kies of Connecticut, who integrated the straw with natural fibres, such as silk.

Sophia Woodhouse did acquire a patent for her bonnet design process in 1821, and obtained an international reputation for her high quality bonnets, which rivaled Italian leghorn pieces, no longer available in the U.S., because of a trade embargo. She gathered, bleached, boiled, fumigated, and plaited the Red Top and English spear grass straws that grew along the riverbank near her home. Some of her work now resides with the *Wethersfield Historical Society*.

Fully lined, black velvet, Pamela bonnet, c.1830. Faded pink velvet bands the hat beneath a bunch of cotton flowers. Velvet under brim. *Mobile Millinery Museum*. $1200-1500.

Pamela bonnets, which reached enormous dimensions, were secured with broad ribbon ties, pressing the widebrims against the wearer's cheeks. The late eighteenth century custom of securing a hat with a diagonally folded kerchief or silk triangle, held firm into the 1820s. Curiously, these silk ties were of red or green, regardless of the color of the hat. Silk kerchiefs were also worn over caps, forming a style known as *en marmotte.*

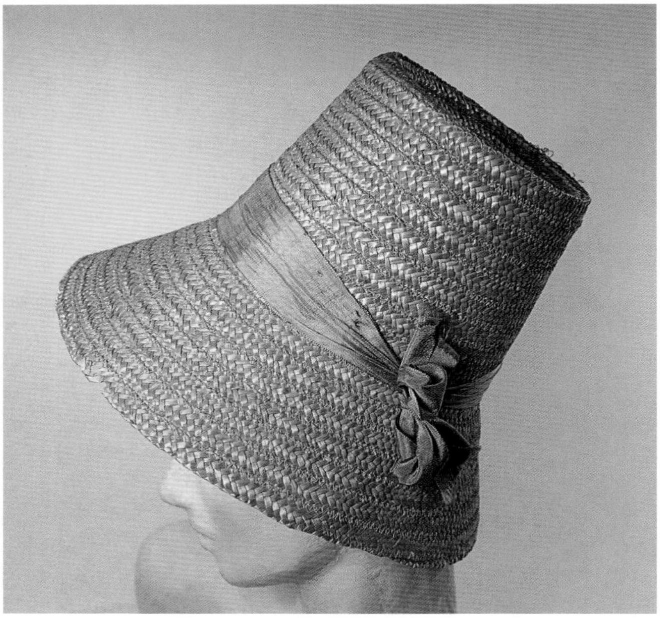

High crowned, French Pamela bonnet, c.1815. Stitches, visible only on the inside, secure a band of teal silk. *Private collection*. $1800-2500.

Caps decorated heads at all times of the day and peeked out from under high-crowned straws when outdoors. Open crowned caps or bonnet frills framed the face under hats and bonnets, many with lace or silk extensions, which lay prettily against the cheek. Morning or day caps, worn indoors, often concealed hair, tied in curls to be released later as ringlets. Fancy, embroidered lace or beribboned caps were worn for sleeping.

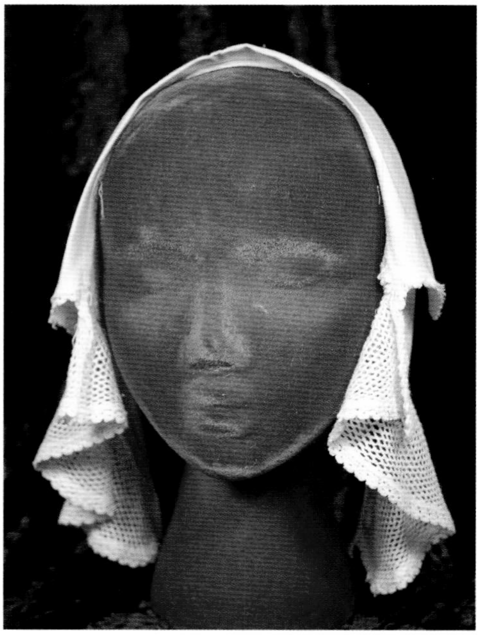

White faille day cap with folded brim. *Mobile Millinery Museum*. $150-250.

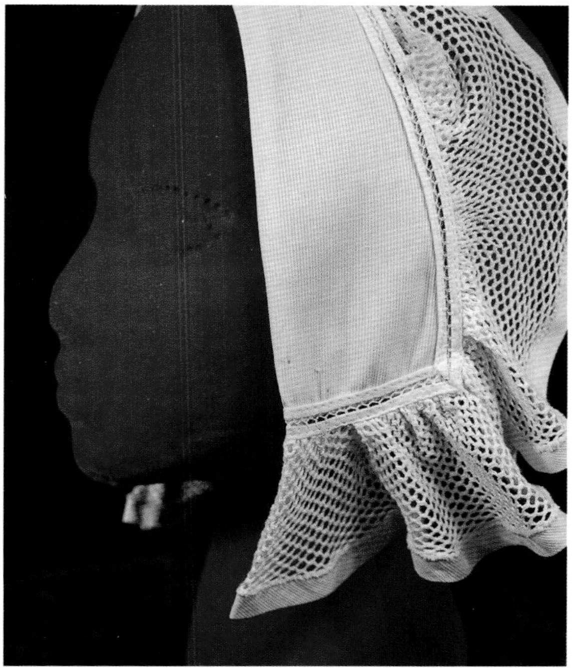

A similar cap of white faille, embellished with cotton, honeycomb lace. *Millinery Museum*. $150-250.

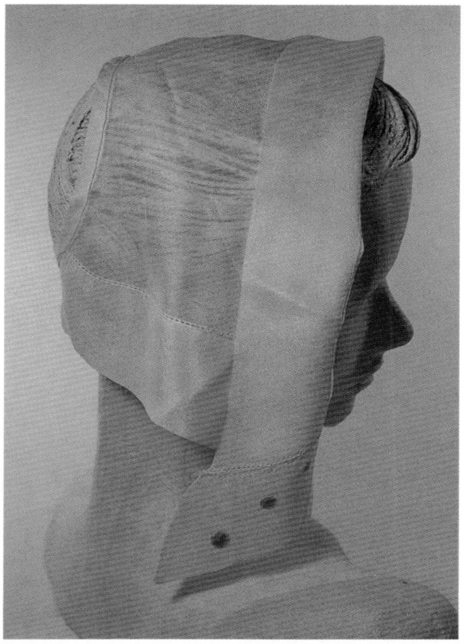

A silk bonnet cap, embroidered with yellow dots, has numerous hatpin holes at the top of the crown. *Mobile Millinery Museum*. $250-350.

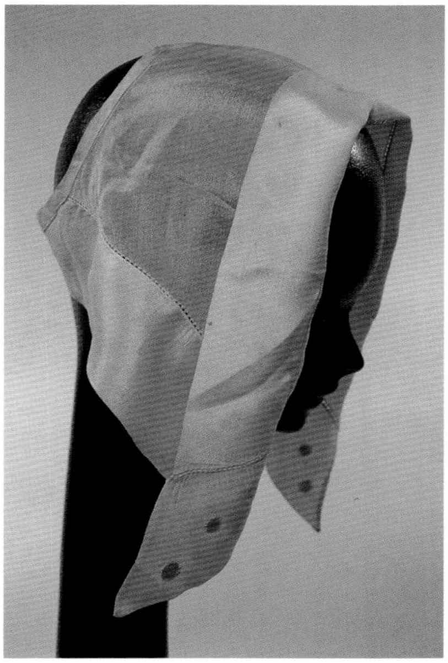

A similar bonnet cap, identical except for the color of the embroidery, reveals several large hatpin holes at the brow line. *Mobile Millinery Museum*. $250-350.

Embroidered cap with folded brim. *Mobile Millinery Museum*. $250-300.

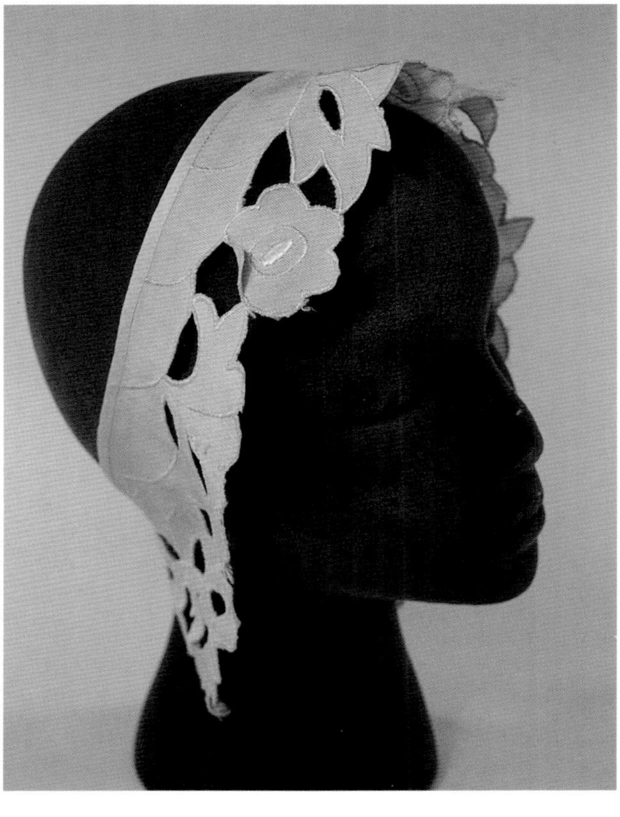

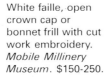

White faille, open crown cap or bonnet frill with cut work embroidery. *Mobile Millinery Museum*. $150-250.

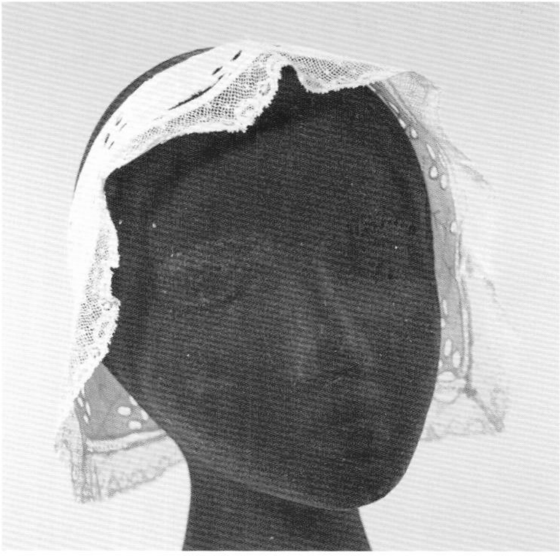

Lace-edged open crown cap to frame the face beneath a bonnet. *Mobile Millinery Museum*. $250-350.

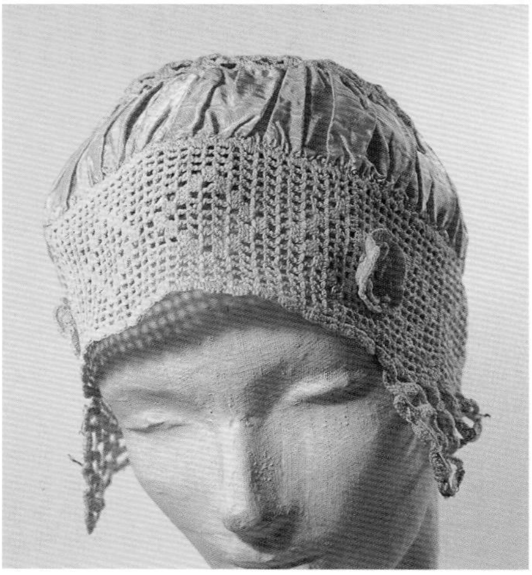

Boudoir cap, fashioned of ecru crochet and watered silk ribbon. *Mobile Millinery Museum*. $300-350.

This tea-colored crocheted cap is fitted along the brow with holes for the placement of ribbon. Open lattice-work covers the hair at back, below which dangles a delicate tassel. *Mobile Millinery Museum*. $200-300.

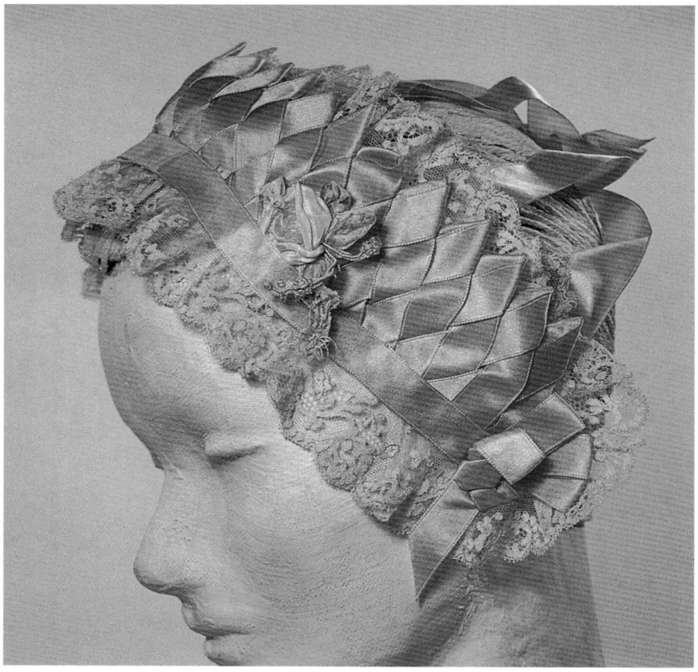

A boudoir cap of lace and woven silk ribbon is decorated with a silk rose bud and tiny blue flowers. *Mobile Millinery Museum*. $300-350.

The lappets of this black silk cap are crocheted from fine cotton. *Mobile Millinery Museum*. $600-800.

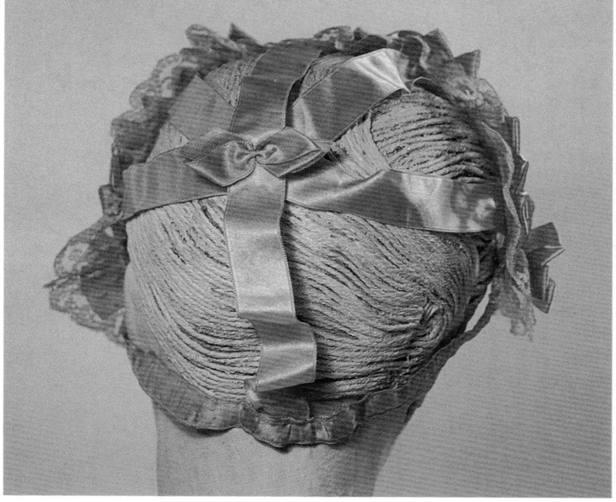

Reverse view showing a lattice of pink silk ribbon.

A boudoir cap of ecru net is encased in a net of cameo-blue tatting. Silk ribbon in Wedgwood-blue forms a border and rosettes. *Mobile Millinery Museum*. $300-350.

French ribbon forms the basis for this Wedgwood-blue boudoir cap, crowned and banded with crochet-work. *Mobile Millinery Museum*. $300-350.

By the mid-1830s, hair, which previously curled at the temples, now framed the face as ringlets and braids. The cornet or starched "fly-away headdress" with flaring fans of lace, muslin, or organdie, complemented evening coiffures for a few years until chignons appeared at the back of the head and decorative combs resumed popularity.

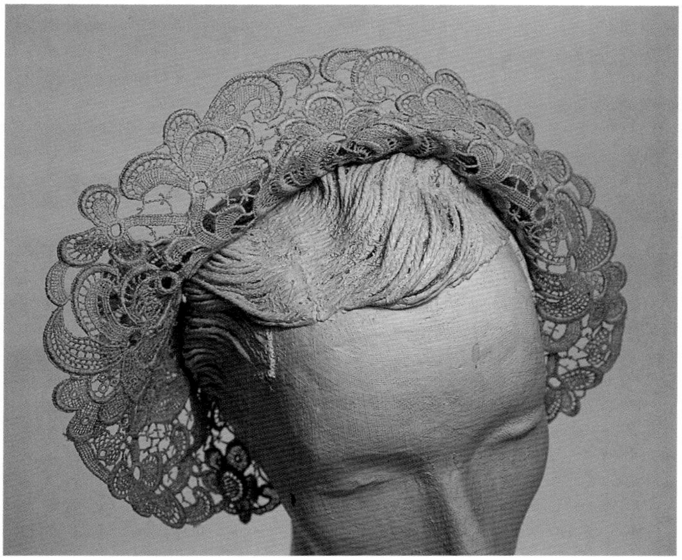

This modest, blue lace, "fly-away" may have been enhanced with feathers when worn as an evening headdress. *Mobile Millinery Museum*. $300-350.

The 1830s saw the poke bonnet diminish in size and make room for the smaller, closefitting, bibi bonnet. This style took its name from the French word for baby (*bébé*) and sat so far back on the crown of the head that some looked as if they might topple off. By variations, ribbon ties secured the bibi under the chin or hung loosely at the back of the head.

The bibi closely hugged the crown of the head at first, then the narrow brim began to rise in the center and protrude slightly in front, eventually morphing into the spoon bonnet.

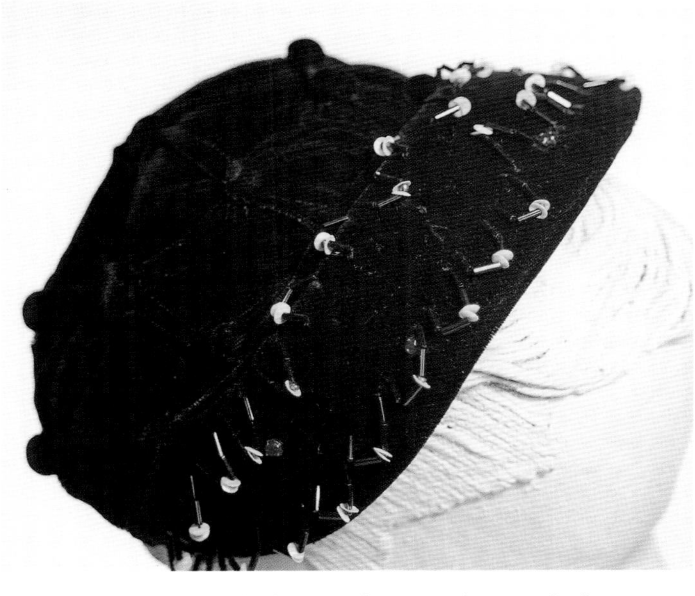

This early, black velvet, bibi bonnet features a button tufted crown. The brim is fringed with bugle beads from which depend seed beads and creamy white sequins. A series of red, semi-precious stones dots the brim. This style of bonnet sat at the back of the head and tied under the chin, resembling a baby bonnet. Label: The Carlotta Hat. *Mobile Millinery Museum*. $800-1000.

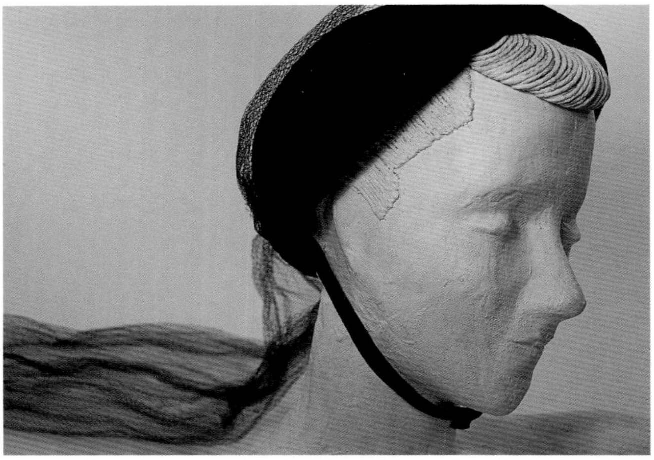

Black veiling trails from the crown of this velvet bibi. *Mobile Millinery Museum*. $400-600.

Toward the end of the decade, a narrow lace or muslin cap called the arcade achieved distinction. This rosebud-trimmed confection tied demurely under the chin, with ribbons, or attached to the hair at ear level, allowing lappets to float behind. Lappets of lace, crochet-work, or broad ribbon also fell from caps and bonnets, while green veiling trailed from riding hats.

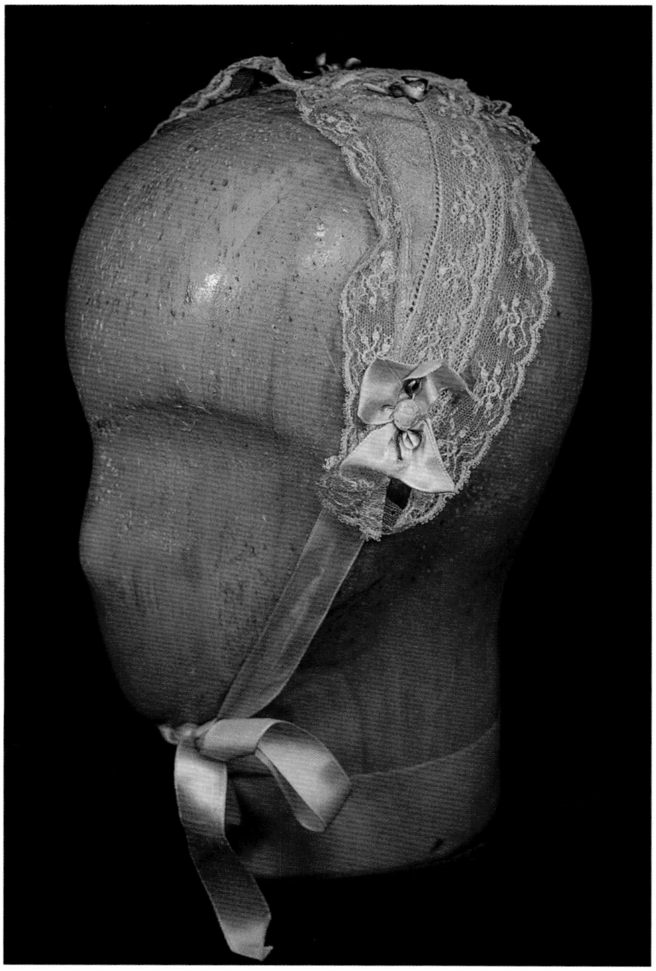

Circa 1840: Sea-green crepe de chine and ecru lace arcade, adorned with ribbon rosettes in yellow, pink, and blue. *Mobile Millinery Museum*. $250-350.

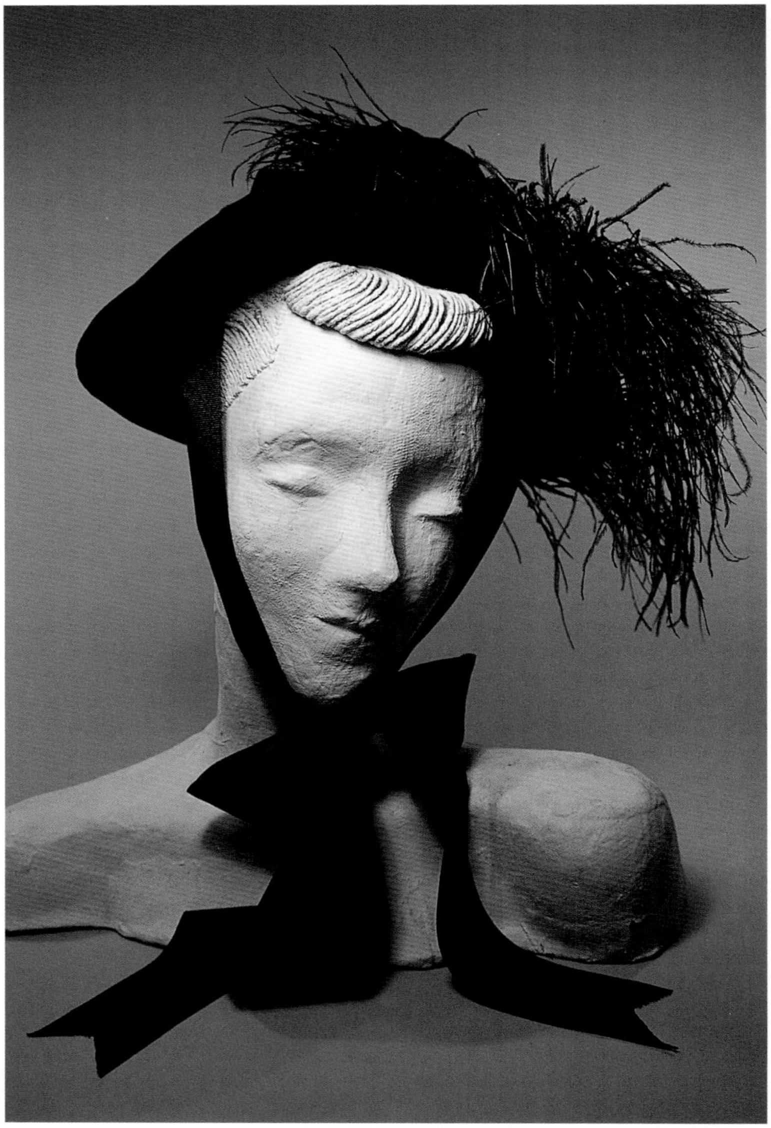

A black, weeping ostrich plume protrudes from a pocket on the brim of this black velvet bonnet with grosgrain ties. *Mobile Millinery Museum*. $450-500.

Ladies of means required small, lacy "party" hats, which they carried with them in fashionable bandboxes, when invited to a social gathering. Upon arrival at the festivities they would exchange their carriage bonnet for a dainty and expensive frivolity.

This jet-beaded, horsehair-lace, party cap would have been an expensive purchase when new, c.1820. *Mobile Millinery Museum*. $1500-1800.

Ribbon dominated fashion; bowknots, ribbons of watered silk, and loops of colored gauze adorned hats generously. Veils appeared in many colors and might be embellished with chenille, embroidery, lace, or jet.

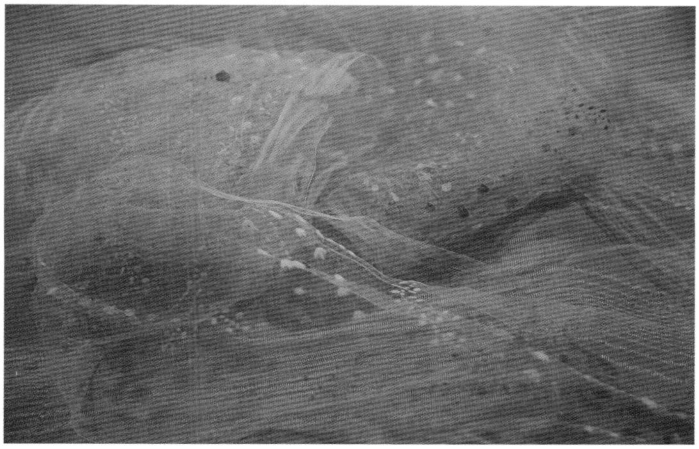

A pair of gauze-ribbon bonnet ties are painted in a delicate floral motif. *Mobile Millinery Museum.* $75-125.

The author's great, great grandmother Ferguson, in a bonnet with broad, printed-silk ribbon ties. *Hillyer Collection, Mobile Millinery Museum*.

A bibi bonnet of navy beaver is ornamented with cookie-cutter, felt flowers along the brow. Grosgrain ribbon ties. *Mobile Millinery Museum*. $250-350.

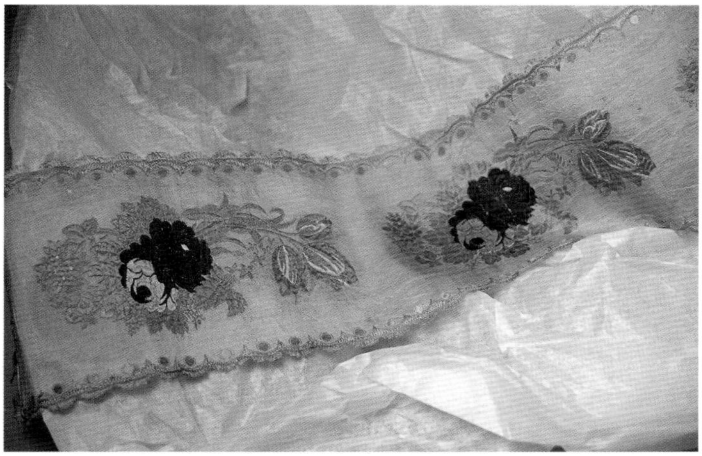

A silk tapestry of pink tulips and navy roses is woven into a length of scallop-edged, French ribbon. *Mobile Millinery Museum*.$100-150.

This French-made, late eighteenth or early nineteenth century, opera hood, beribboned with turquoise grosgrain, may have been worn over a broad-brimmed, Pamela bonnet. *Mobile Millinery Museum*. $1200-1500.

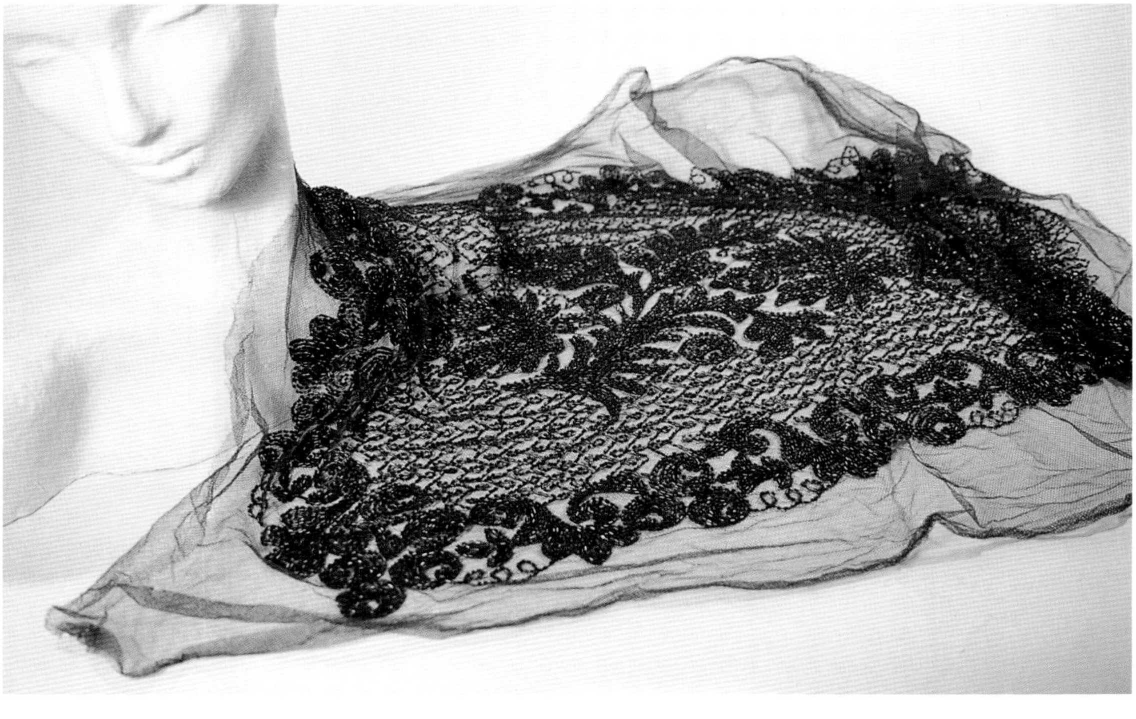

This exquisite bonnet veil of jet-beaded net shows no signs of wear. *Mobile Millinery Museum.* $2000-2500.

Chapter II
Victoriana: 1837 - 1901

"I remember buying and selling the most beautiful, old tin, hat box. It was lined inside with red velvet and contained a lovely, beaver felt hat, positioned on a bunny. It came complete with a brush (stored in the lid), which even had a place for hatpins. I would never break something like that up and sold it complete to a collector."

— Susie, antique shop owner, Hamilton, Ontario

"I bought this old Victorian, millinery cabinet from a woman, years ago, whose mother had owned a hat shop. She told me the piece was one half of a set of two. The other belonged to her sister. Wanting to purchase the complete set, I visited the sister and was about to close the deal, when she enquired as to how I had heard she was selling this item. When I disclosed my source she shouted, 'Get out of my house,' and there ended my chances of owning the complete set."

— Antique shop owner, Hamilton, Ontario

"My grandfather used to walk the baby in the park after church, on Sundays, storing extra diapers inside his top hat."

— A Toronto resident

Caps, designed for various age groups, activities, and times of the day, retained their popularity well into the Victorian era. *Godey's* ladies book introduced a plain lace headdress, c.1850, consisting of a "band of rich lace, which may be fastened at each side, either with ribbons or ornamental hair-pins." The journal advised "many ladies who have a fine braid of hair, prefer this to covering it with a cap." Sketches of caps from the same issue indicate one that might be well suited to "the evening toilette of a middle-aged lady."

Bonnets emerged each season with slight changes in contour or silhouette. The depth of the brim, or angle of its projection, might change. Similarly, through alterations in pleating or dart placement, designers were able to transform the contour or fullness of a crown, or modify the bavolet, making it scant or full, through the addition or removal of ruffles.

An evening cap of crimson georgette is banded with gold-tone lace and studded with pewter-colored beads. *Mobile Millinery Museum*. $200-250.

Victorian coiffure adornment comprised of a trio of feathers in persimmon, Kelly green, and deep orange, bound by a moiré ribbon bow. *Mobile Millinery Museum*. $75-125.

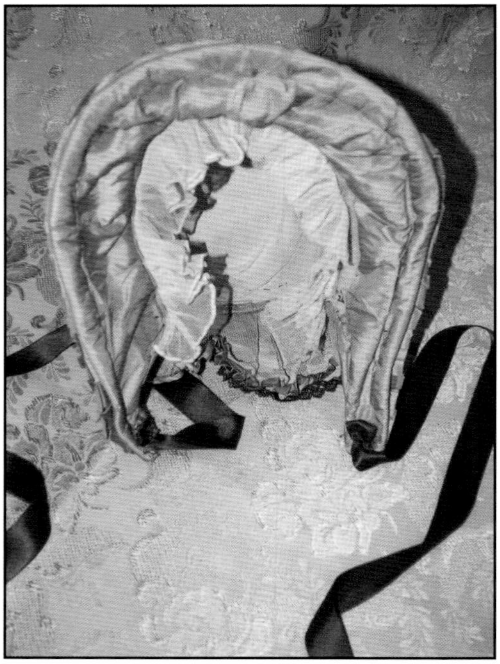

Interior view reveals a face-framing lace frill. Drawn bonnet of verdigris silk is trimmed with narrow black lace along the bavolet. Blue ribbon ties appear to be replacements. *Private Collection*. $500-600.

Drawn bonnet of black silk. Inner brim is lined with white, ruched gauze. *Mobile Millinery Museum*.

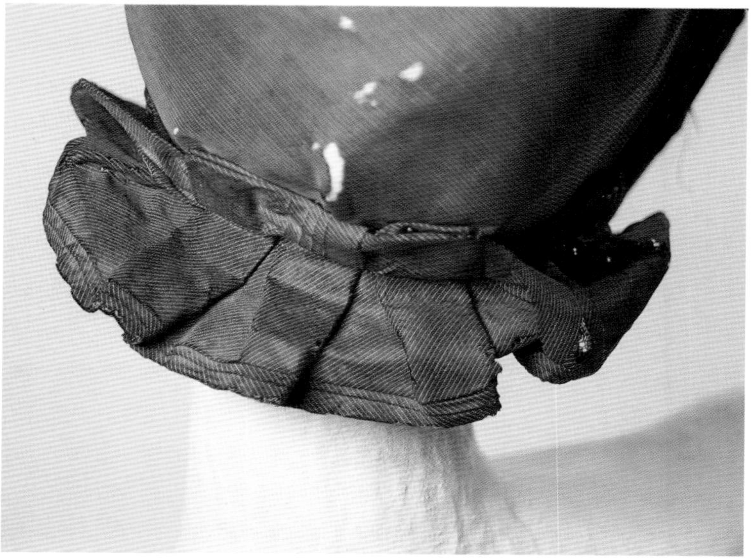

Back view shows a shallow, cartridge pleated, silk bavolet.

Designers applied their creative abilities to bonnet trims as well. The color, size, and arrangement of frills, which adorned the outer bonnet, as well as those which framed the face, altered with the seasons, according to fickle, millinery whims.

Following the *Paris Exhibition of 1855,* artificial flowers were held in esteem. Some were created with matching floral sprays, to be worn on the bodice or waistline of a dress, where fresh flowers were also worn. By 1859, flowers and foliage, fashioned of velvet, formed half-wreaths to brighten brims.

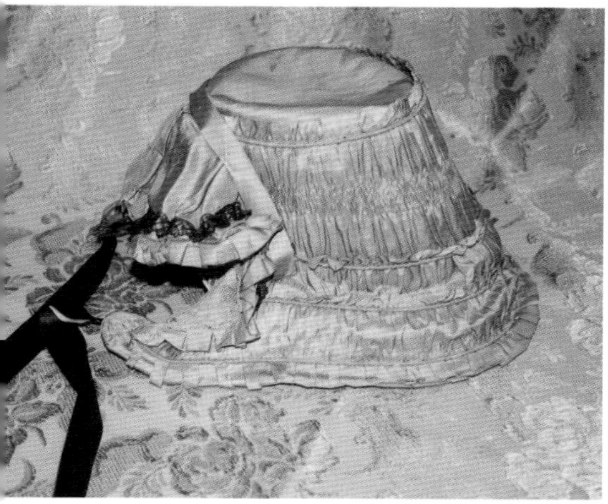

Right:
Poppies line the deep brim of this silk gauze bonnet fashioned on a wire frame. *Mobile Millinery Museum*. $800-1200.

Left:
An unknown woman in a similarly-shaped bonnet. Photo by N. C. LaLonde, Montreal.

A middle-aged woman wears a close-fitting bonnet, which appears to be adorned with berries. Photographed by Oliver Wright, Ingersoll, Ontario.

The development of a felt making machine, in the early Victorian era, enabled hat makers to produce hats in exciting new shapes. William Bowler introduced his hard, melon-shaped hat in 1850 and the style carries his name to this day. Eventually the style was adapted for women's headwear.

Green and black ostrich plumes sandwich the brim of a black felt bonnet (French) with black net lappets. *Mobile Millinery Museum*. $1800 - 2400.

Another of the author's great great grand-mothers in a floral rimmed bonnet with trailing ribbon ties. Photo by N.C. Lalonde. *Hillyer Collection, Mobile Millinery Museum.*

By 1860, the poke bonnet was disappearing and small hats including the kerchief-shaped fanchon, modified spoon bonnet, and pork pie, earned recognition.

Milliners feminized the pork pie with flowers, feathers, and ribbon, tilting them forward, atop upswept hair. Flirtation ribbons appeared on some heads, either streaming from the hat or threading through the hair. In fact, headwear for women reflected not only the social status of the wearer but offered clues as to an individual's personal situation. An eligible maiden would be encouraged to drape flirtation ribbons from the back of her hat, while a recently bereaved widow could be easily identified by her crape-veiled, black, lusterless bonnet.

A cognac-colored bonnet of woven straw with an angular design is strung with a half-wreath of velvet flowers in bottle green and cognac. *Mobile Millinery Museum*. $275-325.

A heart-shaped fanchon bonnet. The faded, yellow tulle confection is fashioned on a wire frame. *Mobile Millinery Museum*. $250-300.

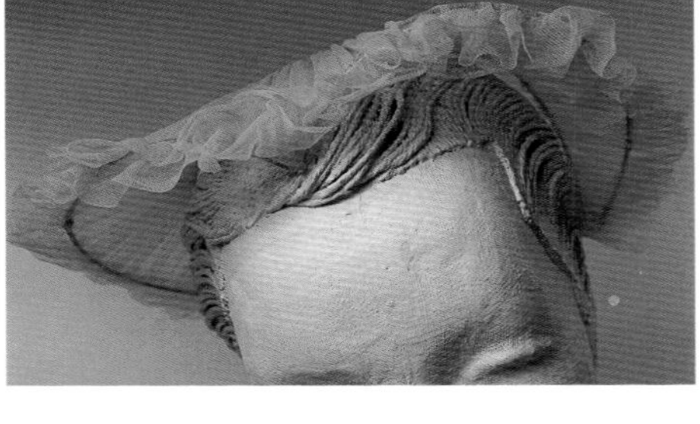

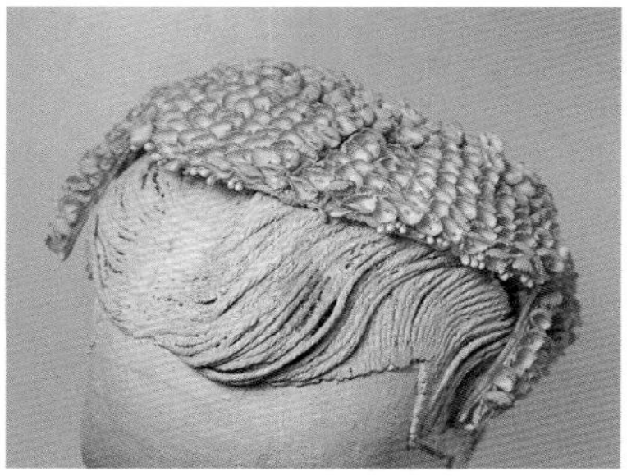

A similar bonnet, strewn with mint-green lily-of-the-valley, reveals the milliners skill at flower making. *Mobile Millinery Museum*. $200-250.

White straw bonnet banded with white grosgrain and fitted with embroidered net along the turned-up brim. *Mobile Millinery Museum*. $150-250.

Delicate pink flowers climb the back of this straw cloth, spoon bonnet. Navy velvet under-brim. *Mobile Millinery Museum*. $325.

A blackberry straw, porkpie hat, from the late Victorian era, sports a trio of faded roses in cheery-blossom pink, deep rose, and robin's-egg blue. Size 22. *Mobile Millinery Museum*. $250-300.

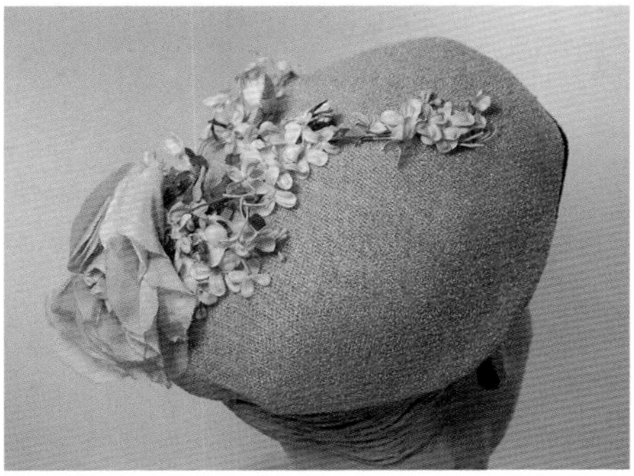

Back view.

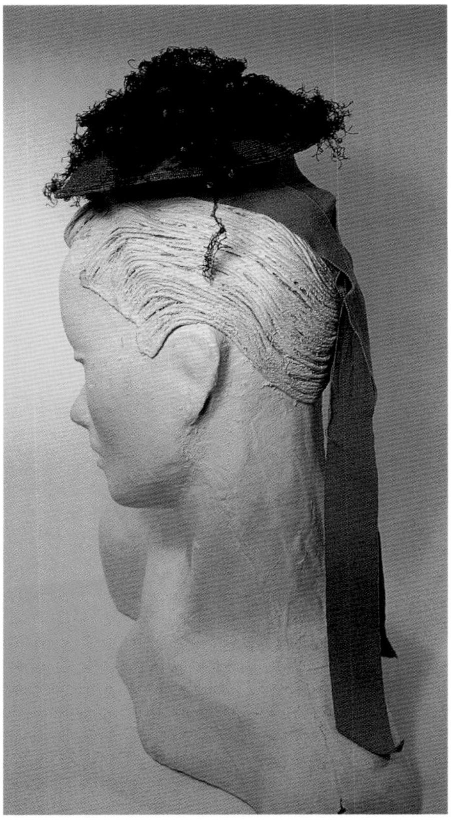

Sea blue flirtation ribbons trail from a straw bonnet topped with straw-dotted, black lace. *Mobile Millinery Museum*. $600-800.

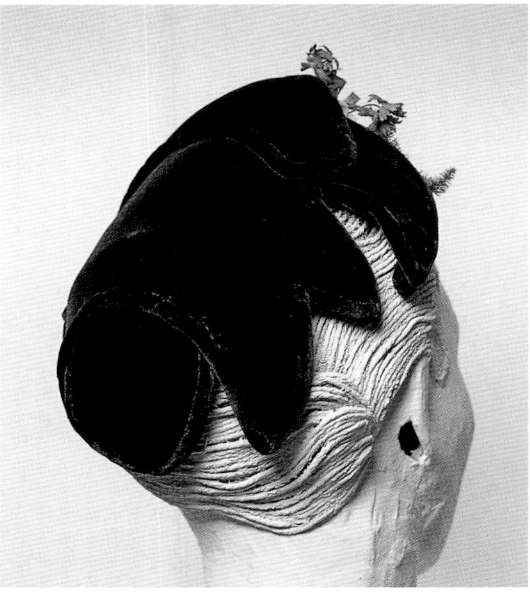

Brown velvet spoon bonnet constructed in segments of bonnet board to resemble an insect. Cotton flowers line the under-brim. *Mobile Millinery Museum*.

Front view.

This daisy-trimmed bonnet fastens with tulle ties. *Mobile Millinery Museum*. $300-400.

A Victorian beauty in black wood straw is banded with black velvet and adorned with an ostrich frond in peach and rust tones. A voilette depends over the brim at front. Label: Glen Mawr Exclusive Model. *Mobile Millinery Museum*. $300-350.

Veils did not completely cover the face until 1863, but existed instead as demi-veils, falling to the nose.

Victorian riding cap festooned with ostrich tips. A fine elastic strap secures the hat at the nape of the neck, beneath upswept hair. *Mobile Millinery Museum*. $200-225.

Circa 1870: A moss-green felt is veiled with a lace scarf, crossed in back and tied at the front in a manner known as Egyptian veiling.

A feather-swept trotteau, comprised of navy ribbon, is secured with a melon colored veil. *Mobile Millinery Museum*. $350.

Detail.

Mourning Hats

In order to identify mourning hats and bonnets of the period, it is helpful to possess a Victorian understanding of the stages and degrees of mourning. These were most commonly represented by the color, length, and arrangement of the veil.

For deep mourning, a lady of means would likely drape a large, black, crape or bombazine bonnet in heavy, black veiling. During second stage mourning, when black, softened with white, was appropriate, a widow might select a white, silk veil, beaded with jet. And during a stage of light mourning, fine black gauze replaced the heavy crape veil, which often moved to the back of the bonnet.

Mourning veils were secured by special, mourning pins – short, flat topped, black-headed pins that could be purchased by the boxful at department stores and millinery salons.

At mid-century, Victorians considered shades of lilac, purple, gray, and lavender appropriate for what was termed half-mourning, but this practice was abandoned and replaced with combinations of black and white, later in the period. French mourning etiquette was equally regulated but looked down upon by the English as too gay or cheerful.

The British also frowned upon North American practices, noting that with no social laws to regulate them, many women made themselves monuments to bereavement, at times wearing full black dress for a period of years. Furthermore, heavy crape veiling, worn over the face, was recognized as being frightening to children and damaging to the health. The fabric, made wet through crying, adversely affected the eyes and at times even caused sores to develop on the skin.

This buckram lined, silk velvet bonnet with mask veil features ink-blue ostrich plumage and a matching silk rose. The mint condition bonnet veil hangs from tiny metal hooks that protrude at intervals from the bonnet's brow. *Mobile Millinery Museum*. $800-1000.

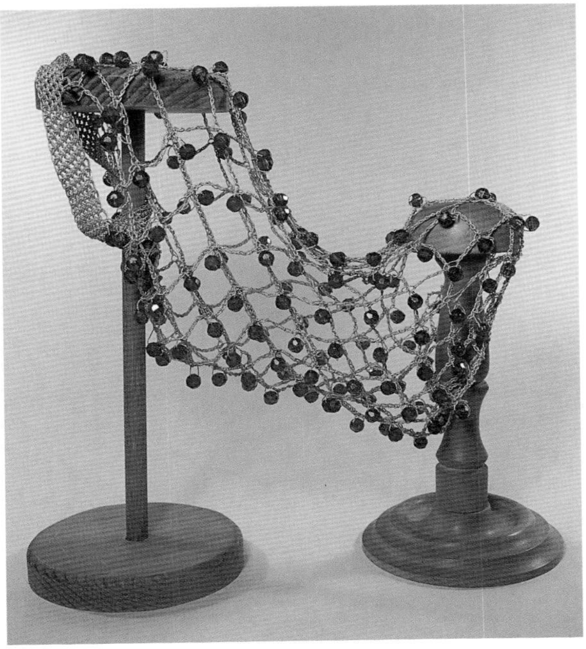

This silver thread, beaded-net, gondolier was likely made to adorn the tresses of a brunette, c.1860. *Mobile Millinery Museum*. $400-450.

During the late 1850s, Paris introduced a beaded, net bag for evening coiffures that consisted of a crocheted or square-knot tube, through which the hair extended at the back of the head. *Godey's* ladies book reported these to be at the height of fashion by September 1859. The fad was short-lived but morphed into the gondolier net, a device, which encased the hair in a caul-like, heavy netting of silk braid, velvet ribbon, or chenille.

As beads began to adorn hair combs, the buckle, a newly devised hair decoration, appeared. Cadogan bows presided over waterfall hairdos, and bonnet ties of flowers, plaited ribbon, and even fur, hung ornamentally.

The chantilly lappets that fall from this woman's stylish trotteau reach her fingertips. *Photo by P. H. Green, Peterborough, On.*

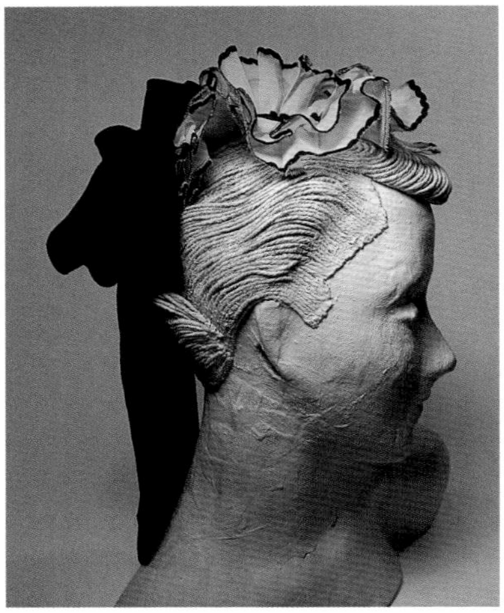

A black taffeta cadogan bow dominates a pink chiffon evening cap, c.1870. *Mobile Millinery Museum*. $350-400.

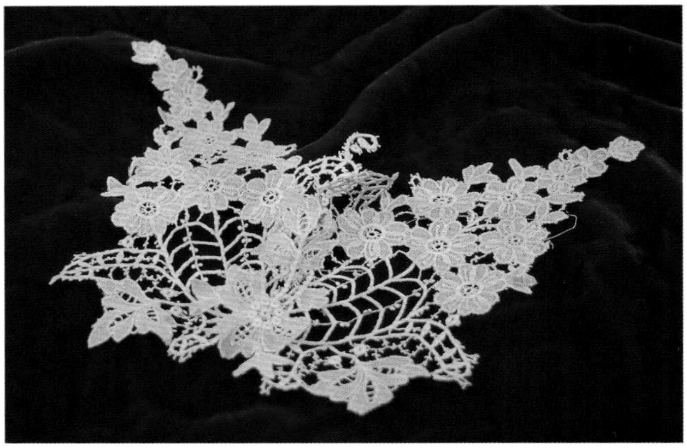

A starched lace butterfly serves as a coiffure ornament, c.1860-1880. *Mobile Millinery Museum*. $75-125.

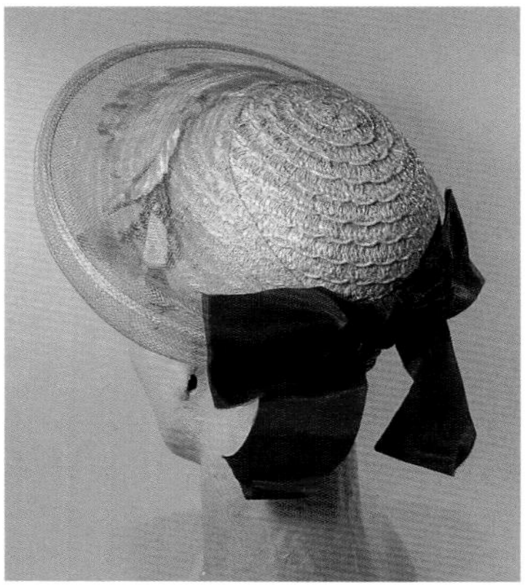

Sprigs of lavender are encased with silk flowers in a horsehair brim to create an airy impression. A burgundy taffeta, cadogan bow presides over the back of a cream straw crown. *Mobile Millinery Museum*. $350-450.

Bloomingdale's, Macys, and *Lord and Taylor's* time-honoured millinery departments served the fashionable women of New York, while mail order catalogues, from companies like *Montgomery Ward*, reached rural areas from the 1880s onward. Although the *Lord and Taylor* department store was established in 1825, the shop did not acquire its elegant, Fifth Avenue & 38th St. location until 1914. Here, Edwardian ladies were able to make stylish selections from elegant, walnut and ebony display cases.

A fad for animal adornment also developed at mid-century. Insects such as beetles, which were also made into earrings, graced milady's hat, as did moths, butterflies, hummingbirds, lizards, and even mice. Some Victorian women took up the hobby of home taxidermy, finding instruction in ladies magazines and periodicals.

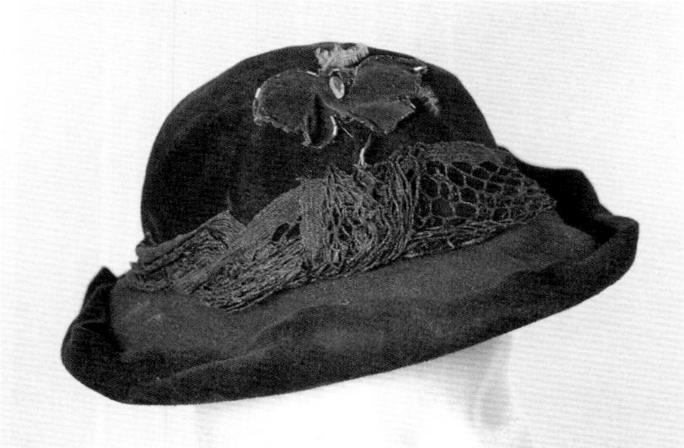

An emerald velour with black satin inner crown is banded in matching honeycomb-net and graced with a self-fabric butterfly. Tiny moss-green feathers serve as antennae while bronze beads outline the wings. Label: Lord and Taylor, Fifth Avenue. *Mobile Millinery Museum*. $350-400.

By 1870, petite composition or "made" birds graced Tyrolean hats, as did small wings. Young women utilized long, jeweled hatpins to secure their hats, until they married or came of age and were permitted to wear bonnets.

A "made bird" perches atop a bonnet of white sewn straw, its red claw beak set against pearls and glass stones. A ring of set-in rhinestones anchors the bird to a cascade of cloth flower petals. Label: Designed by Palmer Hat, Montreal. *Mobile Millinery Museum*. $375-425.

A trio of "made birds" waits to be placed on Milady's hat. *Mobile Millinery Museum*. $75-125 each.

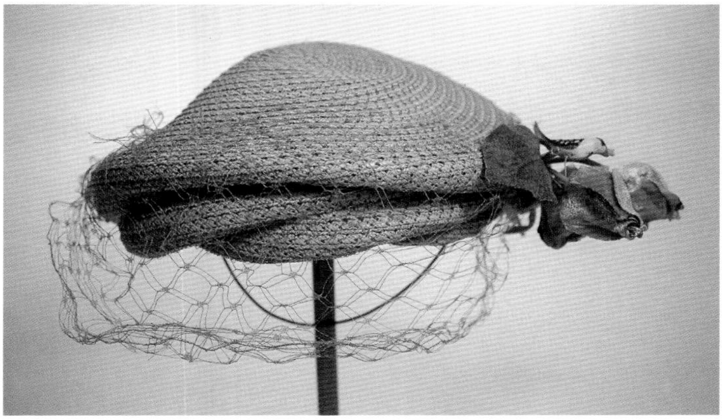

A pale lilac straw with matching lacy veil is trimmed with a trio of lilac velvet rose buds with touches of aubergine. A tiny brown and beige bird perches on a cloth stem. The back strap suggests this hat would have sat atop piled up hair. *Mobile Millinery Museum*. $300-350.

Millinery Bird of feathers, glued to cork, has tiny, green, wire feet. *Mobile Millinery Museum*. $125-150.

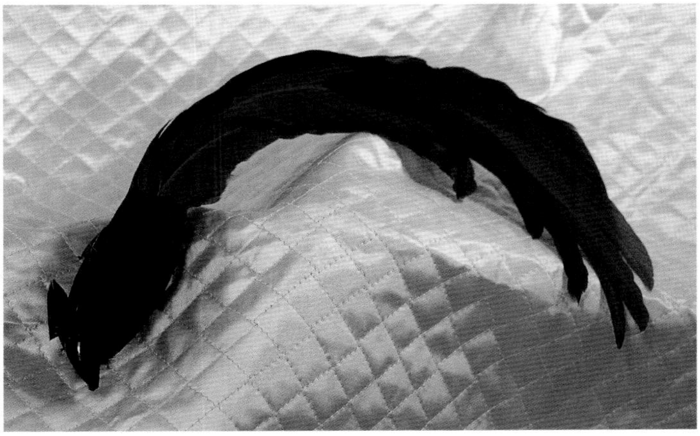

The tail feathers of this millinery bird in shades of blue, green, and black reach a full twelve inches. *Mobile Millinery Museum*. $125-150.

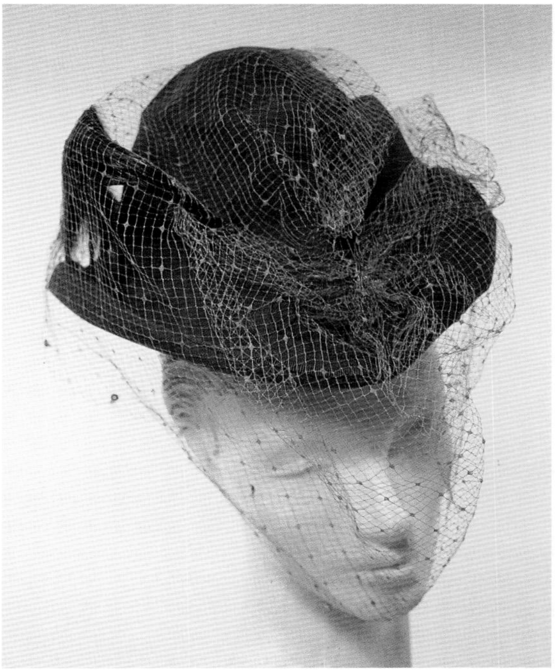

The draped crown of this brown beaver bonnet meets a brim that turns up on the sides to form a peak in front where six medallions have been cut from the felt. A brown feather cockade is secured under chin-length veiling that is sequined along the edge. *Mobile Millinery Museum*. $500-600.

Selection of wing-like adornments, c.1870. *Mobile Millinery Museum*. $60-80 each.

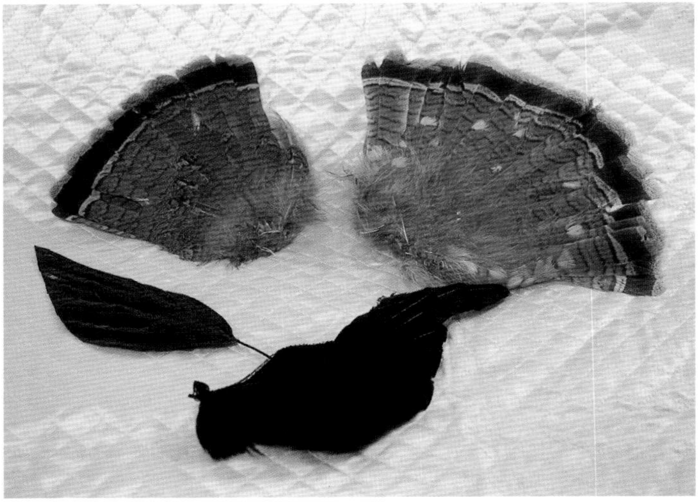

Pheasant tails and large wings, used to adorn hats, c.1880-1910. *Mobile Millinery Museum*. $80-120 each.

With the introduction of aniline dyes came a fashion for dark shades of green, blue, red, and plum and hats were fashioned in these colors to complement the newly popular, jewel-toned dresses. Brown, which was particularly trendy, might be relieved with white lace, ribbon, or feathers.

As the century wore on, hats achieved greater and greater status and were adapted to compliment various sporting ensembles. Large wings and stuffed birds sat on derbies, worn for hiking, hunting, and other sports. Fashionable lawn bowlers preferred the tam o'shanter and chic tennis enthusiasts sported cambric sunbonnets.

Circa 1860: A plaid taffeta cap, banded and bowed with black grosgrain. *Mobile Millinery Museum*. $300-350.

This taffeta and silk, velvet, toque from the 1880s boasts wispy feathers that have been dyed to match and contrast with sumac coloration. The crown is lined with a plaid silk in orange, gold, and green. *Mobile Millinery Museum*. $250-350.

Circa 1890: A two-toned, wood straw, platter is banded in black-to-brown velvet ribbon. A pair of cotton roses with paper leaves, sits atop a swag of spider web veiling. *Mobile Millinery Museum.* $100-150.

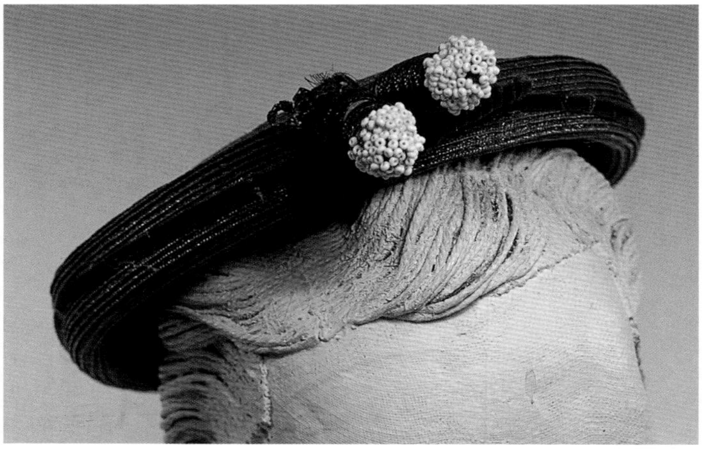

A broad saucer of Milan straw for an outing, c.1880, has faded to antique green. Narrow, brown, velvet ribbon bands a turned-up brim and coils around a pair of wooden beads, appliquéd at the tips with seed beads to look amusingly like cigar butts. Label: Made by Siegel's of Buffalo. *Mobile Millinery Museum.* $175.

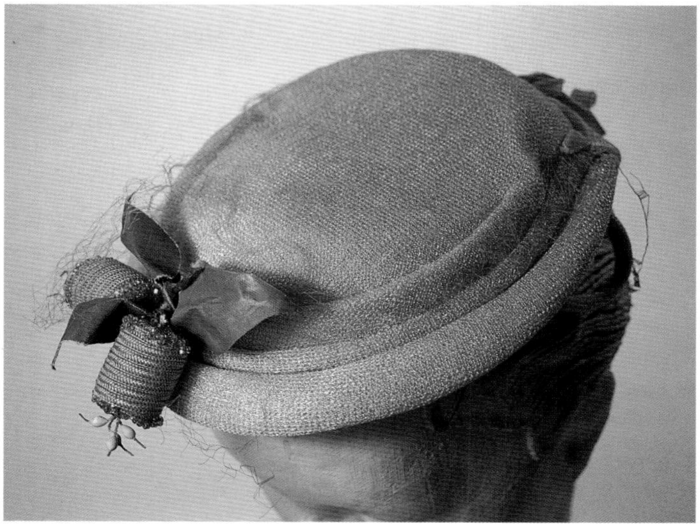

Remnants of veiling cling to this dainty straw cloth bonnet the color of maple sugar. Plaited straw is wrapped around cork to produce cylinder-shaped buds, which adorn the centre front. Green cloth foliage. A small, velvet ribbon bow is draped across the back extension. *Mobile Millinery Museum*. $250-300.

A darling black felt is wrapped in coarse net that is secured with a rhinestone-studded, cut steel buckle. Remnants of blue thread suggest the hat may have been more elaborately trimmed at one time. A ribbon tab reveals a hat size of 7 1/8. This style of riding hat was popular c.1800-1870. Label: Dobbs. *Mobile Millinery Museum*. $250-300.

Victorian bonnet of tempest black sewn straw. The brim is turned up and pleated at back to showcase a bouquet of violets in shades of purple with violet leaves on cloth stems. Black netting wraps the band. *Mobile Millinery Museum*. $320-350.

China-pink and absinthe-green roses peek out from beneath a brim, shaped to frame a nineteenth century face. Black velvet band and streamers. Label: Lady Beatrice Model. *Mobile Millinery Museum*. $300-350.

Historian and dressmaker Margot Dixon in an 1860s reproduction dress and bonnet. *Courtesy of Margot Dixon.*

A strawberry red, beaver plush toque, c.1885, announces its arrival with a spray of beige-to-brown feathers. *Mobile Millinery Museum*. $300-350.

A double grosgrain bow, pressed flat atop a lace jabot, draws interest to the back of this brimmed felt. *Mobile Millinery Museum*. $225.

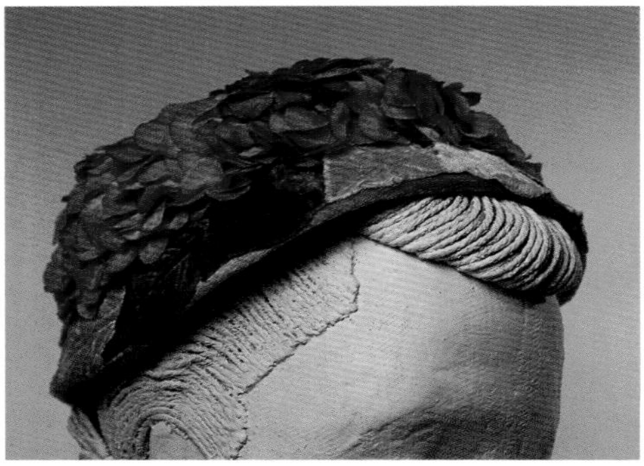

This jewel toned bonnet, c.1880, is made of simulated rose petals, strewn on velvet leaves. The under-brim is of lavender beaverette. Purple silk inner crown. *Mobile Millinery Museum*. $250-350.

Evening hairpiece of gilt foliage on a wire coronet. *Mobile Millinery Museum*. $100-150.

Lavender velvet is shirred and drawn across the crown of this melon-yellow straw bonnet and anchored on each side with cloth lilacs. *Mobile Millinery Museum*. $300-350.

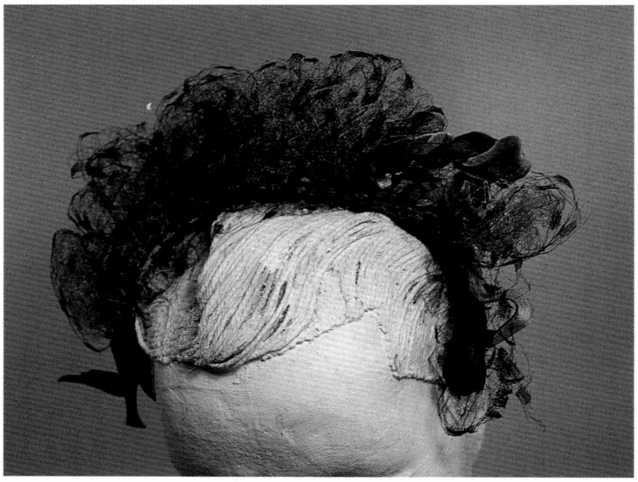

Coils of veiling are secured to a velvet covered band, from which extends a loop of green and blue velvet ribbon, challenging the fashion adage "blue and green should never be seen". *Mobile Millinery Museum*. $200-250.

Cloth-stemmed fuscia feathers are wired onto a black velvet band that ties under the chin. Label: Head Glamour, Made Especially for you by Mitchell. *Aline Banting Collection, Mobile Millinery Museum*. $150-200.

An evening head-piece of velvet leaves and flowers arranged on a wire band. *Mobile Millinery Museum*. $225.

As hairstyles changed and the bun moved closer to the top of the head, bonnet and hat makers adapted their designs accordingly. Hats sat upright or tilted forward, supported by pins or a chignon strap. Bonnets/capotes made room for hair to be pinned in a bun.

An antique-blue summer straw, c.1890, is banded with pink satin and ornamented with handmade bisque roses and paper leaves. Label: Palson Model. *Mobile Millinery Museum*. $300-350.

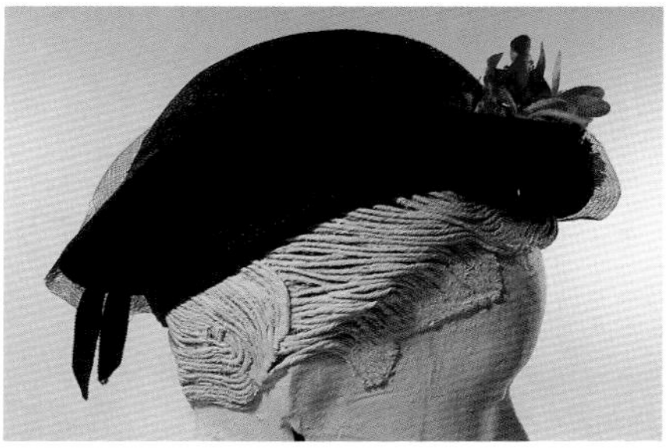

This late Victorian straw presents a forward tilting, rounded crown, which likely sat on upswept hair. A cockade of faded red velvet pinches the brim and catches a delicate spider web veil. Label: Eaton's. *Mobile Millinery Museum*. $300-350.

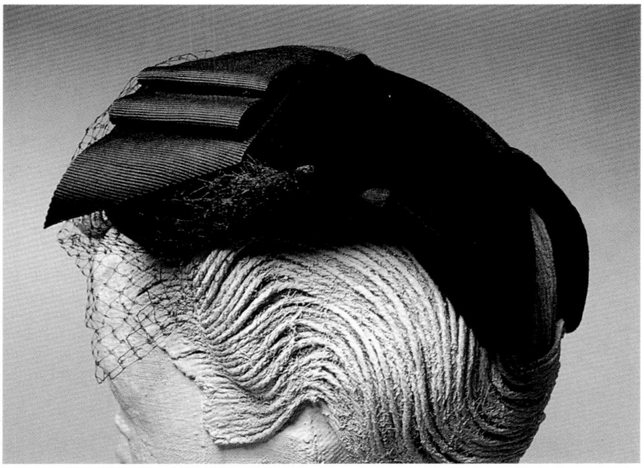

Ribbon-trimmed, black velvet, capote splits in back to allow for a French twist. *Mobile Millinery Museum*. $250-300.

This black silk bonnet is fashioned on a wire frame and trimmed with black leaves along the brow. A layer of black georgette covers the crown, over which is found remnants of a black crepe veil. Bonnet ties are of silk ribbon. *Mobile Millinery Museum*. $350-450.

Peonies and velvet loreilles d'ours (bear's ears) grace the crown of this pink and black velvet topper, c.1890. Remnants of coarse black net suggest that the hat originally trailed veiling from the center back. *Mobile Millinery Museum*. $175-225.

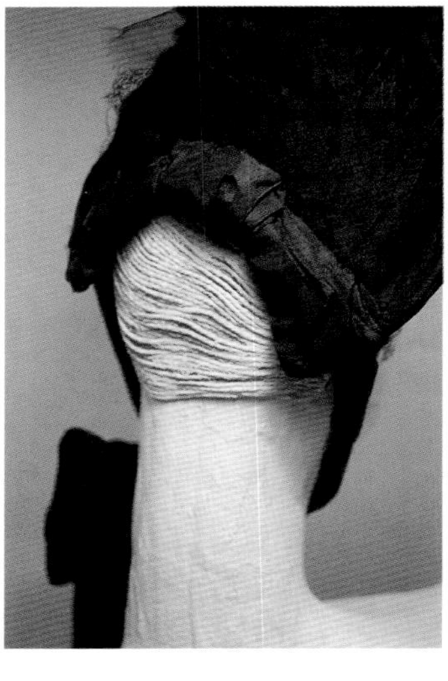

Reverse view showing allowance for the hair to be rolled in a bun.

Navy straw topper, c.1890. Label: Gainsborough Model. *Mobile Millinery Museum.* $300-350.

Interior view. An inner crown of silk gauze is gathered onto a purple ribbon. The occasional bead and steel sequin hints at the bonnet's former glory.

Gainsborough brand hatbox from a later period. *Mobile Millinery Museum.* $120-150.

A bonnet of hair lace over silk gauze, c.1860, ties with a continuous length of chenille dotted, scallop edged, black lace. *Mobile Millinery Museum*. $800-1000.

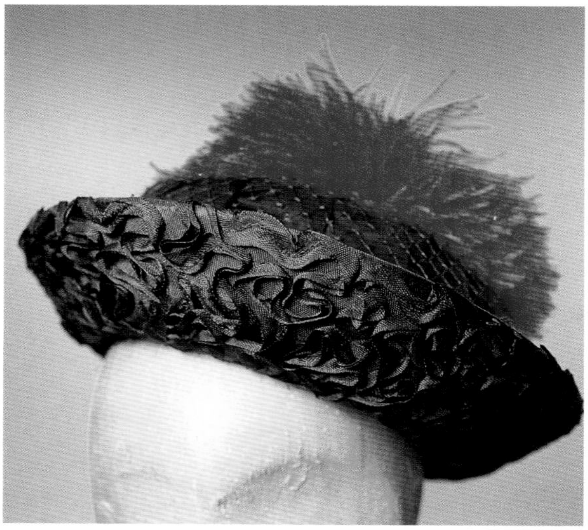

Black satin beauty with soutache under-brim and raspberry ostrich pompom. *Mobile Millinery Museum*. $200-250.

A double velvet bow and stripped coq feathers dangle from the back of this pancake hat of woven chip straw. Label: Evelyn Model. *Mobile Millinery Museum*. $200-250.

Narrow ribbon ties secure a fancy straw dress bonnet, c.1880. *Mobile Millinery Museum*. $600-800.

Detail: Bonnet peak is capped with black lace, tiny florals, and wired jet beads.

A fine quality navy straw from the late Victorian era is banded in cotton and adorned with a huddle of ribbon ends in green, navy, and red. *Mobile Millinery Museum*. $250-350.

By 1880, Canadian stylists took inspiration from architecture and created tall, "three story" hats to perch above upswept hair even as the population debated the ethics of skyscraper buildings. While on vacation in Chicago, Canadian Jennie Philip wrote the following in a letter to her friend, "they have just put up a new building down here; twenty-four stories high, isn't that awful?"

Victorian topper of yellow silk, dressed up with a lacy covering of white straw and horsehair. Satin lining. *Mobile Millinery Museum*. $300-350.

Plum velvet topper with raspberry silk lining boasts a rhinestone-bound, ribbon cockade. *Mobile Millinery Museum*. $250-300.

A crown of lacquered wood straw is covered with popcorn veiling. Label: Boutique, New York, Montreal. *Mobile Millinery Museum*. $275.

This tri-color, woven straw, three-story hat would have sat even higher on the original owner. *Mobile Millinery Museum*. $300-350.

Pink straw skyscraper, capped with moss-green net. *Mobile Millinery Museum*. $200-300.

Bird and feather ornamentation increased as did the use of tulle, lace, and ribbon, secured with strass buckles, and decorative pins. Bronze beads, jet and pearl medallions, and fur remnants competed with ostrich plumes and wired ribbon for pride of place on upright hats and bonnets. Feather quills appeared on tams and fedoras. Female children wore miniature versions of women's hats and bonnets, securing them with elastic under the chin.

This weeping ostrich plume has been lengthened through the addition of hand-tied feather extensions in a second color. *Mobile Millinery Museum*. $40-60.

Alsatian bows dominate these tall settler bonnets, c.1870. A butterfly bow of blue/black grosgrain, faced with white, trims the topper at left. The crown of the black velvet extends four inches above a subtle, sloping brim. Both are fitted with a pleated silk inner band. *Mobile Millinery Museum*. $350-450 each.

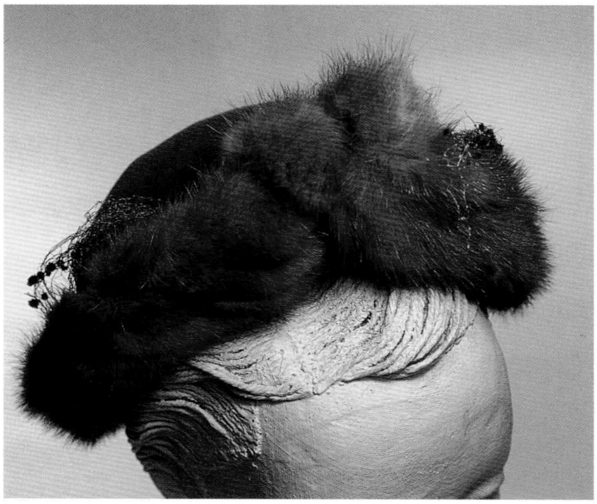

Circa 1890: Mink tails are pieced and coiled to band an orchid velour cap. Damaged spider web veiling boasts deep orchid chenille dots. *Mobile Millinery Museum*. $300.

A young woman rests an ostrich-plumed hat on her knee while she poses for a photograph. Her kid gloves and velvet-trimmed gown suggest she is dressed for winter. Photo by Arthur & Philbric, Detroit, Michigan.

A wood straw boater, banded with black velvet ribbon, proudly displays a vertically wired ostrich tip. A velvet flower in deep claret adds color. *Mobile Millinery Museum*. $300-350.

A dressy little saucer, c.1890, banded and rimmed with black velvet to match the under-brim. A vanilla and cocoa ostrich frond emerges from behind a pearl-studded, velvet rose. *Mobile Millinery Museum*. $250-300.

Chenille and straw-dotted veils added a new dimension to millinery. Moss green, sky, and navy-blue tulle, net, or chiffon veils were usually detached and could be worn in a loose manner, or pulled across the face and anchored at the chin. Ostrich tips, bows, and rhinestone combs stood in for evening headdress.

A young Victorian child sports a fancy bonnet with white ribbon ties. *Thomas Collection, Mobile Millinery Museum*.

A fringe of ostrich tips brims a tall crown of feathers, sewn to felt. *Mobile Millinery Museum*. $200-250.

Headdress of matching velvet ribbon hair-combs. *Mobile Millinery Museum*. $150.

A sapphire-blue "made bird" with touches of slate, maroon, and black, perches on a raisin black, felt topper. A limp, patterned veil falls to nose level. Label: Sanjé, New York, Paris. *Mobile Millinery Museum*. $180-220.

A nicely shaded, brown, beaverette toque. Grosgrain edges the deep, turned-up brim to match a ribbon cockade at the right side. Label: Made in France, Jeanne Le Marechal, 13, R. de Montholon, Paris. *Mobile Millinery Museum*. $275.

Chip straw boater with inner crown extension, c.1890. A black velvet band and streamers support black and white silk flowers with black stamens.

Cloth flowers dominate the brim of this high crowned Victorian straw. Delicate popcorn veiling draws over the chin. *Mobile Millinery Museum*. $350-450.

The fair sex adapted the gentleman's boater for casual wear and schoolgirls claimed an adaptation of the Breton for winter and summer. Picture hats, brimless saucers, and pancake hats replaced bonnets on fashionable heads.

A schoolgirl's Breton in carob beaverette stays secure by means of a narrow elastic chin strap. The mahogany silk ribbon band is marked with giant cross-stitches in canary and sky blue. A strip of antique-blue grosgrain divides a ribbon bow at the center back. The fifteen-inch, weighted silk streamers show deterioration in the form of shredding. Black ladies cloth lines the inner crown. Narrow elastic chin strap. Label (stamped on inner crown): Lady Fair Junior. *Mobile Millinery Museum*. $325-425.

A forward projection of cloth-stemmed petunias graces the brim of this blush-pink, straw cloth, boater. Label: Custom made by Gotham, 175 King E., Hamilton. *Mobile Millinery Museum*. $300-350.

Detail.

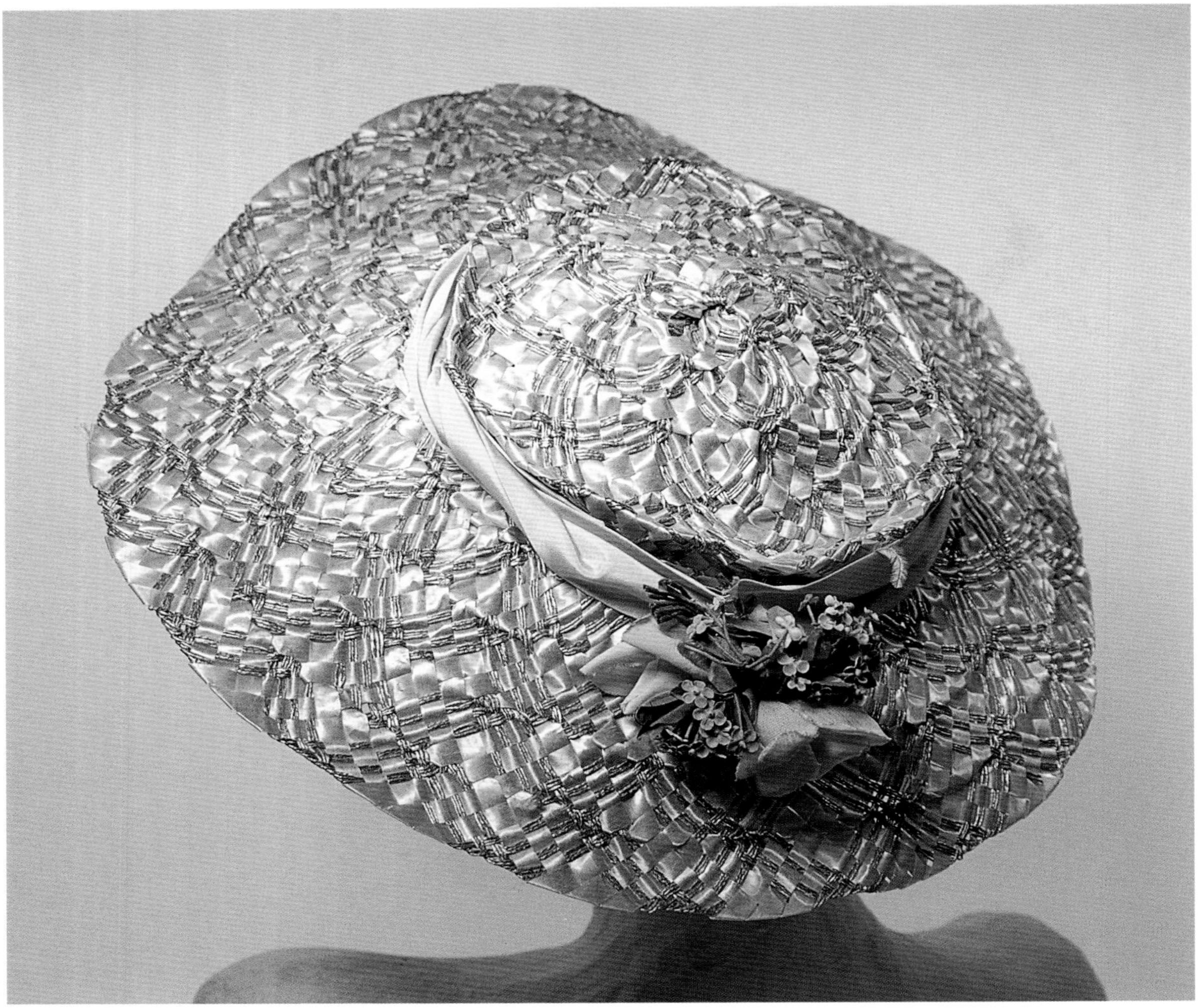

This skimmer of baby blue-straw, wrapped about the shallow crown with barely-pink taffeta, would be literally "gone with the wind" if it were not for hat pins and a fine elastic band. A pink taffeta bow graces the under-brim, while a pair of rose buds and tiny forget-me-nots completes the pink and blue theme. *Mobile Millinery Museum*. $525.

Bow-trimmed under-brim.

A straw skimmer from the late Victorian era, wreathed in realistic-looking wild flowers, rests at the back of the head, providing shade for the face and shoulders. *Mobile Millinery Museum*. $250-350.

Straw sun bonnet embroidered in a floral pattern. Green silk ribbon, attached to an inner crown, ties under the chin. Center crown slits allow for a scarf or fichu. *Mobile Millinery Museum*. $350-400.

Barbie™, as Scarlet O'Hara, in a ribbon-trimmed country straw. *Private Collection*.

Similar, embroidered straw, pagodine. *Mobile Millinery Museum*. $200-250.

An umbrella-brimmed, plaited straw, milkmaid shows off cloth-stemmed Black Eyed Susans. *Mobile Millinery Museum*. $350-400.

Red grosgrain ribbon ties are crudely sewn to the inner crown of this sun-faded, red straw bonnet. The original color can be seen on the under side. Natural straw pinwheels with red straw centers band the hat. *Mobile Millinery Museum*. $375-425.

An open-crowned cartwheel of woven, navy straw is wrapped with a vine of bright red cherries. *Mobile Millinery Museum*. $400-450.

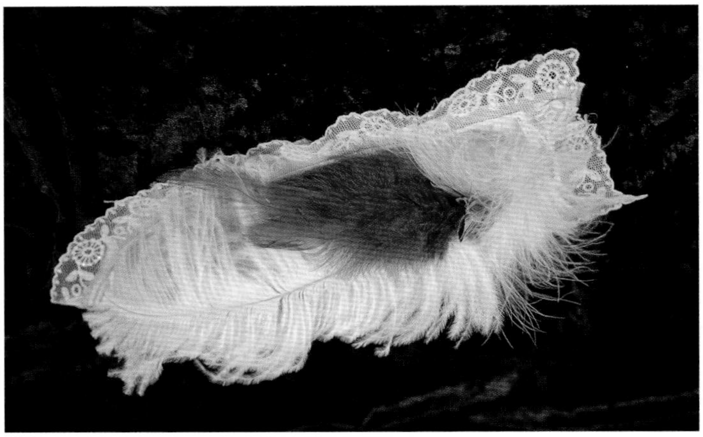

Feather-trimmed ribbon and lace cap, c.1880. *Mobile Millinery Museum*. $150-250.

Gauze-lined pancake hat of pink faille, ornamented with horsehair cats-tails in pink and black. A series of loops at the back of the hat allows for trims to be altered. *Mobile Millinery Museum*. $300-350.

If one possessed an understanding of the language of flowers, millinery trimmings could be interpreted to reveal a woman's mood or intentions. At times, by noting the first letter of each flower, they could also be read to reveal a young lady' first name. This is why original Victorian hats may appear to the modern eye to sport color combinations considered uncomplimentary by today's standards.

Roses, always favored by milliners, spoke their own language. A thorny rose signified hopes and fears, while a rose in bud suggested blossoming love. The cabbage rose represented love's messenger and a moss rose declared love's intention. Tea roses could be interpreted through their shadings; a golden rose admitted jealously while one shaded to apricot asked forgiveness following a quarrel.

The Victorian admiration for all things botanical, combined with a devotion to symbolism, is responsible for that distinct aesthetic, which every fully dressed hat or bonnet from the period, possesses. This aesthetic is not fully appreciated in the marketplace yet, as Victorian hats and bonnets command a considerably lower price than many later pieces; good news for the discerning collector.

In the Victorian era, strict and specific rules of social etiquette governed servant and socialite alike. In addition to being suitably fashionable, a hat was expected to be appropriate in color, style, and adornment for time of day, social station, activity, and, to some degree, age.

Ribbon-straw coils form an airy, summer-white charmer. *Mobile Millinery Museum*. $300-400.

Garden flowers band a dawn-pink, chip straw bonnet. Label: M.I. Gardiner, Ottawa. *Mobile Millinery Museum*. $175-225.

In North America, a woman's hat might also reflect her religious affiliation. One nineteenth century Methodist preacher believed that "no sooner will a woman who wears a bow on her bonnet go to heaven than a toad will climb a greased pole, tail foremost." Quaker bonnets were fairly simple and left unadorned. Hutterite women in western Canada wore a type of embroidered, polka dot kerchief to identify themselves as members of their religious sect.

A millinery bunch of orchid-colored flowers casually graces a similarly hued, straw capote. *Mobile Millinery Museum*. $200-250.

Black Mennonite bonnet. *Private Collection*. $150.

Hat Pins

As bonnets gave way to hats in the 1850s, hatpins were introduced to replace ribbon ties as a means of securing a hat to the head. Long, plain hatpins for this purpose first appeared in 1853. Shortly afterward, they were lengthened and finished decoratively with pearl, enamel, tortoise shell, and jewels. These were not the only sparklers that appeared on hats. Hat baubles included commemorative pins and brooches of precious and semi-precious stones – even the great House of Fabergé produced hat jewelry.

Hatpins reached dangerous lengths in the Edwardian age, necessitating licenses in England for pins longer than nine inches. Germany produced hatpin guards and many a suffragette was stripped of her hatpins prior to a court appearance.

Reddish brown velvet is stitched in a geometric pattern with silver thread, then draped in soft folds over a small-brimmed, high-crowned toque. Pinkish-brown taffeta is folded to band the crown above a narrow, grosgrain ribbon of the same color. Yellowish-brown silk lines the hat, while a pin commemorating the Jubilee of Queen Victoria, pierces the band. *Mobile Millinery Museum*. $400-500.

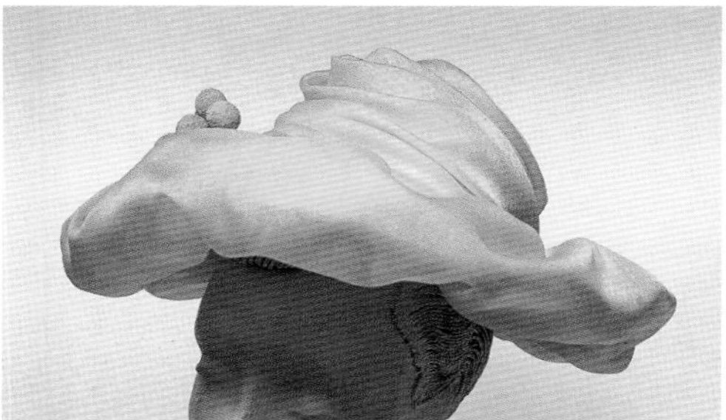

Silk organza, wire-framed Pamela. *Mobile Millinery Museum*. $450-550.

A velvet-trimmed, winter straw with jaunty aigrette. *Mobile Millinery Museum*. $250-350.

Jewel-topped hatpin. *Philip Warde Collection, Mobile Millinery Museum*. $175-225.

A pair of hatpins, lovely at one end, deadly at the other. *Philip Warde Collection, Mobile Millinery Museum*. $150-200 each.

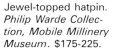

An intricately patterned, ecru veil drapes an orange, straw bonnet, with tucked crown. An organdie, chiffon, and satin rose adds panache. Label: Toronto. *Mobile Millinery Museum*. $375-425.

Late Victorian bonnet of fine, bronze straw. *Mobile Millinery Museum*. $200-250.

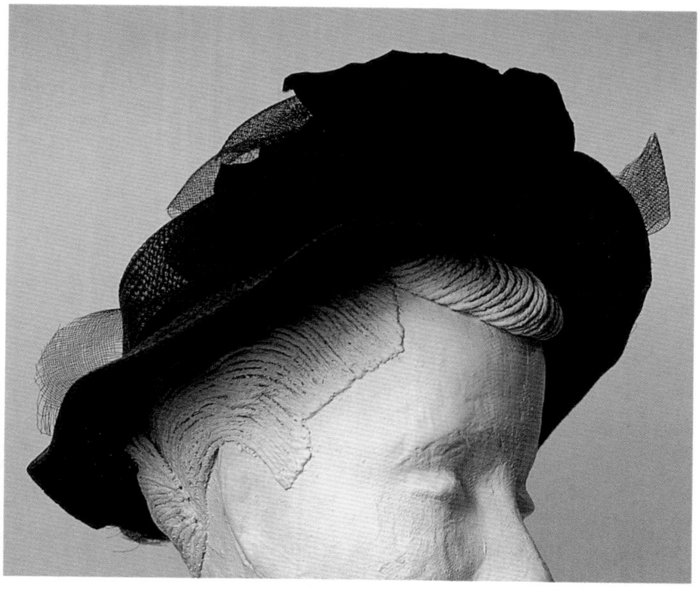

An open-crown hat of brittle, black straw is made lovely with an overlay of horsehair. *Mobile Millinery Museum*. $250.

Circa 1880: In each portrait, the woman on the left favors a three-story confection. All four women wear their hair on top of the head. *Barb Philip Collection, Mobile Millinery Museum.*

Victorian Albina Dunbeau tops her upswept hairdo with a large bowknot. Photo by Bourassa Studios, Montreal. *Barb Philip Collection, Mobile Millinery Museum.*

This young girl looks like a living doll in her enormous, vertically wired headdress. Photo by E. C. Ford. *Barb Philip Collection, Mobile Millinery Museum*.

A young woman models a late Victorian, flat, straw topper with vertical trim. *Barb Philip Collection, Mobile Millinery Museum*.

Natural straw schoolgirl boater of the type made famous by Lucy Maud Montgomery's *Anne of Green Gables*. *Mobile Millinery Museum*. $125.

Chapter III
Edwardian Grandeur: 1901 - 1920

"My aunts were stylish Edwardian ladies who stored their laces, furs, and frou frou in a trunk, from which we extracted special items when making a hat. We referred to this as the 'chest of grandeur.'"

— *Anonymous*

"My mother was a milliner in Wales. I often had to dress up in her creations and parade up and down the street in front of her shop, as a sort of advertisement."

— *Eileen Punnet, Burlington, Ontario*

"At the turn of the century, my father paid as much as $250 a pair for my mother's millinery birds; egrets, bird-of-paradise, etc."

— *Frank Dorsen, Dundas, Ontario*

A box of feather quills, originally belonging to a French milliner. *Mobile Millinery Museum*. $250-300 (box and contents).

This and That

I love the red
blade-like, arrow straight

Lovely too, the lavender
it's silky fronds that undulate

And black coq's oily hue
in sunlight, green
by candle, blue

At crimson quill I sigh and smile
admiring its lustre all the while.

Egret, ostrich
this and that
...feathers
tethered to my hat.

Feather Facts

- The millinery term "aigrette" is from the French, meaning plume.
- The Snowy Egret and Great Egret were shot from ambush, during their breeding season, when the plumage was at its peak. The lengthy, all-white feathers, extending beyond the tail, were highly prized in the millinery trade.
- Ostrich feathers are still used in millinery today as these can be harvested without harm to the bird.
- Supple ostrich plumes were dyed vibrant hues and draped over bonnet brims or used to encircle a crown. On Edwardian high hats, ostrich plumes ascended dramatically to heights of eighteen inches or more. Milliners also clipped and curled the tips to add a flirtatious aspect to their confections.

Extinct Species

Throughout the ages, all cultures have adorned their heads with feathers, either to decorate themselves or to indicate status within a group. During the nineteenth century, the millinery industry took this practice to environmentally tragic extremes. The widespread slaughter of exotic tropical birds for use in millinery led to the endangerment and extinction of many species.

In the late 1880s, a group of Boston-area women, distressed by the profusion of bird-bearing hats, organized to protest an overzealous feather industry. Their efforts eventually led to the establishment of the Audubon society, domestic bird sanctuaries, hunting regulations, the protection of migratory birds, and tariffs on the importation of tropical plumage. The group shared their views door to door and in schools; they instituted inspections of millinery stock, held fashion shows of acceptable headwear, and "white-listed" milliners who sold birdless chapeaux.

By 1901, hats adorned with bluebirds, jays, orioles, terns, owls and owl heads, sparrows, hummingbirds, and warblers fell out of fashion. Soon gull, heron, and tern populations began to recover. Women in Europe and North America followed Queen Mary's lead, early in the century, and discarded their feathered chapeaux. Consequently, there are a limited number of these artifacts available to collectors. A number of them are coming out of storage and showing up at flea markets, antique malls, and rummage sales, however. At one time antique dealers dismantled feathered hats and sold the plumage to fly fisherman. Now vendors are keeping vintage fashion hats intact and feather fanciers are able to amass collections of millinery feathers that are as varied and colourful as the birds they represent.

Circa 1902: A woman named Ellen wears a large, floral-trimmed, straw hat atop abundant, upswept hair. *Hillyer Collection, Mobile Millinery Museum.*

Hats and Hairstyles

The practice of drawing the hair to the top of the head in a bun or braid remained popular well into the first decade of the twentieth century, but enhancements in the form of wire supports, padding, and added hair were used to make the hair appear fuller. The pompadour hairstyle was revived, with hair back-combed and pulled over wire "rats". These also served as a base for what appeared to be free floating hats, of grand proportions, which sat well off the face, by means of crown extensions and integrated bandeaux.

This young girl's large-brimmed hat appears to float above her head. *Thomas Collection, Mobile Millinery Museum.*

Kitty Hillyer, c.1905, under a magnificent, ribbon-crowned topper. *Hillyer Collection, Mobile Millinery Museum.*

The author's Great Aunt Maggie Philip in an ostrich-swept widebrim. *Hillyer Collection, Mobile Millinery Museum.*

Young Irma Newton wears a widebrim, which appears to be suspended behind her head. A ribbon, visible at the center front, is likely drawn across the crown to end in a bow at the nape of her neck.

Edna Combers' double-brimmed hat dominates her winter costume.

This early twentieth century photo depicts women in large hats, which appear almost suspended above their silhouette. The hatless woman in the foreground wears a hairstyle likely enhanced by a pompadour frame. *Ella Philip Collection, Mobile Millinery Museum.*

The Hillyer family, c.1908, in a variety of stylish hats. *Hillyer Collection, Mobile Millinery Museum.*

Postcard, c.1912. A stylish young lady appears to be holding the brim of her rose-trimmed straw against the wind. *Courtesy of Iris Hillyer.*

Postcard of a woman in a posy-trimmed straw skimmer. *Courtesy of Iris Hillyer*.

Postcard of a young maiden in a ruffled blue hat, which perches above a pompadour hairstyle. *Courtesy of Iris Hillyer.*

Postcard, c.1911, of an Irish maiden in an early twentieth century widebrim, secured with a ribbon sash. *Courtesy of Iris Hillyer.*

Postcard, c.1909: This young lady's enormous, flowered hat doesn't fall off despite her perilous circumstance. *Courtesy of Iris Hillyer.*

Postcard sent from McGill University, Montreal, September 30th, 1911. The young lady, dressed in McGill colors, secures her feathered pancake hat with chin-length veiling. *Courtesy of Iris Hillyer.*

The author's great aunt Margaret Hillyer, c.1902, in an ostrich-and-rose-trimmed, satin confection. *Hillyer Collection, Mobile Millinery Museum.*

Early twentieth century postcard of a woman in towering chapeau. Her new husband sports a smart black bowler. *Courtesy of Iris Hillyer.*

Bedford, Quebec, 1909: Three girls in age-appropriate hats pose against the barn. *Thomas Collection, Mobile Millinery Museum.*

The author's great great Aunt Maggie in a scoop-brimmed, horse-hair treasure. The hat originated in Scotland. *Hillyer Collection, Mobile Millinery Museum.*

A winter warmer boasts snow-white ostrich plumage.

Shops and catalogues offered false curls, switches, rolls, plaits, and waves, which women used to elegant effect under plumes, aigrettes, and other evening adornments. Girls, young women, and even brides favored large bows for a time and innovations were made in the hairpin industry, enabling women to arrange their "Marcel waved" hair. Giant tortoise shell combs gained popularity as did the tricorne and the toque.

The Gainsborough made a spectacular repeat performance. These and other hats required a healthy financial investment. In 1902, a gentleman's Homburg felt could be had for 18 shillings, in Britain, while a woman would have to pay 15 shillings for even a poor quality straw. *What's What* of the same year observed "there are no cheap hats for women and no dear (expensive) ones for men."

These photos, taken from Ella Philip's scrapbook, show her stylish Edwardian friends in various grand confections. *Ella Philip Collection, Mobile Millinery Museum.*

Edwardian bride Margaret McCaskill in a lace-brimmed, taffeta, widebrim. *Photo by Carriere Studios, Montreal. Hillyer Collection, Mobile Millinery Museum.*

Widebrims, layered with net, tulle, and lace, held sway for a time but as brims diminished, c.1904, height was emphasized through towering crowns and vertical adornments, particularly feather quills. Milliners hand-tied extra ostrich fronds to existing plumes to lengthen and feminize them. In 1905, America passed the *Audubon Plumage Law*, effectively putting an end to the further use of bird-of-paradise and egret.

By 1907 hat crowns, brims, and ornamentation reached extreme dimensions, complimenting the straight lines of the couture but causing difficulties for theatre owners, who instituted a rule that ladies remove their hats during performances. Hatpins of greater lengths were required to hold these extravagant examples of millinery art in place. The need to skewer hat, hair, false hair, and superfluous wadding created virtual weapons of once simple decorative pins. My own great aunt Millie used to advise me to carry a hatpin for protection. She had once utilized hers to stab a man who had "gotten fresh" with her on a streetcar.

Two women in magnificent widebrims peek through the bars at a zoo. Note the sizeable bonnet on the child in the foreground. *Ella Philip Collection, Mobile Millinery Museum.*

Note the hat with soaring wing adornment on the figure second from the left. *Ella Philip Collection, Mobile Millinery Museum.*

A floral wreath brims this unusual wire-frame hat, worn by stylish Ray Hillyer. *Hillyer Collection, Mobile Millinery Museum.*

Blanche O'Brien's ostrich-plumed hat towers over that of her sister-in-law, Florence. *Thomas Collection, Mobile Millinery Museum.*

You are a bit of all right.

Postcard, c.1910. The young girl is "a bit of all right" in her large striped hat. *Courtesy of Iris Hillyer.*

CORNERED.

Postcard of an Edwardian gentleman, "cornered" by a woman, coiffed for evening, in an aigrette to match her lace-trimmed gown. *Courtesy of Iris Hillyer.*

Olive Mitchell's Edwardian creations sit atop frilled hat stands in her Bruce St. shop window, Thornbury, ON.

A group of friends pose in crown-hugging hats. *Ella Philip Collection, Mobile Millinery Museum.*

Circa 1915: The author's great aunt Mildred poses in a boater with bigeminal floral trim, while her sister Jen (the author's grandmother) sports a lacy, low-crowned, widebrim. Both wear their hair pulled back and covering their ears. *Hillyer Collection, Mobile Millinery Museum.*

Circa 1914: The author's great aunt Ella in a low-crowned, brimmed hat with vertical plumage. *Ella Philip Collection, Mobile Millinery Museum.*

Jane Philip attempts to rock climb, c.1910, in a long skirt and flat-brimmed, straw, sport hat. *Hillyer Collection, Mobile Millinery Museum.*

A pair of women in automobile bonnets stop to picnic with children. *Ella Philip Collection, Mobile Millinery Museum*.

A pair of silk peonies graces a black velvet, Edwardian topper. The brim, wide in front, narrows at the back. An elastic strap secures the hat. *Mobile Millinery Museum*. $300-350.

1915: Beatrice McClarty in an enormous straw widebrim, likely purchased in California when the hat was first in style. *Photo courtesy of Brome County Historical Society.*

A deep-crowned, Edwardian charmer of plush beaverette. The wide velvet, burnt-orange band is secured with a strass buckle. A string-drawn, inner crown allows for removable padding. *Mobile Millinery Museum*. $325-350.

A haphazard array of wildflowers for a silk velvet pagodine. *Mobile Millinery Museum*. $150-200.

A swirl of feathers in black, brown, and pink dresses a hat of black and brown beaverette, banded with black faille. The early twentieth century Dobbs hatbox depicts a street scene outside of the Dobbs & Co. building on Fifth Ave in New York. *Mobile Millinery Museum*. Hat: $150-200.

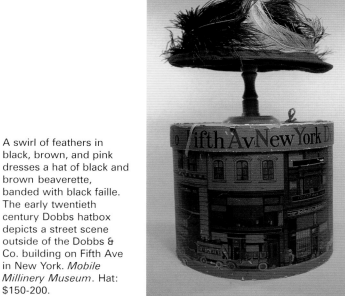

A swirl of feathers in shades of brown and powder blue enhances the brim of this blonde astrakhan homburg. Orange satin lines the crown. *Mobile Millinery Museum*. $350.

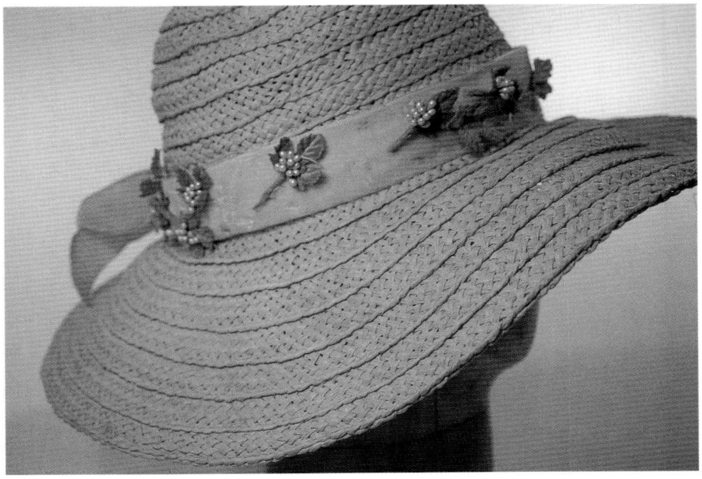

Painted straw Pamela, c.1918. Beaded velvet leaves, sewn to a band of yellow velvet ribbon, please the eye. *Mobile Millinery Museum*. $250-350.

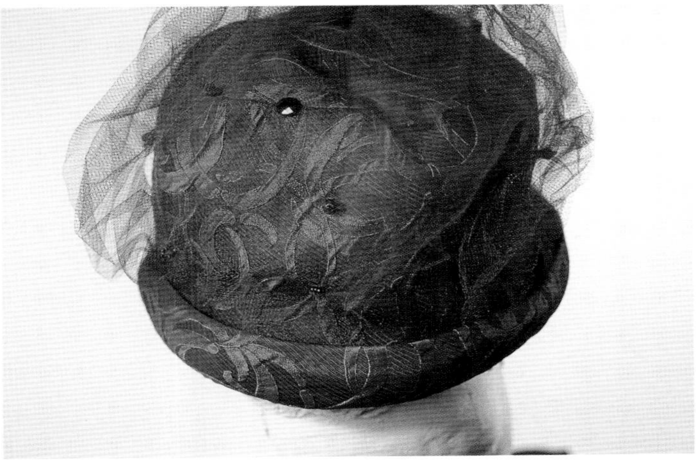

Circa 1910: A crown of black and bronze taffeta, studded with jet beads and medallions, grows taller with a pouf of net. Label: Simpson's. Canada. *Mobile Millinery Museum*. $200-250.

Circa 1914: A military-inspired helmet of red felt with grosgrain band. Label: Glen Mawr. *Mobile Millinery Museum*. $75-100.

Strips of horsehair and lacquered straw spiral from the center crown to produce a stunning, Edwardian confection. Wired brim, tulle band, tuft of wired feathers. *Mobile Millinery Museum*. $350.

An Edwardian widebrim of fine black straw is exuberantly trimmed with powder-blue thistles and a spray of brown rooster tail. Attached chin-ties suggest that the hat may have been designed for motoring. *Mobile Millinery Museum*. $250-350.

Edwardian motoring hat of lacquered straw is secured with a lace fichu. *Mobile Millinery Museum*. $300-350.

A summer garden of velvet, chiffon, and chenille, interspersed with glass balls, is wrapped about a horsehair base, then crowned and rimmed with straw cloth. Label: Custom Made by Gotham. Hamilton, ON. *Mobile Millinery Museum*. $300-350.

This hat style was referred to as a "tall round" by the Edwardians. Woven of blonde green straw, the hat is draped in front with a diagonal spray of flowers and foliage in cabbage, asparagus, and cabaret green. Inner band of velvet ribbon. *Mobile Millinery Museum*. $250-300.

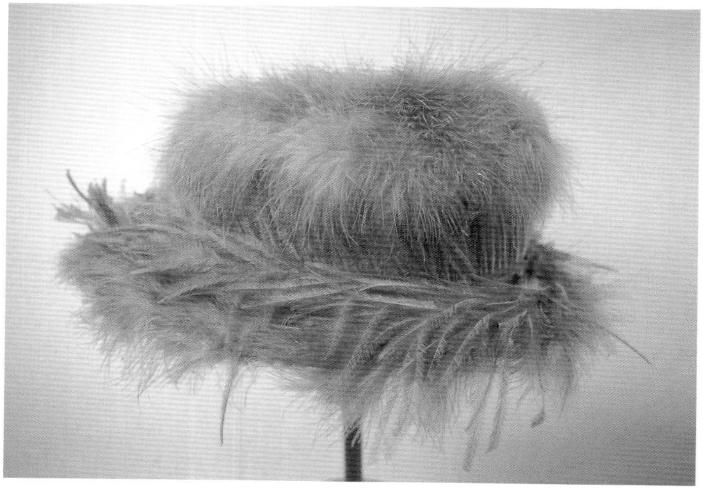

A pink felt boater, swathed in dusty rose marabou, is banded with a matching eighteen-inch ostrich frond. Label: Paris. *Mobile Millinery Museum*. $300-350.

Jewel-toned feathers swirl about a satin-lined, Edwardian toque. Spiderweb veiling helps to hold the feathers in place. *Mobile Millinery Museum*. $250-300.

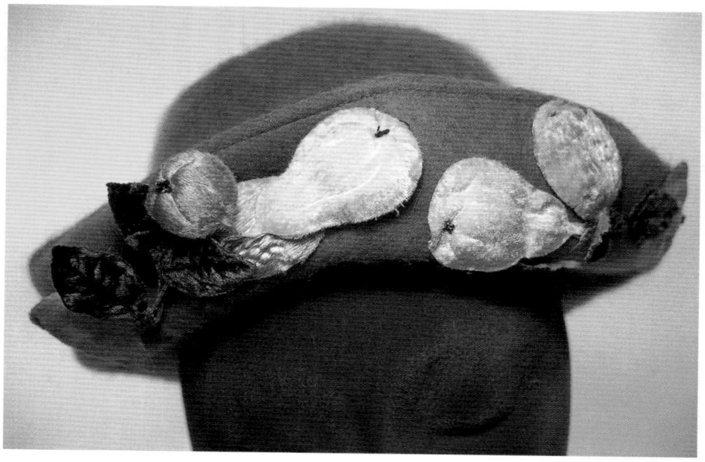

A Breton of tawny wool felt, ornamented with velvet fruit. *Mobile Millinery Museum*. $250.

A piece of hat jewelry, set off against a black chevron, adds panache to this beaverette toque. *Mobile Millinery Museum*. $250.

A chestnut widebrim of woven chip straw possesses a unique tulip-shaped crown. Band and flower of matching organdie. *Mobile Millinery Museum*. $260-300.

The soft yellow color of this Queen Anne style, shallow-crowned, skimmer contrasts nicely with a bottle-green velvet band and streamers. *Mobile Millinery Museum*. $200-250.

Hand painted ivy and a weeping ostrich plume add vitality to this apricot horsehair Pamela. *Mobile Millinery Museum*. $350-450.

A large, brown velvet button anchors a series of narrow velvet streamers to encase a toque in maroon feathers. *Mobile Millinery Museum*. $120-150.

The weeping ostrich plume that drapes the right side of this hat is as velvety as the silk that covers the modified boater, c.1910. A pair of crimson primroses add dramatic color. *Mobile Millinery Museum*. $250-300.

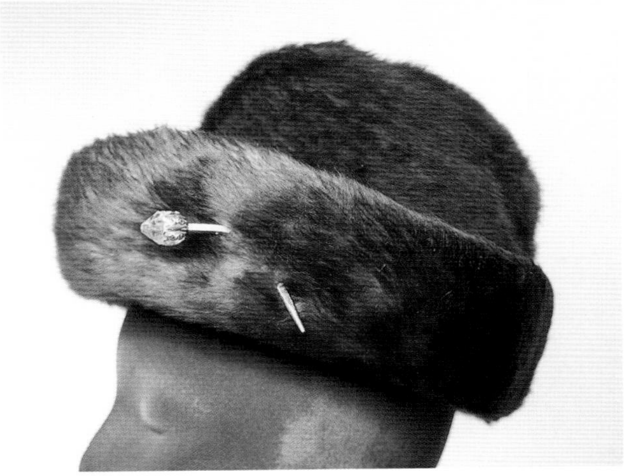

A toque, suitable for winter, is crafted of smoke-gray, long nap beaver on a café-au-lait felt base. A glittery pin rests against a stiff satin tab at the center front. Label: Reproduction of Paulette, Paris. *Mobile Millinery Museum*. $225.

A spiral of grape straw is fronted with a double line of satin, in purple and barely pink. A pair of cloth-stemmed white roses sits atop a cluster of lilacs at the right temple. Remnants of stitching at the center front suggest an absence of further, original trim. *Mobile Millinery Museum*. $200-250.

A coal black, visored, cap is fashioned of chip straw on a net base. An ostrich feather protrudes from a creased crown behind a peach cabbage rose. *Mobile Millinery Museum*. $400-450.

Accordion-pleated organdie covers a pouffed crown lined with black faille. The pinched-back scoop brim is fashioned on a wire frame. *Mobile Millinery Museum*. $280-320.

Flocked net veiling covers the crown of a navy toque, c.1905. Additional veiling ties at the center back. Small white flowers add charm. Velvet inner band. *Mobile Millinery Museum.* $225.

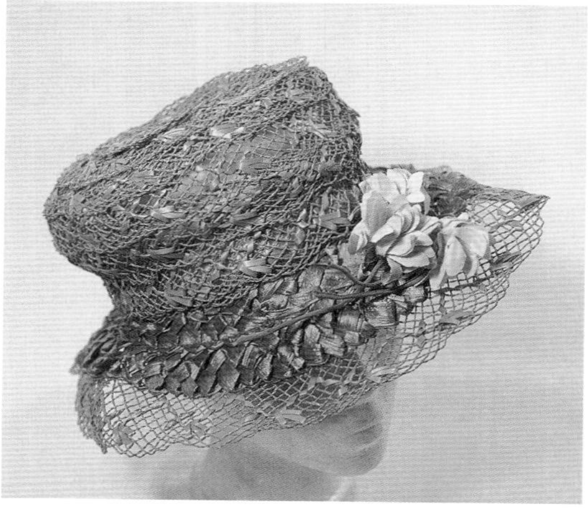

Naturally-colored chip and braid straw alternate to form a fancy sun bonnet, c. 1912. *Mobile Millinery Museum*. $250-350.

Modified bowler, c.1910, is woven of navy chip and white straw. The hat is shaped to perch forward lightly at the brow. Navy eyebrow veiling covers a center front bow. *Mobile Millinery Museum*. $350-400.

Black straw toque, c.1905. A black velvet bow anchors a cluster of burnt orange roses. The crown is also banded with black velvet. Label: Morgan's. *Mobile Millinery Museum*. $200-225.

Circa 1918: A stripped ostrich quill curves along the brow of an oval-shaped orange straw held in place with a tortoise shell hatpin. *Mobile Millinery Museum*. $400-450.

Edwardian high hat of horsehair and straw, banded with olive-green velvet. Early "Eaton's of Canada" label. *Mobile Millinery Museum*. $200-250.

This Edwardian fur has yellowed with age. The original ivory color can be seen in the folds of the brim. Satin lining; narrow leather band. *Mobile Millinery Museum*. $225.

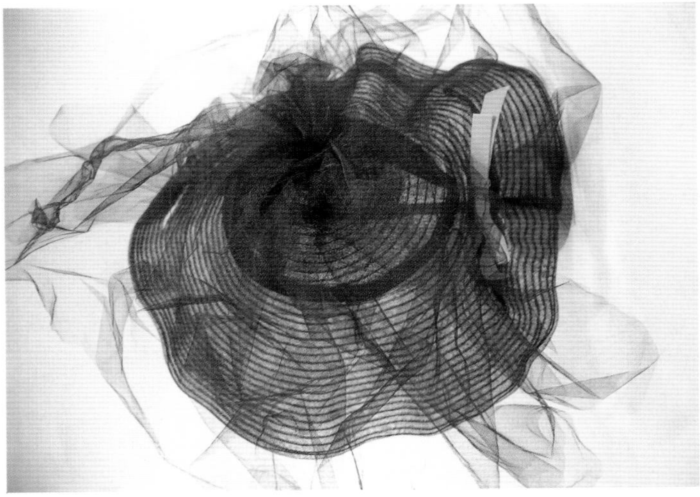

The peek-a-boo brim of this Edwardian horsehair dips seductively over the brow when worn. This unusual hat is given a lighter-than-air effect with the addition of black tulle. *Mobile Millinery Museum*. $650.

Revival Gainsborough of black beaverette features a stuffed inner-crown lining with drawstring. *Mobile Millinery Museum*. $550-650.

The folded brim of this low-crowned, butterscotch, straw dips seductively to support a cluster of nuts. Sandalwood tulle wraps the crown. *Mobile Millinery Museum*. $450-550.

A deep-crowned Edwardian; one of a pair of similarly styled, sleek, navy straws donated by Patty Powel. *Mobile Millinery Museum*. $250-350.

Laurie MacLean poses in a low-crowned hat of similar design. *Laurbelle MacLean Collection, Mobile Millinery Museum*.

Jet-trimmed, Edwardian, gondolier with harem veil, c.1918. *Mobile Millinery Museum*. $800-1000.

Evening headdress of gilded tulle. A cropped aigrette emerges from a rhinestone teardrop at the center front. *Mobile Millinery Museum*. $250-300.

A feathered fantasy, c. 1918. *Mobile Millinery Museum*. $800-1000.

Circa 1914: Glycerined "Mephisto" feathers emerge from the crown of this black tower of silk faille bows. A jeweled hat pin adds distinction. *Mobile Millinery Museum*. Hat and pin $500-550.

Straw motoring hat with red chin-ties and fringed silk puggree. *Mobile Millinery Museum*. $320-350.

A smartly tailored navy felt with vertical quill boasts checkerboard eyebrow veiling. *Mobile Millinery Museum*. $200-250.

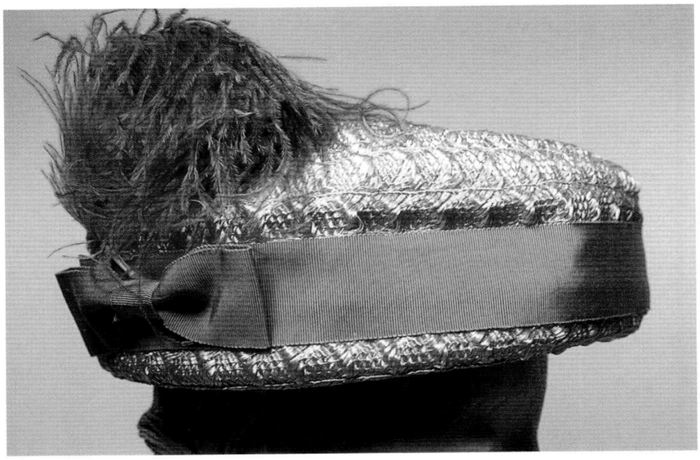

Woven straw toque in complimentary soft pink and brown. *Mobile Millinery Museum*. $350-450.

This black beauty is sewn in alternating rounds of chip straw and horsehair lace. Peach and pink-tinted tulle winds around the brim with black ostrich and a fox fur tailpiece. A chain of jet bead lends a delicate finishing touch. *Mobile Millinery Museum*. $600 – 700.

The dome-shaped crown of this crimson felt is sliced front to back with a black leather stripe. *Mobile Millinery Museum*. $250-300.

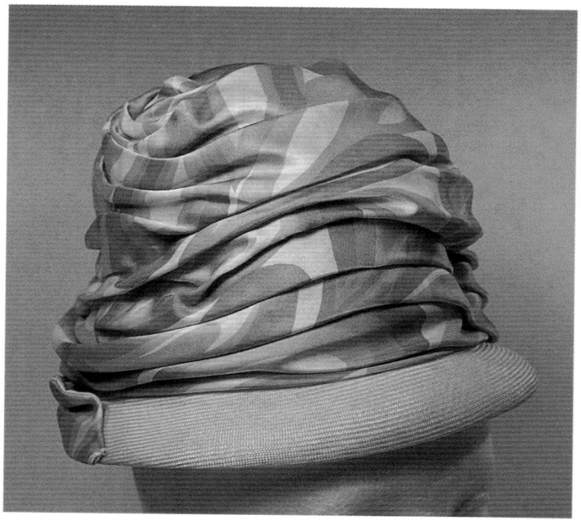

A silk scarf wraps the crown of this white straw "tall round". *Mobile Millinery Museum*. $200-250.

Triangles of straw, woven on horsehair, provide this transitional hat with art deco appeal. Label, printed on silk lining: The Doris Cornwell Hat Shoppe, Barrie, Ontario. *Marg McGuire Collection, Mobile Millinery Museum*. $300-450.

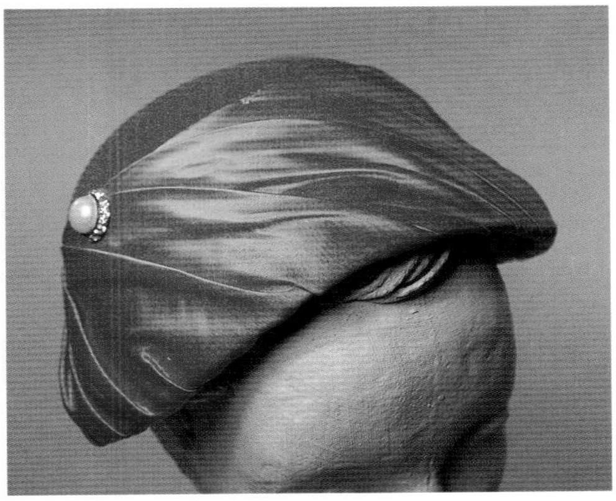

Peach blossom satin wraps an Edwardian hat, fashioned on bonnet board; its velvet crown the color of a cherry popsicle. A rhinestone and pearl pin mimics the dome shape. *Mobile Millinery Museum*. $250-300.

Raspberry ostrich plumes, once owned by Mrs. Harry Clark, grace a black velvet Edwardian worn by Sheila Lewens. *Mobile Millinery Museum*. $450-500.

Reproduction "apple pie" hat. *Private Collection*.

Jewel-toned feathers and flowers trim a black felt, Edwardian tricorne. *Mobile Millinery Museum*. $450-500.

In an age of awakening environmental consciousness, a celluloid wing lies ready to adorn a politically correct chapeau. *Mobile Millinery Museum*. $80.

The author's great aunts Ella (seated) and Mildred in elegant capeline and satin toques, c.1919. *Ella Philip Collection, Mobile Millinery Museum*.

Mrs. Laurie MacLean shows off her newborn in a horsehair-rimmed widebrim with magnificent bow. *Laurabelle MacLean Collection, Mobile Millinery Museum*.

By 1908, wire supports were forsaken for more naturally coiffed hair. Hats and hairstyles began to descend and the side part came into vogue. widebrims returned, paired with dome-shaped crowns and laterally-projecting trims. Lucille's merry widow style was widely copied. Ladies in dusters and goggles employed scarves or fichus to secure their hats, as they motored in open cars, along dirt roads. Some protected their complexions with chic green veils designed specifically for riding in automobiles. Others opted for pouffy, silk, "automobile" bonnets.

At the outset of the 1910s, hairdressing trend setters began covering the ears and pinning the hair at the back of the head. Hats, which covered this new hairstyle, retained the deep, full crowns of the previous decade but sat lower and hugged the crown of the head more closely. Evening turbans mimicked the new, center-parted hairstyles, covering the ears with draped fabric, and adding perpendicular trims.

The outbreak of war, in 1914, introduced the fashion world to military-inspired helmets and toques, which workingwomen found to be practical. Widows draped hats with black veils or attached them to brims, harem style. *Eaton's* department store advertised that even in remote areas of Canada, mourning attire could be obtained in a matter of days through their mail order catalogue.

Following the war, toques, as well as brimmed hats, hugged the crown closely. Black became popular, as did darkly shaded greens, navy, and brown. Looking back, we refer to hats of this period as transitional pieces with elements clearly evident of both the lavish Edwardian widebrim and the crown-hugging cloche, which was to be.

These photos depict three women: Ellen Bethune, Maggie Philip, and Ellen Dewar in similar, early twentieth century hats.

Black velvet, Edwardian, high hat trimmed in the manner of a "Bobby Dazzler". *Mobile Millinery Museum*. $250-350.

Wired ribbon projects skyward from an early twentieth century confection. The children in the picture (Addie, Gertie, and Seaton) also model stylish headwear that typifies the era. *Hillyer Collection, Mobile Millinery Museum*.

Circa 1900: A teacher named Mrs. Ward in a feminine, ribbon-trimmed, sailor. Two of her students sport large hair bows while a third prefers a light-colored helmet, cocked to the right. *Ella Philip Collection, Mobile Millinery Museum*.

Lily Ward's upswept hair has likely been waved and drawn over a pompadour frame or other hair support. She ornaments the back with a large bow. *Ella Philip Collection, Mobile Millinery Museum.*

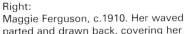

The author's great Aunt Ella wears her hair in a Marcel wave with a stylish side part. The young girl to her left adorns her ringlet-coifed hair with an early, ribbon-trimmed hairband. *Ella Philip Collection, Mobile Millinery Museum*.

Right:
Maggie Ferguson, c.1910. Her waved hair is center-parted and drawn back, covering her ears. *Ella Philip Collection, Mobile Millinery Museum.*

Two women, c.1910, sport the center-parted "waved" hairstyles so popular in their day. *Ella Philip Collection, Mobile Millinery Museum*.

Human hair braid worn by Catherine Snellings and her mother. *Mobile Millinery Museum.*

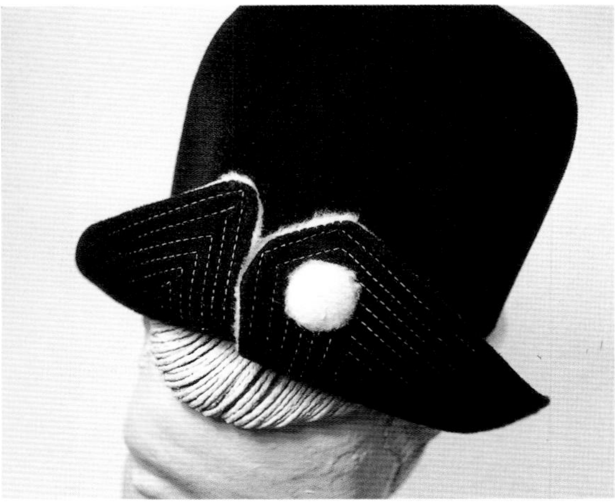

A tall round of black velour and white wool felt . Label: A Palmer Creation, New York, Montreal. *Mobile Millinery Museum.* $350.

Alice Bachelor in an early twentieth century, feather-trimmed widebrim.

A trio of children in early twentieth century chapeaux. *Barb Philip Collection, Mobile Millinery Museum.*

The author in an amazingly similar, yet contemporary, hat.

Edwardian tennis hat with plaited straw brim and crushed peach velvet crown; ornamented in front with a multicolored silk medallion. The silk lining pictures a woman in Edwardian dress swinging a tennis racket. Label: Brentwood Sports. *Mobile Millinery Museum*. $475-550.

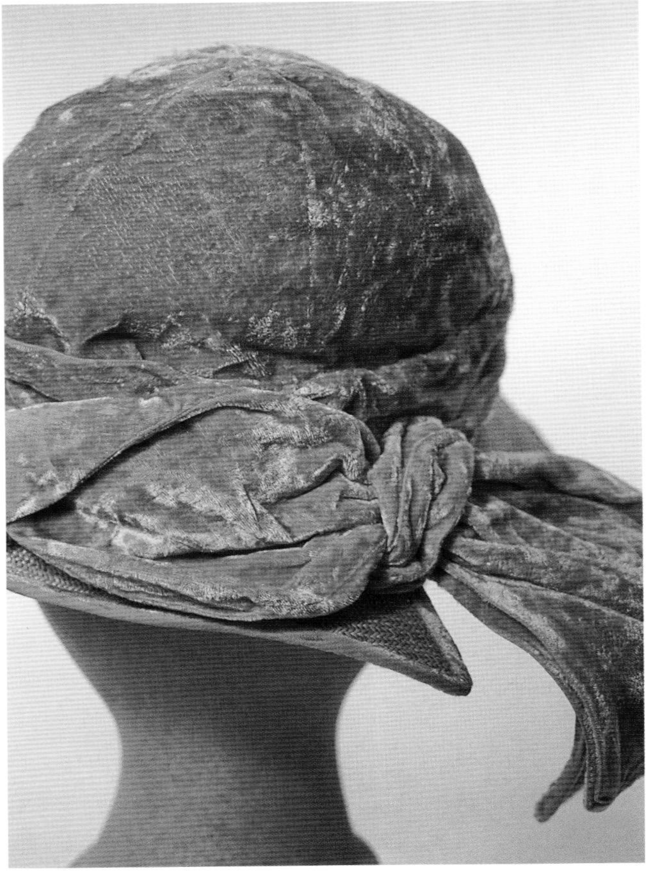

Back view showing practical cut-away brim and large crushed bow.

Gertie White, c.1910, tops her center-parted hair with a face-framing, tucked fabric hat that sits well at the back of her head. *Hillyer Collection, Mobile Millinery Museum*.

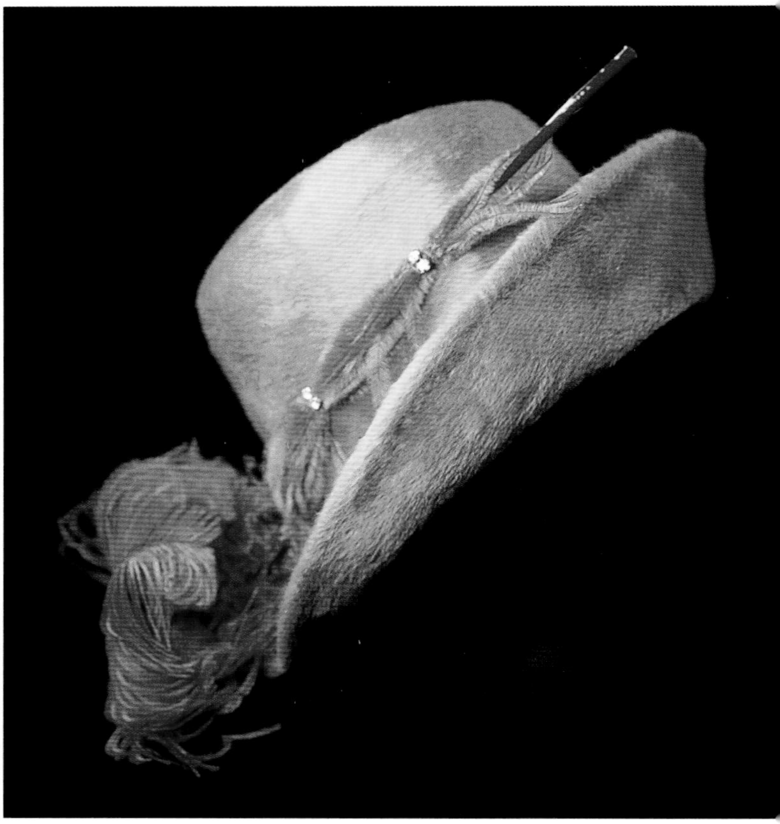

Exquisite beaverette cavalier. A pumpkin-colored ostrich plume, bound with rhinestones, mimics the slope of the brim. Label: Made in Northern Ireland. *Mobile Millinery Museum*. $225-325.

Circa 1910: The author's grandfather takes the arms of her great aunts Ella and Millie, who wear low-sitting, Merry Widow hats, which extend slightly beyond their shoulders. *Hillyer Collection, Mobile Millinery Museum.*

Chapter IV
Flapper Fantasies: 1920 - 1930

"I ran in and looked at Caroline Reboux's exclusive collection of hats the other afternoon. I say exclusive because anything coming from Reboux on the *Rue de la Paix* is stamped with that distinction."

— *Columnist for Mayfair Magazine, February 1928*

"My mother was a milliner who apprenticed at *Milady's Hat Shoppe* in Calgary, c.1926. Whenever someone needed a new hat for a special evening my mother would stitch up a satin tam. She made them in all kinds of wonderful colors."

— *Anonymous*

"One time at the theatre, my husband reached forward and used nail clippers to remove an offensive plume from a large hat in front of him."

— *Anonymous*

The cloche appeared in the early 1920s to complement the new bobbed hairstyles and straight-cut dresses in vogue at the time. The design, which is easy to identify by its characteristic bell shape and crown-hugging fit, is credited to Coco Chanel.

The sleek hat with its narrow brim was molded of straw or felt for a sporting occasion, and fashioned in silk for afternoon, formal wear or restaurant dining. Trim was minimal and might consist of contrast stitching, a band of chiffon or grosgrain, art deco pin, or a nickel ring.

Subtle variations appeared with each new season and designers bestowed descriptive names such as the skullcap, bonnet-hat, beret-cloche, etc. on their creations. The *Dobbs Company*, a famous New York hatter, presented what they termed a "blazer hat" each spring.

The cloche was originally designed with a downward-sloping brim but as the seasons changed so did the hat. The brim might be folded back against the crown or uplifted only in the front, to expose the face and forehead. Irregular brims arrived mid-decade, along with slashes, tabs, droops, and elephant ears. Little could be done to vary the crown, other than lifting with darts or folding the sides.

For a time, the fashionable smart wore hats that were either all black, all white, or black and white, but by the fall of 1928, Paris was showing the cloche to the world in gray, grape, orchid, and leaden blue as well as chocolate, rust, mahogany, and hunter green.

While the cloche can be said to have dominated the decade, other styles such as the Pamela, the capeline, the picture hat, and the turban were also popular. A variation on the cloche was the higher crowned, aviator's helmet. Hatpins were no longer a necessity but were shortened and used decoratively.

Sequined cocktail hats, elaborate "headache bands", and feathered helmets set the stage for evening. Feathered skullcaps, worn extensively throughout Europe, eliminated the need for time spent at a hairdresser.

Of an age when Canadian society was still being presented to the British court, such a candidate might purchase the latest in millinery finery at department stores like *Timothy Eaton* or *Robert Simpson* as well as *Fairweather, The Iris Shoppe*, and milliner *Ruby Cook*; all of whom advertised in *Mayfair Magazine*. In 1928, a felt cloche by *Debway* hats was offered here for the price of $10.50.

Horsehair caps became the rage, c.1928 - 1929, but *Needlewoman Magazine*, June 1930, reported a scarcity of raw material for the making of horsehair lace, which was valued for its stiffness.

In 1929, a fashion for hat/purse, hat/scarf, and other matched sets emerged.

Circa 1920: A black ribbon cloche is brimmed in raffia and adorned with a spray of black feathers. *Mobile Millinery Museum*. $200-250.

Open crown cloche, c.1929. A wavy brim of horsehair lace is secured to a double grosgrain band. Jet beading in a floral and leaf motif adds charm to this well-loved chapeau. *Mobile Millinery Museum*. $250-300.

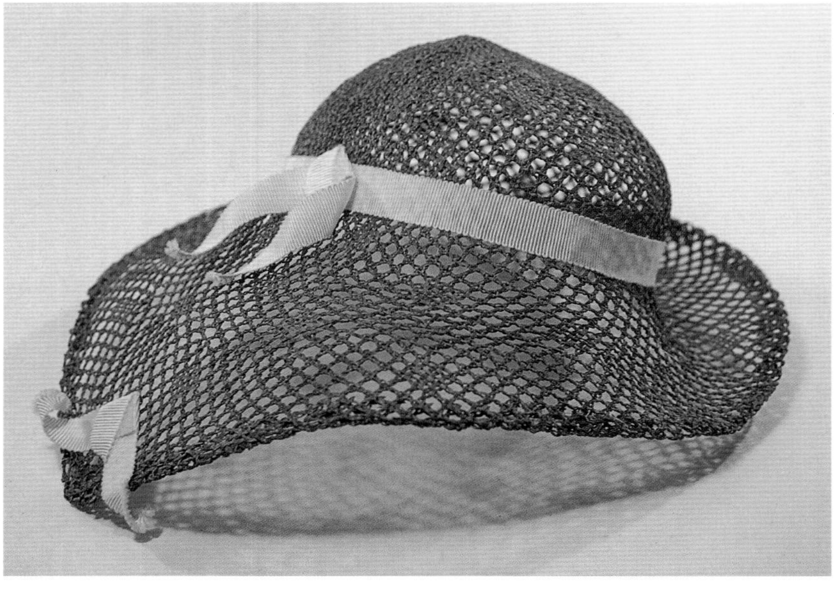

A lacy green straw on a wire frame hugs the crown of the head closely. *Mobile Millinery Museum*. $175-225.

Wheat-colored straw cloche with vertical interest. *Mobile Millinery Museum*. $150-200.

Helter-skelter spikes of cobalt blue on an asymmetric cloche of ice-blue feathers. Velvet under-brim also of cobalt blue. Label: Made in France, Expressly for Abraham and Straus. *Marjorie Wilson Collection, Mobile Millinery Museum.* $200-250.

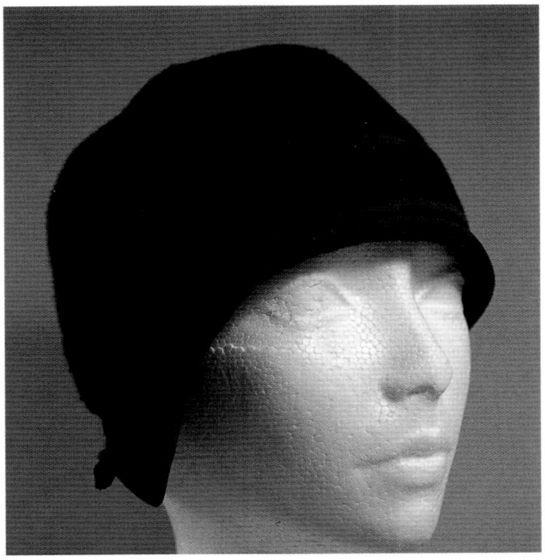

A cloche in chocolate brown, long-nap felt is pinch-pleated above the right ear and trimmed with a trio of grosgrain bows. Label: Exclusively designed by Baron. *Mobile Millinery Museum*. $150.

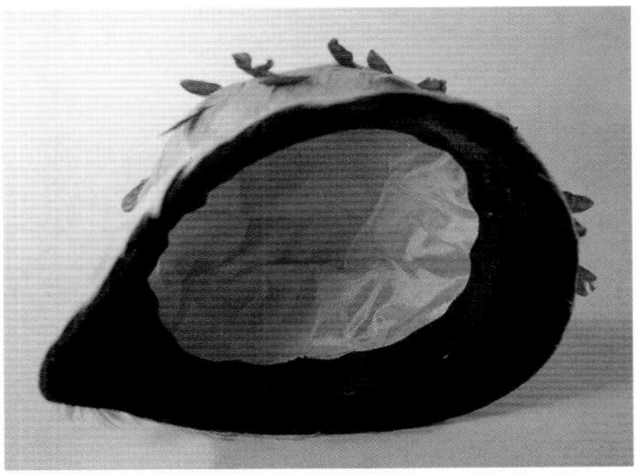

View showing lined crown and velvet under-brim.

The crown of this red suede cloche is pieced in several segments for maximum fit and style. Trapunto-stitched brim turns up along the brow, then dips dramatically over the right ear. Self-fabric band. Label: Original by Jerry Yates, New York, Montreal. *Mobile Millinery Museum*. $225.

This reversible cloche of rubberized fabric is water-resistant. *Mobile Millinery Museum*. $120-150.

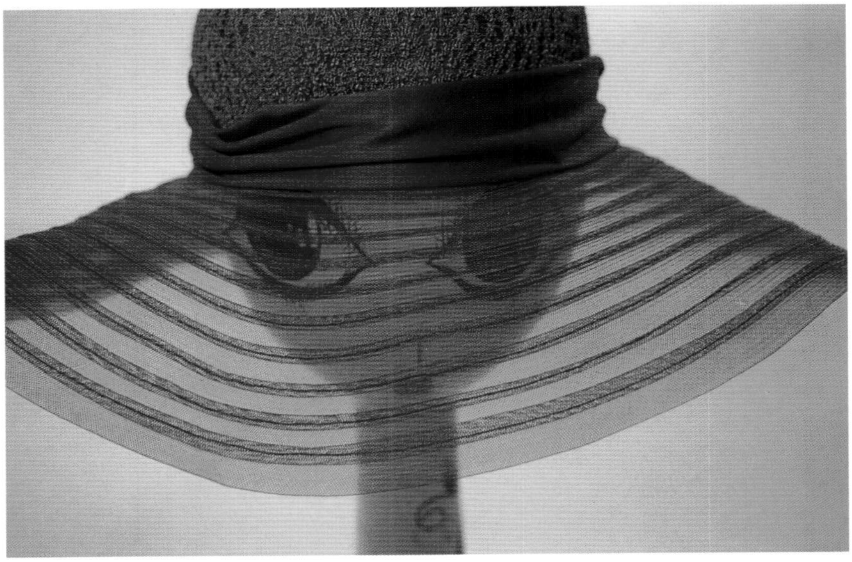

A dressy Pamela of raspberry-colored lace and horsehair. *Mobile Millinery Museum*. $225.

A summer cloche in cream straw is banded with pleated organdie. *Mobile Millinery Museum*. $150-200.

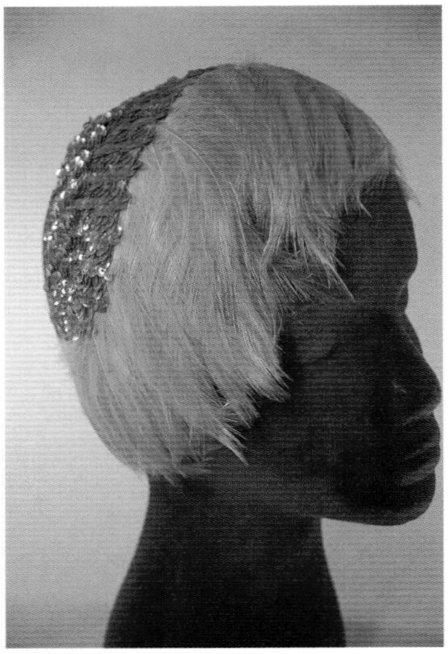

An evening cap of butterscotch sequins sprouts feathers that resemble hair. *Mobile Millinery Museum*. $100-125.

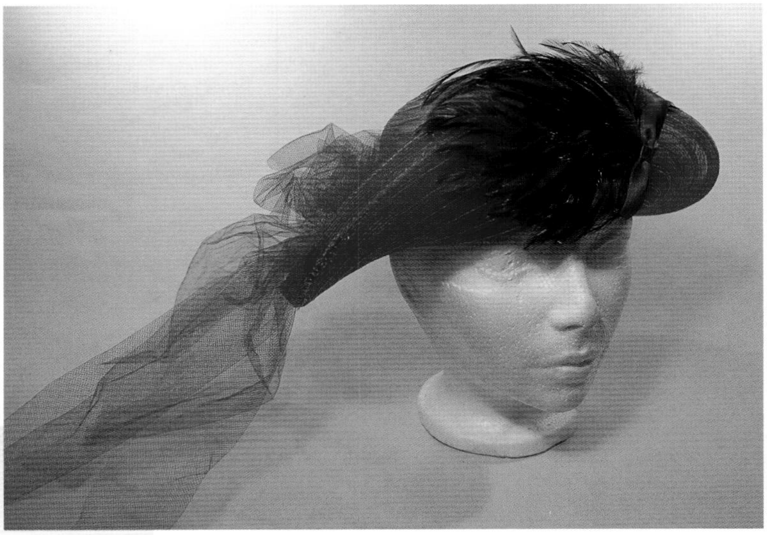

A horsehair bicorn in luscious raspberry is wrapped in matching tulle. A feather spray dominates the up-turned brim. *Mobile Millinery Museum*. $250-300.

A turban of silky green feathers boasts a spiral of red-tipped rooster-tail feathers. *Mobile Millinery Museum*. $250-350.

A variation on the picture hat is fabric-covered in black on a buckram form. A pleated crown and brim make the most of the material's textured striations. *Mobile Millinery Museum*. $225.

A mahogany felt helmet is banded with matching grosgrain and ornamented in a geometric pattern of black beads. *Mobile Millinery Museum*. $150-200.

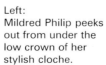

A group of cottagers, two of whom sport slope-brimmed cloches.

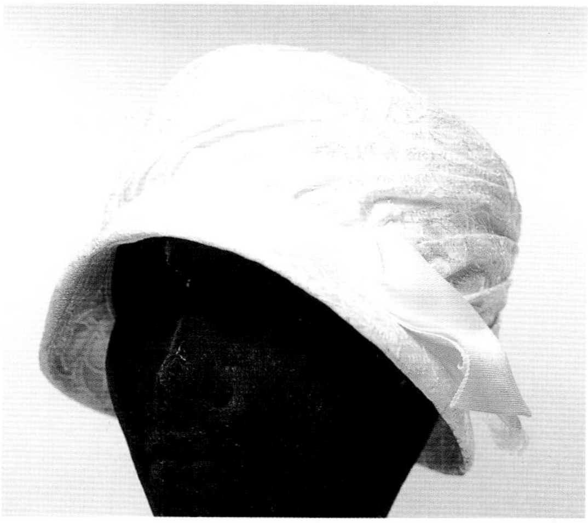

A cloche, draped in winter white brocade with touches of silver, draws the eye downward with its sloping brim and ribbon streamer. Label: Helen Joyce Original. *Mobile Millinery Museum*. $225.

This stiff straw cloche features a brim that turns up in front. Behind it lies a wad of tawny net caged in diamond-patterned straw. Label: Lisette, Abraham & Straus. *Mobile Millinery Museum*. $225.

A dressy cloche of silk velvet is ornamented with a spray of flowers in black and bottle green. *Mobile Millinery Museum*. $250.

Left:
Mildred Philip peeks out from under the low crown of her stylish cloche.

Right:
Kristin Vettese models a vintage straw-cloth cloche purchased at an antiques barn. Velvet petunias in various colors encircle the crown. *Courtesy Kristin Vettese*. $200-250.

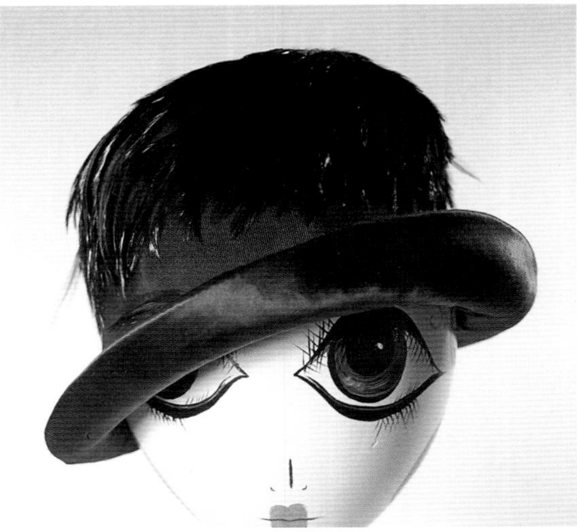

Jet black feathers and heavy satin combine to form a special occasion cloche with diagonal upturned brim. Wide grosgrain band. *Mobile Millinery Museum*. $225.

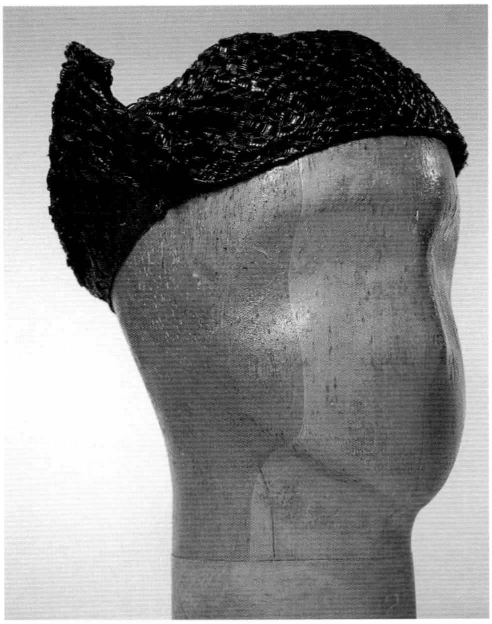

The crown of this 1920s charmer has faded from its original moss-green shade. The brown woven straw band with wing effect has been lacquered. The well worn hat suffers from deterioration. *Mobile Millinery Museum*. $60-80.

A wide band of rich hazelnut velvet separates a crown and downward-sloping brim of tawny straw. Label: Creation by André. *Mobile Millinery Museum*. $200-250.

Orange ribbon cloche. Label: Millinery Import for Eaton's of Canada. *Mobile Millinery Museum*. $250-300.

The high grosgrain band of this navy felt cloche is slipped through a square felt buckle. Label: Parkside, Simpson's. *Mobile Millinery Museum*. $225.

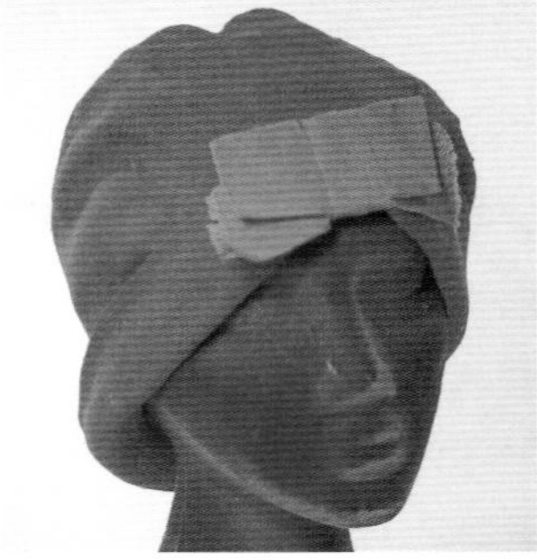

A charming linen beach cap with center-front grosgrain bow. *Mobile Millinery Museum*. $75.

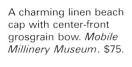

Sequined Juliet cap for an evening of cocktails. Wispy, black, feather tendrils are pulled through the webbing at the right temple for a touch of the dramatic. Label: Piko, Paris, New York. *Mobile Millinery Museum*. $250.

Pearl-centered, velvet flowers ornament a silk faille cloche with straw crown and medallions. Some pearls missing. *Mobile Millinery Museum*. $200-250.

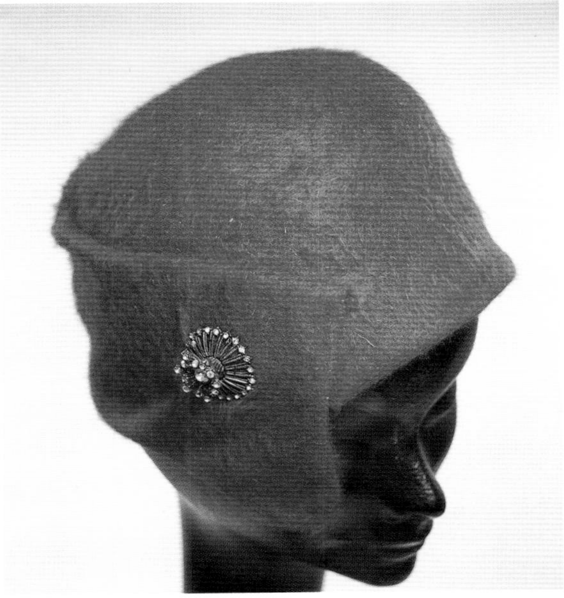

A brilliant wool felt in antique-red is folded on the right side to create a wing effect and finished with an art deco pin; a stylish interpretation of the aviator's helmet. Label: Jeanne et Jacques. *Mobile Millinery Museum*. $320.

Fully lined, navy, silk cloche with upturned brim and self-fabric bow. Union label. *Mobile Millinery Museum*. $200-250.

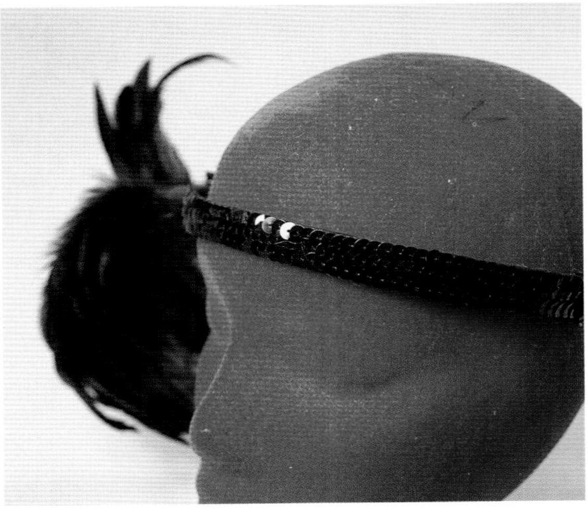

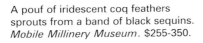

A pouf of iridescent coq feathers sprouts from a band of black sequins. *Mobile Millinery Museum*. $255-350.

Long-nap beaver cloche in hunter-green with narrow, self-fabric band. Label: Genuine Imported Beaver. *Mobile Millinery Museum*. $200-250.

A barely-brimmed cloche of teal felt. *Mobile Millinery Museum*. $200-250.

Reverse view reveals a split crown, laced together with black leather.

An ivory cabbage rose punctuates a similarly-hued cloche with upturned front brim. *Mobile Millinery Museum*. $250-350.

Turquoise beads stand out against a black satin turban. *Mobile Millinery Museum*. $150-200.

A cheerful red and white straw slopes toward the back. *Mobile Millinery Museum*. $225.

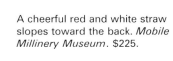

A Christmas greeting, 1921: a young woman named Hilda wears what appears to be a chenille-dotted, embroidered veil, atop a dome-crowned hat.

A young woman, believed to be the mother of designer Philip Warde, sports a floral and berry-trimmed straw cloth hat with her scoop-neck flapper dress. Millinery flowers at the left shoulder set off the dress's filet sleeves. *Philip Warde Collection, Mobile Millinery Museum*.

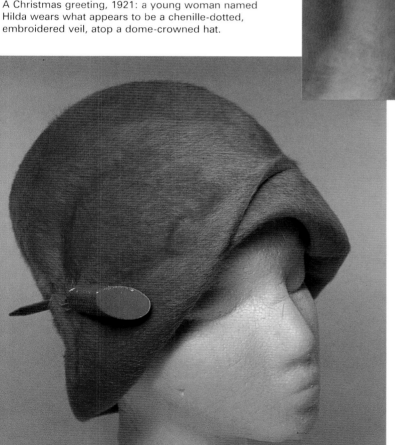

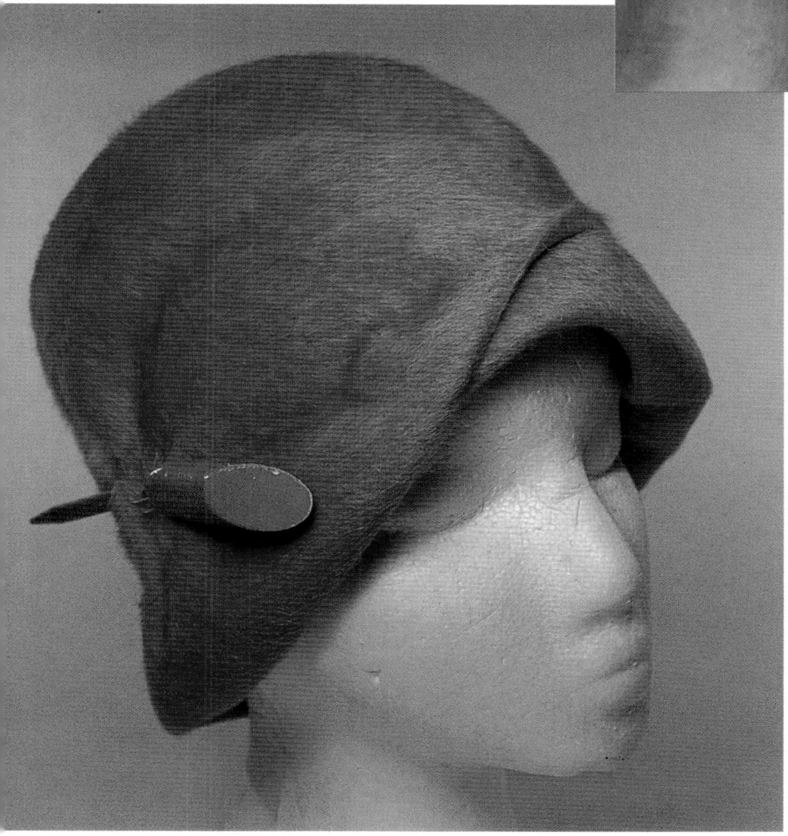

This coral felt cloche is stabbed with a turquoise, wooden hatpin in typical flapper style. *Mobile Millinery Museum*. $325.

A collection of hatpins such as this is easier to amass than longer, earlier examples. These pins range from 2 1/2 to 5 inches in length; some equipped with a safely nub. *Mobile Millinery Museum*. $5-$50 each.

Chapter V
Dignified Beauty: 1930 - 1940

"Hats, this season, are amusing and audacious in style. When they are high they are very, very high and when they are low they are pancakes."

— *Mayfair Magazine, April 1936*

"I simply must do something about a spring hat – this sunshine and the blue skies and pussy willows coming out, make me feel drab in my old felt. Here's a pretty little shop on Portage Ave. I'll just drop in and try on those gay little models in the window ... Just right! I like this one immensely. It makes me feel as happy and irresponsible as it looks!"

— *Miss Eleanor Tennant, modeling hats for the Winnipeg Tribune, April 15, 1939*

Reports from Paris in the early 1930s indicate an evolution from the head-hugging cloche and Pamela of the previous decade, to an even sleeker, more sophisticated arrangement. Hats slip to the back of the head, c. 1930, and lose their brims at first, then tilt to one side to complement the new bias cut in dress design.

For the December issue of the *Delineator*, 1932, Agnes designs a brimless red felt cap, cut out along the tilted brow line. In 1933, Patou announces in *Mayfair Magazine* that he is no longer showing black. Instead, he uses midnight blue with "occasional touches of the lighter blues that are used for my dresses." He is widely copied.

Hairstyles lengthen and curls return but are reserved for the ends of the hair, whether it is worn "down", with a horizontal coil at back, or in an "updo", with curls resting at the brow.

Flat hats are topped with horizontal floral bouquets. By 1935, back bands or straps begin to show for day wear, as do folded-up brims. Brims develop vertically and crowns are manipulated to achieve a tall effect. The September issue of *Vogue*, 1934, features a dark straw duckbill by Maria Guy, on its cover, and discusses this approach of "high hatting" by the French, within its pages. Some designers make chapeaux even taller with the addition of a plume or two.

Hats are created for the beach and for the popular sports of skeet shooting and slalom. As for day wear, the alpine-inspired, Tyrolean felt appears with tailored suits. Slouch hats, the squared pillbox, and halo hats dominate dresses while velvet Bretons, plumed Empress Eugenie derbies, and veiled mortarboards are worn to June horse shows, garden parties, and luncheons. Immense, flat cartwheels compete with floral-trimmed, top hats as women adopt pantsuits for the first time.

With the British court in mourning for George V, black makes a comeback in every collection. Some designers take inspiration from the coronation of George VI, resulting in a trend for forward-projecting brims, c.1937. Fairweather's bridal wear advertises a "Regency Poke bonnet." Hoods become popular and are even adopted with wedding gowns. Magazine ads speak of "dignified beauty", when attempting to sell ranges and refrigerators, but the term can just as easily be applied to millinery.

Veils are reintroduced in 1937; turbans are draped, cuffed, and plumed, and the new shiny straw called cellophane makes headlines. Creased crowns are a novelty in straw as well as felt. Clown hats by Talbot and Schiaparelli sprout pointed crowns. A trend for generous collars or capelets of beaver, silver and blue fox, astrakhan, or marten makes these vertical hats workable. "The hat tall, the head small," instructs *Mayfair* magazine.

Millinery Highlights

- The trend for matched sets of hats with scarves, gloves, wraps, handbags or detachable ruffs is developed in fabric as well as fur.
- Sports and tailored hats are a staple with Stetson and Lady Biltmore.
- By 1936 all manner of trims are thrust into soaring crowns. Iridescent coq feathers are particularly popular and are often clustered together to produce a showy protrusion.
- Flat hats with low brims support bouquets of flowers.
- Large single flowers are seen tucked under one ear.
- Veils cover the face entirely or tie on behind.
- Mary Stuart bonnets dip over the foreheads of brides and bridesmaids.
- By the close of the decade, the most stylish chapeaux are tipped over one eye and referred to as tilt or doll hats.

Designer Profile: Helene Garnell

Helene Garnell was born in New York but spent much of her childhood in Paris. She began her millinery career as a sketcher for the great Jean Patou, after trying her hand for a time at sculpture. After Patou's death she practiced her trade at the Paris salon of milliner Maria Guy, then designed hats for the French theatre and movie industry.

By 1939 Garnell was designing hats in Hollywood for such notables as Greta Garbo, Joan Crawford, and Ingrid Bergman. Her hats can be seen in the movies, *My Favorite Wife, Irene, So Ends Our Night, and Rage in Heaven*.

Garnell admits publicly to have been exasperated by Garbo's penchant for huge, floppy hats. She once said to her, "I might just as well go out and get the straw bonnet off some old horse and sew up the holes for the ears!" Pleasing Garbo was not Garnell's only design challenge. The designer was once assigned to create a hat for an actress who was to fall in a swimming pool, hat and all. The hat had to remain photogenic, even when wet.

Following her career in the movie industry, Garnell opened a millinery salon in New York, then in 1944 she shared her secrets in the instructional book, *How to Make a Hat*.

Bes-Ben: The Mad Hatter of Chicago

The famous millinery label "Bes-Ben" is derived from the first names of a brother and sister design team, Benjamin and Bessie Greenfield, who went into business together in Chicago, c.1920. By 1938, they had moved their shop to Michigan Avenue where a prestigious clientele included Lucille Ball, Marlene Dietrich, Judy Garland, and Elizabeth Taylor.

Bes-Ben was famous for clearing their inventory each summer at a midnight sale, when hat prices, normally in the range of $37.50 to $1,000.00, fell to as little as $5.00. Pieces that went unsold by 2:00 a.m. were tossed into the street to be scooped up by eager scavengers. It is reported that a single Bes-Ben hat, likely owned by a celebrity, sold at auction, in 1999, for $18,400.

Twenty-five rhinestones delineate the center of a 1930s satin cocktail hat. A portion of the original veiling remains. *Mobile Millinery Museum*. $125-225.

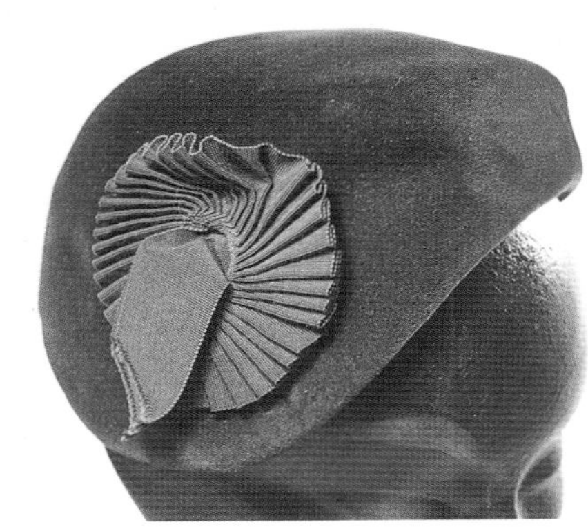

A grosgrain cockade trims a hunter-green velour cap, c.1939. Label: LeClaire, Chapeau De Luxe. *Mobile Millinery Museum.* $150.

A millinery rose adds panache to a shallow-crowned, silk velvet, widebrim edged in hair lace. *Mobile Millinery Museum*. $150-200.

An elegant cellophane straw is widely banded in matching black grosgrain; the brim is doubled at the rim to add weight. Label: A Jan-Dec Hat. *Mobile Millinery Museum*. $150-200.

Circa 1938: A lacy hat of woven jute and cellophane straw is banded in brown velvet ribbon. Label: A Therese Lloyd classic by Crean. *Aline Banting Collection, Mobile Millinery Museum*. $150-200.

A pair of dressy caps, c.1935. The first, a woven straw porkpie with velvet band, is stabbed with an art deco pin. The second, a navy felt, is draped with bow-tie veiling. *Mobile Millinery Museum*. $150 each.

A cap of snowy egret on a felt base by Henry Pollack, New York. A rhinestone swag cinches a cream satin bow. Label: Star Lady, Frank Palma Original. *Mobile Millinery Museum*. $250-300.

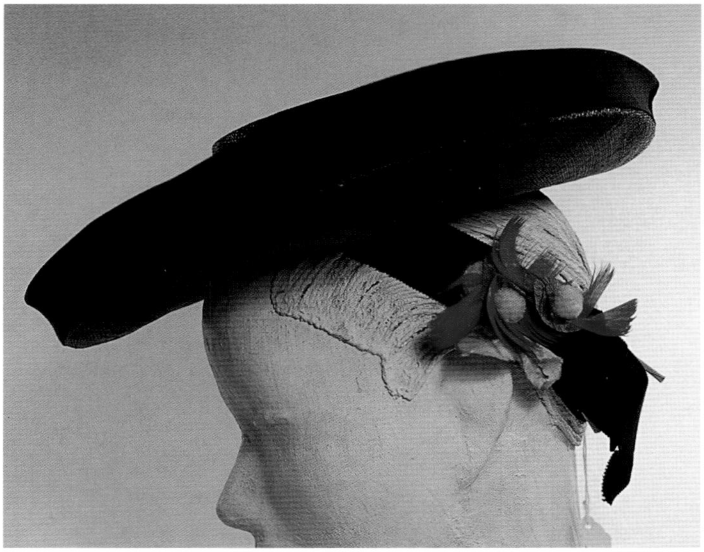

A wagon wheel of fine black straw, c.1938, secures at the nape of the neck with a wide, grosgrain strap. Feathers, chenille dots, and silk leaves decorate the left side. Label: Peggy Model. *Kew Beach Collection, Mobile Millinery Museum*. $225.

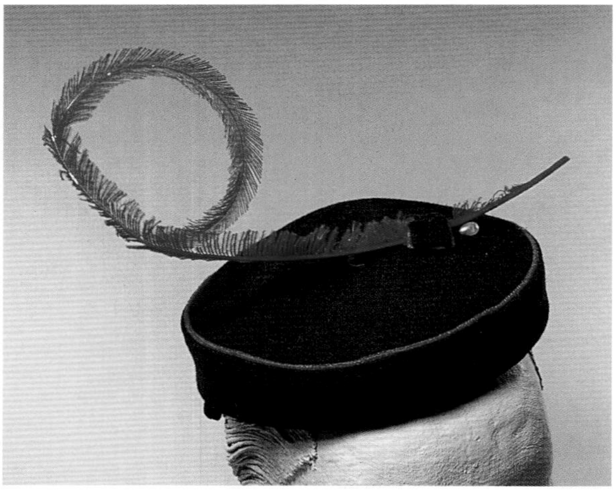

The Bellhop: Red piping on navy wool makes a striking presentation. *Mobile Millinery Museum*. $200-250.

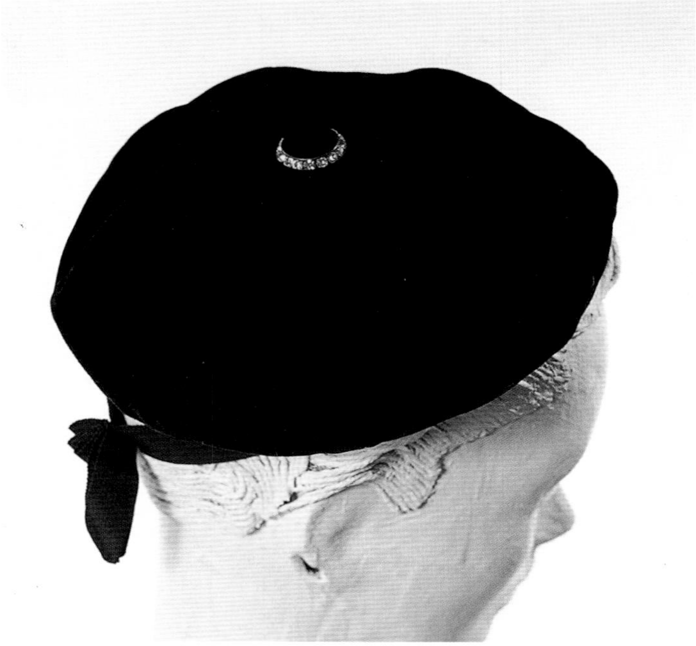

A simple velvet cap from the mid-thirties is crowned with a ring of rhinestones and secured at the back with a grosgrain strap. *Kew Beach Collection, Mobile Millinery Museum*. $225.

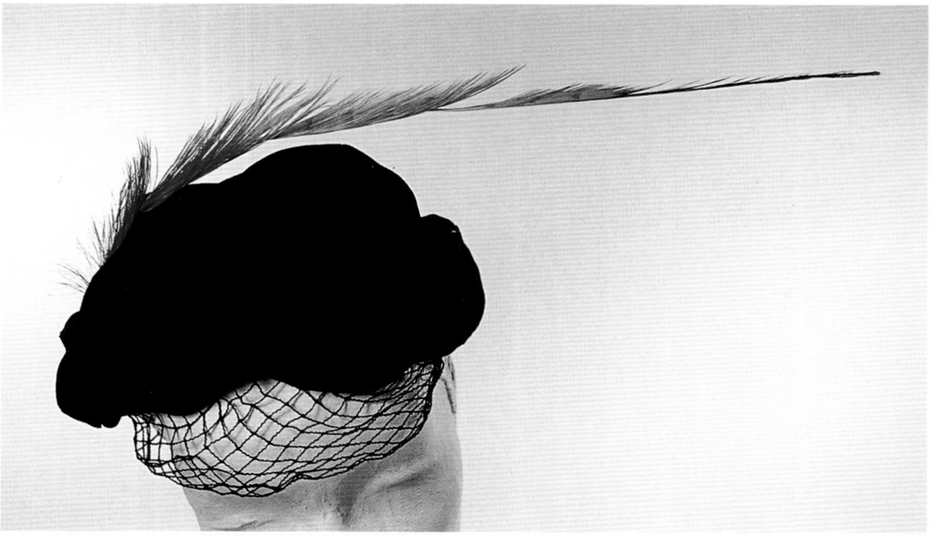

Wings of pleated grosgrain are secured to a black velvet cap. A small coarse veil contrasts with a tricolor, wispy plume. *Mobile Millinery Museum*. $200-250.

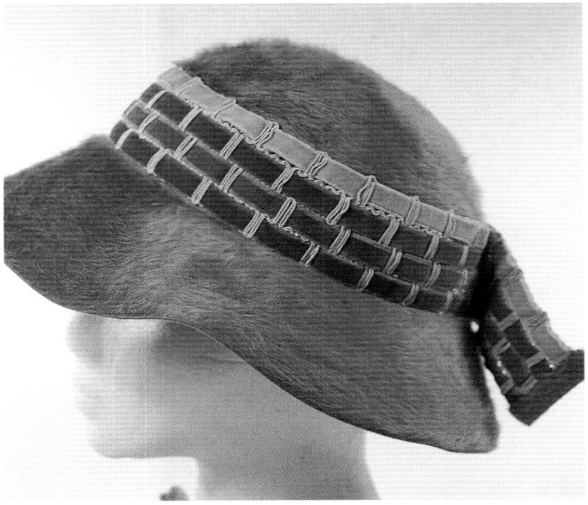

A long nap beaver slouch hat beautifully banded in velvet ribbon of brown, gray, pumpkin, and beige. Label: Leslie Monroe Original, Paris, New York. *Mobile Millinery Museum*. $200-250.

A length of knotted grosgrain secures a pair of jaunty white plumes to the crown of a brown velveteen. *Mobile Millinery Museum*. $150.

Purple posies dominate a lacy straw cap, c.1935. Diamond dot veiling wraps the narrow brim. *Mobile Millinery Museum*. $150-200.

Tiny cloth flowers garland a rigid straw revival bonnet banded in brown velvet. *Mobile Millinery Museum*. $150-200.

A pumpkin-colored felt cap is hand embellished in the art deco style with copper-colored bugle beads and celluloid bells. Matching silk scarf. *Mobile Millinery Museum*. $225.

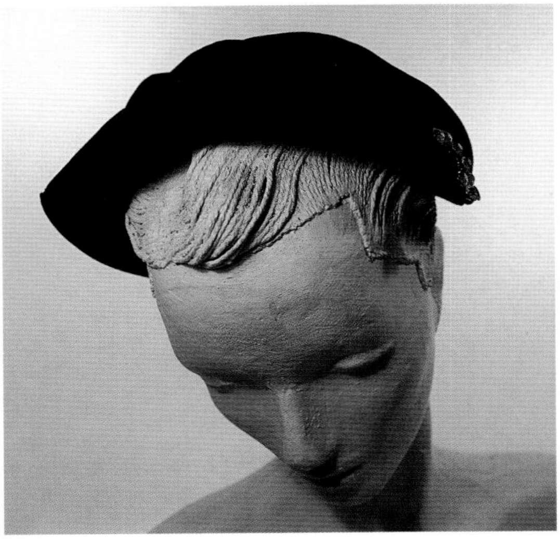

A blue velvet Capulet with asymmetric, pleated brim. Rhinestone pin at the left temple. Label: Macy's, New York. *Mobile Millinery Museum*. $150-250.

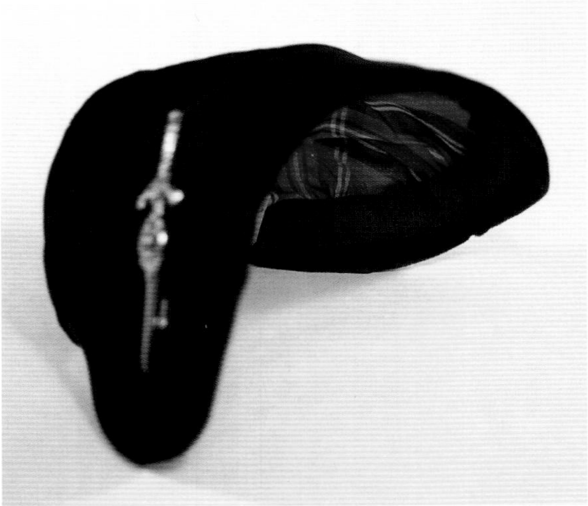

Silk velvet bonnet lined with a tartan plaid. Label: Original Leslie Monroe, Paris, New York. *Mobile Millinery Museum*. $150-200.

Silk velvet, the color of an evening sky, is shaped into a dressy hat, c.1935. A plastic and crystal arch anchors a self-fabric bow. Damaged diamond dot veiling. *Mobile Millinery Museum*. $125-150

A spiral of ribbon straw supports a trio of white organdie roses. Label: Whitehouse Millinery, Trenton, ON. *Mobile Millinery Museum*. $125-150.

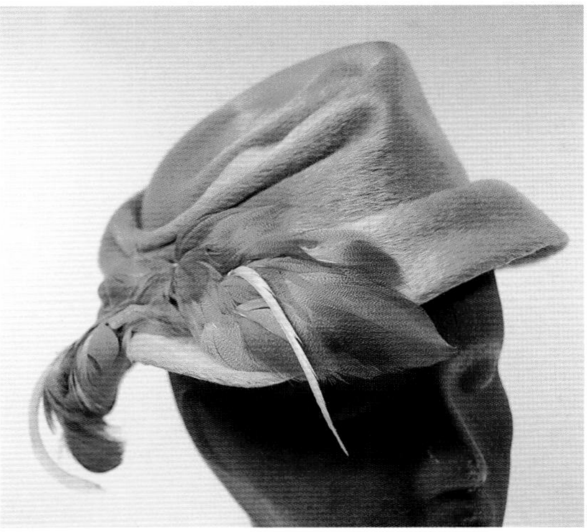

A feather bow in shades of peach to brown rests at the temple of this beautifully draped, beaver, slouch hat. Label: Georgette Original. *Mobile Millinery Museum Collection*. $200-250.

This silk velvet cap from the mid-thirties is the holder for two knife-like, lacquered plumes in butterscotch and caramel. A note inside suggests it was worn by someone named Howes. *Mobile Millinery Museum*. $150-200.

Interior view, showing early rhinestone bejeweled Georgette label.

A black felt disk hat tips forward from a small under-crown, secured at the nape with a grosgrain strap. Delicate spider web veiling, secured with self-fabric hatpins, covers the face. *Mobile Millinery Museum.* $250-300.

Waves of tiny, white, seed beads encircle a navy straw slouch hat, c.1935. Velvet ribbon band and bow. *Mobile Millinery Museum*. $150.

This asymmetric headband would have looked wonderful on a blonde when it was new in the 1930s. Paper leaves and tiny velvet flowers rest on layers of curled lavender feathers. Label: Pasadena Hats. *Mobile Millinery Museum*. $150.

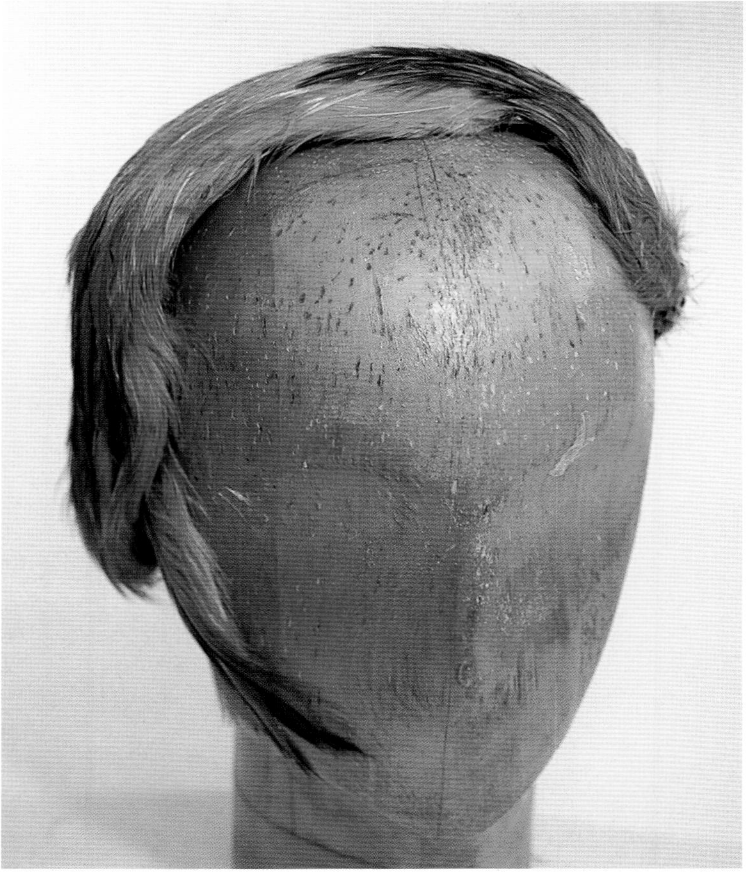

This comma-shaped feather headpiece is reminiscent of early autumn with its orange and green coloration. *Catharine Snellings Collection, Mobile Millinery Museum*. $125-225.

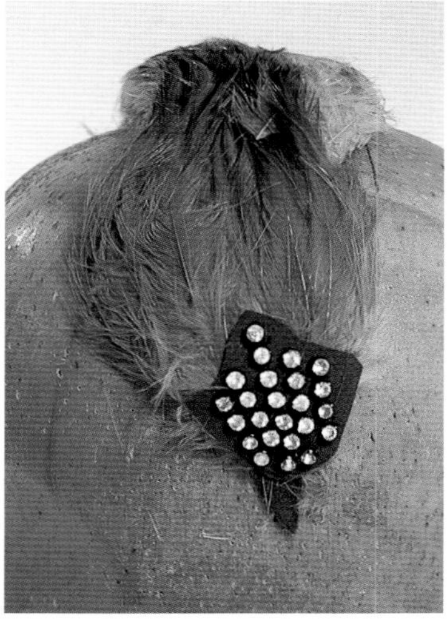

Close-up showing rhinestone studded, leaf-shaped adornment.

An example of high hatting in buttercup-yellow chip straw. Matching grosgrain meanders through a trough along the crown to harmonize with a band and bow of one-inch grosgrain. Yellow velvet bands a fabric-lined inner crown. *Mobile Millinery Museum*. $275-325.

A stiffened felt from the late 1930s possesses military flair. A ten-inch plume of black and red feathers pierces the crown and comes to rest at the temple. Twin labels: "Paris Maid, New York, Paris" and a size 22 union label. *Aline Banting Collection, Mobile Millinery Museum*. $350-400.

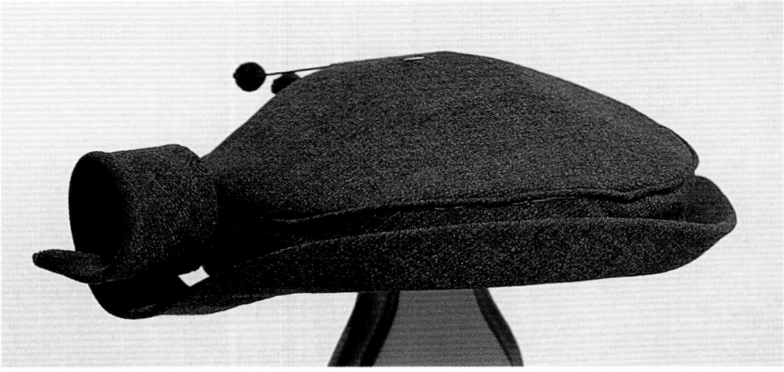

Depression-era cap fashioned from men's suiting. Upturned brim ends in a corkscrew at the right temple. Self-fabric hatpins. Label: Cromie's Fabrics, Woodstock. *Mobile Millinery Museum.* $125-150.

Side view showing a jeweled pin, original to the hat.

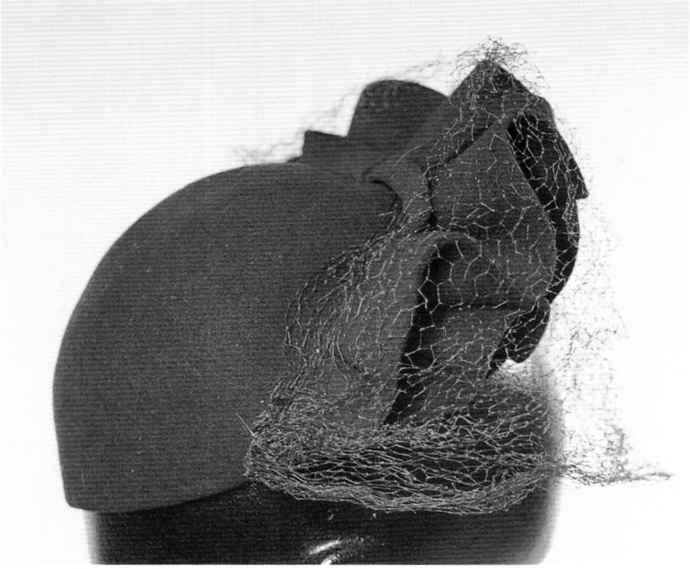

A double ruffle of beaver felt, below a spider web veil, frames the face of this late 1930s, doll hat. *Mobile Millinery Museum*. $200-250.

This crown-hugging wool cap with self-fabric hatpin boasts the MacNeil tartan. *Mobile Millinery Museum*. $150.

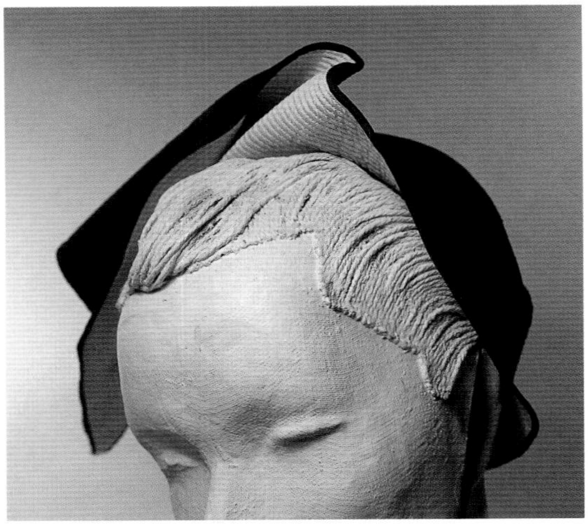

A slouch hat of trapunto-stitched, indigo satin with elastic chin strap. The brim, faced with cream satin, folds up against itself to provide interest at the right temple. Label: Designed by Karen Ross. *Mobile Millinery Museum*. $150-200.

Right:
Chicken coop veiling drapes a felt helmet, shaded midnight blue. A coiled-grosgrain topknot adds the finishing touch. *Mobile Millinery Museum*. $100-200.

A bouquet of white flowers fans out over the crown of this navy straw, pancake hat. *Mobile Millinery Museum*. $150-200.

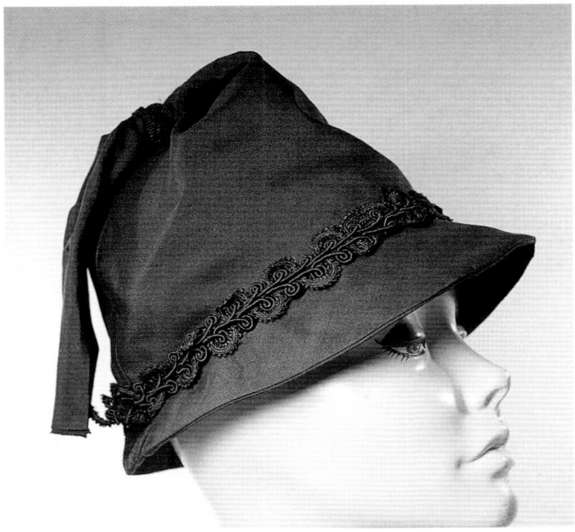

A 1930s ink-black cotton bonnet trimmed with matching passementerie. Satin lining. Label: Evelyn Tuck Hats, Barrie – Canada. *Marg McGuire Collection, Mobile Millinery Museum*. $200-300.

Left:
Ensemble, borrowed from the men: a plaid, wool bowler and matching ascot. *Mobile Millinery Museum*. $200-250.

Right:
The milliner's skill is revealed in this dramatic felt slouch. Rust-colored grosgrain trims a double brim and binds a folded crown. Label: Marion Altman, Toronto. *Marg McGuire Collection, Mobile Millinery Museum*. $350-450.

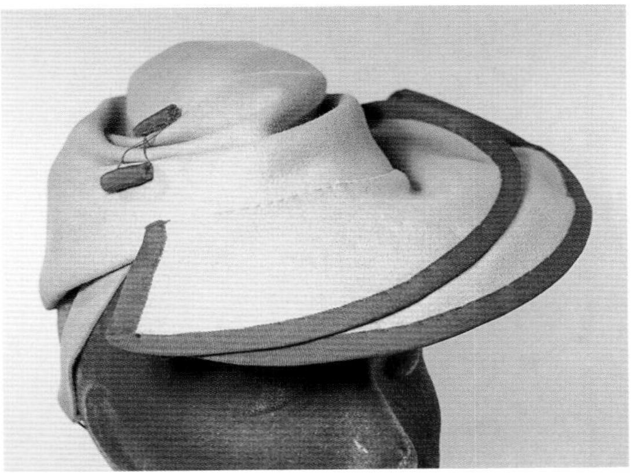

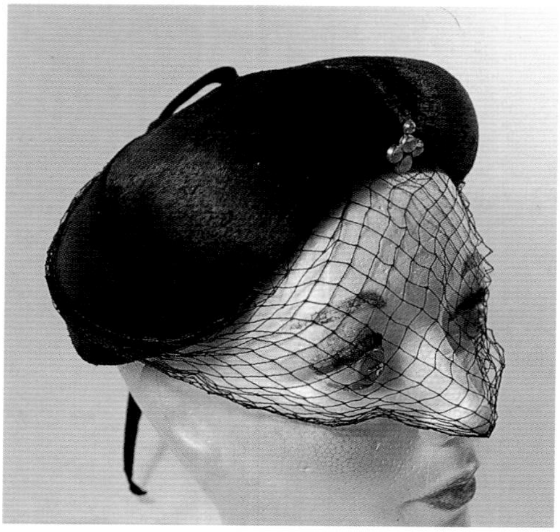

A black voilette ties behind an exquisite, heart-shaped cap of peau-de-pêche beaver. Label: McCreary, 5th Avenue & 34th Street, New York. *Marjorie Wilson Collection, Mobile Millinery Museum*. $225.

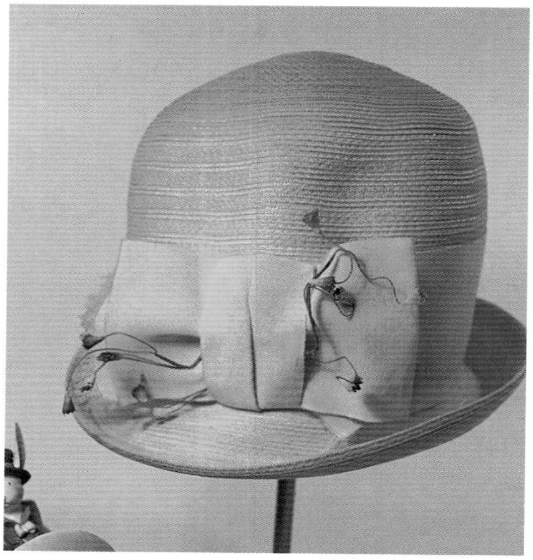

This sunshine-yellow straw bowler sprouts tiny bell flowers from a grosgrain bow at the center front. Label: Boutique. *Mobile Millinery Museum*. $125.

A pair of orange cartwheels, c.1938: one trimmed with rhinestones; the other sports a silk and velvet rose, it's green, thorny stem wrapped about the shallow crown. *Mobile Millinery Museum*. $300 and 350 respectively.

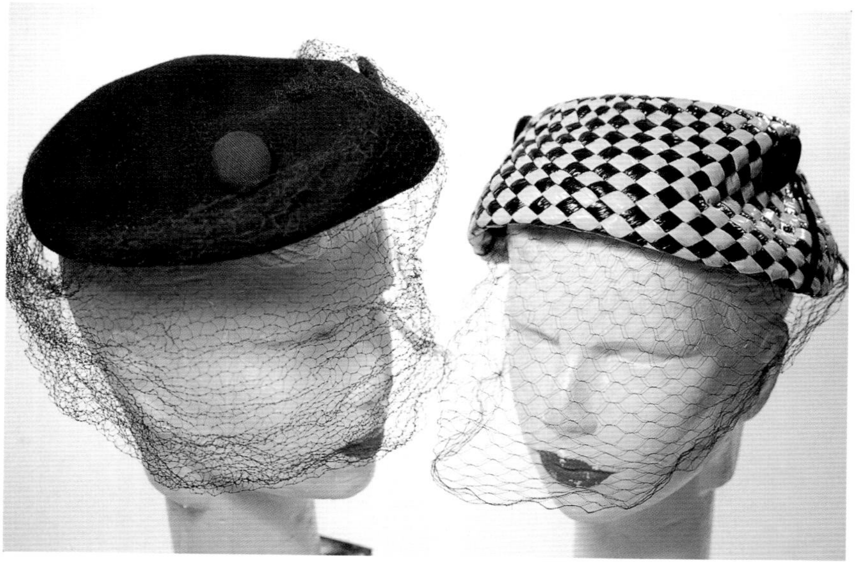

A pair of button-trimmed caps from the mid-1930s: the first, a navy and white cellophane straw; the second, a modified beret of black wool felt. Both are graced with chin-length hairline veiling. *Mobile Millinery Museum*. $125 each.

This asymmetric helmet of turquoise-tinted beaver felt is intriguing from every angle. Most unusual is the folded crown. A velvet ribbon marks the crease of the pieced crown, to match a stylized, velvet bow. *Mobile Millinery Museum*. $300-350.

This stiff little flat hat shines with rhinestones and jet beading. A double, self-fabric bow sandwiches a knife-like, navy plume. *Mobile Millinery Museum*. $150.

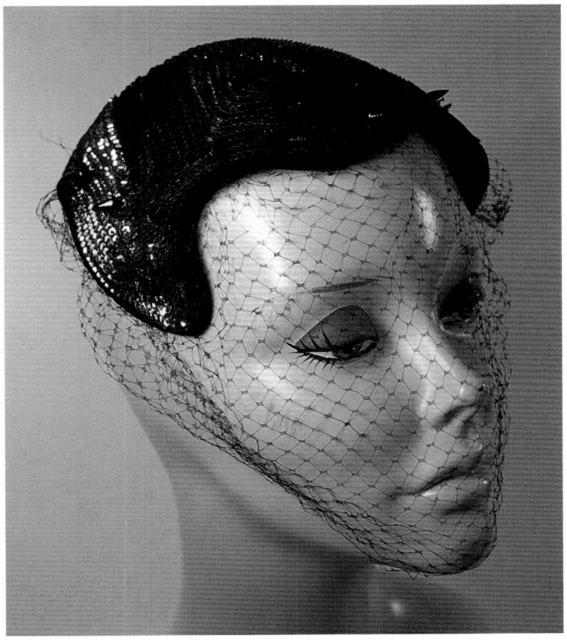

A sparkling Juliet cap for evening, c.1935. Panels of sequins are sewn in opposite directions, creating an impression of alternating segments of black and silver. Black, honeycomb veil. *Marg McGuire Collection, Mobile Millinery Museum*. $350-450.

Feather tendrils in various shades of brown band a tall brown felt. Label: By Eleanor Mack, Oakridge – Park Royal. *Mobile Millinery Museum*. $100-150.

Pipe-cleaner chenille bands a beautifully-molded, chocolate brown felt beneath an arrangement of orange and brown feathers. Label: Deer skin finish by Variety Hat Co. *Mobile Millinery Museum*. $225-250.

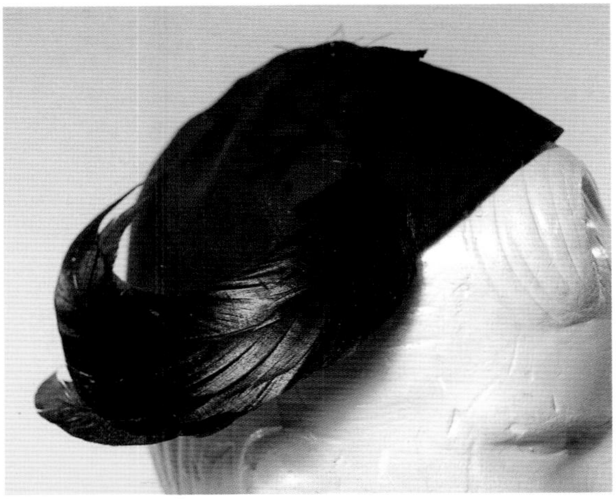

Black faille calot constructed of six wedge-shaped sections and lined with net. Twin grosgrain bows anchor a swirl of iridescent coq feathers. A small comb has been stitched to the inside front edge. *Mobile Millinery Museum*. $150-250.

A cheerful cellophane straw fedora, the brim of which is pinched in the front, providing a base for a floral spray in patriotic colors. *Mobile Millinery Museum*. $200-250.

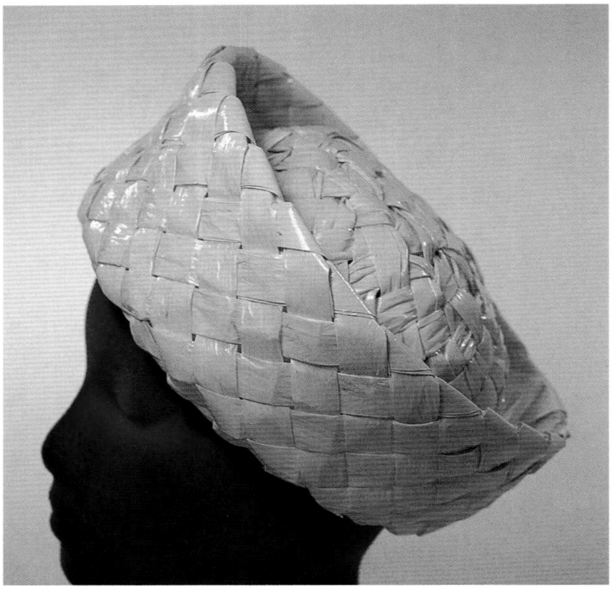

Late 1930s Breton woven of creamy-white cellophane straw. *Mobile Millinery Museum*. $175-225.

This early 1930s felt reveals elements of both the cloche and the slouch. An ornamented grosgrain ribbon slices through the crown to suggest a band. *Mobile Millinery Museum*. $250-300.

Opaline straw cartwheel. Label: Piko, Paris, New York, Montreal. *Mobile Millinery Museum*. $350-400.

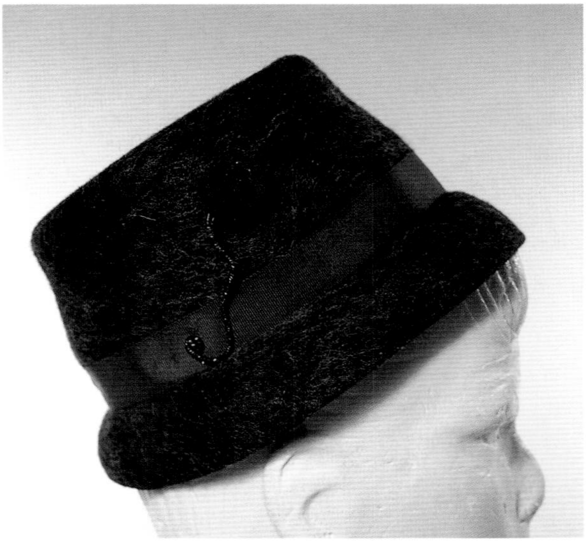

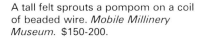

A tall felt sprouts a pompom on a coil of beaded wire. *Mobile Millinery Museum.* $150-200.

A dressy velvet beret in black and Peking-blue is banded only along the brow line. Label: Designed by Betty Henderson, Toronto. *Mobile Millinery Museum*. $175-225.

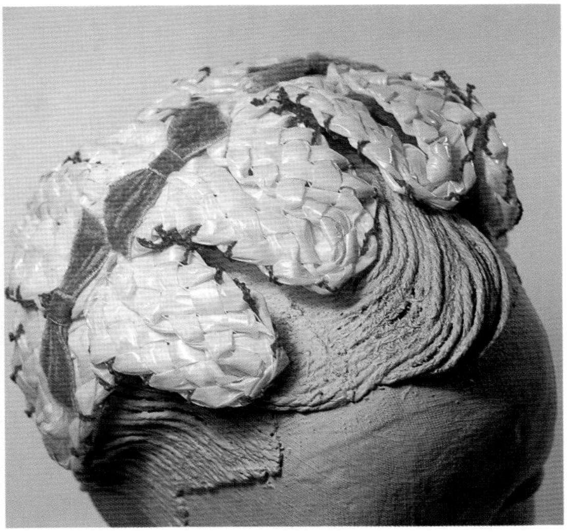

White cellophane straw hat edged in carnelian straw and dotted along the crown with small, salmon-colored, velvet bows. *Mobile Millinery Museum*. $100-150.

Left:
A pair of miniature millinery birds nestle in the fold of this hat's beret-shaped, crown, adding a touch of carnelian, oyster, and silver to a black, velour base. Label: Reine Model. *Mobile Millinery Museum*. $120-150.

Right:
Slate-gray astrakhan slouch banded in black velvet. Label: Dor-Lee. *Mobile Millinery Museum*. $175-225.

White chip straw hat with sloping crown and grosgrain band and bow. Shown with a jeweled hatpin fashioned in the shape of a mouse. *Mobile Millinery Museum*. Hat and Pin, $250.

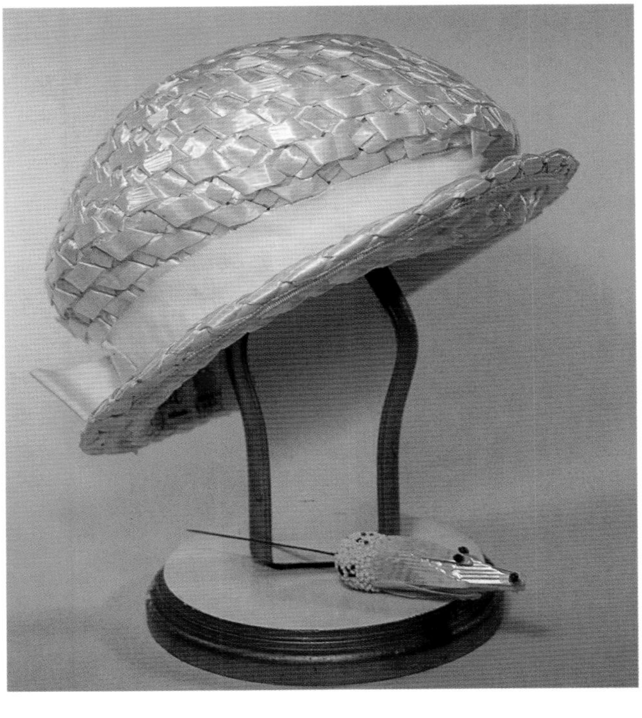

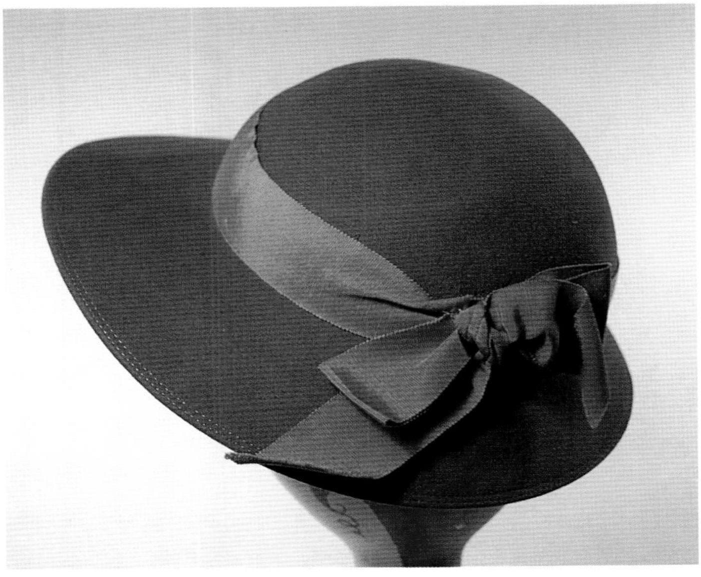

Camel-colored grosgrain bands and bows, a felt slouch of the same coloration. Label: Lady Biltmore. *Mobile Millinery Museum*. $175-225.

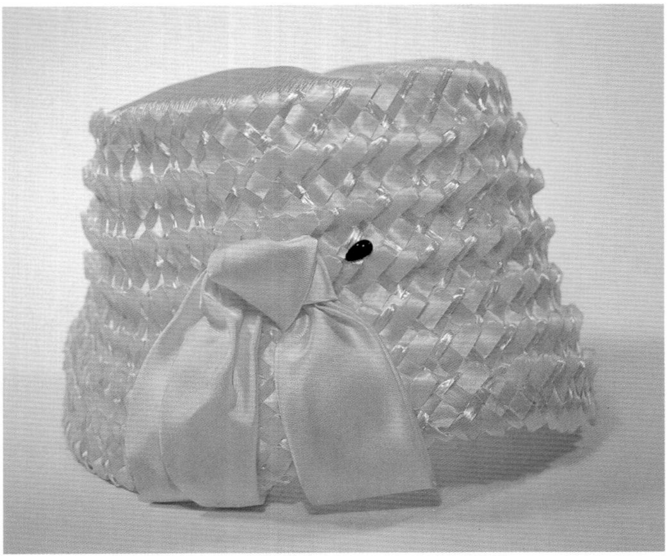

A bonnet of crisp, white, cellophane straw looks all the whiter as a backdrop for an eggshell satin bow. Label: Darcel Exclusive. *Mobile Millinery Museum*. $100-150.

This Italian-made felt, trimmed with navy grosgrain and a double row of rhinestones, presents a wonderful example of the diagonal millinery line of the 1930s. Some fading has occurred. *Mobile Millinery Museum*. $200-250.

Strips of mustard, cherry, and dove-gray felt band a charcoal beaver felt. *Mobile Millinery Museum*. $150-200.

Celestial-blue revival bonnet, c.1930. The upturned, synthetic straw brim folds the right side to hold a cluster of cotton-stemmed, pink and blue flowers. *Mobile Millinery Museum*. $200-250.

A charming straw in American Beauty red is sewn with white thread and banded with black velvet ribbon; the tucked and folded crown is cleverly shaped through a series of interior stitches. Label: Eaton's of Canada. *Mobile Millinery Museum*. $150-250.

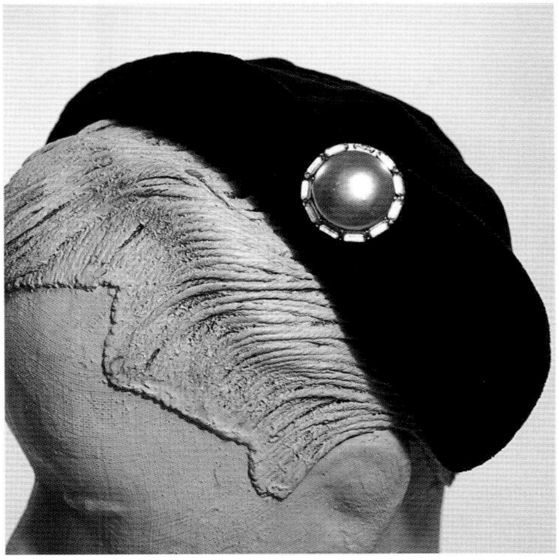

An art deco pin secures the narrow, upturned brim of this deep plum, silk velvet cap. *Mobile Millinery Museum*. $225.

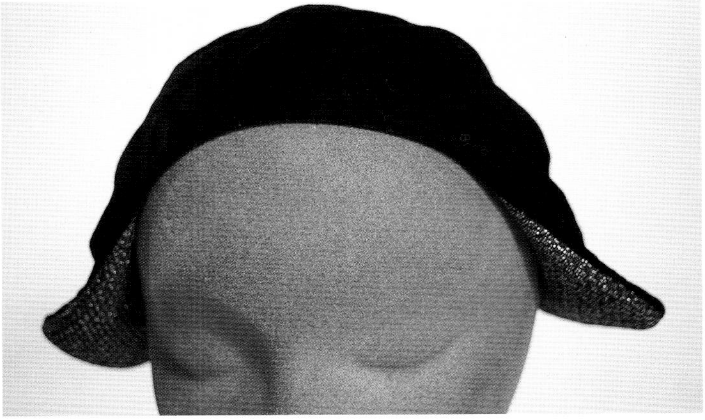

This undersized version of the Dutch cap, in black silk velvet, hails from the mid-1930s. Gold lamé lines the wire-shaped, crown extensions. Label: Created by Linda Farell, New York. *Mobile Millinery Museum*. $200-250.

A spiral of trapunto-stitched ribbon climbs a tower of deep brown velour. A flat bow droops to the side, extending the diagonal line. Label: Ellen Faith Original. *Mobile Millinery Museum*. $225.

This black velour Juliet cap oozes Hollywood glamour. Crystal-encrusted pheasant feathers add warmth, with their warm coloration, while tiny mirrors add sparkle to the quills of a pair of black pointers. Twin labels: The Emporium, Studio of American Design, San Francisco, California/By Barbara Lee. *Mobile Millinery Museum*. $300-400.

Deep turquoise linen bonnet banded with white straw and set with white paper lilacs. *Mobile Millinery Museum*. $150-200.

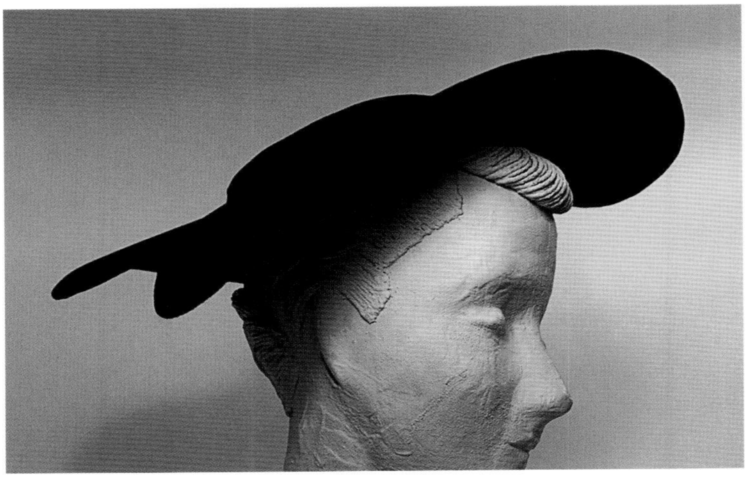

Black felt was never so stylish as in this bow-trimmed widebrim with self-fabric hatpin. Label: Crean, Canada. *Mobile Millinery Museum*. $350-400.

Pea, olive, and grass-green felts are stacked to form a alluring cone hat. A bronze silk tassel falls to the back. Label: Alpine Hats, Toronto. *Mobile Millinery Museum*. $200-250.

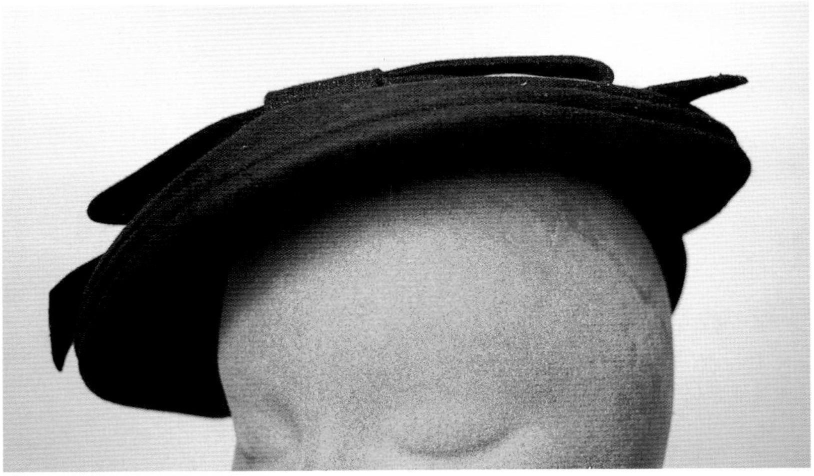

A saucy navy saucer. *Mobile Millinery Museum*. $200-250.

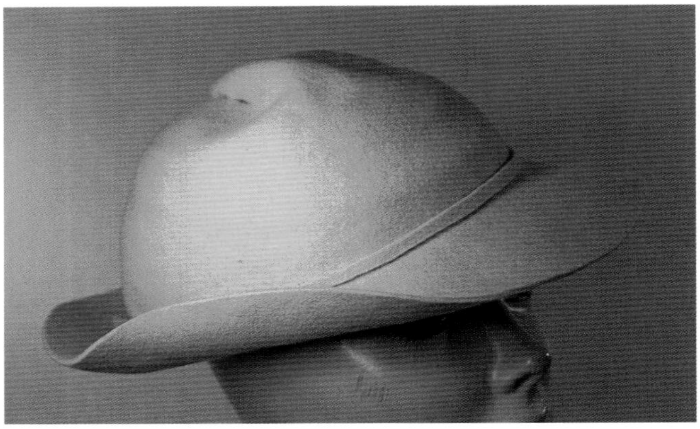

A cheerful yellow felt slouch. *Marg McGuire Collection, Mobile Millinery Museum*. $150-200.

Velvet roses fall over the rolled brim of this veiled navy straw. *Mobile Millinery Museum*. $200-250.

A dramatic feather helmet in black and burnt orange is made all the more spectacular with the addition of a sweeping rooster tail. *Mobile Millinery Museum*. $350-450.

Depression-era remake: a turquoise felt covered with banana yellow fabric and trimmed with muskrat. *Mobile Millinery Museum.* $200.

A bumper-brimmed Juliet cap of dove-gray straw cushions the brow with a navy velvet under-brim. Navy, diamond dot, voilette. Label: Evelyn. *Mobile Millinery Museum*. $200-220.

White straw banded simply with navy grosgrain. Label: Bonwit Teller. *Mobile Millinery Museum*. $200-250.

Black felt beret with open-weave snood or crepinièr decorated on top with mink tails. Matching mink muff, banded with black ruched satin, simulates a bow. It is very likely that the pelts for this ensemble were ranched by the author's grandfather. Gift of Madelene Dover of Cowansville, Quebec. *Mobile Millinery Museum*. $600-800.

Wool tartan Dutch cap and brass-trimmed matching muff; these items were custom made in Montreal, c.1935, and worn by Mary Bach. Label: Ray Spires, Montreal. *Vicky Bach Collection, Mobile Millinery Museum*. $300-450.

Dainty floral trimmed hat of brown bonnet board. *Mobile Millinery Museum*. $150-200.

A dear little bonnet and drawstring bag fashioned of natural straw and chocolate-brown satin. *Mobile Millinery Museum*. $250-300.

The flattest of cartwheels, in midnight black Milan straw. Cloth daisies grace the small, flat crown. A narrow elastic chignon strap provides security. Label: Valentine Modiste Français, 288 St. Catharine O. (Montreal). *Mobile Millinery Museum*. $300-350.

Carnival figurine of a smartly dressed gal in a slouch hat. *Private Collection*.

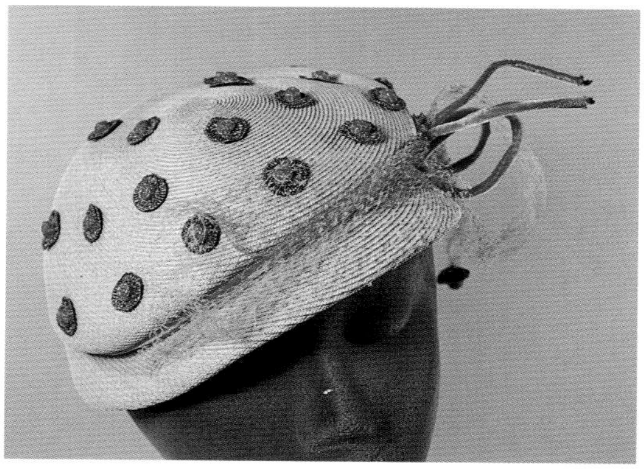

An intriguing, dove-gray straw, dotted with tiny straw medallions, features a narrow, wired band and bow with gray sen sen veiling. Early Strathmore label. *Mobile Millinery Museum*. $150.

A taupe velour cap, accented with red, boasts hat jewelry of brilliant rhinestones. *Marg McGuire Collection, Mobile Millinery Museum*. $120-150.

The wide collar of this woman's fur coat sets off her close-fitting wool Tyrolean. Note the tilt and downward-sloping aigrette. *Photo courtesy of Iris Hillyer.*

Feather trim and a tie-on veil dotted with bits of brightly colored-straw feminizes an otherwise masculine-looking fedora. *Mobile Millinery Museum*. $350-450.

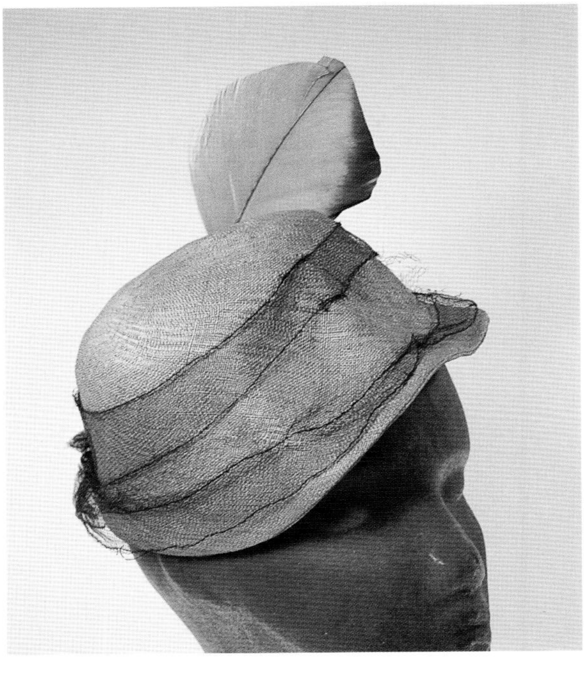

A subtly shaped straw topper, wrapped in black hairlace, exhibits great élan. A matching plume is singed with just the right touch of black. Triple labels: Made in France/Fine Mouche/Annie, 3 Rue Du Cirque, Paris ELY.38.01. *Marg McGuire Collection, Mobile Millinery Museum*. $175-225.

Chapter VI
War and Post-War Ingenuity: 1940 - 1950

"After the war a friend and I were looking for a project to take on – something important; not just some type of sewing group. We heard of a man on the street who had Multiple Sclerosis, a mysterious disease at that time, which left him and others like him, unable to work. We strongly wanted to help this man so we got in the car and drove to Toronto where we boldly approached the hat factories and asked for donations of new hats. To our amazement they accepted our appeal. For a period of years we presented hats for sale to ladies groups in church halls and basements. We were able to raise funds for these people to support their families. This was the beginning of the present *MS Society*."

— *Fran Richardson, Stoney Creek, Ontario*

Iris Hillyer in a contour-brimmed hat, c.1945. *Courtesy of Iris Hillyer.*

"As a young minister's wife in the '40s, I was introduced to my husband's congregation one Sunday, and made to walk down the aisle on his arm. I wore a red suit with a silver fox collar and a fabulous hat, which prompted a wolf whistle from one of the parishioners. We never found out who was responsible."

— *Iris Hillyer, Burlington, Ontario*

"Miss Schuler was a wonderful milliner. Mother always went there and I'd go with her: In those days you would have a hat for the four seasons and more if you could afford it."

— *Valerie Denton, Hamilton resident*

"To this day I remember the hat I wore to my cousin's wedding over fifty years ago. It was a sweet little thing that tilted over one eye and was covered in Black-Eyed-Susans. I've always loved Black-Eyed-Susans."

— *Laurabelle McLean, Richmond Hill, Ontario*

"I was walking in downtown Montreal during the war, when my large red beret blew off into the street. I watched in amazement as a group of young soldiers ran off to retrieve it."

— *Iris Hillyer, Burlington, Ontario*

The Spring collections of 1940 reveal a variety of small hat styles to compliment the new lean silhouette. Most, including the pagodine, tilt forward or to one side. Red and green are seen and blue is prevalent in shades of teal through navy, but white makes headlines. *Ladies Home Journal*, in bold print, proclaims "White, white, very right" and "White hats very, very wise".

As the conflict in Europe escalates, millinery turns to the military for inspiration and designers reinterpret the helmet and the beret for women. The fedora, the turban, the kerchief, and the snood become popular for day wear and serve a practical purpose for the many women employed in factory work. Because milliners utilize fabric remnants faithfully, many variations on the turban appear, including a pleated halo style, which mimics headgear worn by native chieftains.

As designers are forced to contend with government restrictions on allowable yardage, small hats make big statements through the application of frou frou. Like the dresses they are designed to accessorize, hats are carefully cut and constructed to make the greatest impact with the least amount of material.

Iris Thomas and her cousin in separate interpretations of the 1940s beret. *Courtesy of Iris Hillyer*.

A large spider web veil is hand-embroidered in coffee and cream-colored silk and secured with a hatpin, adding drama to a 1940s velour chapeau. Label: Made in France. *Mobile Millinery Museum*. $500-700.

The tilt or doll hat of the late 1930s is carried into the war years and becomes all the more charming with the addition of various transparencies. The glamour bug bites even the tailored Lady Stetson hat, with one model completely enveloped in shoulder-length veiling.

Millinery designs, c.1940-1945, reflect many of the consequences of war. Despite shortages, hats are not rationed in Britain or Canada as it is argued, in parliament, that a hat can be made out of anything and, after all, a cheery chapeau is a vital spirit booster. Many of the metal molds, used for centuries in the production of petals, leaves, and flowers for millinery trims, are broken during the conflict, and the metal recycled for the war effort. Plastic buttons and buckles make an appearance and millinery roses are set on plastic stems, complete with realistic-looking thorns. Some hats are held in place with small plastic combs, sewn to the inner crown, as bobby pins made of high carbon steel become scarce.

Jen Hillyer and Mildred Philip are dressed for a wedding in early 1940s chapeaux. *Courtesy of Iris Hillyer.*

This doll hat, c.1940, would have been expensive when new. Velvet roses in grape, lavender, rose, raspberry, beige, and soft pink tumble over the brow as black beauty-marked veiling cascades over sleek tresses. *Mobile Millinery Museum*. $250-300.

By the fall of 1945, the line of a hat, rather than its trim, begins to make fashion headlines. Hats with rounded contours become the order of the day: domes, derbies, pouffs, and soufflés. Lilly Daché produces a brimmed hat that sweeps forward at the side, and labels it a "profile bonnet". Turbans and berets are manipulated to new heights that include side width, and brimmed pieces acquire new dramatic contours.

Hat jewelry returns to adorn cartwheels, toques, boaters, and turbans, while flowers and bowknots perch on hats and evening coiffures. Small bandeau, known as half hats and curvettes, hug hair worn in chignons, long bobs, and pageboys. Small veils fall from all manner of elegant chapeaux and large transparencies drape brimmed hats, falling to shoulder level and beyond.

By 1948, magazines offer alternatives to hats in the form of twisted scarves, veils, ribbons, and flowers, which are worked into shorter, waved hairstyles. Thus, the seeds are planted for a hatless age that is to come.

"In the 40s, we freshened our feathers by rubbing them with crayon."

— *Anonymous hat owner*

With exotic plumage at a high premium, or no longer available, the feathers of garden-variety birds are altered in various ways to enhance their appearance. Pigeon, turkey, sparrow, and goose feathers are curled, waxed, glycerined, or glued together to form "made birds" or "breasts". Domestic poultry feathers are also treated with dyes, acids, and starch. Innovative post-war milliners use plastic, leather, and other materials to create "fake" plumage.

Designer Profile: Peggy Claire

Peggy Claire, a well-known Hamilton milliner, apprenticed during WWII. She said she was sick of farm work. Once established in her career, Claire employed clever tactics for marketing her designs. By wearing flamboyant hats in public, she and her assistant became walking advertisements for *Peggy's Hats*. One day a man from Montreal asked her where she had obtained the hat she was wearing, then came round to her shop and bought five of her creations.

Like all milliners, Claire made winter hats in the summer and summer hats in the winter. The designer was adamant about not wearing a summer hat after August 15.

Circa 1945: White wool has been crocheted to form a stylish sweater hat. A cluster of short mahogany feathers adds contrast. *Mobile Millinery Museum.* $125-150.

A black, rayon velvet, dish hat, c.1948, is banded with a narrow strip of passmenterie and finished with a self-fabric bow. Silver-tone balls, set with rhinestones, add sparkle. *Mobile Millinery Museum*. $120-150.

Black on black: Deep-pile, black velvet, Juliet cap, beautifully trimmed in the same hue, with a mix of textures and shapes, which include: a cotton velvet rose, clusters of papier-mâché berries, and lacquered paper leaves. Brown, thorny stems add the only touch of color. Label: Strathmore by Newton, Paris, New York. *Mobile Millinery Museum*. $150-250.

A bumper pillbox from the early 1940s in chocolate brown wool felt. Nose length hairline veiling. Self-fabric pin may have been used to affix floral bouquets to the crown, as was the fashion at the time. *Mobile Millinery Museum*. $175-225.

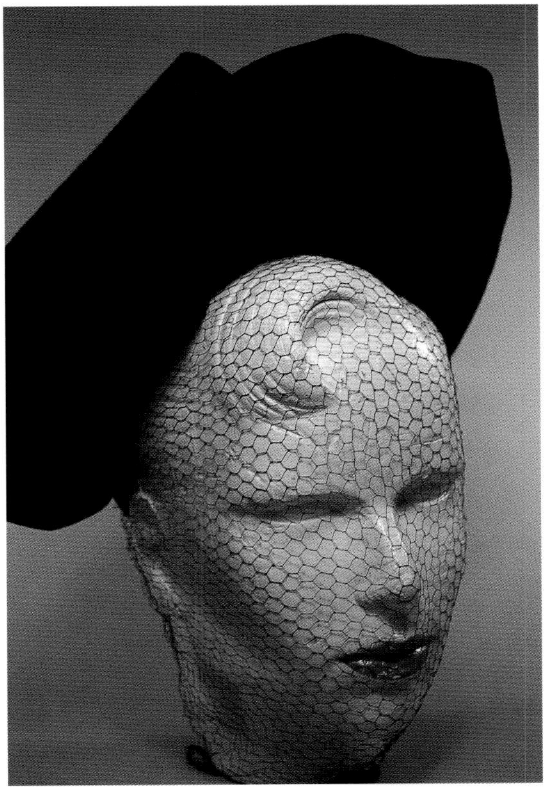

Stylized vertical bows dominate this black felt beretta from the early 1940s. Label: Fur felt in the English Manner – Wimbledon Hats. *Mobile Millinery Museum*. $250-350.

A double bow adds the finishing touch to a black beaver disc hat with bumper brim. *Mobile Millinery Museum*. $225-325.

A late 1940s straw turban. Straw cloth is folded and draped across the crown, ending in a swirl that droops over the right ear. A curled aigrette repeats the contour. Label: Lilly's Hat Shop, Burlington. *Mobile Millinery Museum*. $225.

A turban of warm brown velvet exhibits a flat, wired crown. A jeweled pin medallion marks the center front. Original paper price tag, c.1945, reveals a cost of $8.95. *Mobile Millinery Museum*. $175-225.

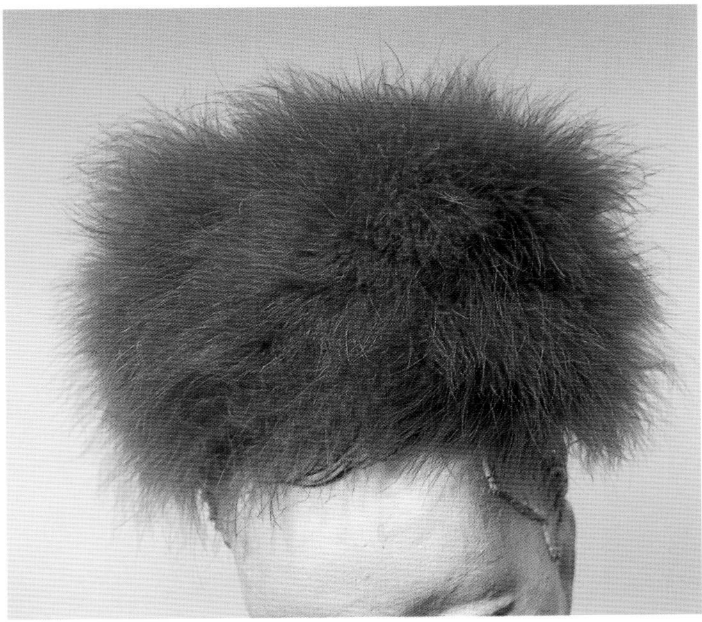

Deep pillbox of golden brown marabou. Label: Brae Burn, New York, Montreal. *Mobile Millinery Museum*. $150-175.

A net toque, bound with fine navy straw that crisscrosses at the center front, is covered with giant chiffon petals in pink and lavender. The dotted veil shows significant damage. Label: Creation by André. *Mobile Millinery Museum*. $60-80.

These bow hats for evening make the most of black velvet and veiling. *Mobile Millinery Museum*. $150-200 each.

A dramatic periwinkle wool felt is enveloped in Russian veiling and dotted with blue velvet bows. A grosgrain strap secures the hat at the nape of the neck. A similar hat, in pink, was shown in the spring issue of *Ladies Home Journal* in 1948. Label: Henry Pollack Inc., Fifth Ave., New York. *Mobile Millinery Museum*. $350-450.

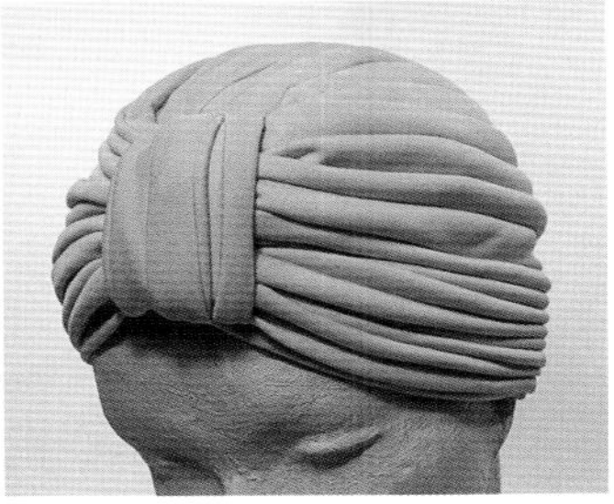

An elegant turban of baby-pink nylon tricot. Label: Simpson's. *Mobile Millinery Museum*. $225.

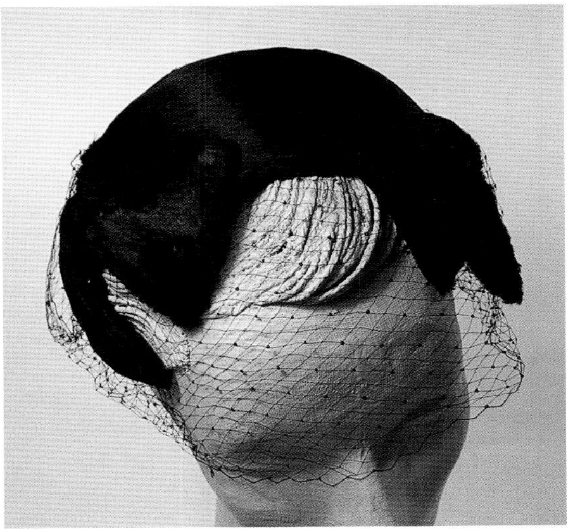

An evening cap of brushed beaver felt is made to shine in artificial light. Self-fabric bows mark the temples and center back. Nose-length, diamond dot veiling. Label: Piko, Paris, New York. *Mobile Millinery Museum*. $150-250.

A navy velvet band and bow make a dramatic statement against this loose-weave, red straw toque. Label: Paradise Model. *Mobile Millinery Museum*. $125-150.

This doll is fashionably dressed in a silk tilt hat to match her colorful gown. Her seamed nylon stockings suggest she was made in the 1940s. *Mobile Millinery Museum*. $125.

Details.

An open crown widebrim of midnight-black velvet is pierced with a triangular, mother-of-pearl hatpin. *Mobile Millinery Museum*. Hat and pin: $250-300.

A cream straw, summer fedora proudly displays a spray of violets, forget-me-nots, starflowers, and other blossoms, anchored at the left temple with a small, black velvet bow. The hat lacks a label but appears to be the work of a meticulous and artistic milliner. *Mobile Millinery Museum*. $250-300.

A winter hat of cherry velvet, from the mid-1940s, bears a union label. *Mobile Millinery Museum*. $150-200.

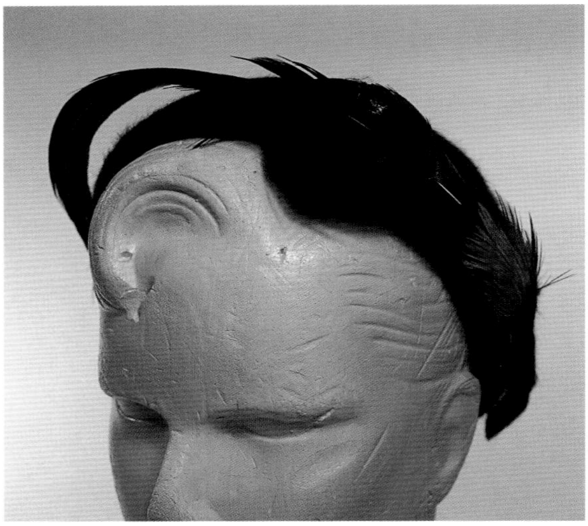

The brow of this brimless, black felt is wrapped with a glycerined feather, which passes through a black feather donut. Label: Strathmore by Newton of Canada. *Mobile Millinery Museum.* $120-150.

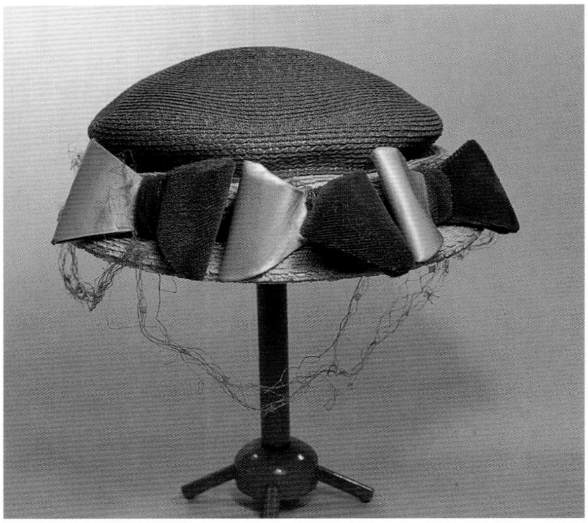

A striking coffee-and-cream straw topper makes a statement with stiff satin and velvet bows. Remnants of matching veiling are secured to a velvet band. *Mobile Millinery Museum*. $125-150.

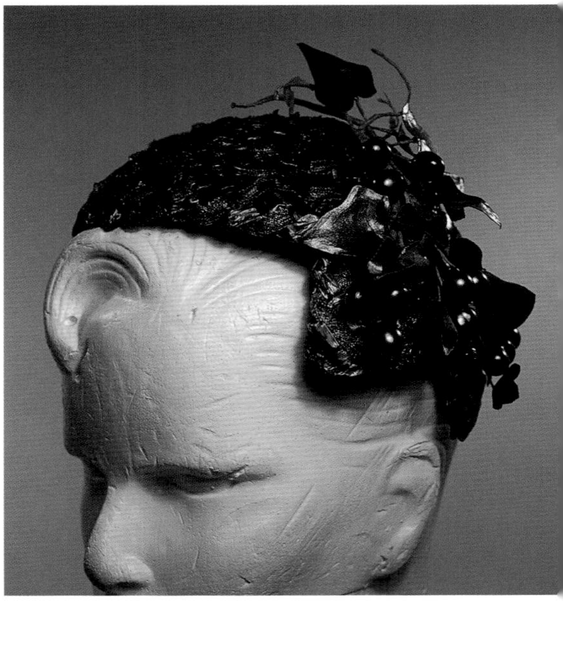

A woven straw, saddle-brown, bandeau, festooned with berries that resemble black pearls and brown leaves, shines with copper highlights. *Mobile Millinery Museum.* $150.

Black velvet rims an open-crown horsehair with upturned brim. Center-front, pearl and rhinestone button. *Mobile Millinery Museum*. $225.

This high-crowned, crimson straw, picture hat has a more recent look to it but must have been made before 1948, as it bears a John Frederics label. The millinery partnership of John Piocelle and Frederic Hirst ran from 1929 to 1947. The tall crown, banded with wide, black grosgrain, finishes with a bow at the right side. *Mobile Millinery Museum*. $200-250.

Buckram cap, swathed in heavy, deep persimmon satin, is bedecked with a pair of taupe cabbage roses with yellow and orange stamens and wired, silver-gray leaves. *Mobile Millinery Museum*. $150-200.

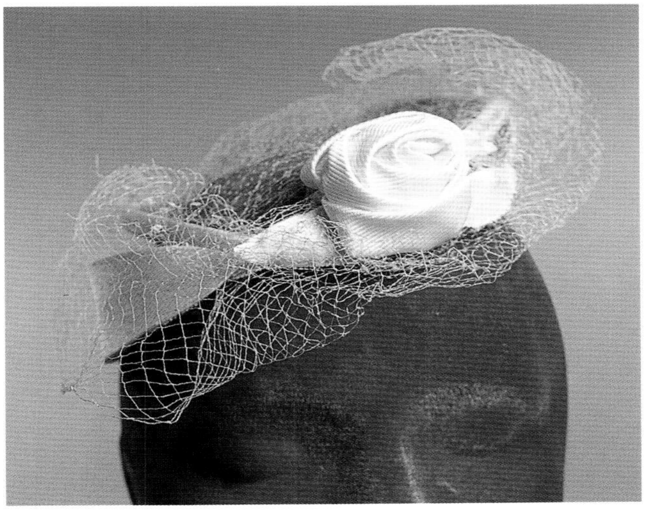

Ivory faille, fashioned as a rosebud, presides over a cage hat with double veiling. Label: Norman Paulvin, New York. *Mobile Millinery Museum*. $150-200.

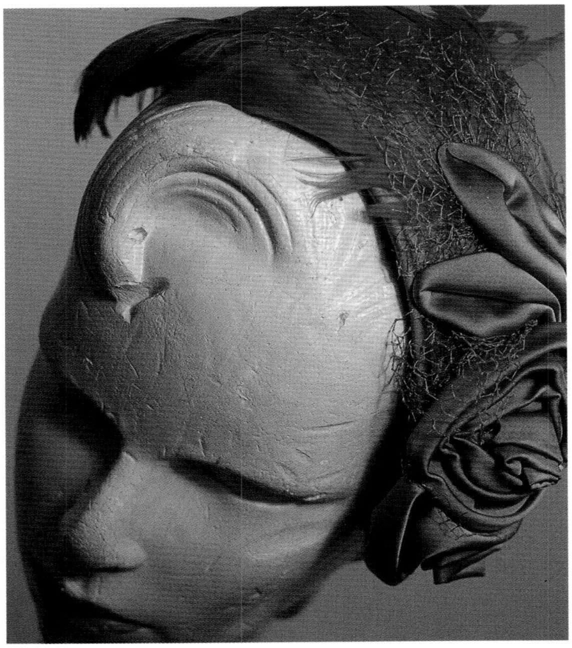

A satin and feather fantasy in acorn and deep amber with moss-green net. *Mobile Millinery Museum*. $125-150.

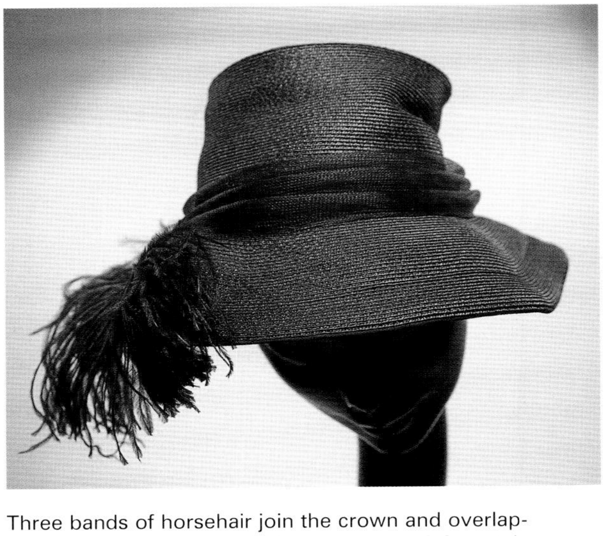

Three bands of horsehair join the crown and overlapping brim of this chocolate-brown fedora. A forward-projecting ostrich plume in beige and brown is secured above a pair of horsehair loops. Label: Creation by André. *Mobile Millinery Museum*. $200-250.

Two types of veiling, layered over a trio of velvet discs, makes an engaging doll hat. *Mobile Millinery Museum*. $150-200.

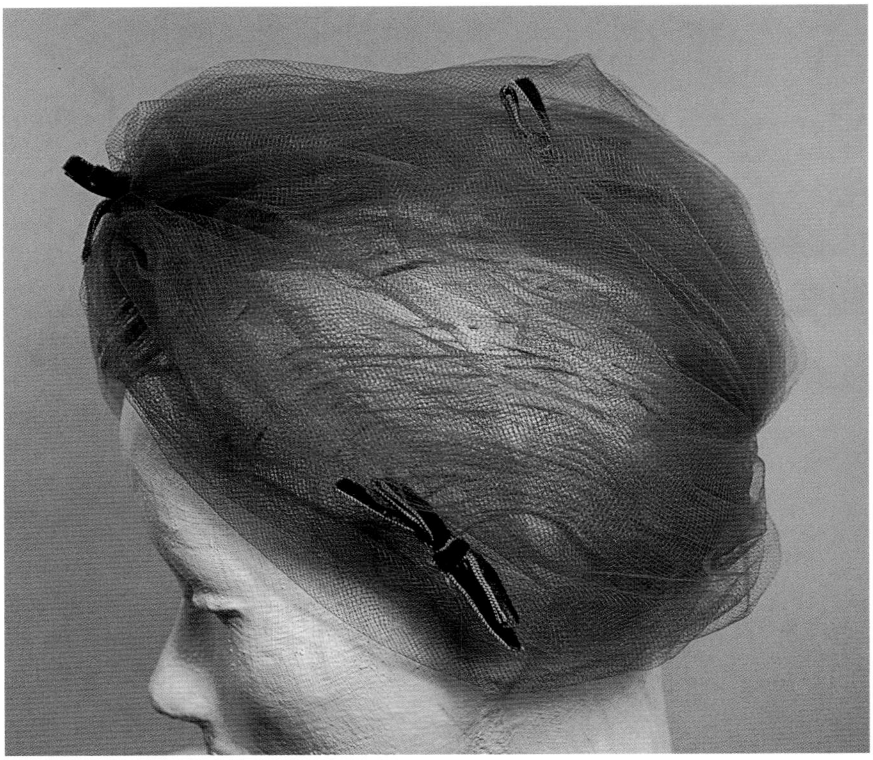

A turban of peacock tulle separates in back, allowing the hair to tumble out, perhaps in a pageboy. Velvet ribbons have faded with time. *Mobile Millinery Museum*. $150.

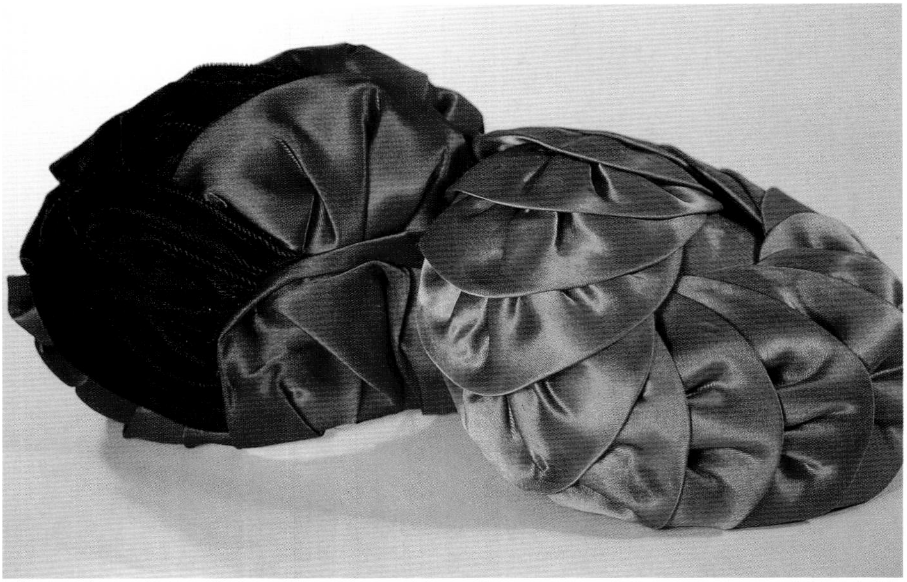

The original owner of these satin and velvet petal hats maintained them in perfect condition. *Mobile Millinery Museum*. $75-150 each.

This black satin calot, beaded with jet, was worn at a jaunty angle by its original owner. *Mobile Millinery Museum*. $120.

An inner crown supports a saucer of beaded satin with a center-crown pearl button. *Mobile Millinery Museum*. $150-200.

Horsehair bands a sewn straw widebrim, which would look new if worn today. *Mobile Millinery Museum*. $250-300.

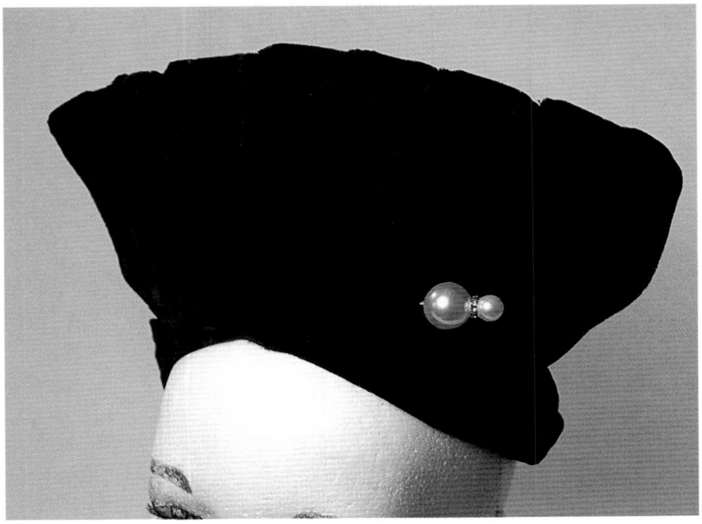

A black velvet cap with pleated, vertical crown is dressed up for evening with a pearl-and-rhinestone hatpin. *Mobile Millinery Museum*. $425.

This battleship-gray, wool felt, widebrim shows great style with its double band of velvet and horsehair, set above a chenille-dotted checkerboard veil. *Mobile Millinery Museum*. $350.

Black velvet headband with rhinestone-centered topknot. *Mobile Millinery Museum*. $150-180.

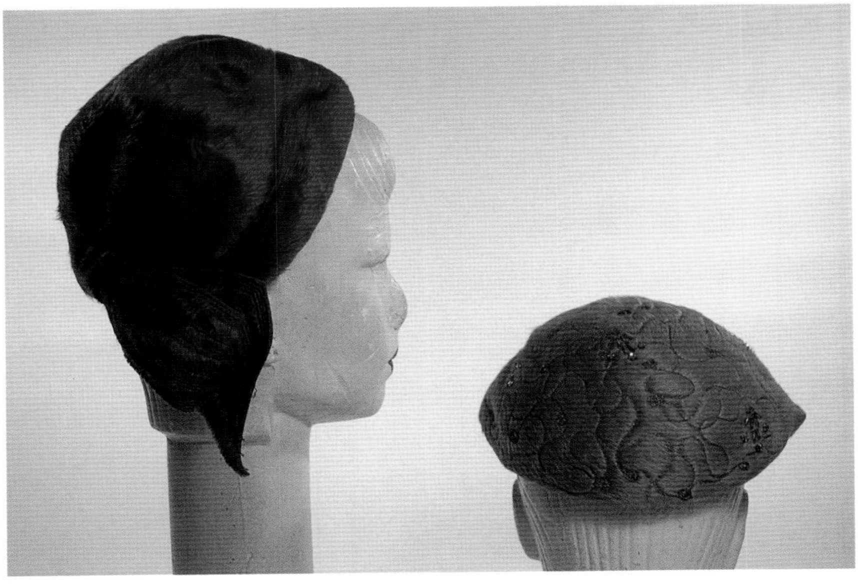

For an autumn afternoon: a pair of embroidered capulets. *Mobile Millinery Museum*. $80-120 each.

Left:
Although it bears no label, this coral felt curvette may have been custom ordered. Its rounded crown sweeps gently forward to the right. A matching, diamond dot, coral wimple frames the chin. *Mobile Millinery Museum*. $250.

Right:
Pinkish-brown roses and orange blossoms ring an elegant, scalloped-edge topper. *Mobile Millinery Museum.* $180-220.

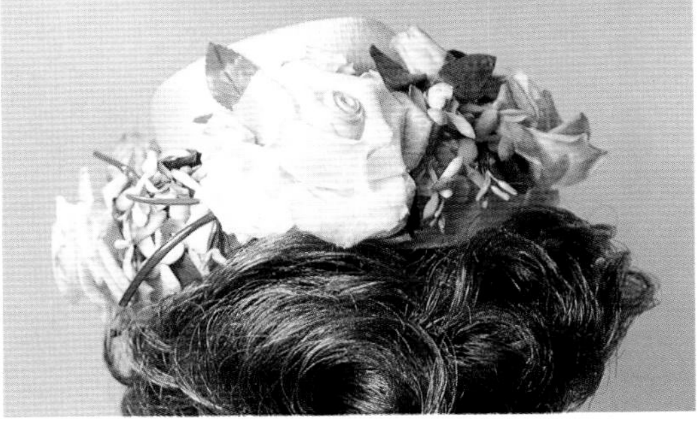

Vertical bows dominate an almond-shaped felt cap in perfect condition. The bow motif is repeated in flocked chiffon on a black lace veil. Label: Simpson's. *Mobile Millinery Museum*. $800-900.

Back view.

Side view.

Grape felt tilt hat with self-fabric bow and chignon strap. Label: Furfelt reg'd. *Mobile millinery Museum*. $300-350.

This fully-lined salmon felt is swept with a trio of black aigrettes and finished with nose-length chenille-dotted veiling. *Mobile Millinery Museum*. $240-260.

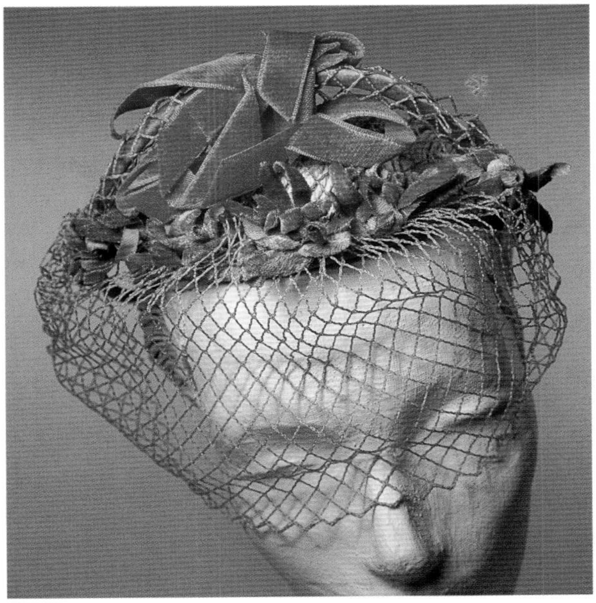

An apricot doll hat, brightened with orange velvet bows, is made all the more dramatic with the addition of bright orange chicken coop veiling. *Mobile Millinery Museum*. $220.

A silk velvet treasure in pumpkin and autumn brown. *Mobile Millinery Museum*. $150.

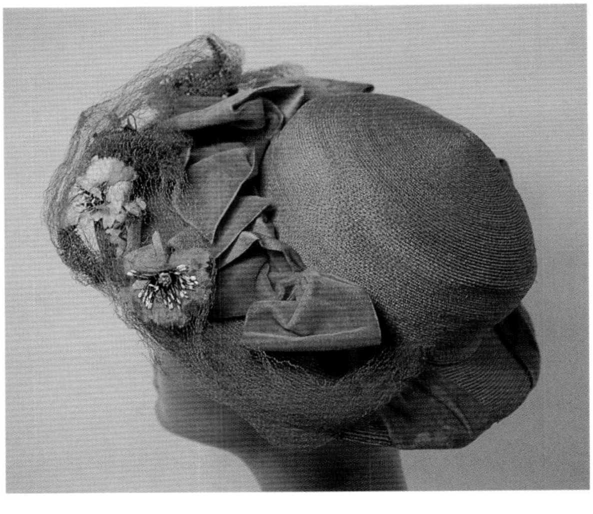

A natural straw, brimmed with golden velvet ribbon, traps fabric flowers, bottlebrush trees, and horsehair sprays inside a fine, taupe, horsehair veil. Label: Custom Made, Laddie Northridge Inc., 1 W. 57th St., New York. *Mobile Millinery Museum*. $350-450.

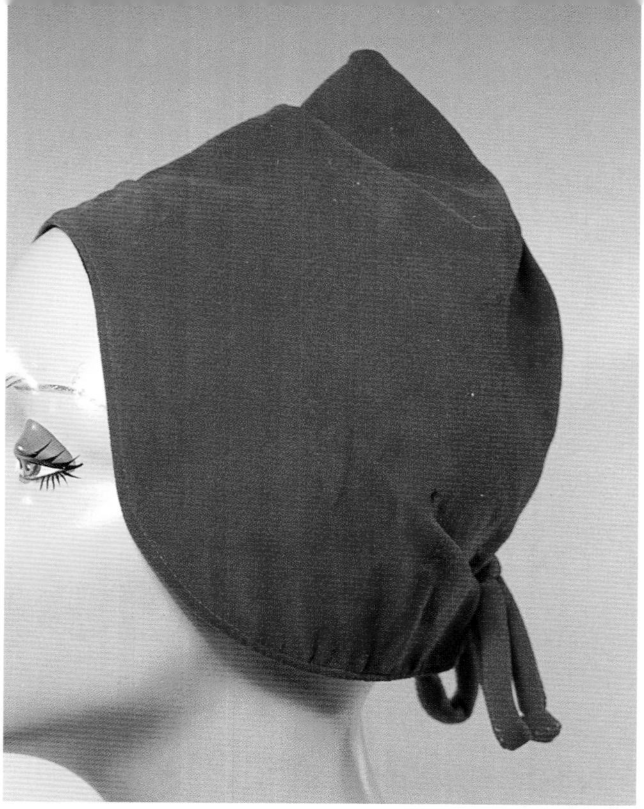

An impish pixie confection in cherry velveteen. *Mobile Millinery Museum*. $250-300.

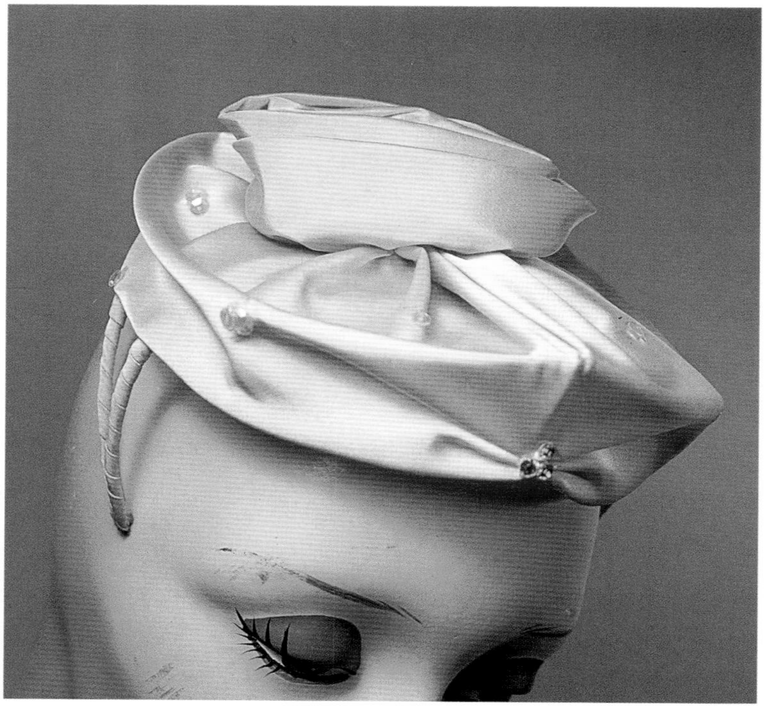

A crown of cotton-candy taffeta on a white wire frame is cut away in a deep vee at back to allow for an elegant coiffure. A rhinestone trio marks the center front. *Mobile Millinery Museum*. $200-250.

This ruffle-rimmed dish hat has the allure of lingerie. *Mobile Millinery Museum*. $250-350.

This advertising poster by the *Wabasso Cotton Co®*. features a white, floppy-brimmed, beach hat.

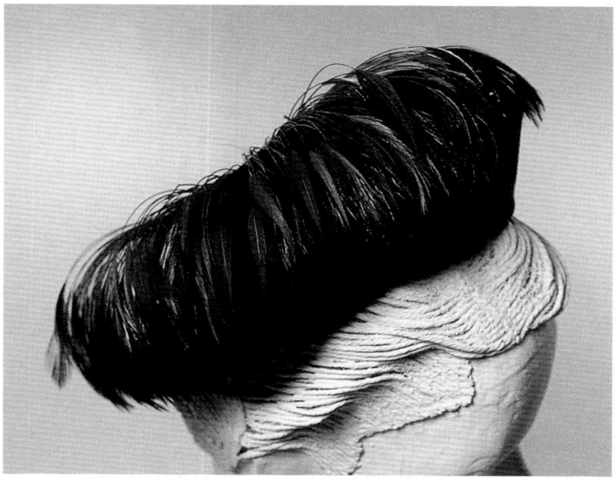

Goose feathers ring a black velvet crown. *Mobile Millinery Museum*. $200-250.

An endearing confection in indigo felt. *Mobile Millinery Museum*. $300-350.

"Wig hat" of game feathers. *Mobile Millinery Museum*. $200-250.

A revival cloche of black felt is trimmed simply with a self-fabric bow and strip of black sequins. *Mobile Millinery Museum*. $80-100.

Left:
A superb example of the stand-up beret or beretta; this one in brown mink. Orange satin lining. *Mobile Millinery Museum*. $400-450.

Right:
This cheerful orange straw was worn to business meetings in the late 1940s. Organdie ties, in eggshell and sienna, intertwine under matching fabric roses. Label: Strathmore by Newton, Paris, New York. *Mobile Millinery Museum*. $125-225.

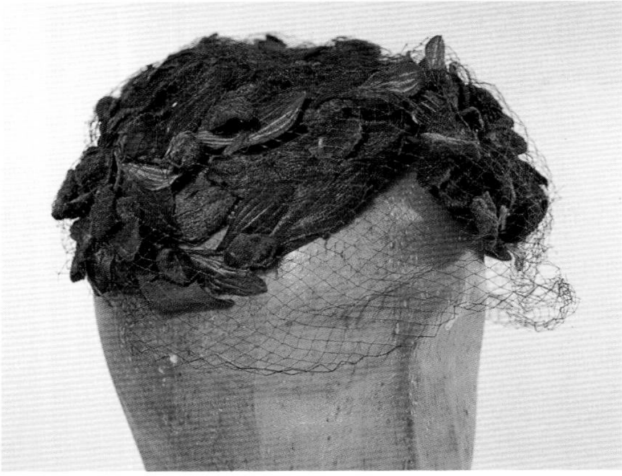

Royal blue "half hat". *Mobile Millinery Museum*. $100-150.

A beautifully shaped, long-nap, beaver felt is banded in reddish-brown grosgrain. The wrap-around brim allows for the addition of a feather or two. Label: Creation by André. *Mobile Millinery Museum*. $180-240.

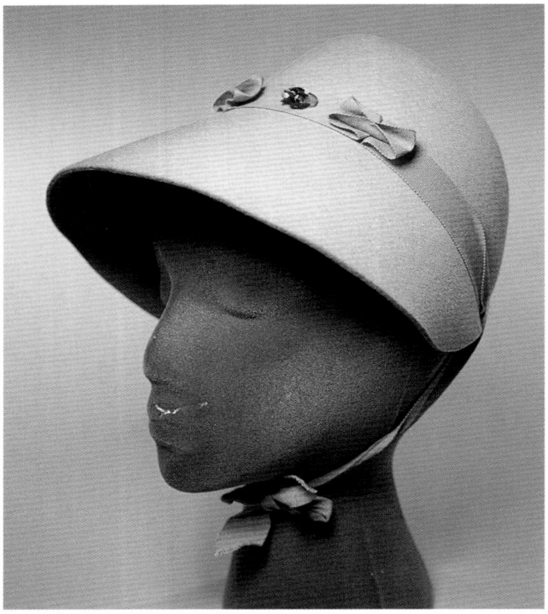

This child's revival bonnet of baby-pink felt is a nod to the Regency period. *Mobile Millinery Museum*. $150-200.

Osprey feathers sweep the brow-line of this delightful cage hat. *Mobile Millinery Museum*. $180-220.

Black and white was never more striking than this late 1940s, dish hat, edged in accordion-pleated grosgrain and offset with a pair of rhinestone flowers. A spider web veil ties at back. *Mobile Millinery Museum*. $150-200.

Black velvet "Statue of Liberty" hat, cut to sit at the back of the head. Satin lining, small jeweled hatpin. *Mobile Millinery Museum*. $250-300.

Crimson jersey bourrelet. *Mobile Millinery Museum*. $100-150.

A chinstrap of black veiling adds a military air to this confederate-gray felt. A rooster-tail spray adds panache. *Mobile Millinery Museum*. $300-350.

An evening curvette in bronze satin boasts hand beading. *Mobile Millinery Museum*. $225.

Winter hat of plum velveteen banded in casually-tied grosgrain. *Mobile Millinery Museum*. $150.

Kathleen Baird in a stylish 1940s kerchief. *Photo courtesy of Iris Hillyer*.

Circa 1940: The author's grandmother in a tilted disc hat. *Photo courtesy of Iris Hillyer.*

A velvet half hat is treated to a feathery, vertical arrangement. *Mobile Millinery Museum*. $250-300.

The milliner's skill with fabric is evident in this late 1940s stunner with pinch-back brim. Crown and upper brim are of ribbed, black rayon; band and under-brim of abstractly striped, black and white satin. Label: Jo-Anne, Designer, 1566 Yonge St. –Toronto. *Eleanor Auld Collection, Mobile Millinery Museum.* $200-250.

Mary MacLean in a wool funnel hat. *Photo courtesy of Iris Hillyer*.

Iris Hillyer models this hat.

Business cards of milliner Eleanor Auld, a.k.a. Jo Anne.

Jo Anne announces the "festive season" with an invitation to view the latest models.

Announcement card interior.

A pair of matrons sport a dressy canotier and a tilted Breton to shop in downtown Montreal, August 1941. *Barb Philip Collection, Mobile Millinery Museum.*

Henriette Leroux's pansy-trimmed church hat, c.1945 - 1955, is of fine black straw, sewn in concentric circles from the center crown. Black diamond-dot veiling wraps an upturned brim. The small, brass-and-jet hatpin hails from a much earlier era. *Barb Philip Collection, Mobile Millinery Museum.* $250-350.

Detail.

A mound of paper-white mums crowns a navy brim. Label: Made in USA. *Mobile Millinery Museum*. $300-350.

Left:
Unlabelled, handmade, red straw beauty, banded with melon-colored grosgrain. *Mobile Millinery Museum*. $300-350.

Right:
A pixie of green-black velvet, joined by bugle beads, finishes with a double tassel. Label: Strathmore. *Mobile Millinery Museum*. $225.

Palm-green wool felt bucket, banded high on the sloping crown, is finished with a jeweled double bow. *Mobile Millinery Museum.* $80-120.

This hat of almond-green jersey, with its dramatic turkey plumage cascade, may have been created to resemble Scarlett O'Hara's famous drapery hat. Hers, however, was further adorned with black coq feathers and gilded chicken bones. *Mobile Millinery Museum*. $1200-

This bumper pillbox, trimmed with a crystal fan, is constructed of long nap wool felt. Label: Evelyn Original, Paris, New York. *Mobile Millinery Museum*. $80-100.

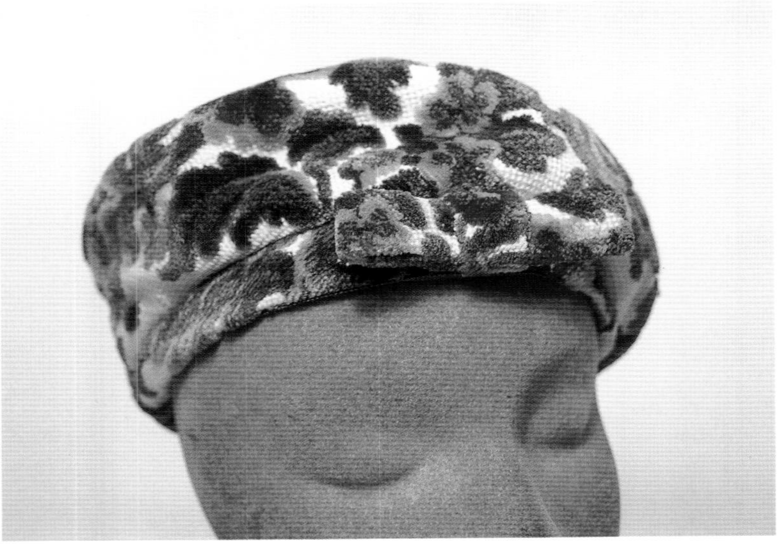

A winter charmer of richly-textured autumn leaves is set against a white background. *Mobile Millinery Museum*. $80-100.

Four girls attend a Montreal nightclub in 1947. One wears an ostrich-plumed half hat. *Laurabelle MacLean Collection, Mobile Millinery Museum.*

Frances Kavanaugh (second from the left) wears a small, dark, gardenia-trimmed hat to the St. Andrew's Ball at the Windsor Hotel in Montreal, November 29th, 1940. Mrs. Florence Clark holds an ostrich feather hat in her lap. *Laurabelle MacLean Collection, Mobile Millinery Museum.*

Chapter VII
Socialites, Church Ladies, and Debutantes: 1950 - 1960

"My mother was known as the *Hat Lady of Kingston*. She used to tell me to put on a hat and gloves every time I left the house with my father, because I was 'going out with an officer of the King's army.' We were usually on our way to the beer store."

— *Daughter of Mary Elliot, Kingston, Ontario*

"We always bought our new spring hats in February – and wore them with our fur coats!"

— *Catherine Sherlock*

"Our minister always arrived at the church early, to prepare for the morning service. One Sunday he noticed a woman wearing a hat identical to the one his wife had selected that day. Like a good husband, he raced home before the service, to tell her to choose another hat."

— *Anonymous*

"I remember when we were in competition with at least thirty hat factories in Toronto alone."

— *Lillian Lieberman, wife of Variety Hat Co. Owner*

"*Klein's* department store was my *Lord and Taylor* when I was growing up in Clark, New Jersey. Mother and I frequently visited the *Kleins* on Canal Street in New York City, long after our move to New Jersey. Naturally, we were thrilled when they opened a store in Woodbridge. These feathered hats, purchased during the late '50s and early '60s, made a fabulous fashion statement: they framed the face, flattered the hair styles, and added true panache to spring suits and coats."

— *Arlene Allen, Clark, New Jersey*

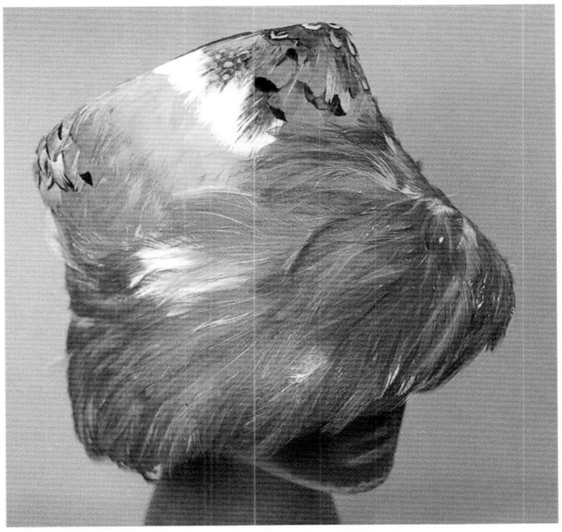

Caramel lampshade with touches of red and green-dyed guinea plumage. Union label. *Arlene Clark Collection, Mobile Millinery Museum.* $200-250.

Halo hat of dyed pheasant and guinea plumage. Label: Evelyn Varon Exclusive. *Arlene Allen Collection, Mobile Millinery Museum*. $200-250.

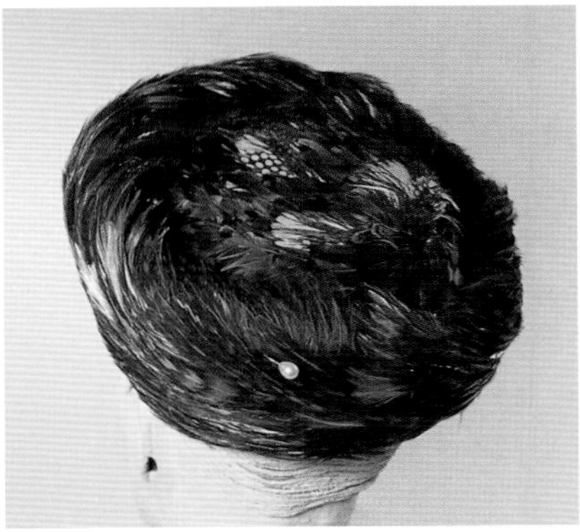

Christmas-green pheasant feathers with sprinkles of white, red, and ginger brim a bumper pillbox to complement a crown of green and black pheasant, relieved with red, white, and yellow guinea plumage. Label: Evelyn Varon Exclusive. *Arlene Allen Collection, Mobile Millinery Museum*. $200-250.

"I gave a fashion show at the Trenton Air Base one year and the models switched hats to throw me off, but it didn't matter because I knew my hats."

— *Rita Minion, milliner*

"When I summered in Lake Megantic in the '50s, the stores were in competition for summer clearance sales. One offered a free hat with each $5 purchase. At that time many women did not want to be seen wearing the same hat twice so this was an effective marketing strategy."

— *Kathleen Baird*

During the 1950s the dish, the platter, the whimsy, the close hat, the clip, and countless other styles filled the pages of fashion magazines. Many of these models carried over into the early sixties. Department stores maintained entire millinery departments and women could select from custom pieces, factory made hats, or haute couture. In Canada, quality hats bearing labels like *Lady Cavendish* and *Lady Warrick* were produced at *Variety Hat* in Toronto, while *André, Henri*, and *Georgette* labels reflected the Montreal chic of pieces from *Canada Hat* and other companies.

Hat label, Canadian Hat Co. Ltd.

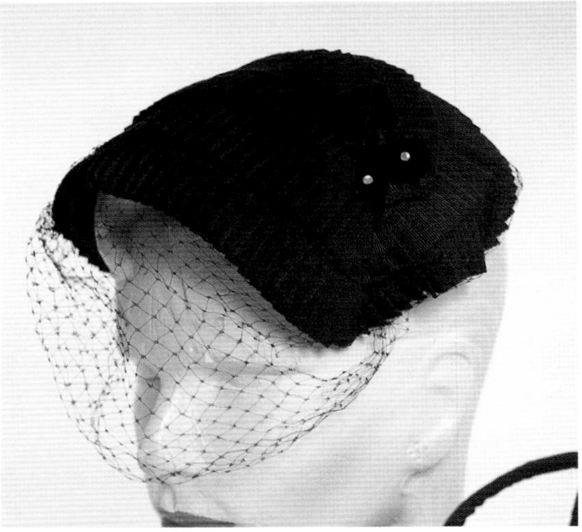

This 1950s close hat of pleated grosgrain has attended many a luncheon. The diamond-dot veiling is damaged slightly. *Mobile Millinery Museum*. $75-125.

French couture models from Chanel, Dior, and Schiaparelli were displayed alongside those of John-Fredericks, Lilly Daché, Sally Victor, and the like; American designers who had risen to prominence through the influence of Hollywood and the wounding effects of the Second World War on the French fashion industry.

Designers marketed select styles to young debutantes and to even younger girls whom *Ladies Home Journal* termed "sub-debs". Every town had its milliner and city shopping districts were peppered with hat salons. Four or five millinery boutiques might be clustered on a single city block and in some urban centers hat shops competed side by side.

Milliners invited the public to spring and fall "showings" and advertised their latest models in the women's section of the newspaper. Those who could afford it had their confections custom made each new season. Patrons were loyal to their personal hat makers, speaking of them with fondness and admiration to this day.

Roses and yellow rayon buds encircle a wired opencrown, c.1958. Fine yellow veiling covers all. *Mobile Millinery Museum*. $50-75.

A lattice crown peeks through a sprinkling of pale pink posies. *Mobile Millinery Museum*. $60-80.

Designer Profile: Irene Burstyn (Irene of Montreal)

Irene of Montreal had a reputation for making any woman look beautiful. "It is the not-beautiful ones I remember most," she told me some time ago, when recalling her days as a leading millinery designer. "It is that feature, which is unique about a woman, that makes her beautiful," she instructed. "Most women do not want to draw attention to a big nose, or high forehead – a long neck whatever it might be. They might feel awkward but different – unique is good," she advised, and explained that she took this factor into consideration when fashioning a hat.

The Montreal designer kept a file on each of her 3,000 clients and insisted that no woman leave her shop after the final fitting until she herself was satisfied with the custom creation. Perhaps that is why, often after dark, competitors lurked outside of Irene's Sherbrooke St. Salon, sketchpads in hand, trying to understand her magic. Burstyn occasionally spotted them herself as she taxied home late at night. "I took it as a compliment," she said. "After all, I was not in the business of selling hats, I was a designer!"

And what a designer she was. Irene of Montreal's clients numbered among North America's social elite. A Montreal woman who apprenticed in the millinery trade in the 1950s, remembers "a buzz would go through the industry whenever someone was seen wearing one of Irene's hats."

"We made them out of the air," Irene told me in an effort to explain the creative process. When asked about her favorite, she described a tremendous Breton style in tulle and organza, the brim of which rose three inches above the hair, then fell in back to touch the shoulders. The girls in the workroom had difficulty with it at first, insisting they could not achieve what she demanded. "Yes, you can" Irene insisted, and layer after layer of bias organza was pressed and placed flat, one on top of the other, until Irene of Montreal's vision was a reality.

Inspired, artistic, creative, self-confident, and dramatic, Irene's speech reflected her enthusiasm for excellence. When asked to comment on women's factory-made hats, she quickly replied, "I can't answer that, I never touched the things." Irene's distaste for mediocrity can be excused as she had seen a lot of the world before settling in Montreal for the first time in 1944. In 1939, she and her first husband, a doctor seventeen years her senior, fled Nazi-occupied Warsaw with faked passports. They settled in Italy, then moved on to Greece, Turkey, Syria, and Palestine, where they divorced. Irene remarried and moved with her second husband to South Africa. There they successfully farmed tobacco before being accepted into Canada, by special order of the cabinet.

In Montreal, Irene ran a more than successful millinery atelier from 1948 until 1976, when the entire hat trade fell into a decline. She turned her talents in later years to the craft of writing, publishing *Picking Up Pearls* in 1977.

The Easter bunny shows off a white feather headpiece, designed to wrap a bun or encircle a ponytail. *Mobile Millinery Museum*. $100-125.

A spray of red roses spans the brim of a black, bouclé straw. *Mobile Millinery Museum.* $125.

Black sequined halo turban, with a dramatic sweep of aigrette. Label: Christian Dior Chapeaux, Paris-New York. *Mobile Millinery Museum*. $300-350.

A simple bonnet of starflowers on a wired, velvet frame. *Mobile Millinery* Museum. $75-100.

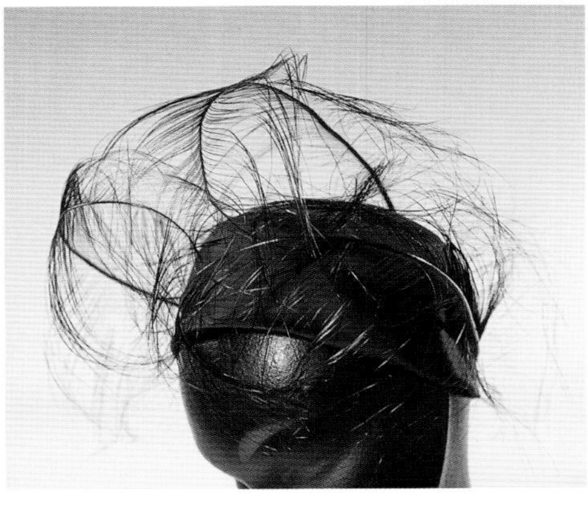

This domed, satin pillbox, reminiscent of Schiaparelli's famous eyelash hat, becomes a showstopper with the addition of curved aigrettes. Label: Georgette. *Mobile Millinery Museum*. $250-300.

A minaret of black sequins on a velvet band erupts in a spray of black feathers at the center crown. *Mobile Millinery Museum*. $250-350.

Hats were a must for church services and women's meetings and were required by law for women attending court proceedings. Former judge Edra Ferguson had her bailiff keep a box of cast-offs handy, for anyone improperly attired.

Some women in the 1950s made their own hats after taking one of the many correspondence or home millinery courses offered at the time. Hamilton's Bev Brown remembers donning one of her homemade creations to appear in court regarding a traffic violation. According to Brown, the judge, upon seeing her hat, declared, "If you can light up my courtroom in such a way, you don't deserve a fine!"

Many of the hats of the 1950s were close fitting: Juliet caps, shallow pillboxes, half hats, eggshells, and feathered clips. Turbans, berets, pancake, and halo hats closed in on the skull and took on a symmetry that was lacking in the previous decade. In March 1958, the Women's section of the *Toronto Star* carried the headline, "Smartest Easter Paraders Will Wear Gay Flowered Hats". Pictured were a Flemmish bonnet, a wired floral, an Edwardian-style widebrim and a cloche.

One of the most enduring styles to emerge from the 1950s was the all-over floral hat. A wonderful example by Sally Victor was first shown on the cover of *Vogue* magazine in 1950. Other designers weighed in with their own versions, knockoffs appeared, and home milliners even got into the act.

There are plenty of these flowered confections hanging about and the good news is that they are inexpensive, as vintage millinery goes. Hat fanciers will find all-over florals interpreted as bandeaus, stiff bubble toques, and wig hats. A small grouping in the different spring colors makes a wonderful collection or one can display them as a centerpiece in place of fresh flowers.

Designer Profile: Constance Lachance

In 2004 the *Welland Historical Museum* mounted an exhibit of the work of Constance Lachance, whose millinery salon was a fixture in this Ontario city for many years. Local residents supplied the museum with over thirty felt, straw, and cloth hats, many in their original boxes.

Lachance was born into a family of twenty-one children in Thetford Mines, Quebec. She learned her millinery skills from her mother and used them to establish a successful enterprise when she moved to Ontario, c.1958.

As a single mother of five, Lachance employed her offspring in the boutique as they were growing up. Her children remember the handwork required to complete the millinery creations – gluing hundreds of individual feathers in place, for example. Daughter Edith says her mother worked long hours in the shop, getting up at five and often labouring past midnight.

Former patrons of Madame Lachance still rave about her creations and are happy to reminisce about how good they felt in one of her pieces.

The *Mobile Millinery Museum* is home to some Edwardian examples that may have been made by Lachance's mother. The faded labels are of tan-colored, grosgrain with "Constance Lachance" inked in cursive script. Lachance's hats from the 1950s and '60s bear more modern, woven labels.

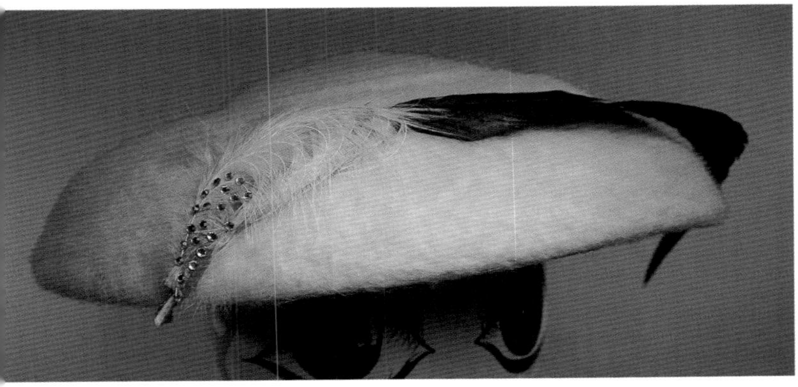

A plush beaver dish hat in winter white is draped with rhinestone-speckled "made bird". Label: the Ostrich, Made in Italy. *Mobile Millinery Museum*. $200-250.

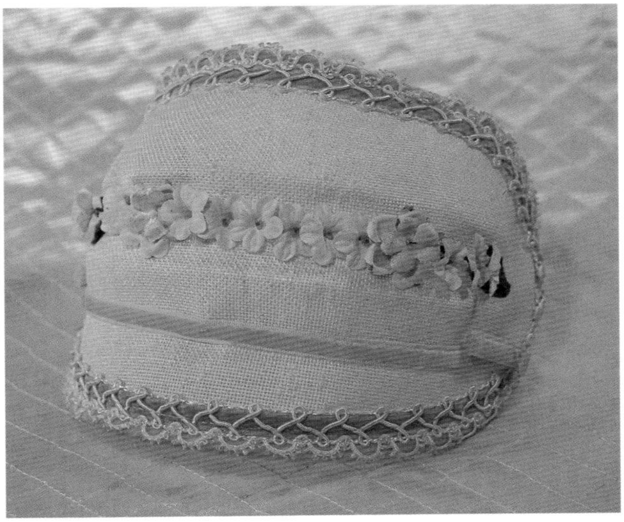

Child's buckram bonnet, edged in pink velvet and ornamented with a row of factory-cut flowers. *Mobile Millinery Museum*. $75.

A floral bandeau of roses and starflowers, from the mid-1950s, is covered with a fine layer of chenille-dotted veiling. *Mobile Millinery Museum*. $80-100.

A demure, blush rose drapes elegantly across the brow of this stiff, pink, factory-made cap. Eyebrow veiling, visible staples. *Mobile Millinery Museum*. $50.

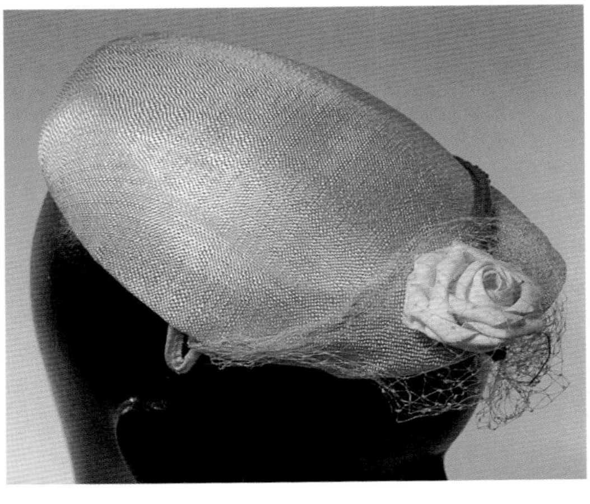

This all-over floral pillbox is particularly pleasing to the eye, with its profusion of colors and shapes representing summer flowers. Stiffened net base. *Mobile Millinery Museum*. $200-250.

A delightful cone hat. Four velvet, beige-tinted leaves hide beneath pendulous, sky-blue petals, tipped with pearl-white drops. Label: Susan Carol, Paris, Roma, New York. *Mobile Millinery Museum*. $75-125.

Rose petal cone hat in dark-to-light azure-blue, topped with a bronze-tipped rose and deep azure, velvet leaves. Label: Susan Carol, Paris, Roma, New York. *Mobile Millinery Museum*. $200.

Child's nylon sun bonnet with satin ribbon ties and band. *Mobile Millinery Museum*. $60-80.

Giant roses in orange, taupe, ecru, and grass-green form an all-over floral c.1958. *Mobile Millinery Museum*. $225.

Molded rubber bathing cap crowns the owner with a rose and leaf motif. *Mobile Millinery Museum*. $60-80.

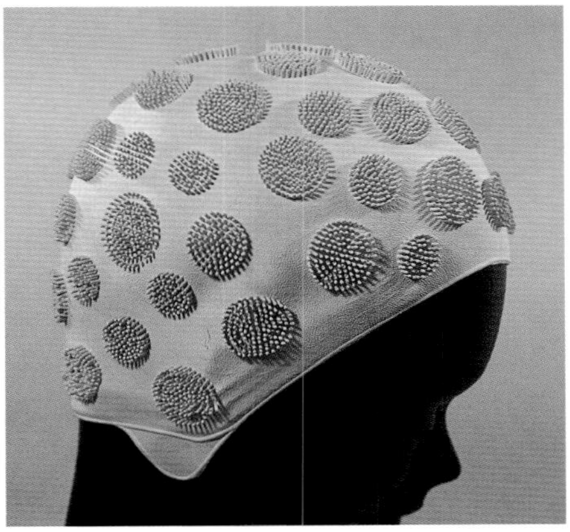

White rubber swim cap with medallion motif. *Mobile Millinery Museum*. $60-80.

A Schiaparelli hat of black brushed felt is shown with the great designer's signature hatbox. The original owner has listed the contents of the box on its lid. *Mobile Millinery Museum*. Hat, $250-300.

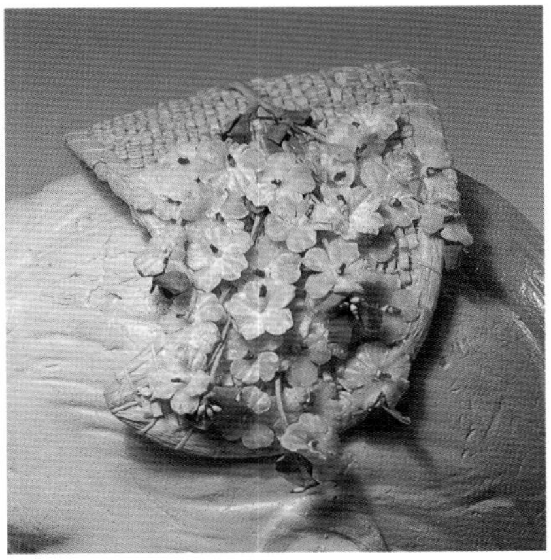

An irregularly-shaped bandeau of soft beige raffia is the backdrop for a spray of tiny, white, velvet flowers with fuscia centers. *Mobile Millinery Museum*. $125.

A miniscule diadem of salt-and-pepper tweed is overlain with coarse netting and finished with a black feather sprig. *Mobile Millinery Museum*. $80-100.

A crinkled, black fabric hat on a felt base is shredded at the crown/brim join to generate finger-like tendrils. Label: Bessie Irwin's Hat Shop, Church St., Oakville.

A stiff velvet head hugger, edged along the brow with ruched satin. Small velvet bows, a nose-length veil, and the occasional rhinestone add detail. *Mobile Millinery Museum*. $125.

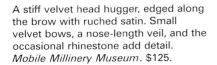

A band of rhinestones secures a china-pink ostrich tip to a black velvet hairband for an evening of cocktails. *Mobile Millinery Museum*. $325-350.

This white organdie kerchief, with self-fabric ties and floral petals, can be tied under the chin or at the nape of the neck. These were made in all colors and marketed as "convertible caps". Although they were designed to be worn over a pony tail, many women wore them, in public, over curlers, and they soon fell out of fashion. *Mobile Millinery Museum*. $60-80.

Dusty-pink angora Breton. A black tassel, ringed with set-in rhinestones, dangles from a pleated-grosgrain column. Label: Hudson's Bay Company. *Marie Minaker Collection, Mobile Millinery Museum*.

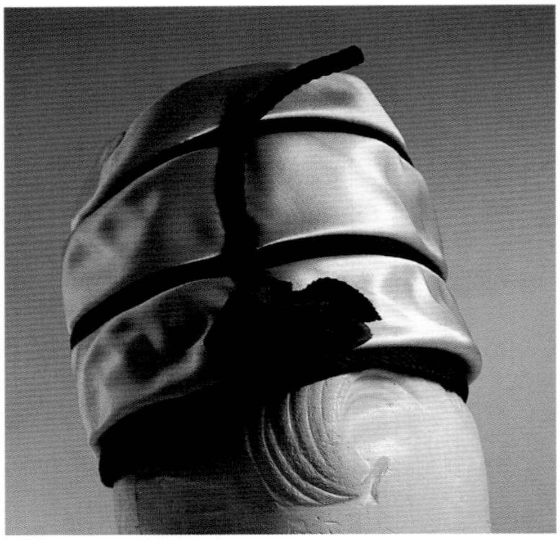

An exquisite toque of ice-blue satin is twice banded with black, cut velvet. The same fabric forms a stem for an upside-down, black velvet rose. Label: M'Sieu Léon, Paris, Roma, New York. *Mobile Millinery Museum*. $360-400.

A striking blend of black and white chip straw is banded high on the crown with black and red velvet. Label: A Charm Model, Montreal. *Mobile Millinery Museum*. $325.

Left:
This jeweled cocktail hat resembles a spider on its web. *Mobile Millinery Museum*. $175.

Right:
Black chip straw is fashioned into medallions and layered to produce a textural bandeau, then covered with a black, nose-length veil. *Mobile Millinery Museum*. $150.

A salmon organza turban forms a nest for a trio of chenille-centered poppies. Label: Jo-Anne Designer, 1566 Yonge St., - Toronto. *Mobile Millinery Museum*. $150-180.

A triple layer of leaves, made of fabric-bonded-to-felt, is dotted with the occasional pearl and draped with fine green veiling. Likely a custom creation. *Mobile Millinery Museum*. $180-220.

An exquisite black bird rests along the brow of a silk velvet platter. *My Fair Lady* album cover depicts a similar hat worn atop a sleek sheath dress. *Mobile Millinery Museum*. $500-550.

Miss *Bearilyn Monroe*® in a sequined, polka dot turban to match her stylish satin dress. *Private Collection.*

Watteau blue beaverette cap with front bumper brim, casually trimmed with blue daisies. Triple labels: Henry Morgan & Co. Ltd./ Francine: 5. Rue Du 4 Septembre, Paris, Made in France/Tricolor label. *Mobile Millinery Museum*. $300-350.

Interior view.

The softly-pleated brim of this midnight-black peau-de-pêche beaver folds onto the crown at back to create a horizontal line, off-setting the trim. A spiral of multicolored glass stones encircles a self-fabric bow. Label: Simpson's. *Mobile Millinery Museum*. $225.

A black velour cap is draped with feathers and dotted with the occasional rhinestone. Label: Riviera. *Mobile Millinery Museum*. $120-150.

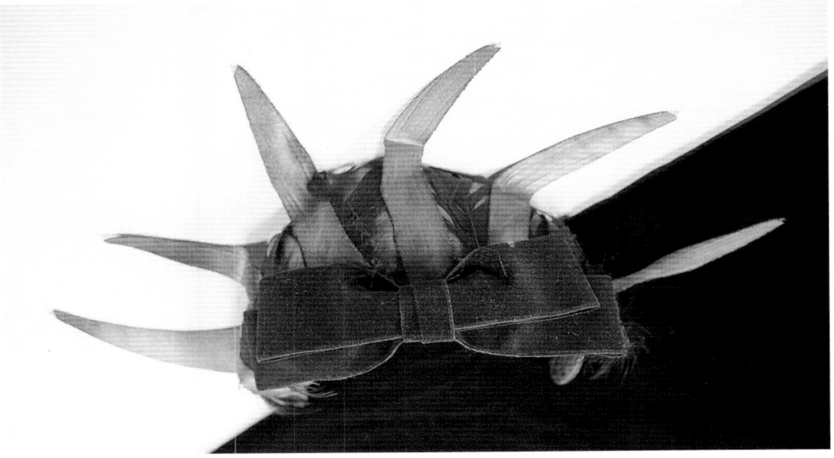

Purple feathers are placed between a series of orchid silk petals and united with a double velvet bow. Remnants of marabou suggest that this hat has lost some of its original glory. *Mobile Millinery Museum*. $80-100.

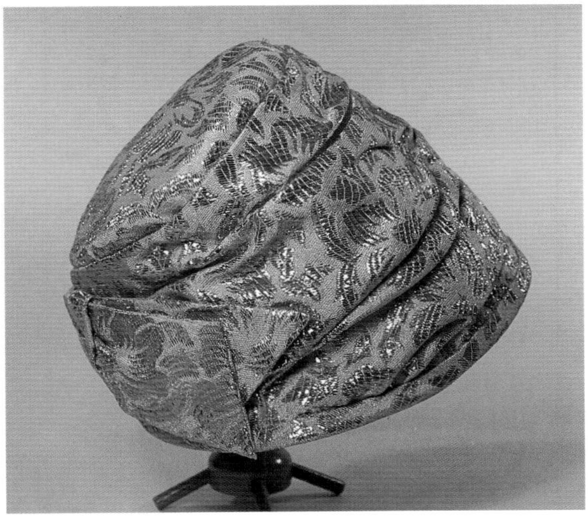

A revival bonnet in pink and gold brocade boasts an elegant double bow at the center back. *Mobile Millinery Museum.* $125-150.

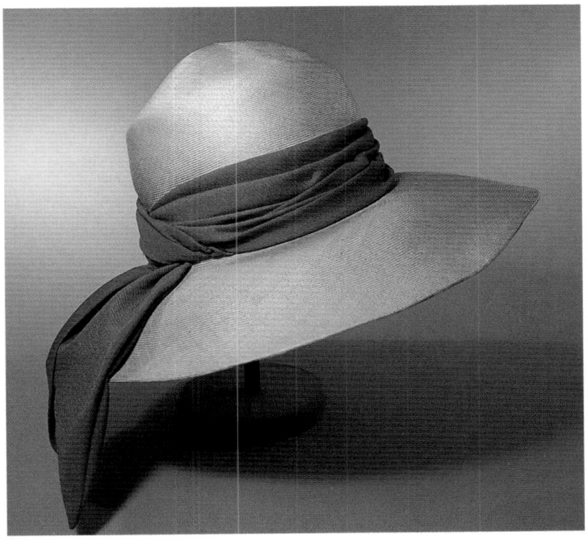

Panama straw picture hat, banded in deep turquoise rayon silk. *Mobile Millinery Museum*. $150-200.

Emerald green feathered "wig hat". *Mobile Millinery Museum*. $225.

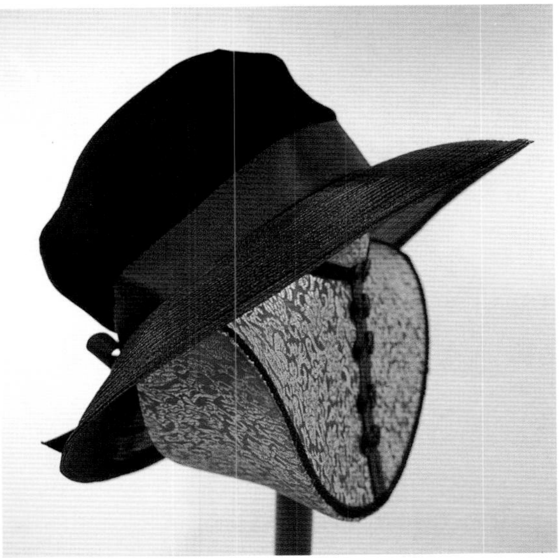

A dressy picture hat of silk velvet with a horsehair brim. Label: Astor Chapeaux, Ottawa. *Mobile Millinery Museum*. $150-200.

A picture hat of bright turquoise organza on a buckram frame is banded in deep turquoise straw. Label: Made in Canada. *Mobile Millinery Museum*. $125.

Star flowers, of powder-to-peacock blue, envelop a bonnet designed to top a chignon or French roll, c.1955. Label: Leopold Original. *Mobile Millinery Museum*. $150-250.

The milliner's skill at dying feathers is evident in this magnificent black and red fabric turban. *Mobile Millinery Museum*. $400-600.

Velvet-covered wire supports an array of spring flowers. *Mobile Millinery Museum.* $150.

Chip straw is plaited to create two very different black beauties from the 1950s. The first is an unlabelled picture hat, banded in wide, black grosgrain. The second, a flowerpot by Maggy Plouffe, is banded in black velvet and finished with an organza brim. *Mobile Millinery Museum*. $200-250 each.

A sloping brim is pleated onto a grosgrain-bound crown, all in navy felt. *Mobile Millinery Museum*. $200-250.

A red straw close hat with saw-tooth brim is lined with black lace and fitted with delicate black veiling. Matching hand-crocheted gloves. Label: Simpson's. *Mobile Millinery Museum*. Ensemble: $150-200.

The crown of this cheerful cruise hat is laced together at the peak to resemble a drawstring bag. *Mobile Millinery Museum*. $300-350.

A child's factory-made, white wool, bigonette. Colorful paillettes surround a pom pom at the center crown. *Mobile Millinery Museum*. $60-80.

The author, c.1954, in one of her first hats, a scallop-brimmed wool bonnet.

A pair of dress hats in stylish black and white. On the left: a plush beaver beret, banded and crowned in white jersey. Black passmenterie adds Zhivago-inspired detailing. Label: Georgette. On the right: a square revival cloche in patterned velvet, banded and bowed with black and white satin ribbon. Label: Lady Silhouette, New York, Paris, Montreal. *Mobile Millinery Museum*. Value: $200 and $150 respectively.

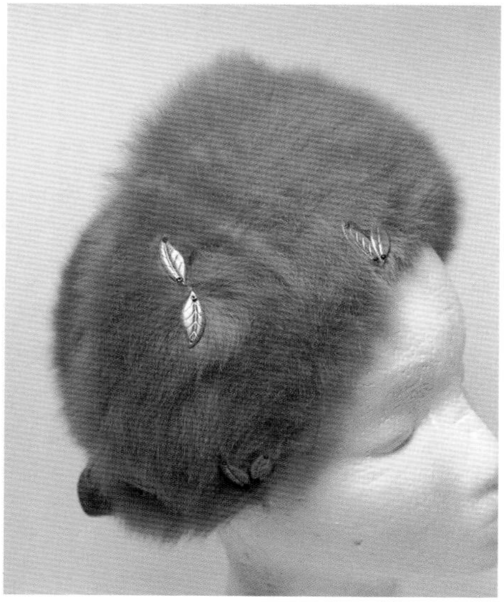

Pewter leaves nestle in a halo hat of orchid mohair. Label: Schiaparelli. *Mobile Millinery Museum*. $250-300.

Melon-colored factory straw banded with cinnamon organdie. *Jean Keough Collection, Mobile Millinery Museum.* $150.

A veiled platter or dish hat in striking pink and black. *Mobile Millinery Museum*. $150-200.

Strips of red, yellow, and green straw are sewn into this navy straw dome. *Mobile Millinery Museum*. $150.

A feather and satin pillbox by designer Elizabeth Ford. *Mobile Millinery Museum*. Hat and boxes: $200-250.

All over floral in delicate pink tints. *Mobile Millinery Museum*. $50-100.

Variegated velvet leaves are clustered amidst grass-green marabou to create an elegant bandeau. A paper Paris label reveals model number 6555. *Mobile Millinery Museum*. $150.

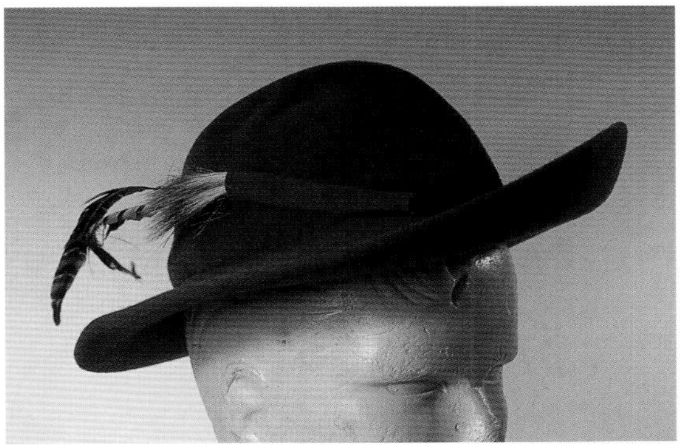

A jaunty, reddish-brown velour strikes a pose with brown-toned plumage. Label: Frank Olive. *Mobile Millinery Museum*. $220-250.

A crown-hugging fantasy erupts in a fountain of turquoise feathers. *Mobile Millinery Museum*. $250-350.

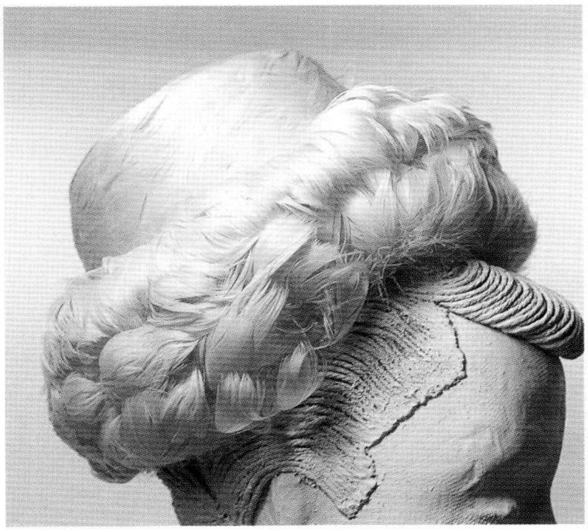

A 1950s feathered top hat with bumper brim. Label: Mary Corene, New York. *Mobile Millinery Museum*. $200-250.

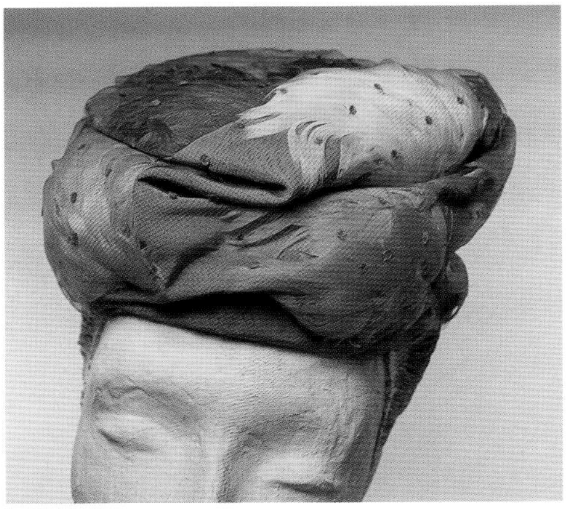

Unusual avocado taffeta turban encased in green chenille-dotted net to protect a succession of feather breasts in orange, squash, yellow, green, peach, steel, and pale turquoise. *Mobile Millinery Museum*. $320.

Navy linen cartwheel with floral motif and rhinestone hatpin. Label: Parkside, Simpson's. *Mobile Millinery Museum*. $300-350.

Lemon straw pancake, narrowly banded in brown ribbon. *Mobile Millinery Museum*. $75-125.

Bev Brown's late-1950s homemade treasure saved her from paying a fine. *Mobile Millinery Museum*. $80-120.

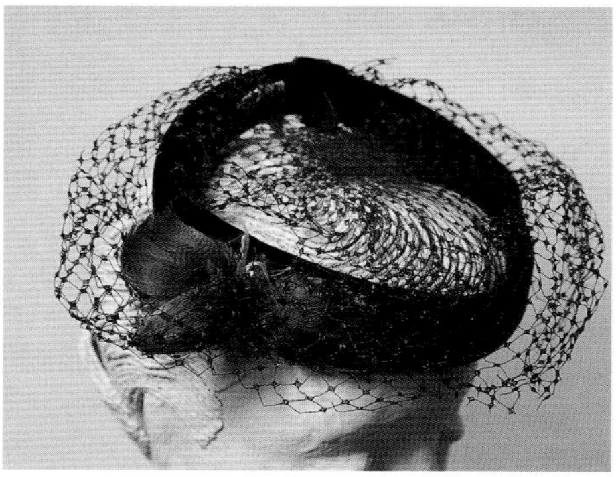

A cork-bodied, emerald-green bird graces the right brow of a black velvet bandeau within a nest of black veiling. Label: Original Design by Madcaps, Paris, New York. *Mobile Millinery Museum*. $125-150.

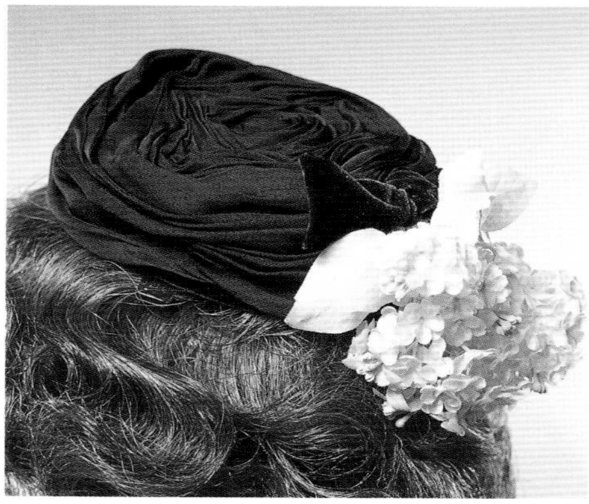

A cloth pillbox by Rose Broderson. *Mobile Millinery Museum*. $100-150.

Pink posies are set against navy straw on a style seen frequently in the mid-1950s. *Mobile Millinery Museum*. $100-150.

An elegant turban-cloche, lined with satin. *Mobile Millinery Museum*. $150-200.

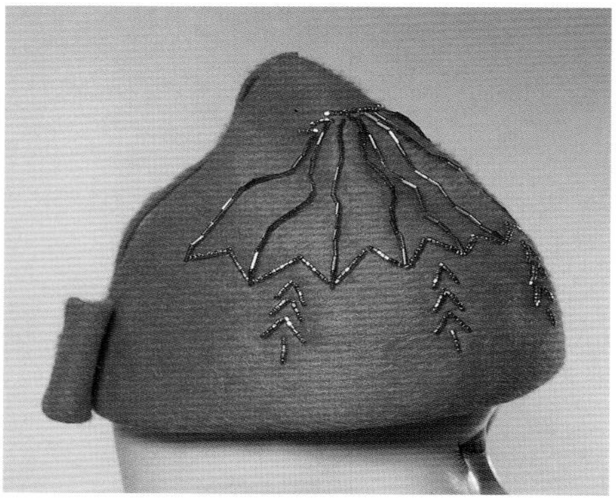

A cozy, rose-colored felt features bugle-bead embroidery and self-fabric bow. *Mobile Millinery Museum*. $225.

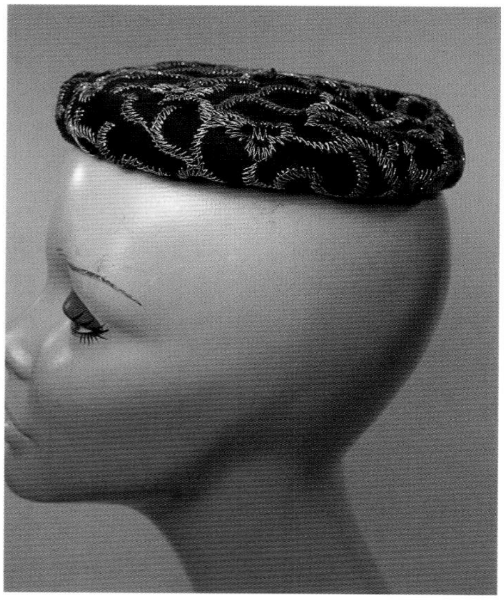

A pancake hat of black and bronze brocade. *Mobile Millinery Museum*. $125-175.

The black velvet under-brim of this shiny straw matches the band and bow. *Mobile Millinery Museum*. $400-450.

Painted straw beach hat with olive-green nylon ties. A trio of plastic stars adds whimsy. *Mobile Millinery Museum*. $60-80.

The author models one of her very first hats, a baby bonnet, c.1953.

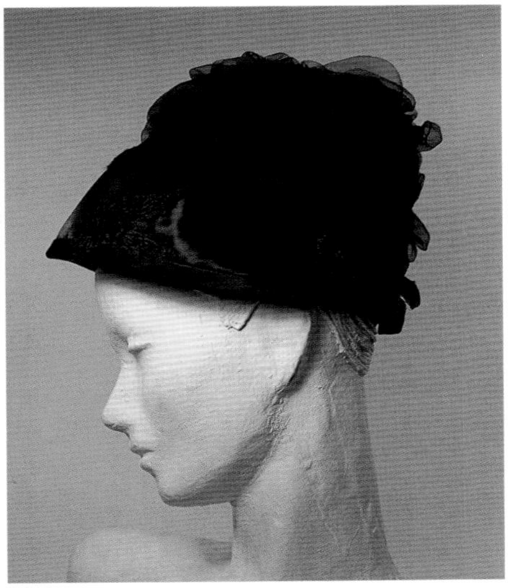

Circa 1958: The stiff crown of this satin, reproduction bonnet is wrapped in gently-tucked chiffon. Embroidered, silk flowers and foliage adorn the brim. *Mobile Millinery Museum*. $200-250.

A child's satin majorette's cap and uniform. *Mobile Millinery Museum*. Ensemble: $120-150.

Chapter VIII
The End of an Age: 1960 - 1970

"I wore a pink and black plaid, horsehair widebrim to a military air show in Ottawa one year. The Commanding Officer's wife commissioned me to make one like it for her. The finished hat was delivered to Ottawa in an air-force plane."

— *Rita Minion, milliner*

"I used to carry a red pen with me when I went shopping. I would keep the sales tag on after I bought a hat, but mark the price down myself before I showed the new purchase to my husband. I was able to buy more hats that way."

— *Anonymous*

"In the early 60s, my mother bought a deep-pink straw to wear for the Easter Parade in New York City. She and her friend went out shopping and left their hats in their hotel rooms. They never wore the hats because they got a front row place for the parade and didn't want to lose their position."

— *Shirley Brooker*

"Literary guru Aldous Huxley ... is chiefly remembered here for near-sightedly sitting on the Editor's hat, causing some loud and unladylike anguish."

— *Vogue Magazine, British edition, March 15, 1963*

The styles of the 1960s evolved naturally from among those of the previous decade. Pillboxes retained their popularity but became deeper. The crowns of other brimless styles began to rise as cone shapes, flower pots, lampshades, and bubbles toques dominated. Those who preferred brimmed confections adopted lofty Bretons and sou'westers.

More than ever, hairstyles influenced design with milliners having to contend with the craze for high, rigid coifs. A tall-crowned, brimless hat, called the beehive, encased a hairstyle of the same name. Whimsies and cage hats sat atop teased hair, "bomb buns", and spirals. These weightless confections of veiling were simply decorated with flowers, bows, sequins, or ribbon.

It is by no coincidence that many hat styles of the swinging sixties resemble those of the Belle Époque. Fashion magazines of the day freely admit to Edwardian influences within their pages.

Left:
1966: The author and her sister attend a wedding in veiled whimsies.

Right:
A spectacular whimsy to cap a beehive hairdo. Diamond-dot veiling, studded with the occasional rhinestone, cascades beneath a giant silk posy. Ostrich fronds add movement, while a trio of cherry-colored velvet ribbons anchors the back. Label: Morgan's. *Marjorie Wilson Collection, Mobile Millinery Museum.* $200-250.

Original Value

Elda Revell remembers paying eighty dollars for a Persian lamb toque in 1965. The Kingston area resident modeled the hat for a large outdoor fashion show put on by the *Mobile Millinery Museum* some years ago. As commentator, I was happy to share the original price of the hat with the audience but, after the show, Elda was not pleased with me. "My husband was in the audience," she said, "and until today he had no idea I spent so much on that hat."

In describing hat trends for the summer of 1963, the British edition of *Vogue* magazine declared that "the biggest hats are the biggest news" and showcased examples such as Balmain's "Mexican sombrero" and Dior's "halo beret." Decreasing in size but not in popularity were newsboy caps, dubbed "Jackie Cougans", bowlers, shakos, tall straw helmets, and pillboxes, worn back on the head. Otto Lucas showed rear-tilting, straw turbans, some veiled to the nose.

Sequined halo beret, c.1963. *Mobile Millinery Museum*. $200-250.b

Bun caps and tambourines were introduced for late afternoon. These were meant to be worn back, on a chignon. The tambourine was also veiled and carried to the top of the head, in a variation of the whimsy.

"Ten-gallon" felt in Navaho red, resembling Balmain's "Mexican sombrero". Narrow black patent leather is threaded through a gold-tone chain to form a liquorice-whip band. Liquorice-whip detail is repeated at the brim's edge. Label: M'Sieu Léon, Paris, Roma, New York. *Mobile Millinery Museum*. $250-350.

Circa 1963: Berry clusters dangle from a loop of black velvet that tops a tambourine of looped chip straw. Label: By Rose De Paris, Toronto. *Myra Krangle Collection*, *Mobile Millinery Museum*. $220.

Camel-colored tulle tambourine, trimmed with matching cord. *Myra Krangle Collection, Mobile Millinery Museum*. $225.

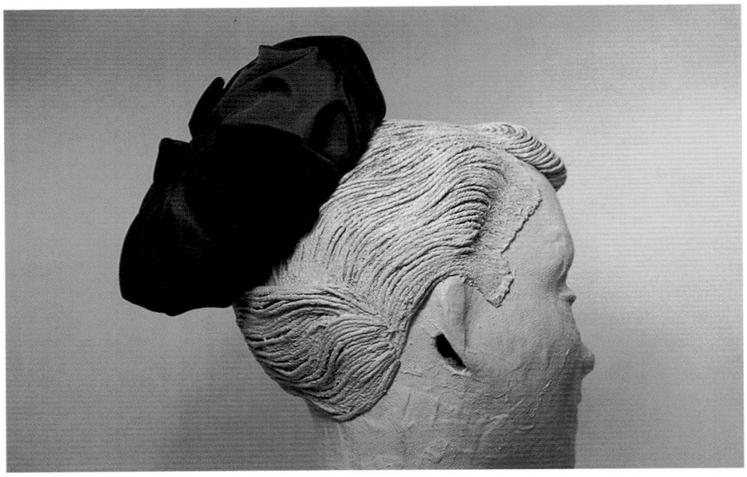

Gold and silver embroidery graces a black taffeta tambourine. Label: Spencer. *Mobile Millinery Museum*. $180-220.

A spray of pink posies decorates an open-crowned tambourine/whimsy. *Mobile Millinery Museum*. $100-150.

A similar hat in royal blue. *Mobile Millinery Museum*. $100-150.

If fashion mavens had previously followed Parisian trends, now their eye was on London. Helmets, resembling those worn by British Bobbies, were turned out in felt, fabric, fur, and leather. High-crowned postillions topped mini skirts and "go go" boots. The American experience affected fashion as well with military influences like camouflage prints appearing during the Vietnam War.

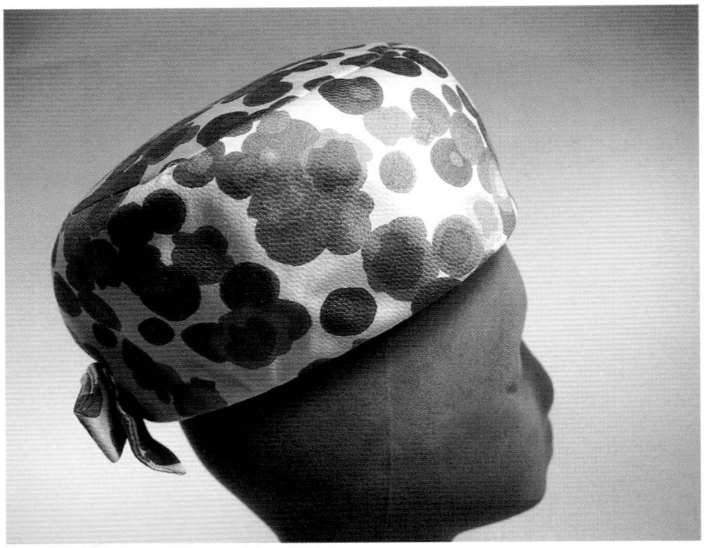

Camouflage-print deep pillbox, c.1968. Label: Custom Made by Erica's Hat Salon, 42 Hughson St. N., Hamilton. *Mobile Millinery Museum*. $225.

Perhaps sensing the dissolution that was to come, many of the couture houses began to market to a younger clientele, with less expensive bridge lines such as *Adolpho II, Mr. John Jr.,* and *Lilly Daché Debs*. As women chose hair over hats, however, these efforts were doomed to failure and an entire industry fell into decline.

Daché's bridge line label.

A plastic-stemmed white rose sits off-kilter at the back of a molded navy straw. Decorative veiling. Label: Lilly Daché Debs, New York, Paris. *Mobile Millinery Museum*. $250.

A smart autumn fedora in rust-shaded felt with beige grosgrain trim. Label: Lilly Daché Debs, New York, Paris. *Mobile Millinery Museum*. $175-225.

Designer Profile: Philip Warde

"Philip could carry colors in his head the way nobody else could."

— *Joy Drew, friend and client of Philip Warde*

Toronto designer Philip Warde showed a natural talent for millinery from a young age. In an interview with the *Toronto Star* he tells of refashioning an expensive cartwheel, that his mother had paid "an arm and a leg" for into something he considered much smarter. "I begged her to let me take the hat apart," said the designer, whose reworked creation caught the attention of an established, downtown milliner. She invited the boy into her workroom and thus began his millinery apprenticeship.

Warde learned the basics in Toronto but when his aunt suggested he study in New York he bolted for the States and took instruction in interior design and millinery, completing a three year course in just eighteen months. "My funds were pretty low," he confided to a reporter in 1953, hence the twenty-four-hour swing shifts, which enabled him to finish the course in record time.

Warde's hats speak for themselves. Vibrant in color, innovative in form, and pre-eminent in suitability, his felt, fur, straw, and fabric confections are as wearable today as they were in the 1940s, '50s, '60s and '70s. Warde's regular clients purchased as many as thirty hats a year.

Pauline McGibbon, in her capacity as Ontario's Lieutenant Governor, supplied Warde with autographed photos of herself in his creations. These include shots of her with Princess Anne and the Queen Mother. Elizabeth Taylor also counted among the designer's many patrons, having purchased a yellow, daisy-bedecked headpiece for her wedding to actor Richard Burton.

Amateur milliners were able to benefit from Warde's expertise as well. A Toronto newspaper held a hat-making contest in the late forties and appointed Warde as judge. He shared his design philosophy with contestants, advising them to work directly with their material. "Merely slapping material on a buckram form is not creating," he instructed, and encouraged entrants to allow their own creativity to emerge.

Photos of Warde show a handsome, dark-haired gentleman in heavy-rimmed glasses, looking not unlike a 1950s game-show host, but by all accounts he was a modest individual. "Philip was not given to bragging about his accomplishments," explains long-time friend Ernie Paglietti.

Former client Joy Drew remembers Warde as a creative designer and cordial host. She visited his home studio often, following the closure of Warde's Bloor St. Salon, c. 1970. "Philip was a gracious, marvellous host," Drew says. "He served me elegant lunches on beautiful serving pieces and I never came away without buying a hat."

A Philip Warde model in a 1960s, beaverette cloche. Note the hat jewelry. *Philip Warde Collection, Mobile Millinery Museum.*

Designer Philip Warde in his Bloor St. Salon. *Philip Warde Collection, Mobile Millinery Museum.*

A psychedelic sou'wester of iridescent paisley and black velvet. *Mobile Millinery Museum*. $150-250.

A beautifully draped rayon satin turban shaped on a buckram form. *Mobile Millinery Museum*. $150.

An apple blossom beehive, c.1964, boasts shades of beige to cinnamon. Label: Jo-Anne, Designer. 1566 Yonge St., Toronto. *Eleanor Auld Collection, Mobile Millinery Museum.* $125.

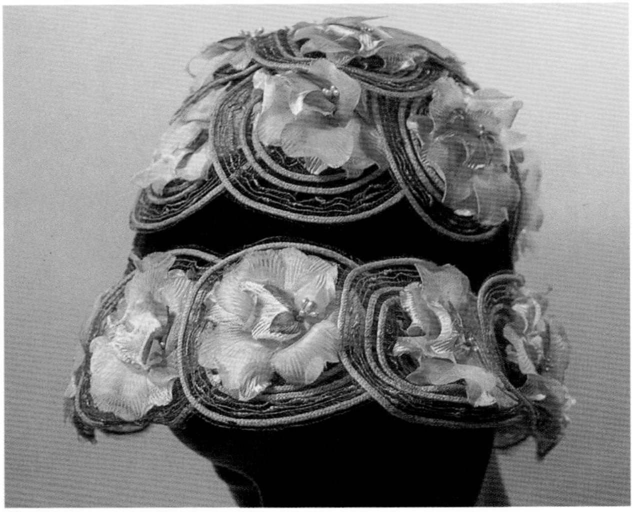

This tower of floral-centered medallions is constructed of synthetic horsehair and banded with chocolate-brown velvet. Label: Styled by Nadelle, Montreal. *Mobile Millinery Museum*. $100-125.

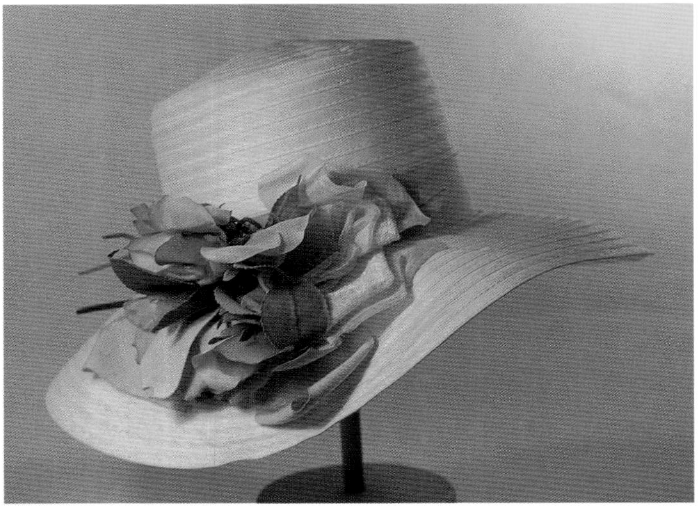

Circa 1968: A wide-brim confection in summer white is banded in chartreuse grosgrain ribbon. A cluster of blue roses in silk and velvet adds to its charm. *Mobile Millinery Museum*. $200-300.

A rose-trimmed beauty for a mother-of-the-bride is fashioned on a stiffened buckram form. Six roses of variegated organza and velvet surround a cloud of pink tulle. Label: Sanjé, New York, Paris. *Marjorie Wilson Collection, Mobile Millinery Museum*. $225.

A spectacular hat and handbag set of hand-embroidered jute. *Marjorie Wilson Collection, Mobile Millinery Museum*. $250-300 for the set.

Purse is completely handmade.

Detail.

A 1960s sou'wester in long-nap beaver. Vinyl band allows for the placement of a quill or two. *Mobile Millinery Museum*. $125-225.

Pink, rabbit-felt, high hat with self-fabric bands. Matching gloves by Kayser. *Mobile Millinery Museum*. Ensemble $125.

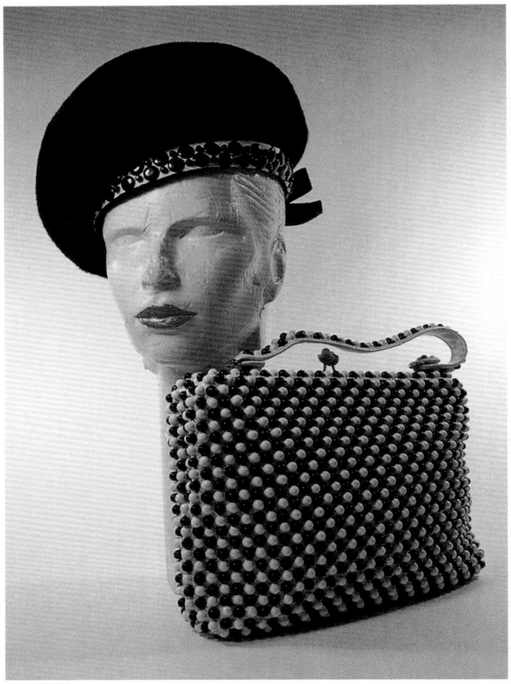

Black plastic beads dot the band of a long-nap beaver-felt beret, c.1965. Label: M'sieu Léon, Paris, Roma, New York. Matching beaded bag by Grandee bead. *Mobile Millinery Museum.* Ensemble: $150-250.

This Milan straw in pigeon-gray, Wedgwood, white, red, and navy tapers at the back where a navy satin wing extends from a straw braid. *Mobile Millinery Museum*. $125-225.

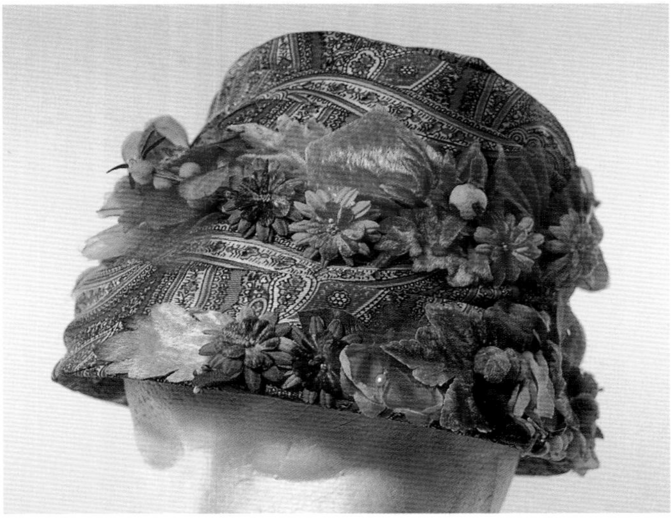

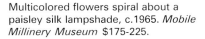

Multicolored flowers spiral about a paisley silk lampshade, c.1965. *Mobile Millinery Museum* $175-225.

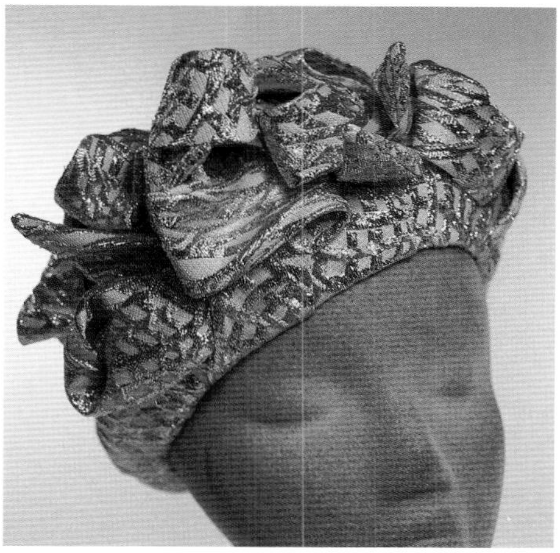

Pink and gold brocade is draped, looped, and tied to produce an elegant crown. Label: Vera Anne Millinery, The Kingsway. *Marjorie Wilson Collection, Mobile Millinery Museum*. $150.

A high-crowned topper for a bouffant hairdo, c.1968. Red and white bouclé straw is banded with black and white grosgrain that trails at center front. Black grosgrain laces the crown. *Mobile Millinery Museum*. $125-225.

Navy straw bowler, c.1965, banded and buttoned with pink and white printed rayon. Label: A Palmer Creation, New York, Montreal. *Mobile Millinery Museum*. $125.

A 1960s department store bonnet in lavender and white. Matching, machine-embroidered gloves. *Mobile Millinery Museum*. Ensemble: $75.

Side view.

A stunning sou'wester in natural suede and black velvet is as lovely to touch as it is to look at. Black grosgrain band and bow, black velvet under brim. Label: Mr. John Jr. Shown with contemporary faux fur handbag. *Mobile Millinery Museum*. Value (hat) $300-350.

A band of velvet ribbon peeks through a cloud of cotton-candy tulle. A pink and white variegated rose adds drama. *Mobile Millinery Museum*. $125-225.

A pair of high-crowned beauties in ecru straw. The first, fashioned of ribbon loops, mimics a giant bow. Label: Green Room Millinery, Bloomingdale's. The second, a flowerpot style on a buckram frame, is banded in velvet ribbon. Label: A Palmer Creation, New York, Montreal. *Mobile Millinery Museum*. $200-250 each.

The crown of this high hat measures six inches in depth. A trio of grosgrain ribbons in white and burnt orange makes a dramatic 3 1/4 inch band. Two off-kilter plastic buttons add to the drama. Label: A Peggy Claire Original (Hamilton, On). *Mobile Millinery Museum*. $125-150.

Back view of a floral bubble toque, likely made by a home or amateur milliner. Deep rose grosgrain bow. *Mobile Millinery Museum*. $60-80.

A winter turban in cerise-colored cotton velvet is styled by Nadelle of Montreal. *Mobile Millinery Museum*. $100-150.

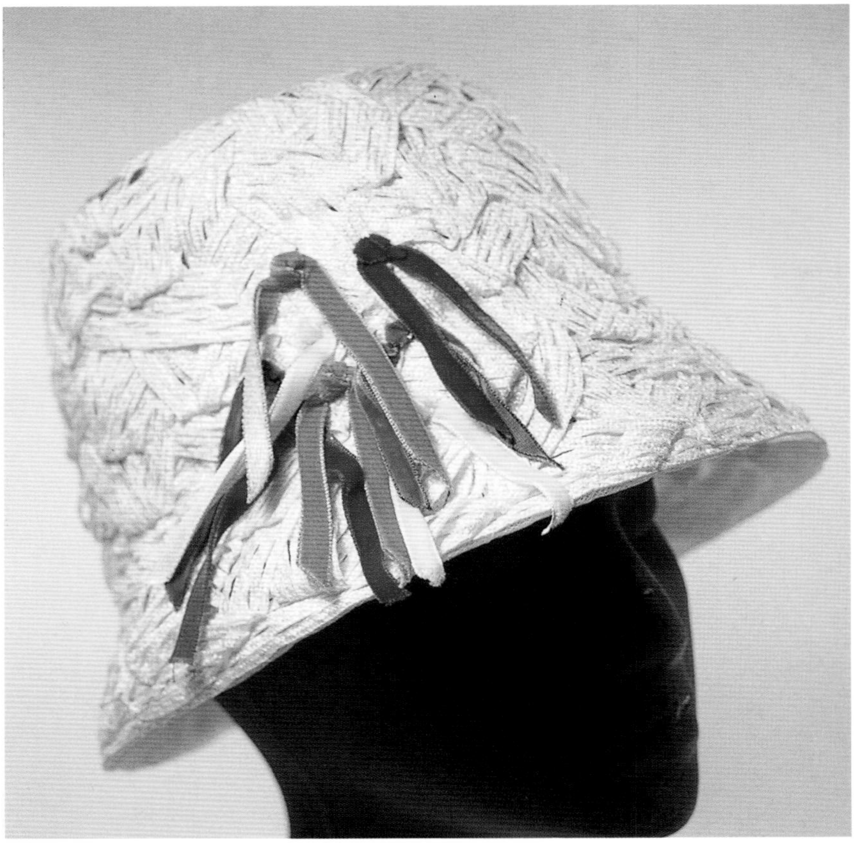

This straw lampshade in brilliant white was worn by a Toronto-area woman when she was presented to the Queen in the late sixties. Velvet ribbon ties punctuate the right temple. Label: Schiaparelli. $300-350.

A crown of garden flowers in peach, yellow, white, and cream on a narrow, satin, avocado brim. Label: Gwenn Pennington Exclusive. *Mobile Millinery Museum*. $200-250.

The crown of this apple blossom casque measures 5 inches deep. *Mobile Millinery Museum*. $150-200.

Carnations dominate this union-made bubble toque, which also sports tiny bell flowers in pink and lavender. *Mobile Millinery Museum*. $100-150.

A feathered whimsy in electric-blue receives added support from a velvet-covered demi headband. *Mobile Millinery Museum*. $60-80.

A puritan hat of amber, long-nap, felt is banded in contrasting shades of two-inch grosgrain. A three-inch square plastic buckle dominates the band. Label: Creation by André. *Mobile Millinery Museum*. $150.

A vine of tiny, beige, velvet flowers borders a lattice of puce velvet. A voilette of fine sen sen is secured with tabs of rhinestone-studded yellow velvet. *Mobile Millinery Museum.* $125.

The outer crown and upper brim of this "special occasion" straw are encircled with alternating strips of trapunto-stitched white felt and straw braid in yellow, grape, and crimson. A cluster of bell flowers in vibrant pink, sumac, lemon, white, and purple is secured to the hat with a strand of yellow straw. Label: Adolpho, New York, Paris. *Mobile Millinery Museum*. $250-300.

This exquisite lime-green cloche by Frank Olive is constructed of nubby straw, which folds back on itself at the brim's edge. A pink rose with deep green cloth leaves dangles from a straw stem at the brim's deepest point. A paper tag announces that the hat was purchased at Abraham & Straus for $15.00. *Mobile Millinery Museum*. $225-325.

This sou'wester of vibrant beaverette is banded with a royal blue grosgrain ribbon and a large ribbon-covered button. Label: Creation By André. *Mobile Millinery Museum.* $250-300.

An exuberant floral baseball cap, in shades of pink-to-deep rose, shows just the right touch of green and yellow for contrast. *Mobile Millinery Museum*. $300-350.

A magnificent claret flowerpot in plush beaver announces its arrival with an array of black and claret feathers between a pair of velvet bows. Twin labels: Creation by André/Lillie's Hats, Burlington, Ontario. *Mobile Millinery Museum.* $125-150.

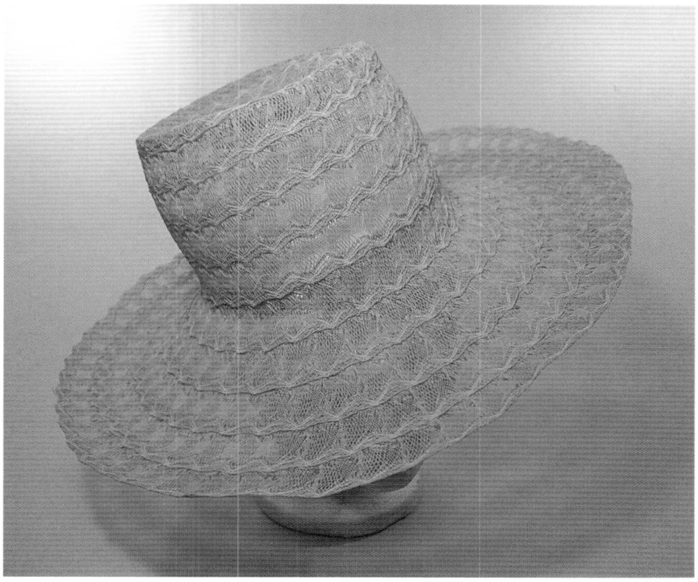

Square-crowned picture hat of cotton-candy nylon lace. *Mobile Millinery Museum*. $150-200.

A pair of elegant cage hats. *Mobile Millinery Museum*. $125 each.

A variation on the all-over floral. The roses that cover this bubble toque are of white chiffon. Navy chiffon bows, dotted throughout, provide contrast. This may have been selected for a mother-of-the-bride. *Mobile Millinery Museum*. $150.

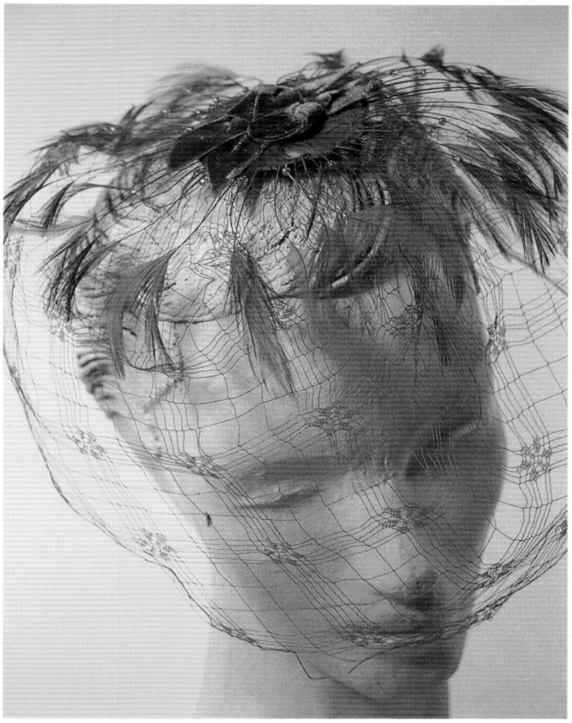

A salon whimsy is constructed of moss-green velvet, beaded feathers, and intricately-patterned veiling. *Mobile Millinery Museum*. $225.

A second salon whimsy, in similar tones, features a pair of twenty-inch feathers, curled seductively beneath a velvet ribbon bow. *Mobile Millinery Museum*. $225.

A psychedelic bowler by Maggie Plouffe. *Mobile Millinery Museum*. $175.

This apple blossom flower-pot in pinkish-brown tones, with matching velvet ribbon, appears to be factory made. Label: *Made in U.S.A. Mobile Millinery Museum*. $150-200.

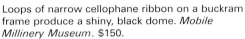

Loops of narrow cellophane ribbon on a buckram frame produce a shiny, black dome. *Mobile Millinery Museum*. $150.

A dome of rayon and velvet leaves in autumn browns and greens. Black feather fronds and silver-capped pods peak out from amid the foliage. *Mobile Millinery Museum.* $225.

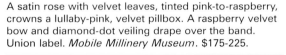

Synthetic horsehair is looped about the crown of this lavender confection, c.1968. *Mobile Millinery Museum*. $225.

A satin rose with velvet leaves, tinted pink-to-raspberry, crowns a lullaby-pink, velvet pillbox. A raspberry velvet bow and diamond-dot veiling drape over the band. Union label. *Mobile Millinery Museum*. $175-225.

Shocking-pink confection, c.1960, fashioned from chip straw and coarse net. A plastic-stemmed rose, variegated in tints of pink-to-blush, nestles against the brim. *Mobile Millinery Museum*. $225.

Banana and orange-colored velvet ribbons wrap a deep, ecru straw pillbox to form a small extension at the center back. Label: Grace Spencer Original, Vancouver B.C. *Mobile Millinery Museum*. $150-200.

Picture hat of navy straw, banded with white grosgrain. Label: Lady Silhouette, New York, Paris, Montreal. Shown with matching crocheted gloves and spiked leather heels. Hat $125-150.

An all-over floral of dark to light, woodland-green fabric. Green wire coils are dotted throughout, to form three-inch, antennae-like extensions. Label: Styled by Lois. *Mobile Millinery Museum*. $200-250.

A modified bowler in Panama straw is turned up in back and secured with a cream-colored, grosgrain ribbon. Label: Madcaps, New York, Paris. *Mobile Millinery Museum*. $150-200.

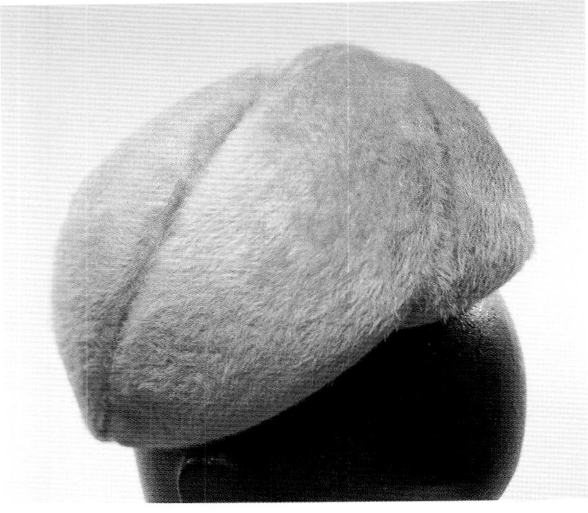

Smoke-gray bubble toque of long nap beaver. Label: Mr. Fredericks, Young Sophisticates. *Mobile Millinery Museum*. $100-150.

A white ribbon, summer charmer with grosgrain topknot. *Mobile Millinery Museum*. $125.

A towering, honeysuckle lampshade is dotted with the occasional magnolia. Deep green leaves are shaded with touches of beet-red. Olive-green tulle band. Label: Elizabeth, Bonwit Teller. *Mobile Millinery Museum* $200-250.

Carmine velvet bows are piled atop a ring of striated, pink and white, rayon petals. Label: Creation by André. *Mobile Millinery Museum*. $225.

A felt postillion is shaded carnelian and draped with a weeping ostrich plume in flat-black. This beauty was purchased at a Grimsby, Ontario, hat shop in the late 1960s and worn with a black, Persian lamb coat by Ontario resident, Elaine Yerex. Label: Hand Made, Bernice *Mobile Millinery Museum*. $250-350.

Designer cavalier of adobe felt with velour finish to the crown and under-brim. A pair of feathers and a short horsehair brush emerges from a felt casing on the right. Label: Frank Olive. *Mobile Millinery Museum*. $225.

A narrow-brimmed crown of dandelion straw is encased in hand-painted, yellow tulle and bound with olive-green, velvet ribbon. Label: Hand made by Marion Woon. *Mobile Millinery Museum*. $150-175.

White cotton blossoms are shaded blueberry along the edges and overlain with chiffon petals in light turquoise. White stamens and wired leaves add texture and interest. *Mobile Millinery Museum*. $150-250.

Pandora-pink organza wraps turban-like about a buckram beehive. A cluster of primroses with grass-green foliage marks the center back of this hat, which was originally owned by Beulah Paisley. Label: Jack McConnell Boutique. Gift of Ann Higgins. *Mobile Millinery Museum*.

This toque is made special by the shape of the crown, molded to simulate a bow. Tiny touches of black are sprinkled throughout the fine, cherry-pink straw. A tailored grosgrain bow stretches across the crown for an elegant, sophisticated look. *Mobile Millinery Museum*. $150-200.

Navy straw Breton with patent leather crown. *Mobile Millinery Museum*. $120-150.

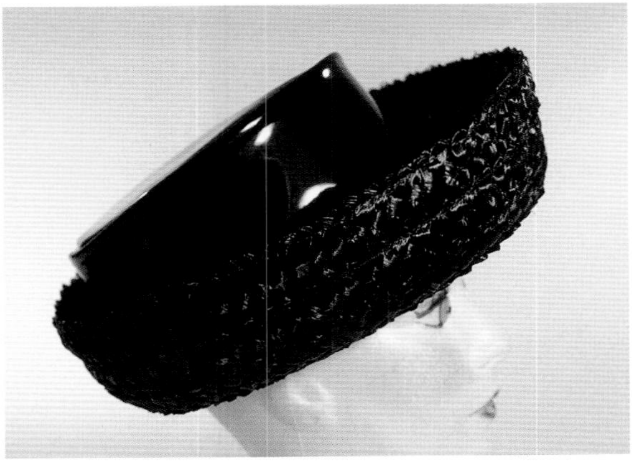

This sombrero, c.1963, looks smashing with its patent leather rim, band, and streamers. *Label: Georgette. Mobile Millinery Museum*. $225-325.

A ten gallon hat in rich chocolate brown is banded with grosgrain and pocketed to allow for the addition of a plume. Label: Borsalino, size 22. The Borsalino hat company has been in business since 1857. *Mobile Millinery Museum*. $250.

A domed crown of black lacquered straw is set against a black velvet band to preside over a brim that is covered in striated petals. Paper-white flowers sweep to the right on strands of lacquered straw. Label: Creation by André. *Mobile Millinery Museum*. $350-400.

A similar look in wool felt is double-banded with grosgrain and finished with a bow and half streamer. Twin labels: Georgette/ Simpson's. *Mobile Millinery Museum*. $150-200.

A vanilla confection comprised of a variety of straw. The Toronto designer has selected 5 1/2-inch, cognac, satin ribbon to band the hat and form a continuous ribbon bow. Label: Vera Anne Millinery, The Queensway. *Mobile Millinery Museum*. $300-350.

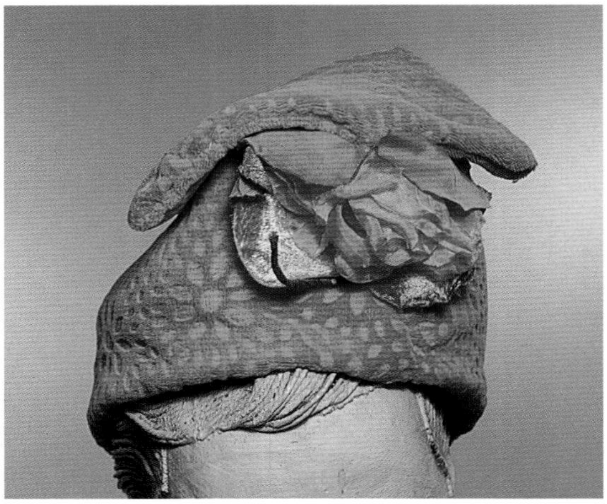

A turban of flamingo-pink velour, cut in a floral pattern, is wrapped, towel-fashion, about the head. A rose, tinted blush-to-flamingo, sports yellowish-green velvet leaves. *Mobile Millinery Museum*. $220-250.

A pair of pieced-felt bubble toques by milliner Anita Pineault. *Mobile Millinery Museum*. $175-225 each.

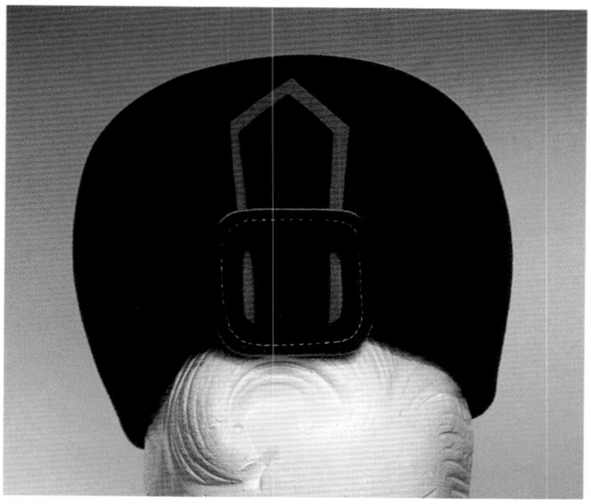

A buckle marks the center-front of this high hat in navy, and squash-colored, felt. Label: Cecelia Francis, Toronto. *Mobile Millinery Museum*. $200-250.

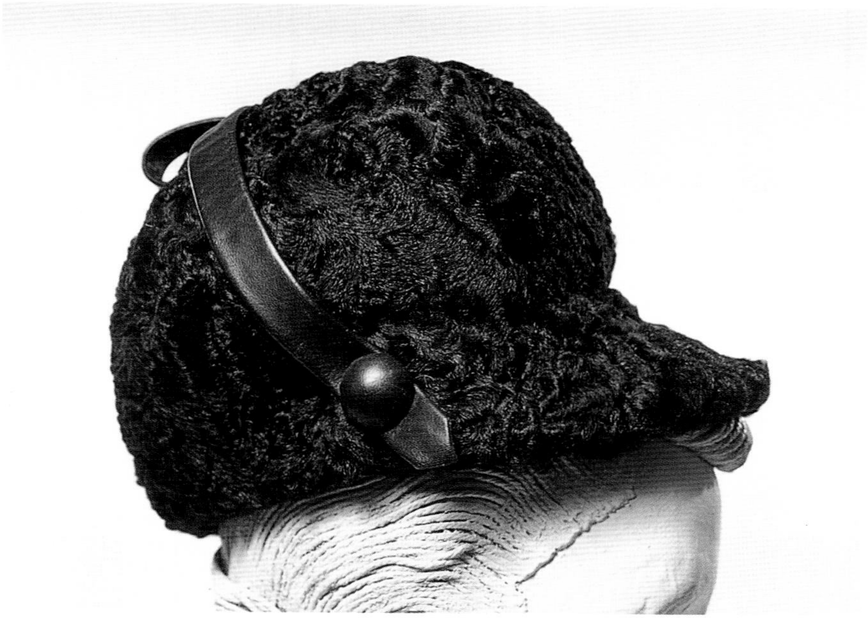

A visored helmet of black Persian lamb is trimmed with a horizontal band of black velvet, then finished with buttons and a pair of leather loops. Black lace lining. Label: Irene Hat Salon.(Irene of Montreal.) *Mobile Millinery Museum*. $450-500.

This mallard-green cuffed hat perches on the back of the head. The satin crown is studded with aluminium beads to top a turned-up brim with trapunto stitching. Label: "Dachettes", Designed by Lilly Daché. *Mobile Millinery Museum*. $350-450.

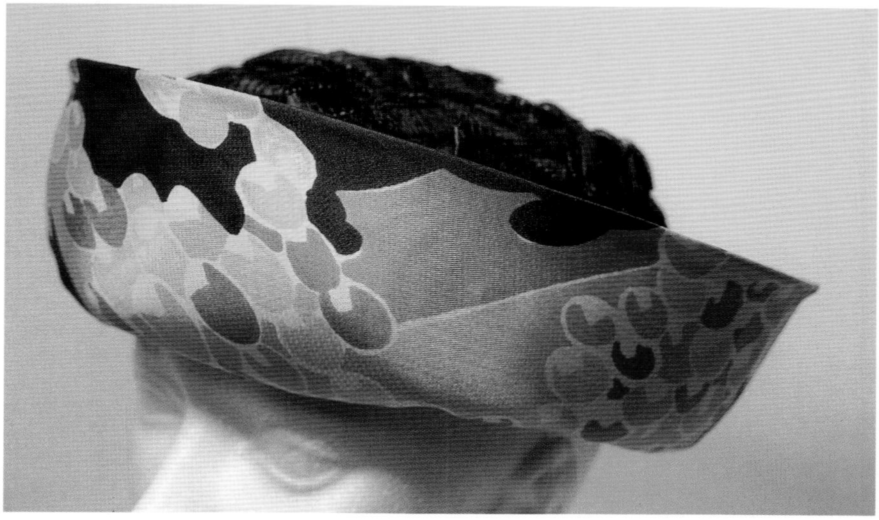

Halo Breton, c.1965: Black straw crowns a brim of simulated tie-dye fabric. *Mobile Millinery Museum*. $200-250.

Lacy black braid bands a high-crowned, 1960s hat of plum-colored beaver plush and darkens the under-brim. Label: Custom made by Erica's Hat Salon, 42 Hughson N., Hamilton. *Mobile Millinery Museum*. $220-260

Silk poppies supply eye-popping appeal to this green and white floral casque. *Mobile Millinery Museum*. $275-325.

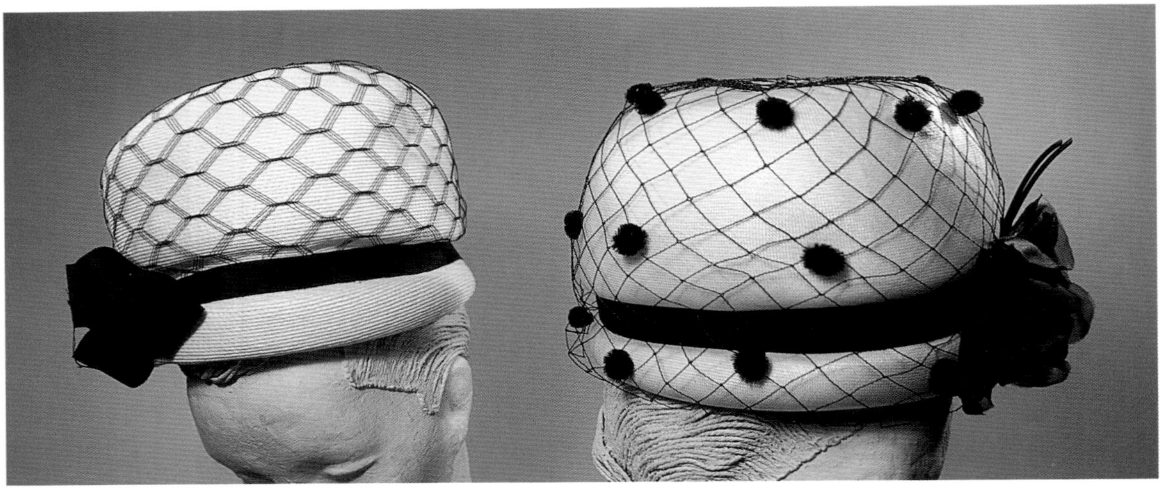

A pair of similarly-styled, straw bubble toques. The first is encased in large-gauge, honeycomb veiling, while its mate, also veiled, receives an added punch from dollops of chenille. *Mobile Millinery Museum*. $150-180 each.

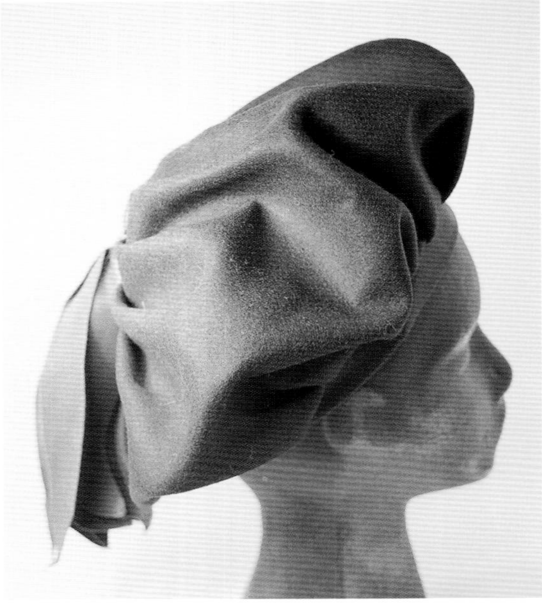

Chocolate-brown halo beret with grosgrain topknot and streamers. Label: Mr. Fredericks Young Modes. *Mobile Millinery Museum*. $250-300.

Modified chef's hat of hazel organza, shown with two hat boxes by the same maker. Label: Darcel Exclusive. *Mobile Millinery Museum*. Hat and boxes: $250-300.

This variation on the chef's hat in plaid organza must have looked great with a mini dress and "Go Go" boots when it was new. *Mobile Millinery Museum*. $200-250.

Right:
A print fabric picture hat with the look of cross-stitch. Label: Jacqueline Original, Toronto. *Mobile Millinery Museum*. $300-350.

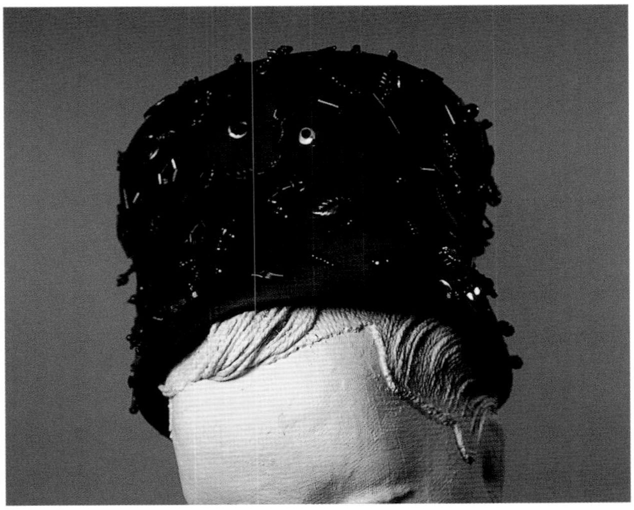

This towering crown of beaded satin has been lovingly preserved in its original hatbox since the 1960s. *Mobile Millinery Museum*. $300-350.

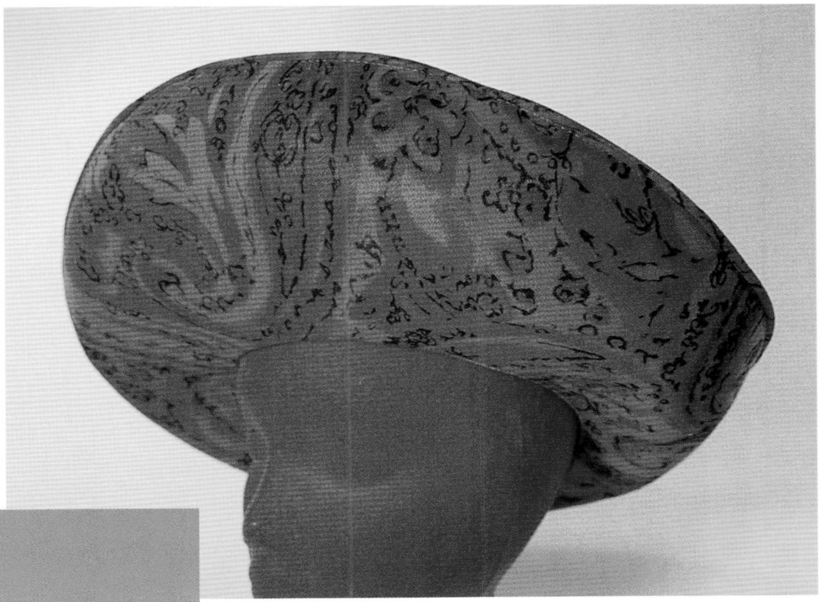

Halo sombrero, c.1963, skillfully crafted of psychedelic jersey print in shades of claret, deep coral, black, and taupe. Satin-lined crown. Label: Mr. Charles, New York. *Mobile Millinery Museum*. $400-450.

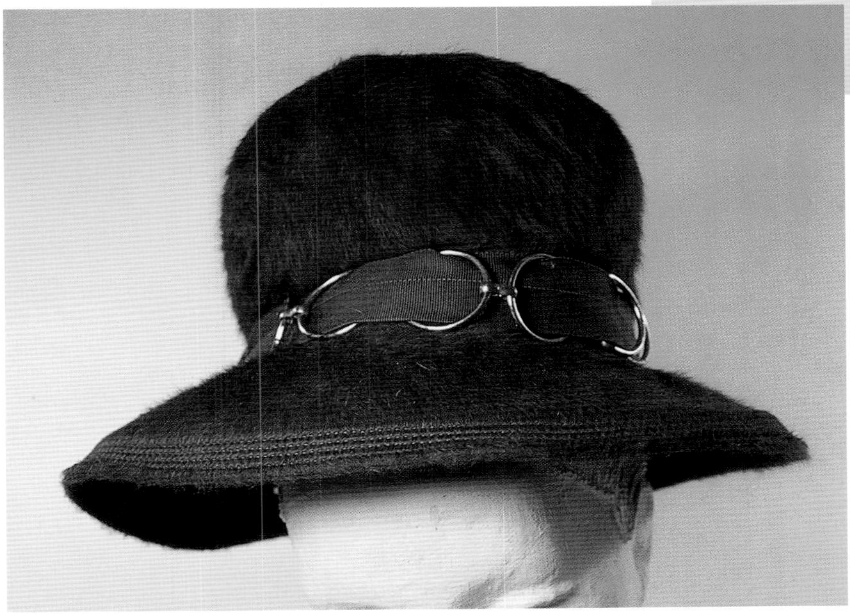

Lillian Lieberman remembers this electric-blue felt to be one of the designs of the *Variety Hat Company*, owned by her husband. Metal embellishments like the hat's linked-chain band were popular, c.1968. *Mobile Millinery Museum*. $300-350.

A fantasy in raspberry felt. Raspberry ostrich tendrils dot a white marabou brim. Label: Ellen Faith, Paris, New York. *Mobile Millinery Museum*. $450-550.

A designer velvet in cherry-blossom-pink features contrasting leaf-green band and trapunto stitching. Twin labels: Mr. John Jr./Millinery by Jennie L. Willis, Hamilton, Ontario. *Mobile Millinery Museum*. $300-350.

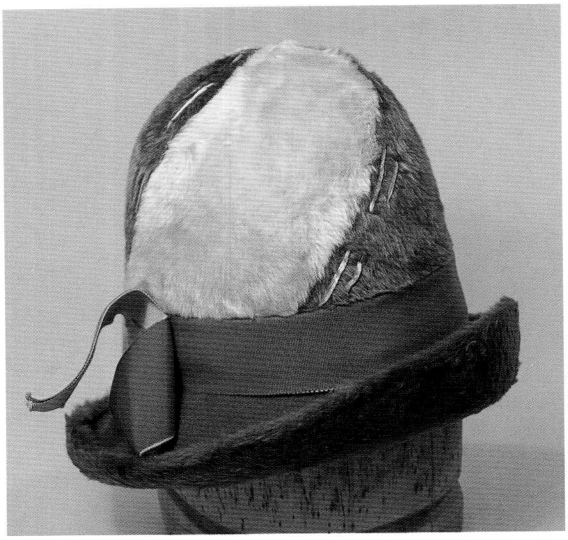

The crown of this postillion is pieced from contrasting colors of beaverette and laced with long, running stitches in cream-colored silk. Label: Creation by André. *Mobile Millinery Museum.* $220.

Taupe stroller of high-quality felt. Label: Irene of New York. *Mobile Millinery Museum*. $200-250.

Essence of witch: Bronze straw, floppy brim, c.1963. A spray of tea roses, shaded gold-to-orange, rests on a soft brown silk medallion. *Mobile Millinery Museum*. $450-500.

A feather-trimmed velour from the late 1960s has down-turned brim. *Mobile Millinery Museum*. $180-200.

Left:
The taupe, peach, and green roses that cap this chenille-dotted whimsy represent a color combination popular c.1960. *Mobile Millinery Museum*. $150.

Right:
A turban of winter-white twill by Mr. Fredericks (Young Sophisticates Line). *Mobile Millinery Museum*. $250.

Slate gray beaver felt with matching rose. *Mobile Millinery Museum*. $80-100.

Cranberry beaverette cloche with black lacquered band. Label: M'Sieu Léon, Paris, Roma, New York. *Mobile Millinery Museum*. $150.

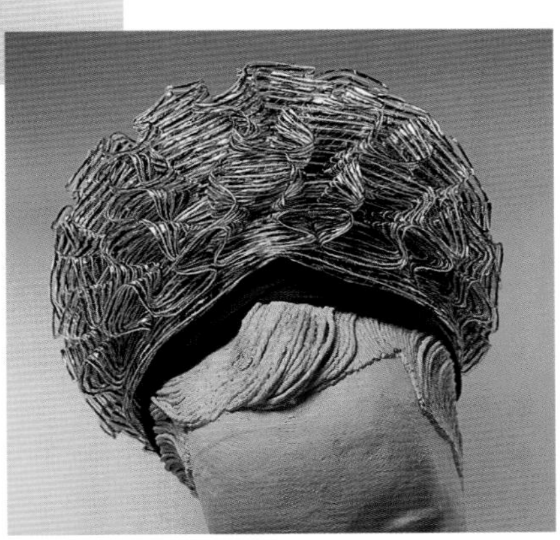

Ruffles of ribbon straw crown a band of navy satin. Label: Country Club Creation, Toronto. *Mobile Millinery Museum*. $180-220.

Celluloid paillettes dangle from a woolen casque, c.1966. Label: 100 % wool, Hand Made in Italy. *Lillian Lieberman Collection, Mobile Millinery Museum*. $100-150.

The crown of this olive-drab flower pot is carefully shaped to follow the contours of the head and provide a backdrop for a magnificent band and bow of deep goldenrod satin. Label: The Club Woman Hat by Piko of Montreal, Paris, New York. *Mobile Millinery Museum.* $275-325.

A treasure in pumpkin velvet, c.1968. *Mobile Millinery Museum*. $250-300.

Reproduction of an Edwardian, fore-and-aft, hunting helmet. Brown felt is buttoned and banded with matching satin. Label: Mr. John Classic, New York, Paris. *Mobile Millinery Museum*. $200-250.

Straw bubble toque, banded with white-on-black velvet ribbon and finished with a pair of black and white satin peonies. Label: Mr. John Jr. *Mobile Millinery Museum.* $225.

Whimsy, c.1965; a ring of velvet bows tops a hairline veil. *Mobile Millinery Museum*. $50-80.

Coffee and cream-colored sou'wester. Trapunto-stitched vinyl brim. Grosgrain band, crushed bow. Label: Leopold Original. *Mobile Millinery Museum*. $250-350.

Black velvet beauty: a millinery brooch joins the hatband extension to the center brim. *Mobile Millinery Museum*. $225.

Afternoon hat of bone-white felt with brushed crown and upper brim. Grosgrain band ends in fringed streamers, turned up to mimic the left brim. Label: Georgette. *Mobile Millinery Museum*. $80-100.

A smart little hat in eggshell and avocado straw. *Mobile Millinery Museum*. $100-150.

Circa 1960: A wired chip-straw brim supports a fabric crown of colorful stripes. *Mobile Millinery Museum*. $100-150.

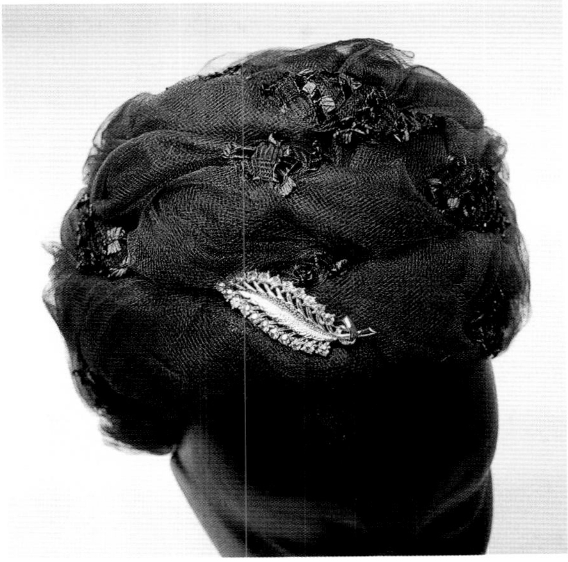

Black net is woven with ribbons of cellophane straw to produce an elegant bubble toque with a leaf-shaped rhinestone pin. *Mobile Millinery Museum*. $80-100.

An astonishingly realistic rose dominates the brim of this straw-cloth beauty. *Mobile Millinery Museum*. $200-250.

A cousin to the Cossack in tulle and satin. *Mobile Millinery Museum.* $80-100.

A turban toque with a casual floral air. *Mobile Millinery Museum*. $120-150.

Flower pot in vivid shades of blue. *Mobile Millinery Museum*. $250-300.

This tulle and fabric confection resembles an inverted nest. *Mobile Millinery Museum*. $120-150.

Feather-trimmed halo beret of mustard beaverette. *Mobile Millinery Museum*. $150-180.

A cool, white, summer confection is banded with chartreuse and weighted with colorful choux. *Mobile Millinery Museum*. $250-300.

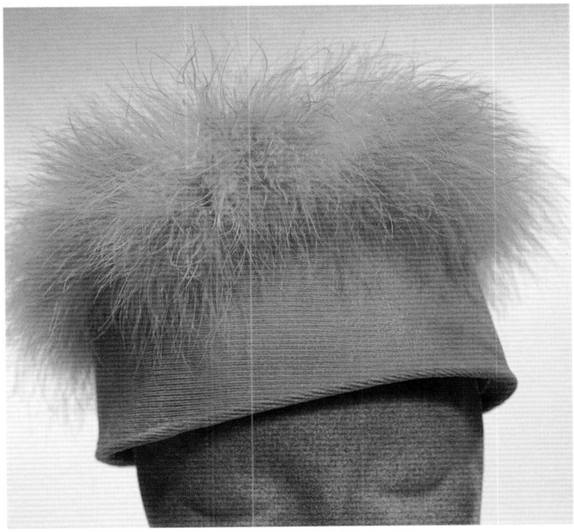

The right touch of red on a straw and velvet charmer. *Mobile Millinery Museum*. $250-300.

This deep velvet pillbox, in autumn-squash, is rimmed with matching marabou. *Mobile Millinery Museum*. $150-180.

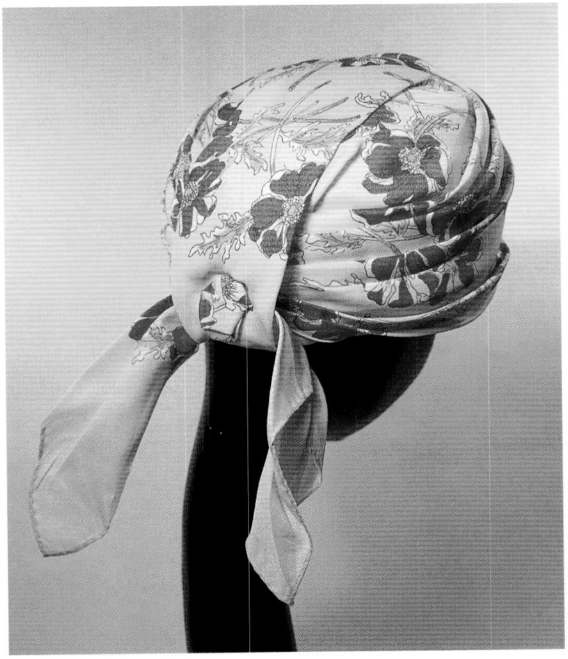

Left:
A turban toque of rayon silk. Label: Frederick Fox, by appointment to Her Majesty the Queen. *Mobile Millinery Museum*. $200-250.

Right:
A crimson felt winter lampshade. *Mobile Millinery Museum*. $150-200.

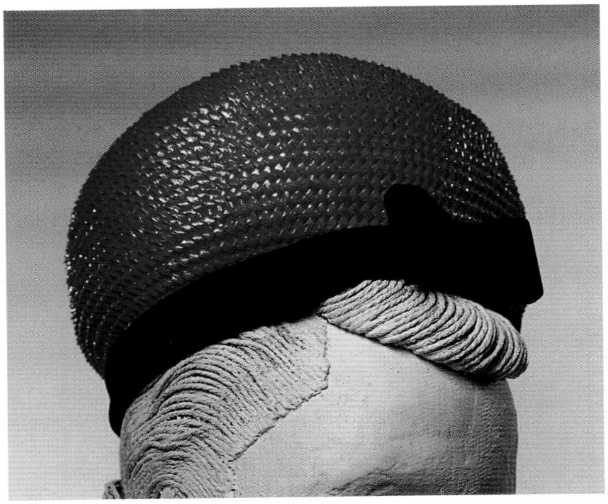

A trio of black velvet whimsies. *Mobile Millinery Museum*. $50-80 each.

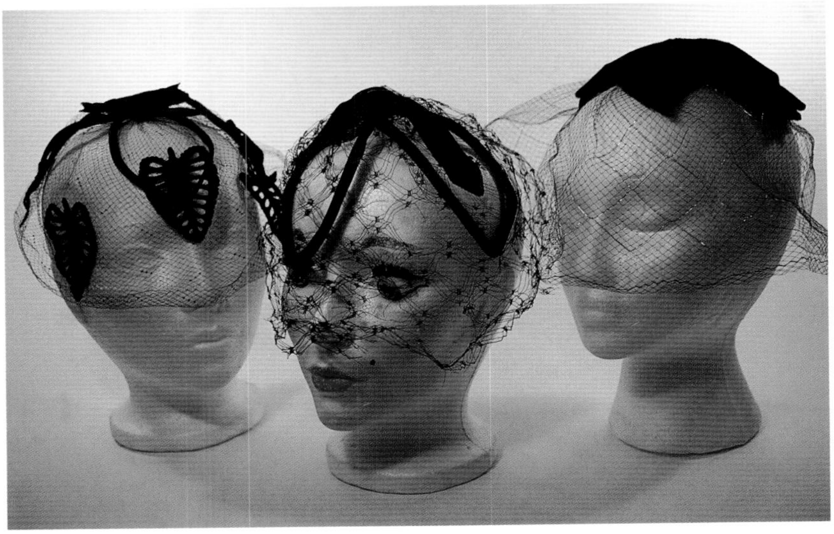

A red lacquered dome rests on a black velvet band, ready to be paired with a mini skirt. *Mobile Millinery Museum*. $225.

This black and white velvet sensation exudes an Edwardian design influence. *Mobile Millinery Museum*. $250-350.

Bumper-brim paisley pillbox. *Mobile Millinery Museum*. $80-120.

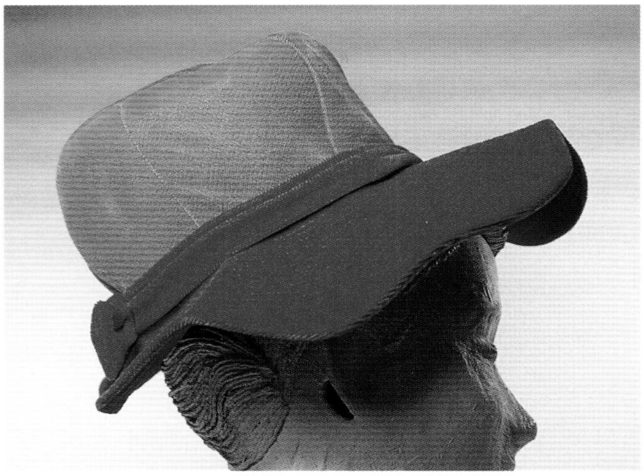

A stiff, undulating brim of cherry velvet supports a peppermint-pink crown. Label: Jacqueline Original, Toronto. *Mobile Millinery Museum*. $250-300.

White straw, banded in ice cream colors, shows off a trio of organdie roses. *Mobile Millinery Museum*. $250-300.

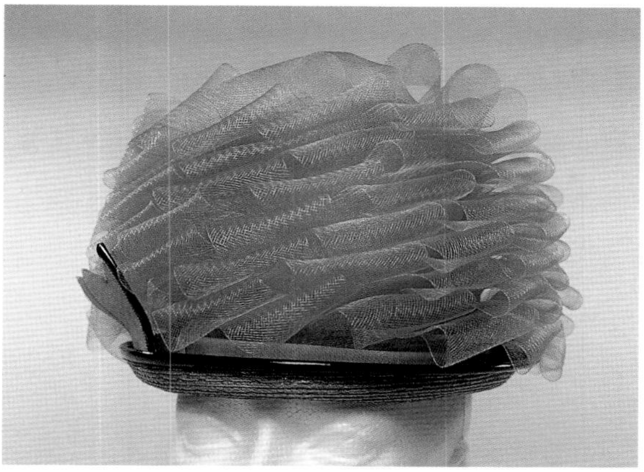

Loops of synthetic horsehair soften a stiff, turquoise straw, bubble toque. Narrow patent leather band and rim. *Mobile Millinery Museum*. $200-250.

White straw revival cloche, banded simply with navy grosgrain. Label: Frank Olive for Bonwit Teller. *Mobile Millinery Museum*. $250.

A late 1960s showstopper in battleship and dove-gray felt. Label: Jacqueline Original. *Mobile Millinery Museum*. $250-300.

A frizzled tassel extends the line of this dome-crowned beaverette. *Mobile Millinery Museum.* $150.

This cuffed gold dome is encased in fine-gauge veiling. A spray of black leaves draws attention to the back. *Mobile Millinery Museum*. $150-200.

The crown of this crisp navy widebrim is bound with narrow white straw. *Mobile Millinery Museum.* $200-250.

The author in a floral bandeau, c.1963.

Green straw Puritan with rhinestone buckle. *Mobile Millinery Museum*. $250-300.

A helmet of deep brown, long-nap, beaver is banded with caramel-colored snakeskin. A pair of buttons surrounds a tapering panel of stitches to simulate the eyes of a cobra. Label: Creation by André. *Mobile Millinery Museum*. $225.

Chapter IX
The Demise of Millinery: 1970 - 1980

"I remember when I wore a hat just to walk past three houses to the post office."

— *Jean Lemay*

"It makes me want to cry that people don't wear hats anymore. I always continued wearing them even though people laughed."

— *Fran Richardson, Stoney Creek, Ontario*

"I've been in hat shops where women try on hats and they look fabulous, but hats draw attention, and a lot of people want to be anonymous."

— *Walter Gosk, president of Biltmore Hats, in an interview with Kerry Thompson for an article in the Grand River Life, April 19, 2003.*

With the struggle for women's liberation came the desire by women to be free of the dictates of fashion and social convention. In one sense they were following in the footsteps of their male counterparts who, for centuries, were so bound by etiquette and social convention that a man's decision of when and where to remove his hat was not his to make. As recently as the 1960s, a man could step onto an elevator without removing his hat unless there was a woman present. He would be expected to remove his hat when entering a public building or when flying or traveling by train. He would wear his hat for a bus or subway ride. The dos and don'ts of doffing and tipping one's hat would fill a book, the content of which was common knowledge.

Millinery Law

Over the centuries, various hat regulations have even been written into law including the manner of a military salute. In 1702, the following rule was issued to the Royal Scots. "As nothing disfigures hats or dirties the lace more than taking off the hat, the men are, for the future, only to raise the back of their hand to them when they pass an officer."

For women, the social imperatives were equally stringent. Wearing a hat to call at the home of a friend was a sign of respect, out of which developed the rule that a woman might not wear a hat indoors after 5 o'clock. This was to ensure that a visitor did not overstay her welcome and interfere with the supper hour of her hostess. Women bore the added burden of being expected to purchase new hats each season as style changes were practically up to the minute.

Several social factors were responsible for the decline of millinery, c. 1970, but two events in Rome during the 1960s would foreshadow the ultimate demise of this once thriving industry. The granting of papal permission for Catholic women to attend mass bareheaded, and the egg pelting of fur-wearing *La Scala* patrons are often cited as the death knells to the trade. More accurately, these events are reflections of a shift in consciousness.

Women did not so much rebel against the wearing of hats as against the obligation to do so. By the 1980s, when a mild resurgence in the popularity of hats occurred, there were no longer any social, legal, or religious imperatives to determine their suitability.

Although millinery was kept alive in North America by race goers and strict religious groups, the wearing of hats was, and is, no longer a part of everyday dress. Just as large hats and larger hatpins were symbolic of women's emancipation during the first women's movement, so hats themselves came to signify rigid confinement during the feminist movement of the 1970s and were thrown off altogether.

The resulting decline and subsequent demise of millinery is a significant and unprecedented event in centuries of fashion history. Although designers attempted to keep the millinery wheel turning through the introduction of unisex styles and other strategies, the early 1970s saw the end of a two hundred year period, considered to be the great age of millinery; a period when the hat held its place as the cornerstone of fashion, a means of personal expression, and an art form.

During the decline, many milliners turned their talents to bridal headpieces; some went out of business altogether, and some survived the market shift by focusing on a niche market. Designer Frank Olive, famous for Kentucky Derby hats, marketed a round, rolled brim straw hat in 1979 that he termed the wedding ring.

A 1970s casual blue straw dressed with a gold-edged grosgrain band and a cluster of posies on plastic stems. Label: Boutique Kates, Canada. *Mobile Millinery Museum*. $50-60.

Circa 1973: Narrow strips of cellophane straw are sewn in concentric circles to form this crisp, navy and white, topper. A decorative loop at the crown can also be utilized to carry the piece. Label: Georgette. *Mobile Millinery Museum*. $125.

Circa 1974: Pauline McGibbon wears another of Warde's designs in her official capacity as Ontario's Lieutenant Governor. *Philip Warde Collection, Mobile Millinery Museum*.

Ontario's Lieutenant Governor, Pauline McGibbon, wears a similar hat by Philip Warde as she accompanies England's Queen Mother on a state visit, July 1st, 1974. It is inscribed: "To Philip Warde, really to show his hat." *Philip Warde Collection, Mobile Millinery Museum.*

A variation on the fedora in barely-green felt. Self-fabric daisies descend from the crown to the brim, which is upturned at back. *Mobile Millinery Museum*. $125.

A caramel fedora sports a sweeping feather adornment. Satin inner crown. *Mobile Millinery Museum*. $180-200.

Lavender bubble toque, relieved with touches of soft green. Shown with a fabric swatch and bill of sale from Simpson's-Sears. Mrs. Alan Heywood purchased the hat in January of 1970, for $14.70. *Mobile Millinery Museum*. $60-80.

Wool-felt topper with silver-toned metal studs. Label: Hand Made for Holt Renfrew. *Mobile Millinery Museum*. $250-300.

Chapter X
The Return of Millinery: 1980 and Beyond

"What store, other than a hat shop, can you leave happier than when you went in, especially if you didn't buy anything?"

— *Kevin Neufeld, Niagara-on-the-Lake, Ontario; owner of BeauChapeau® Hats*

"I remember the first time I saw a couple dancing in my shop. They each chose their hat and with no words at all just came together and started waltzing around the store. All the customers stopped what they were doing and just looked on in inspiration. It made me so proud to see that, and I was inspired to never lose that feeling in our store... That's what we hope for, people to come to our store for 'date night', not just to buy hats, but also to play."

— *Kevin Neufeld, Niagara-on-the-Lake, Ontario; owner of BeauChapeau® Hats*

Millinery is a recovering industry. The centuries old production of women's fashion hats fell into an unprecedented decline in the last three decades of the twentieth century, with the result that by the year 2000, an entire generation of women had grown up without hats. Hats fell into such disfavor that even some mainstream museums failed to display headwear with the historic costumes they were originally designed to complement. Others refused to accept hats into their archives and many beautiful works of millinery art were donated instead, to theatre groups.

One of the Canadian hat factories that survived the millinery decline of the 1970s, '80s, and '90s is the *Biltmore Company* of Guelph, Ontario. They have been producing felt hats since 1917 and recently developed a line of straw hats for women. Many of these are golf wear, exported directly to the U.S. and Japan.

A mild resurgence of millinery interest occurred during the Princess Diana years as young women emulated her style, but with the disappearance of hat stores, patrons were left to find their treasures in bridal salons or home parties.

Many North Americans who entered the millinery trade during the final decades of the twentieth century did so after apprenticing in Britain or Australia. Specialty hat shops were a rare find in most locations but a treasure to loyal hat wearers.

Disco fever: This sequined visor from the 1980s adjusts with an elastic strip in back. Label: Made in Indonesia. *Mobile Millinery Museum.* $125.

A skyscraper turban by Simon Chang, c.1990. Label: Simon Chang for Kates Millinery Ltd. *Mobile Millinery Museum.* $250-300.

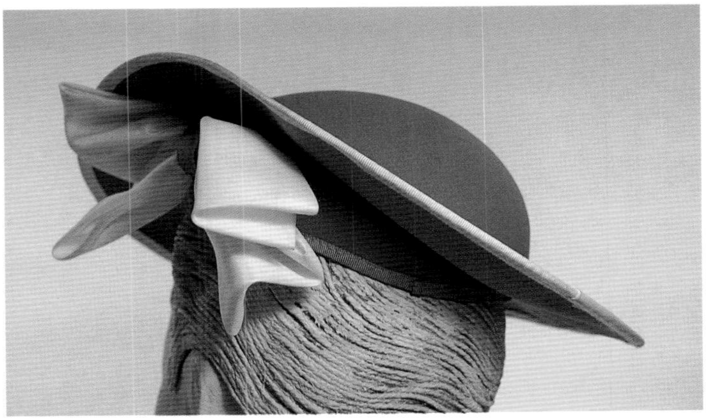

A 1980s peacock-blue brimmed saucer of a style favored by Princess Diana. Label: Connor, Made in England. *Mobile Millinery Museum*. $150.

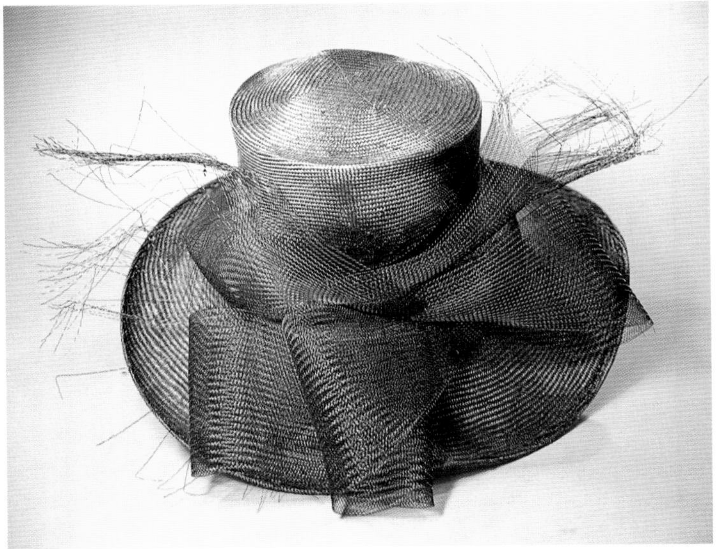

Black duckbill straw with large horsehair bow; a variation on the short-back sailor. Label: Original-custom Lilliput Hats, Toronto, Canada. *Private Collection*. $200.

A trio of 1980s saucer hats for evening. *Mobile Millinery Museum*. $75 each.

Lilliput label with the original price of $200 listed on the reverse.

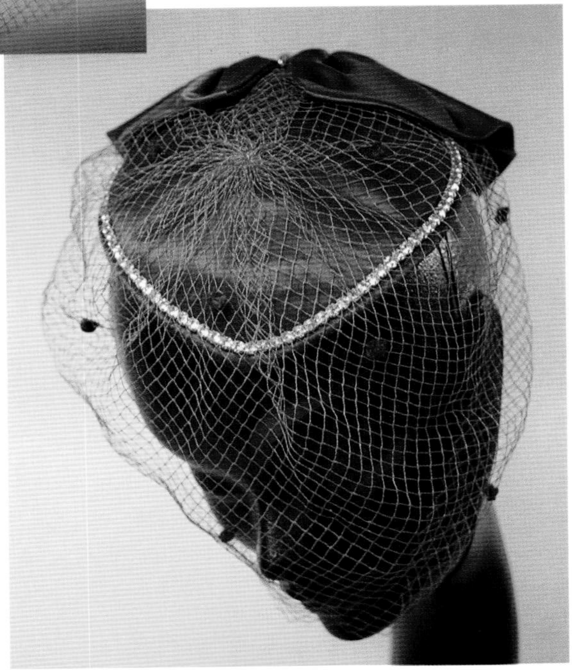

This saucer of rhinestone-trimmed purple satin was worn by Karen McClendon to her grade eight graduation dance. Label: The Hattery, Hamilton, Ontario. *Mobile Millinery Museum*. $80-100.

A variation on the boater in brilliant white. Label: Designed by Sylvia, New York, St. Louis. *Mobile Millinery Museum*. $320-350.

This contemporary straw provides shade and great style for under $15.00! *Private Collection.*

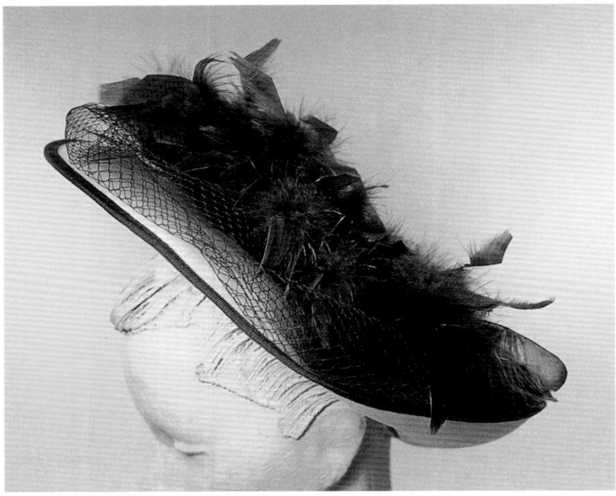

A feathered, pinch-back brim in navy, white, and national blue. Crown and brim are of buckram, covered with a double knit fabric. Made in England, c.1995. *Private Collection.* $300-350.

The halo brim of this green-black velvet cap boasts iridescent rooster tail. Hat designed and made by the author, c.2002. *Private Collection*. $450-550.

A factory-made split-brim straw hails from the 1990s. *Mobile Millinery Museum*. $125-150.

In 1997, Kevin Neufeld of Niagara-On-The-Lake, Ontario, established *BeauChapeau®*, the first men's and women's hat shop south of Toronto, since the decline. "It was a time of retro; the cigar was enjoying an unparalleled resurgence, the Chrysler PT Cruiser® was a concept car, and retro fashions were all around," remembers Neufeld, whose 1000 square foot boutique now attracts shoppers from a wide geographic area and serves an international clientele by mail order.

The images of hats on these BeauChapeau® promotional postcards are difficult to resist. Postcards *courtesy of Kevin Neufeld*.

Beyond Fashion: Margo

Margo's Hat Shop has been in the Yonge and St. Clair area of Toronto for forty years. Milliner Efstathia Xynnis-Hall has occupied the space since the late 1980s and serves a clientele of chemotherapy patients and church ladies, Orthodox Jewish, strict Catholic, and other women who wear hats for religious reasons. They call her Margo and she doesn't correct them. The previous owner, Lillian Fletcher, also went under the millinery name of Margo, believing it sounded exotic.

After an initial fitting, a custom *Margo's* hat is completed in two or three days, then placed in a hatbox, ready for pick-up. Xynnis-Hall, who made hats for the 1996 Canadian Olympic team, instructs her customers to carry their hat boxes "delicately, like paper, like gold".

This whimsical, hand-crafted lamp is evidence of a returning hat craze.

Nylon veiling covers the crown of this white straw boater, banded in moiré silk. Pink, plastic-stemmed roses add back interest. *Edith Mitchell Collection, Mobile Millinery Museum.*

Chapter XI
The Sketch Pad

"Madame Reboux will have neither photographs nor sketches of her models."

— *Columnist for Mayfair Magazine, February, 1928*

Many a hat began and ended its life cycle as a sketch. The inspiration for a hat might have first leaped onto paper from the imagination of a designer or milliner, in the form of an outline or draft. At a later stage the same hat, now finished and ready for sale, might be sketched again and appear as an advertisement in a newspaper or magazine. Finally, many a hat, when received into the archives of a costume museum, is examined, described, and photographed or sketched onto an accession sheet for identification purposes.

Sand Tagal with pale Pink Lancer Feathers finished with flowers made of Tagal.
WILLIS, NELSON & CO.

Advertising sketches for Willis, Nelson & Co. Millinery, c.1912. *Jennie Willis Collection, Mobile Millinery Museum.*

Grey Tagal small pink Rose buds, striped Ribbon with Rose Colored Edge.
WILLIS, NELSON & CO.

Putty Tagal lined Black Velvet, shaded Lilac and Pale Roses round crown.
WILLIS, NELSON & CO.

Pearl Straw shrouded with Black Calais Lace, Coque Velvet round crown finished with Poppy of same shade.
WILLIS, NELSON & CO.

The following drawings by contemporary artists reflect their vision of the millinery experience. The hat sketches are by Corinne Shephard, while the sketches depicting hats and faces are the work of Catharine DeLuca.

Chapter XII
Special Collections

"I love the way delicate straw hats filter light as it falls on a woman's face. I always say make sure you stand in the sunlight, and your hat will be like a halo."

— Patricia Underwood, designer
(Victoria magazine, June 2003)

"An operator can make only about ten hats a day, so we sell them for five hundred and fifty dollars."

— Shellie McDowell, designer
(Victoria magazine, June 2003)

"For churchgoing women, Sunday is an event and they greet it in style. So the fancier the hat, the better."

— Patricia Underwood, designer
(Victoria magazine, June 2003)

Throughout the years, hats were fashioned for every occasion in a variety of materials and styles, with the result that a splendid collection can be built around any number of themes. You may want to focus on feathers or furs, elaborate mother-of-the-bride hats, or go Hollywood with the sensational styles set by the glamorous movie stars of old.

Some collections reveal a preference for a famous designer while others favor a particular color or adornment – roses perhaps.

A collector may even select hats based upon how or where they will be displayed. Straw hats add charm to a door, porch, or cottage, while elegant cocktail hats may be exhibited in the most formal of rooms.

What follows is a series of mini collections based around various themes.

The Aline Banting Collection

In 2004, the *Mobile Millinery Museum* accessioned nearly 200 haute couture hats and an equal number of coordinating shoes from the estate of the late portrait artist Aline Banting. The collection, the museum's largest single acquisition of quality millinery to date, presents a mini history of twentieth century Toronto, Paris, New York, and Montreal fashion.

Mrs. Banting, who signed her work "Myles," was a regular annual exhibitor at many major Canadian shows and she received invitations to show at the *Canadian National Exhibition* and at *Grand Central Art Galleries* in New York City. Globally, her work may be found in Florence, Calcutta, Capetown, New York, Boston, Los Angeles, and Vancouver. Important private collections such as A. Bronfman, Montreal; W. Watson of the *Watson Gallery* in Montreal, and J. Bauer of Waterloo have acquired her works.

Banting's hats and shoes, worn to gallery openings and art shows, are as vibrant as her paintings. Many still bear their original price tags, a real boon to the museum's documentation efforts. Banting's daughter-in-law remembers that Aline would tuck the attached price tag up under a hat when she wished to wear it. Perhaps she possessed foreknowledge of their ultimate destination.

Self-portrait by Aline Myles Banting, c.1940. *Photo courtesy of Peter Banting.*

A Schiaparelli label peeks through the green, open-weave, velour crown of this posy-trimmed summer straw. Shown with hand crocheted, banana-yellow glove. *Mobile Millinery Museum*. Hat: $250-300.

A jaunty felt in winter white, shown with white leather, rabbit-trimmed boots. *Aline Banting Collection, Mobile Millinery Museum*. Hat: $150.

Caramel straw dish hat, c.1948. Label: Georgette Originals. Matching jewel-studded leather pumps by Feet Flairs. *Aline Banting Collection, Mobile Millinery Museum*. Hat: $125.

Mid-1950s cherry straw with navy velvet band and navy diamond-dot veiling. Label: Rachael-Mack, Hamilton. *Aline Banting Collection, Mobile Millinery Museum*. $125.

A posy-trimmed straw close hat, c.1955, rests on a pair of navy stilettos. *Aline Banting Collection, Mobile Millinery Museum*. Hat: $100-150.

Navy straw bubble toque contrasts stripes with medallions. Label: Lady Beatrice Model. *Mobile Millinery Museum*. $80-100.

Turquoise straw close hat with rosebud trim, c.1955. Label: Leslie Monroe, Paris/New York. *Mobile Millinery Museum*. Hat: $150-200.

A turban of bronze satin and gold lamé bears its original $13.95 price tag. Label: Henri Original. Shown with gold and silver spiked heels by Pancaldi. *Aline Banting Collection, Mobile Millinery Museum*. Hat $125-150.

Rose-trimmed yellow straw embellished with hand beading and embroidery. Label: Raphael-Mack. Seed beads adorn matching leather stilettos. *Aline Banting Collection,* M*obile Millinery Museum*. Hat: $120.

Circa 1955: A nest of blue and white bias tape crowns a brim of bell flowers and apple blossoms. *Aline Banting Collection*, *Mobile Millinery Museum*. $225.

Black straw halo hat, banded with white organza. Label: Charmaine. Original. Montreal, Paris. A style tag indicates the hat was made by Charm Hats Inc., 651 Notre Dame W., Montreal. Price tag reveals the hat was purchased at Eaton's for $3.97, reduced from $18.00. *Aline Banting Collection, Mobile Millinery Museum*. $125-150.

Inner view showing a band of organza along the under-brim.

Horsehair straw wreathed in a vine of papier-mâché buds. Label: Brandt. New York. Alligator shoes by Barbara Gay. *Mobile Millinery Museum*. Hat: $125-150.

Navy straw cartwheel by Darcel. Purchased at The Right House, c.1955. *Aline Banting Collection, Mobile Millinery Museum*. $300-350.

Giant peonies cap, a 1950s straw "special occasion" hat. *Aline Banting Collection, Mobile Millinery Museum.* $225.

Silk cartwheel brimming with cherry blossoms and the occasional rhinestone. Label: Flo-Raye, New York. *Aline Banting Collection, Mobile Millinery Museum*. Hat: $350-400.

A provocative, posie-trimmed straw from the 1940s rests on green leather, open-toes from the same era. *Aline Banting Collection, Mobile Millinery Museum*.

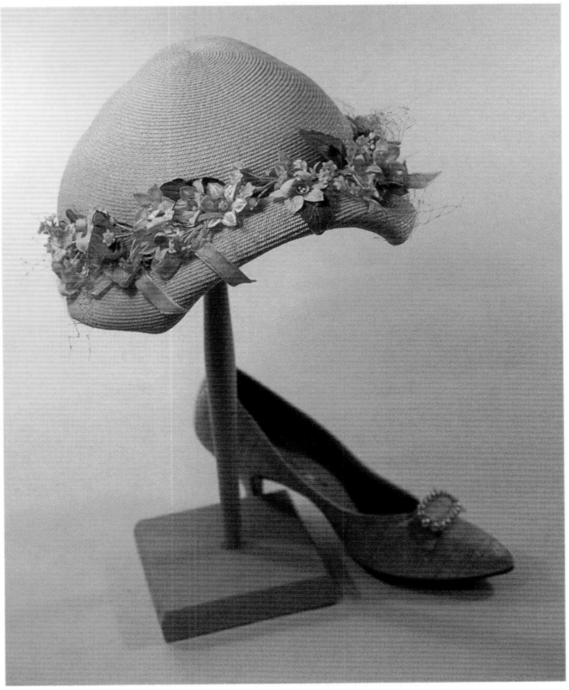

Pretty in Pink: a crown-hugging straw, casually strewn with flowers along the brow. Shown with matching shoes. *Aline Banting Collection, Mobile Millinery Museum*. Hat: $150-200.

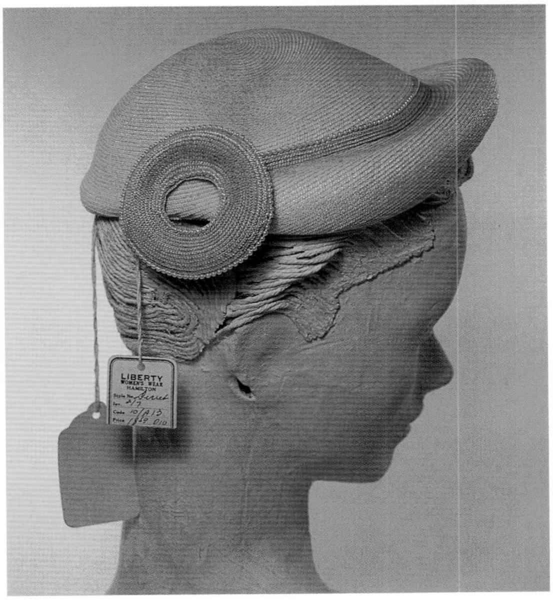

The identical hat in lemon-yellow and soft turquoise. Original paper tags. Label: the Maybrook Hat. *Aline Banting Collection, Mobile Millinery Museum*. $225.

This cream straw, c.1960, is brimming with roses, carnations, lilacs, and sweet pea. Label: Peggy Anne Original. *Aline Banting Collection, Mobile Millinery Museum*. $150-250.

This 1950s turquoise and navy straw bears the original price tags. *Aline Banting Collection, Mobile Millinery Museum.* $225.

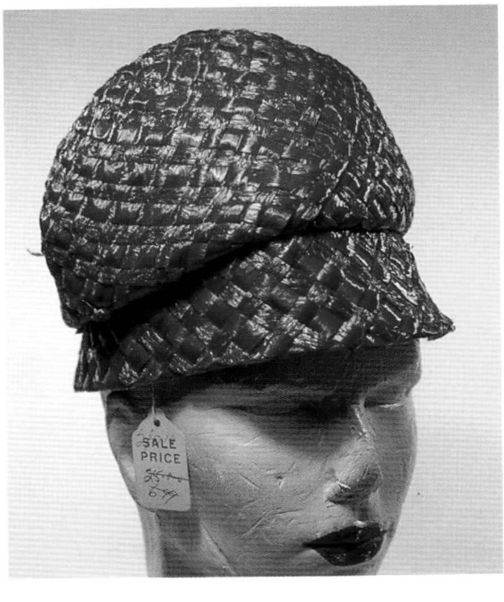

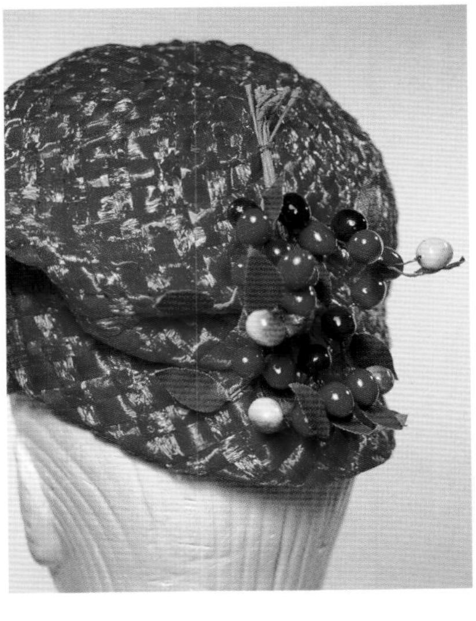

Right:
Red cello tallboy, c.1968, bears an original price tag of $6.99, marked down from $25. *Aline Banting Collection, Mobile Millinery Museum*. $150-200.

Far right:
A cluster of papier-mâché choke cherries adorns the back.

A Milan straw cartwheel, c.1950, is banded with navy velvet and a variety of garden flowers in pink, purple, and white. Label: Strathmore, Paris/New York. *Aline Banting Collection, Mobile Millinery Museum*. $225.

The back is the best feature of this 1960s gold print turban with touches of green, yellow, brown, and white. *Aline Banting Collection, Mobile Millinery Museum*. $80-120.

Cone hat, c.1950, lavished with peonies and lilacs, with green, satin leaves, pearl stamens, and red faux jewels. *Aline Banting Collection*, *Mobile Millinery Museum*. $225.

A close hat, c.1955, is banded in wild flowers. Label: Darcel. Matching lavender stilettos by Pancaldi. *Aline Banting Collection*, *Mobile Millinery Museum*. Hat: $80-100.

Water lilies grace a shell-shaped navy straw, c.1938. Label: La Salle Model. *Aline Banting Collection, Mobile Millinery Museum*. $250-300.

An exquisite rose of coral silk and navy velvet punctuates a 1940s widebrim, swathed in coral veiling. *Aline Banting Collection, Mobile Millinery Museum*. $250-300.

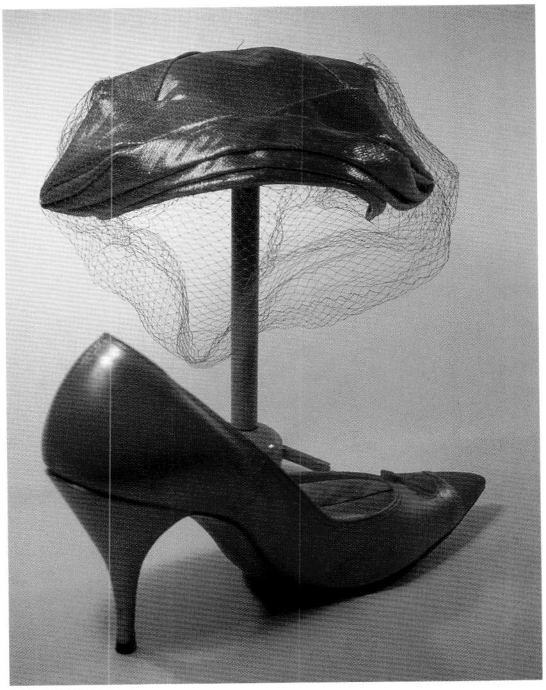

A 1950s evening hat, with nose-length veiling, rests on a pair of suede and leather spiked heels by Gleneaton. *Aline Banting Collection, Mobile Millinery Museum*. Hat: $125.

Winter cap of velvet pansies, c.1950. Label: Schiaparelli. Matching purple suede boots sport wool cuffs. *Aline Banting Collection, Mobile Millinery Museum*. Hat: $225.

Pink and green satin roses anchor a moss-green veil to finish a coral, felt topper by Vanity. Matching boots in coral leather by Brevitt of Bond Street, London. *Aline Banting Collection, Mobile Millinery Museum.* Hat: $80-120.

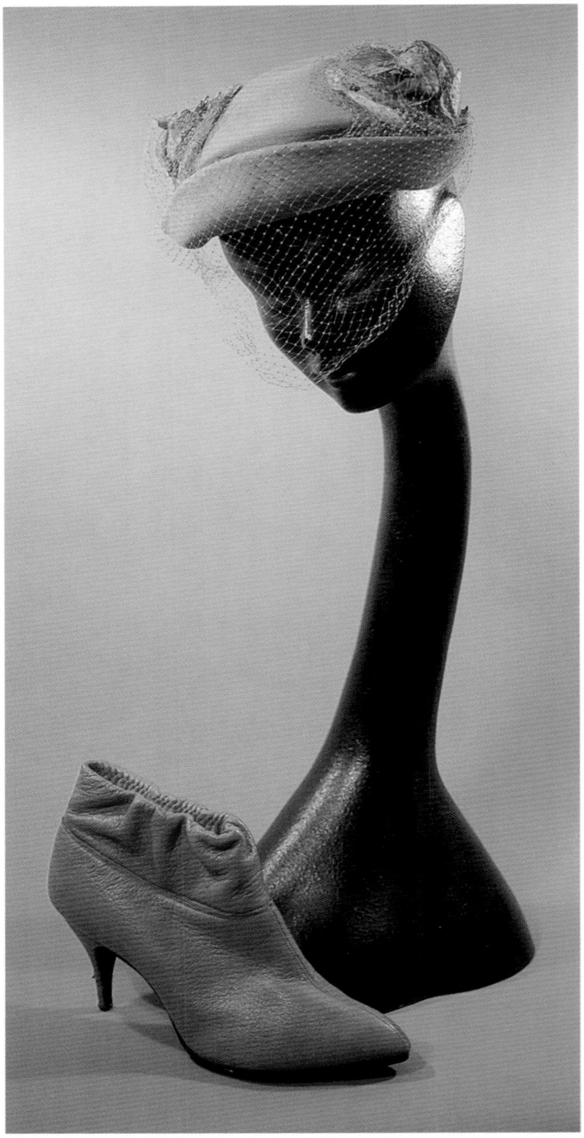

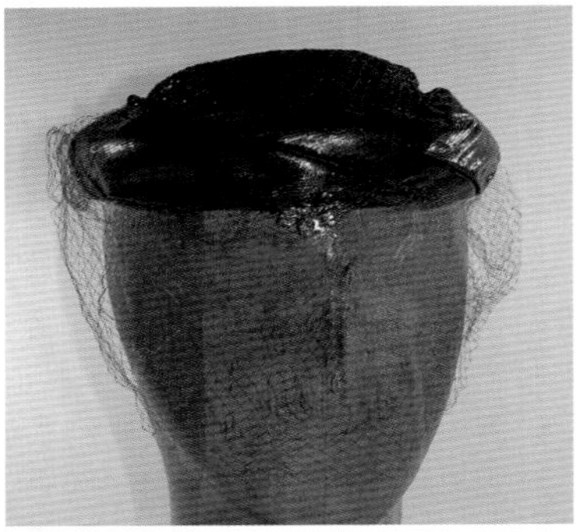

Sea-green evening hat with matching, chin-length veiling. *Aline Banting Collection, Mobile Millinery Museum*. $100-120.

Gold lamé evening hat with chin-length veiling. Morgan's price tag shows an original value, c.1950, of $15.95, reduced to $4. Gold lamé t-straps by Fitzgerald. *Aline Banting Collection, Mobile Millinery Museum*. $125.

A daisy-studded cap, c.1965. *Aline Banting Collection, Mobile Millinery Museum*. $50-75.

A hot-pink, daisy-trimmed straw, c.1960. Label: Eaton's Fashions. *Aline Banting Collection, Mobile Millinery Museum*. $150-200.

Raspberries and cream-inspired open-weave straw, banded and edged in velvet and topped with Russian veiling. Label: Winner Original, c.1940. *Aline Banting Collection, Mobile Millinery Museum*. $150-200.

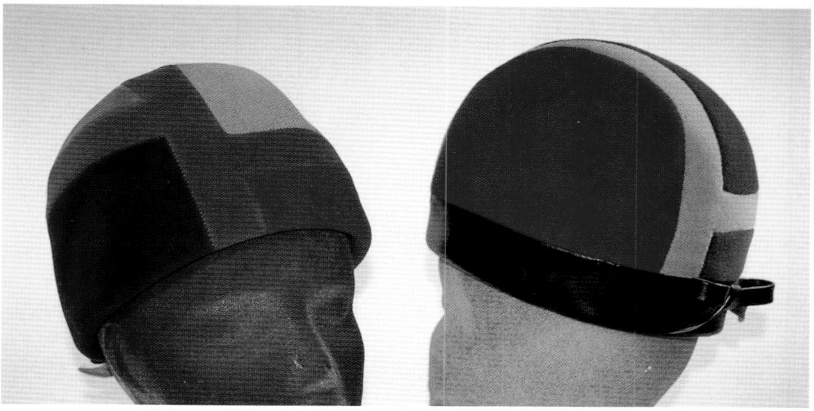

Two 1960s helmets of pieced felt. The red/blue/purple/pink example is a New York Import for Eaton's of Canada. The green/gold/red helmet is banded in black vinyl and bears a Simpson's-Sears label. *Aline Banting Collection, Mobile Millinery Museum*. $150-200 each.

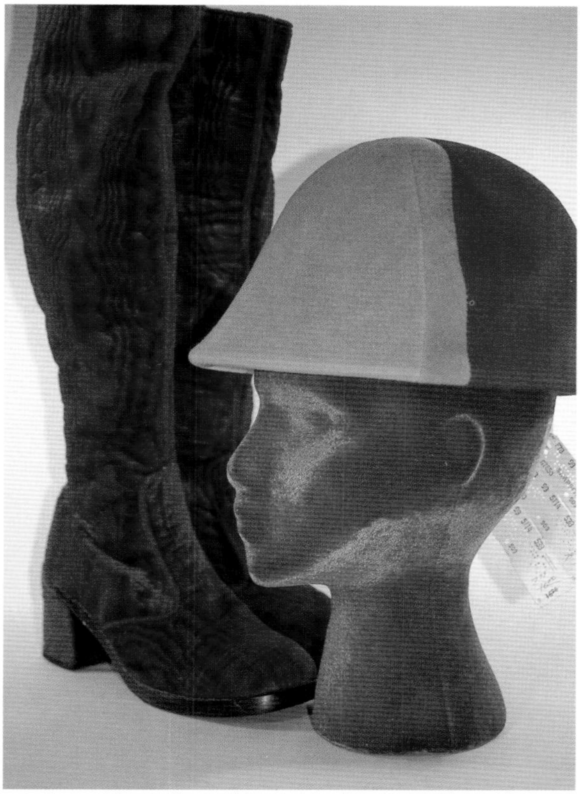

Multicolored felt helmet shown with raspberry suede vamps. *Aline Banting Collection, Mobile Millinery Museum*. Hat: $150-200.

A helmet of pieced felt in elephant gray, camel, and creamy white bears its original sale tag of $7.99, reduced from $16.98. Label: Simpson's Sears. *Aline Banting Collection, Mobile Millinery Museum*. $100-125.

Purple, lavender, and grape velvet toque, c.1968. Shown with patchwork suede vamps. Label: Mr. Arnold Junior. *Aline Banting Collection, Mobile Millinery Museum*. $100-120.

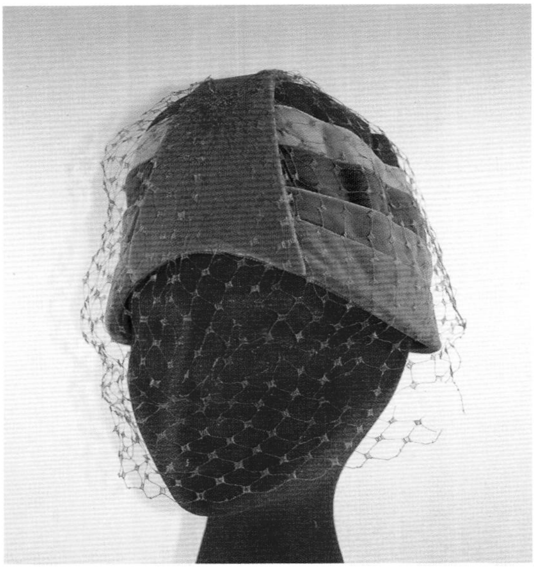

A helmet, c.1960, in five vibrant velvets with chin-length diamond dot veiling. Label: Created by Marilyn. *Aline Banting Collection, Mobile Millinery Museum*. $80-120.

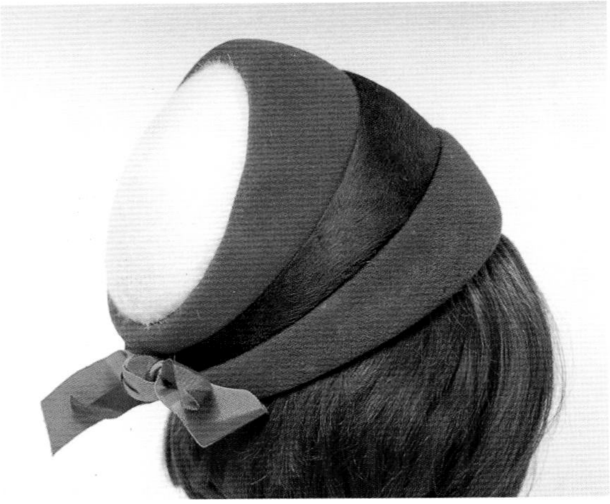

A 1960s toque in alternating bands of brushed and matt felt. The color combination of raspberry, hunter green, and taupe is repeated on the grosgrain, which is knotted at the nape of the neck. Label: Simpson's Canada. *Aline Banting Collection, Mobile Millinery Museum.* $150.

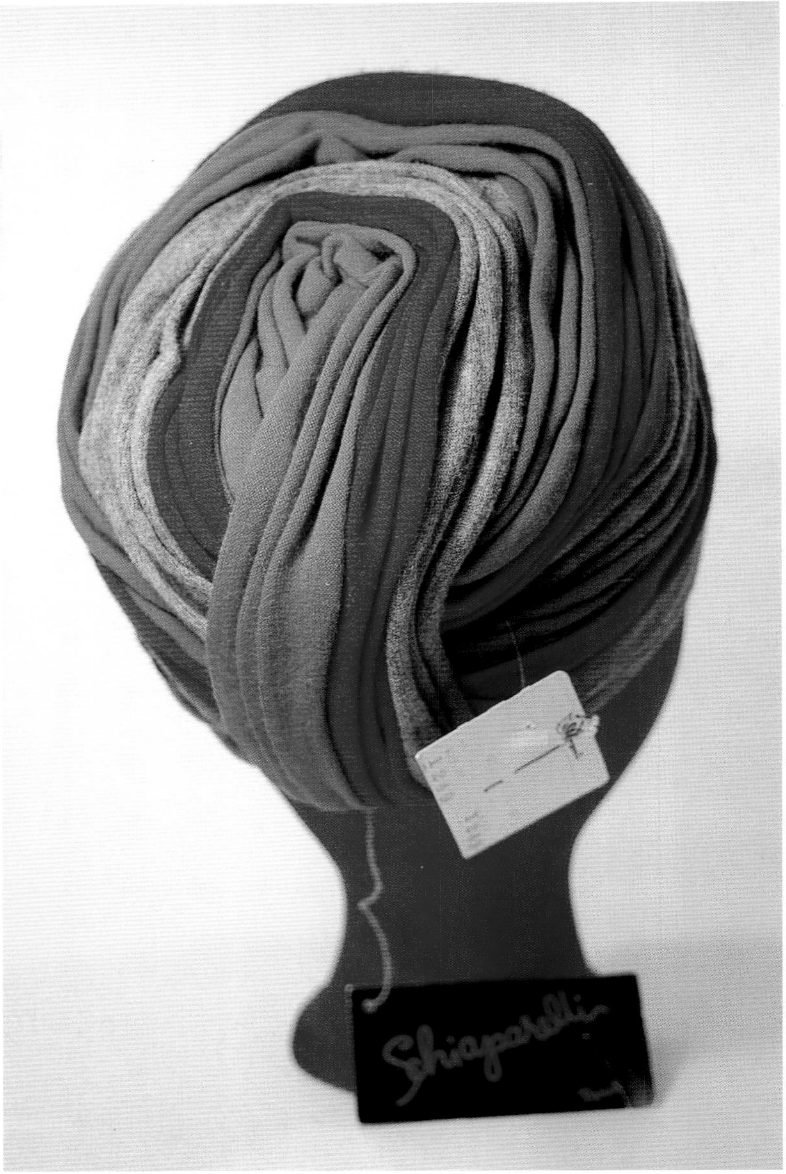

Alternating lengths of turquoise, crimson, and steel-gray jersey have been joined to form a turban, then hand stitched to a stiffened-net, beehive form. Twin labels reveal that this richly colored hat was designed by Schiaparelli and sold through the Hudson's Bay Company. A black and pink cardstock tag depends from the back, revealing Schiaparelli style number S6113. A Morgan's price tag, attached to the crown, shows that the hat was purchased, on sale, for $12.49, from an original price of $25.00. This hat was never worn. *Aline Banting Collection, Mobile Millinery Museum*. $250-350.

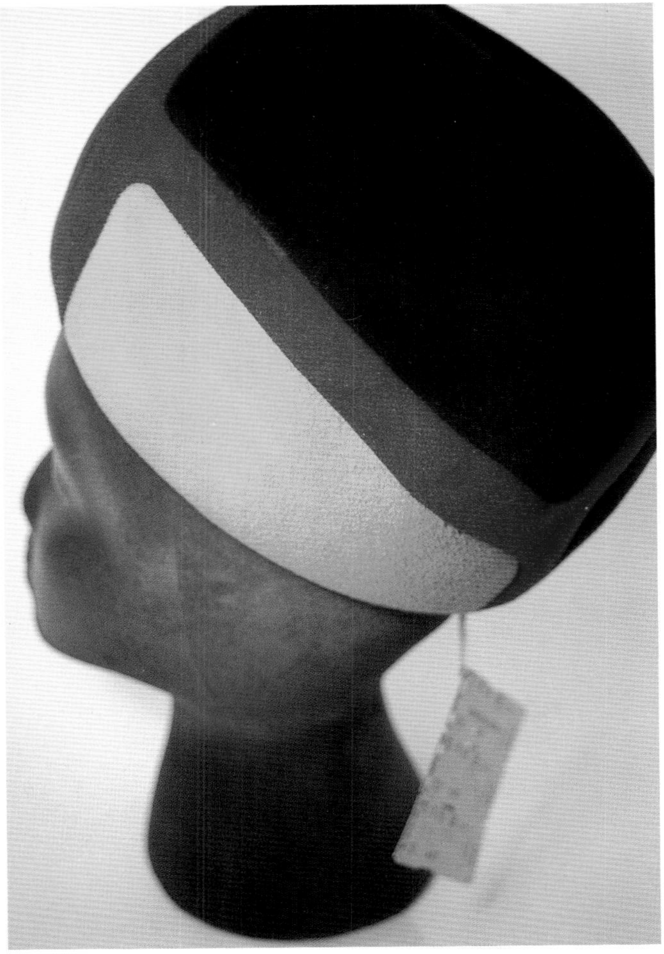

Four irregularly shaped felt panels in cocoa, goldenrod, teal, and hunter green are stitched to a red felt tripod to form a bubble toque. Label: Simpson's Sears. Original style tag and computer-generated price tag are intact. This hat was purchased in the mid-1960s for $7.99, reduced from $16.98. *Aline Banting Collection, Mobile Millinery Museum*. $100-150.

A wool blend of psychedelic colors is pieced and banded in cherry velvet for a stylish turban, c.1965. Label: Jacqueline Original, Toronto. *Aline Banting Collection, Mobile Millinery Museum.* $125.

A halo hat of sand-colored straw is banded in yellow velvet to match the posies that nestle in its brim. Purchased at Robinson's in Hamilton, c.1960, for $15 from $19.95. *Aline Banting Collection, Mobile Millinery Museum*. $125.

A natural straw halo hat is rimmed in black velvet to match unusual black foliage, which winds over the crown and under the brim. Two tiny red bows provide the finishing touch. Label: Miss Carnegie by Hattie Carnegie, c.1968. *Aline Banting Collection, Mobile Millinery Museum*. $225.

A 1930s feather-brimmed halo hat. Label: Liberty Women's Wear, Hamilton. Leather pumps by Golden Pheasant. *Aline Banting Collection, Mobile Millinery Museum.* Hat: $80-100.

Dish hat of coq feathers, c.1950. Label: Originals by Flo-Raye Jrs., New York. *Aline Banting Collection, Mobile Millinery Museum*. $225.

A 1950s turban of orange-print brocade is studded with faux jewels. Label: Cele Logan, New York. Original price $6.99 reduced from $18.99. *Aline Banting Collection, Mobile Millinery Museum*. $80-120.

A magnificent floral bubble toque, in fall colors, by Elizabeth Ford, New York. *Aline Banting Collection, Mobile Millinery Museum*. $150-220.

Detail.

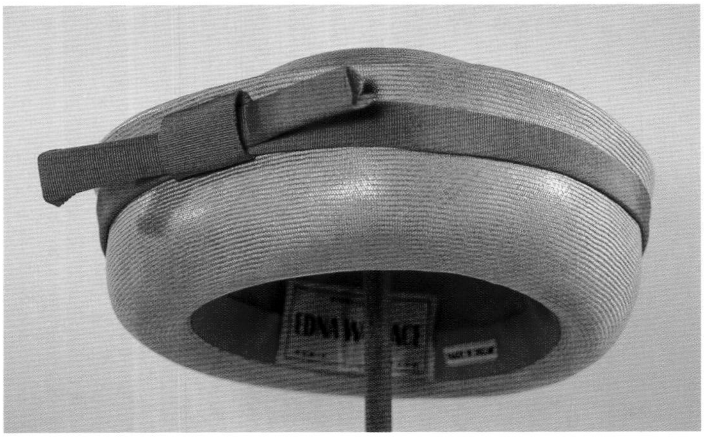

Afternoon straw in cotton-candy pink, banded simply with a matching grosgrain band. Purchased on sale at Eaton's, c.1960, for $9. Label: Millinery Import, Made in England. *Aline Banting Collection, Mobile Millinery Museum*. $80-120.

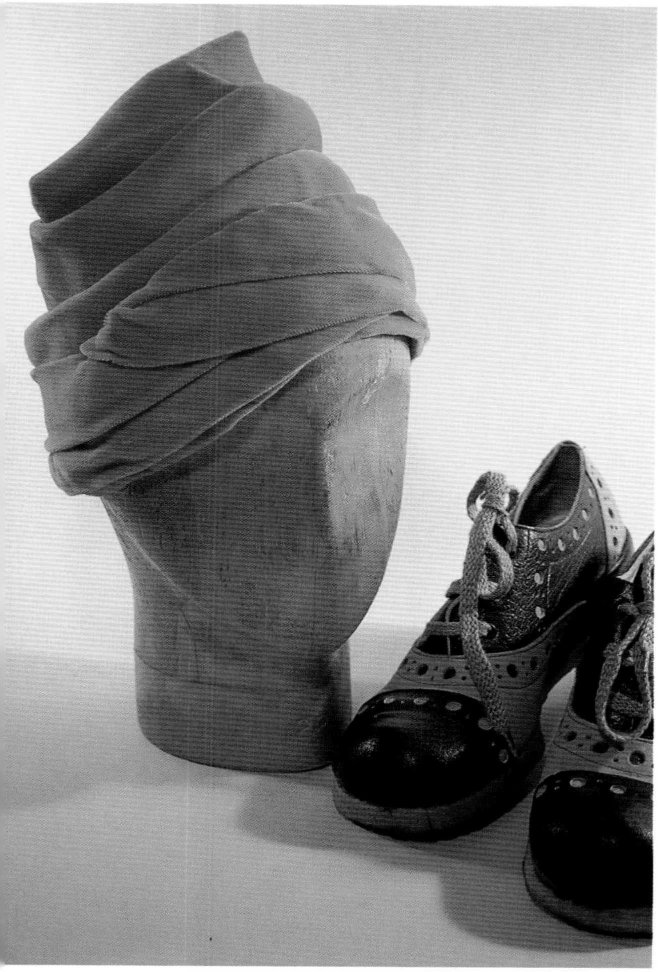

A 1960s paisley velvet pillbox by Elizabeth Ford, New York, is made special with the addition of beads in red, gold, black, and amber. Shown with cranberry, patent leather pumps from the same era. *Aline Banting Collection, Mobile Millinery Museum*. $150.

A 1940s draped velvet turban in pink, for a winter walk, and green saddle shoes. *Aline Banting Collection, Mobile Millinery Museum*. $120.

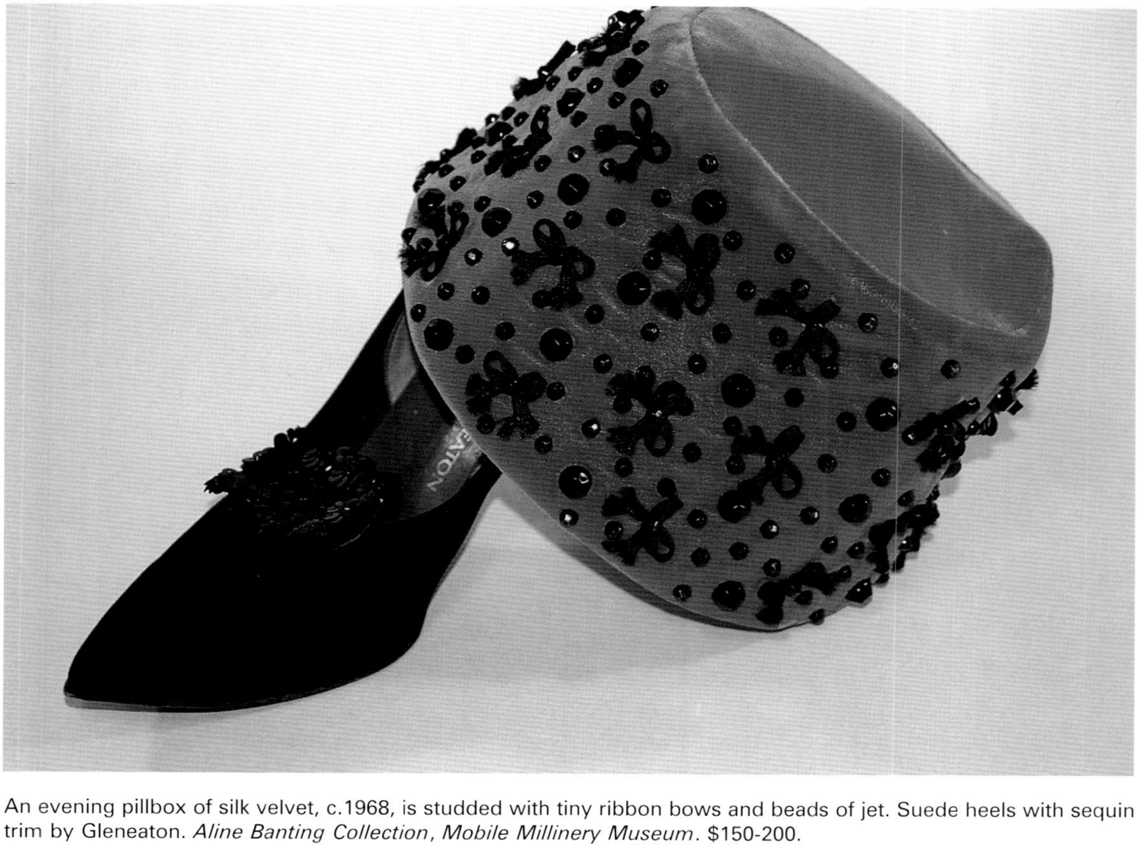

An evening pillbox of silk velvet, c.1968, is studded with tiny ribbon bows and beads of jet. Suede heels with sequin trim by Gleneaton. *Aline Banting Collection, Mobile Millinery Museum*. $150-200.

A beehive turban in silk velvet, c.1965. Italian heels by Pancaldi are flocked with velvet leaves. *Aline Banting Collection, Mobile Millinery Museum*. $75.

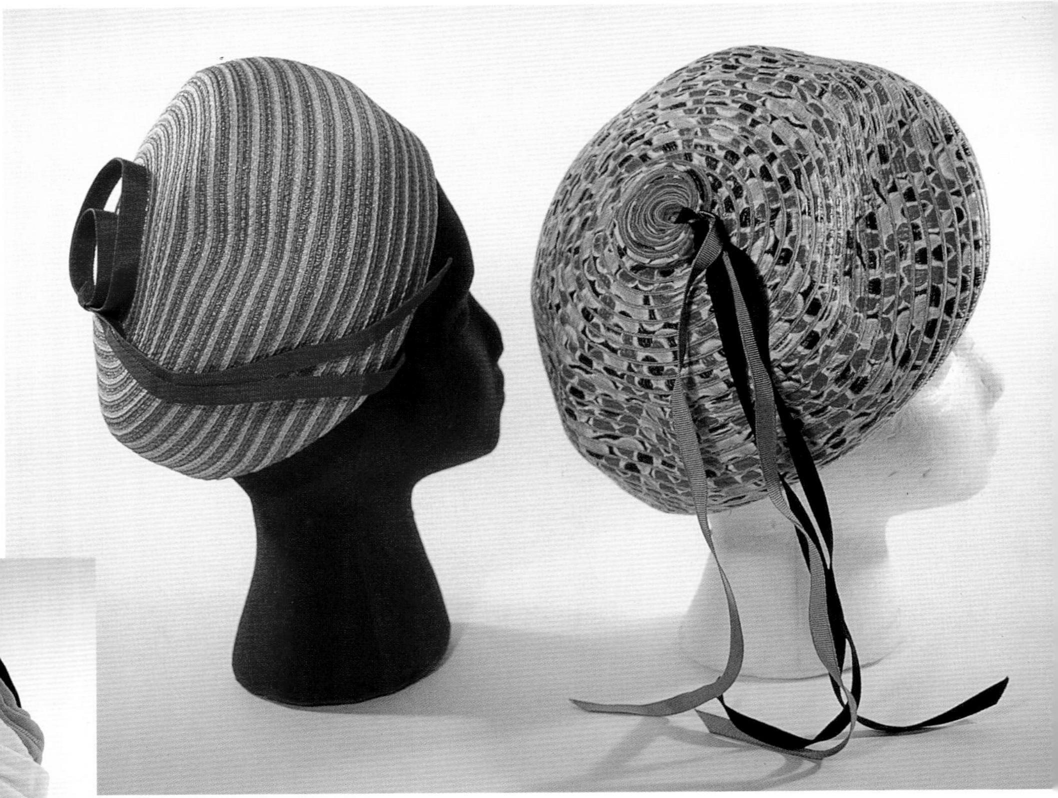

Two similarly constructed bubble toques, c.1965. The first is a ribbon-straw creation by Mr. John, New York, Paris. The second is an unusual multicolored print straw, coiled and shaped from the center crown. Label: Jacqueline Original, Toronto. Purchased at Eaton's Toronto for $2.97, marked down from $5.99, $8, $10.67, and $16. *Aline Banting Collection, Mobile Millinery Museum*. $100-150 each.

A single rose adds a touch of pink to this wildflower-rimmed navy straw. Label: The Raphael-Mack, Hamilton. *Aline Banting Collection, Mobile Millinery Museum.* $100-120.

Circa 1955: Orange straw toque, rimmed with posies. Label: Raphael-Mack, Hamilton. Leather heels by Charles Jourdan, Paris. *Aline Banting Collection, Mobile Millinery Museum*. $125.

A deep 1960s pillbox with silver thread and eyebrow veiling is punctuated with blue stones. Label: Boutique. *Aline Banting Collection, Mobile Millinery Museum*. $75-100.

A satin turban in avocado, turquoise, and royal blue on a stiffened lace form. Label: Lady Charm Original. *Aline Banting Collection, Mobile Millinery Museum*. $125-150.

An interesting variation on the calot. Pumpkin-colored, long-nap, beaver with an ostrich-tip pompom and spider web veiling. Label: Vanity Model. *Aline Banting Collection, Mobile Millinery Museum*. $150.

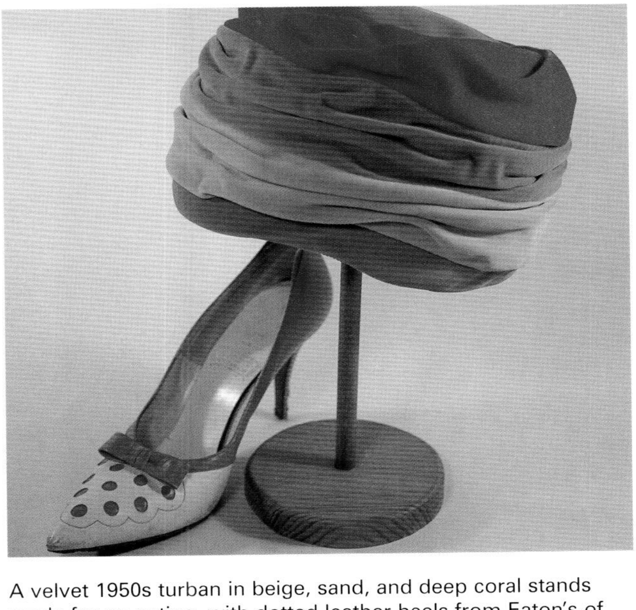

A velvet 1950s turban in beige, sand, and deep coral stands ready for an outing, with dotted leather heels from Eaton's of Canada. *Aline Banting Collection, Mobile Millinery Museum*. $60-80.

A crimson flower pot of plaited wood straw is banded in contrasting navy velvet. *Aline Banting Collection, Mobile Millinery Museum*. $125-225.

Reverse view showing original price tag of $6.99.

A high-crowned confection, woven of black and green cellophane straw. Matching grosgrain band and bow. Label: Harridege's. Original price tag $25. Matching leather kitten heels by Bachelor Girl. *Aline Banting Collection, Mobile Millinery Museum.* Hat: $125-150.

Right:
This blue skyscraper of woven chip straw demonstrates a Puritan influence. Green grosgrain band with navy trapunto stitching. Label: Peggy Claire Original. *Aline Banting Collection, Mobile Millinery Museum.* $150-200.

This widebrim straw in brilliant orange was purchased in the 1960s for $4, reduced from $12. *Aline Banting Collection, Mobile Millinery Museum.* $100-150.

Reverse view. Sales tag reads $6.99.

Italian-made fedora of hunter-green plush beaver, c.1968. Label: Millinery Import for Eaton's. *Aline Banting Collection, Mobile Millinery Museum*. $125-150.

A 1950s picture hat of woven crinoline straw. Label: Made in Switzerland. *Aline Banting Collection, Mobile Millinery Museum*. $100-150.

Circa 1950: A carefully pieced, aqua and sea-green straw. Label: André, Haute Mode, Paris. 49 Rue De Richelieu. *Aline Banting Collection, Mobile Millinery Museum*. $125-150.

A high-crowned boater with swinging sixties attitude. Chenille-centered flowers of cotton and organza in blue, yellow, orange, and white rest stop a brim, which is rimmed in yellow grosgrain. Label: Eaton's Fashions. Original price: $22. *Aline Banting Collection, Mobile Millinery Museum*. $150.

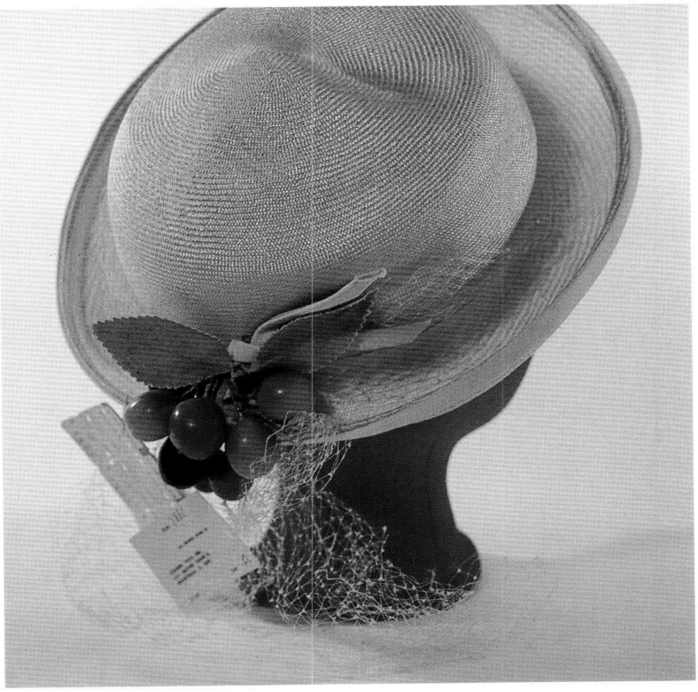

Diamond-dot veiling bands this 1950s yellow straw and trails from beneath a cluster of papier-mâché grapes at center back. Label: Charmaine Original, Montreal-Paris (Size 22, Charm Hats Inc., 651 Notre Dame W., Montreal). Eaton's tag shows an ultimate sale price of $3.97, reduced from $15. *Aline Banting Collection, Mobile Millinery Museum*. $150.

Grapes and summer flowers encircle a 1930s hat with a hint of orange veiling. Label: Duby, New York, size 22 1/2. *Aline Banting Collection, Mobile Millinery Museum*. $125-150.

A 1930s navy straw sports vines, berries, and orchids. Open-toed shoes of genuine cobra. *Aline Banting Collection, Mobile Millinery Museum*. Hat: $125-150.

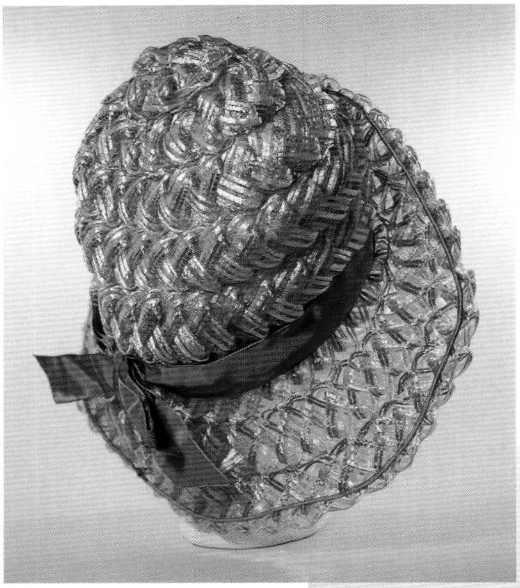

Back view.

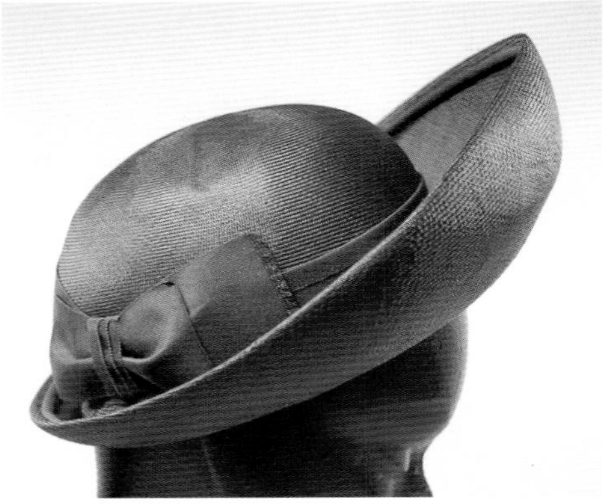

A jaunty, scoop-brimmed, halo hat, c.1965, is banded in navy grosgrain and decorated with an off-center bow. Label: Eve-Marie, Paris, New York. *Aline Banting Collection, Mobile Millinery Museum*. $80-100.

A 1960s wide brim cellophane straw. Label: Made expressly for Harridge's, Toronto. Final price tag: 2 for $9.99. Original price tag: $35. *Aline Banting Collection, Mobile Millinery Museum.* $125.

A stunning confection of poppies, c.1968. Label: Boutique, New York, Montreal. Suede heels by Charles Jourdan, Paris. *Aline Banting Collection, Mobile Millinery Museum*. Hat: $150.

Circa 1968: Ten gallon hat of creamy white felt and Mongolian lamb. Label: Michel Robichaud. *Aline Banting Collection, Mobile Millinery Museum*. $300.

Detail.

This 1930s stiffened felt resembles a cornucopia. Trimmed with pearl-tipped satin petals. *Aline Banting Collection, Mobile Millinery Museum.* $125.

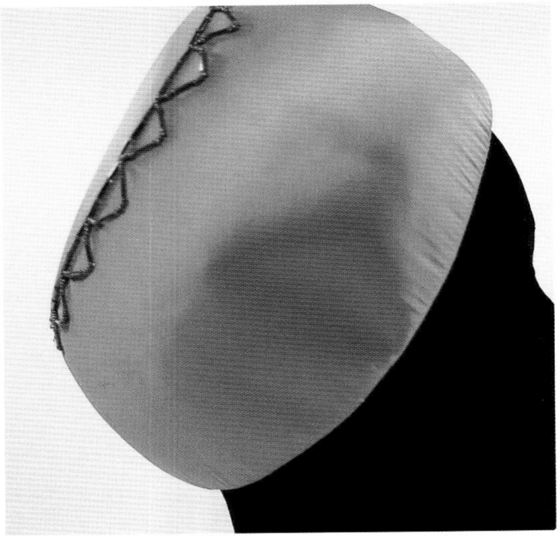

The seam-line of this beautifully shaped, satin bubble toque is outlined in bronze and pewter seed and bugle beads. Label: Nadelle, Montreal. *Aline Banting Collection, Mobile Millinery Museum.* $60-80.

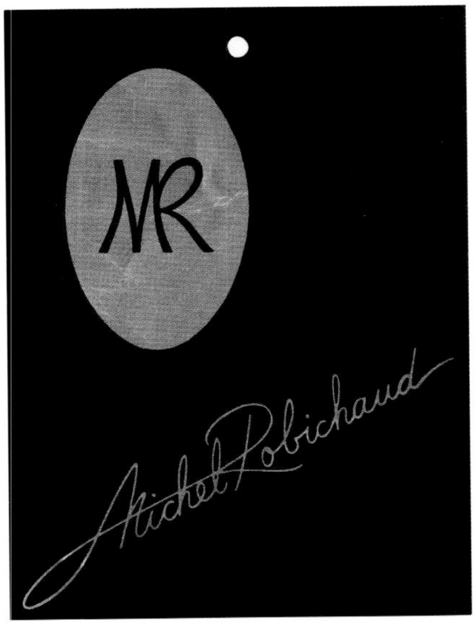

Michel Robichaud label.

A 1930s revival bonnet with matching pink velvet band. *Aline Banting Collection, Mobile Millinery Museum.* $75-100.

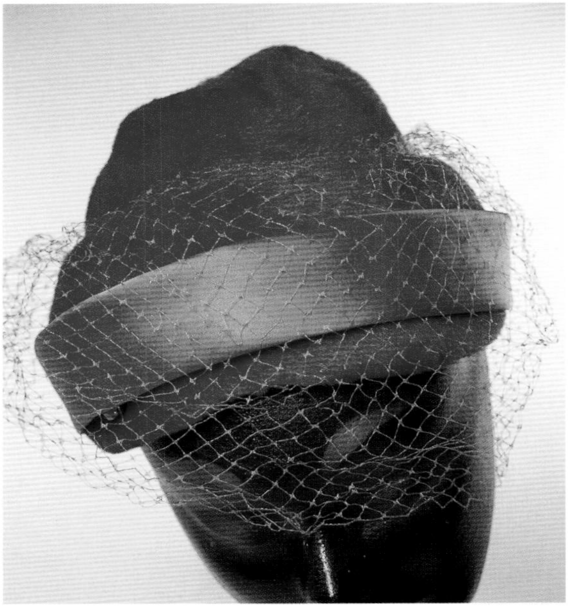

A crimson toque of long-nap beaver is banded with satin and graced with diamond-dot veiling. Purchased at Robinson's of Hamilton, c.1960, for $9.00, reduced from $15.95. Label: Brae Burn, New York, Montreal. *Aline Banting Collection, Mobile Millinery Museum.* $80.

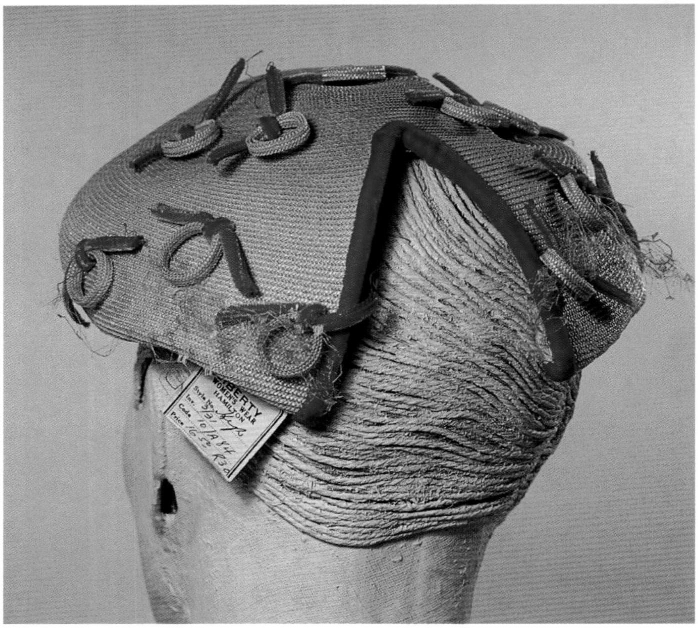

An apple-green Milan straw by Eve Marie parts at the back to allow for a chignon. Straw rings are tied to the crown with strands of cherry velvet. Purchased at Liberty Women's Wear, Hamilton, c.1960, for $16.50. *Aline Banting Collection, Mobile Millinery Museum.* $150.

Circa 1965: A leaf-patterned gold lamé pillbox, purchased at Robinson's for $6.99, reduced from $10.95. Matching black and gold stilettos. *Aline Banting Collection, Mobile Millinery Museum.* $80-100.

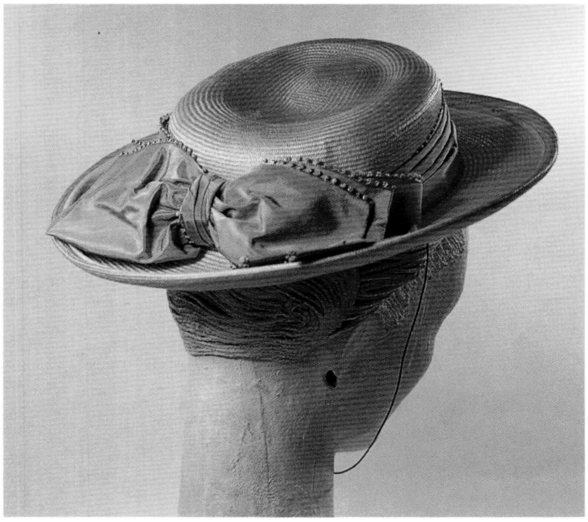

Circa 1960: A triple crushed bow of picot-edged satin ribbon adorns a sand-colored straw schoolgirl boater. Label: Creation by André. *Aline Banting Collection, Mobile Millinery Museum.* $80-100.

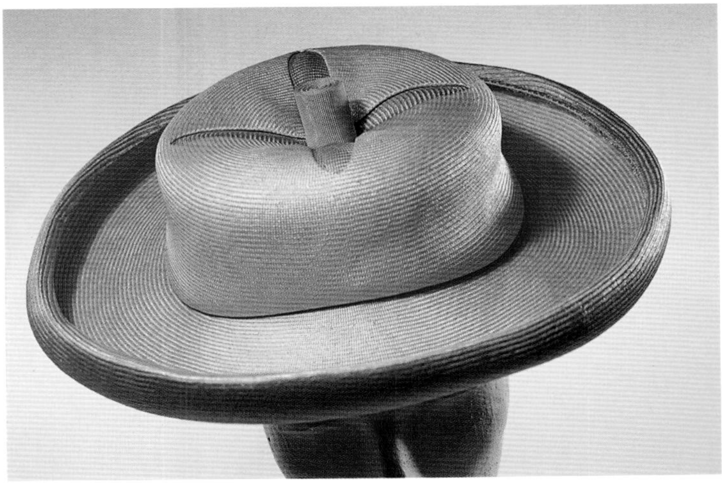

A halo hat in cotton-candy pink and powder-blue sprouts a topknot of coiled grosgrain. Label: Eaton's Fashions. *Aline Banting Collection, Mobile Millinery Museum*. $100-125.

A long-nap felt, banded and button-tufted, with coffee and cream-colored grosgrain ribbon. *Aline Banting Collection, Mobile Millinery Museum.* $60-80.

This unusual, orange straw pillbox is segmented by narrow bands of black satin. Label: Eaton's Fashions. Sold as a sample in the 1960s for $2.97, reduced from $10.99. *Aline Banting Collection, Mobile Millinery Museum*. $80.

A sand-colored straw from the 1930s by Raphael-Mack of Hamilton. Straw blades are banded narrowly in multicolored striped ribbon. Original coiled-metal hatpin. *Aline Banting Collection, Mobile Millinery Museum.* Hat and pin: $150.

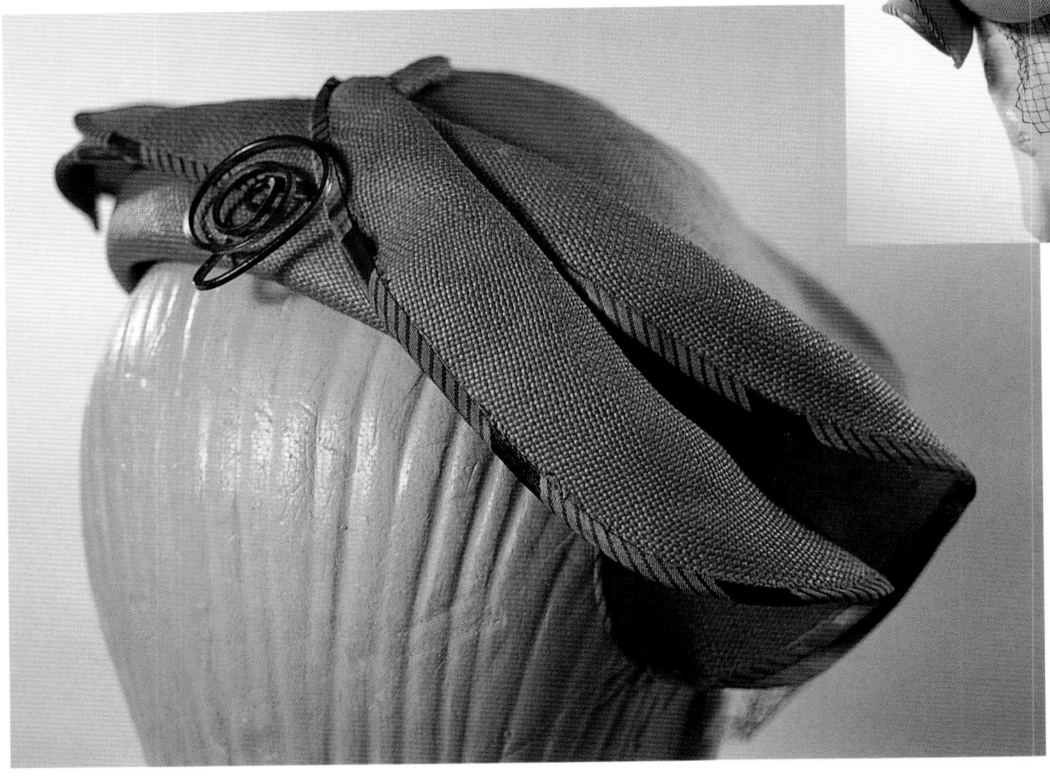

Back detail.

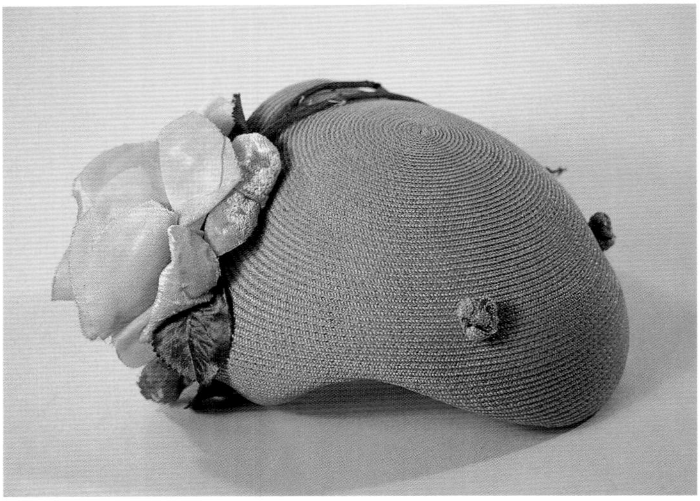

An eggshell of powder blue straw is difficult to resist with its silk and velvet rose with realistic looking, thorned stem. Label: Devonshire Model. *Aline Banting Collection, Mobile Millinery Museum.* $125-150.

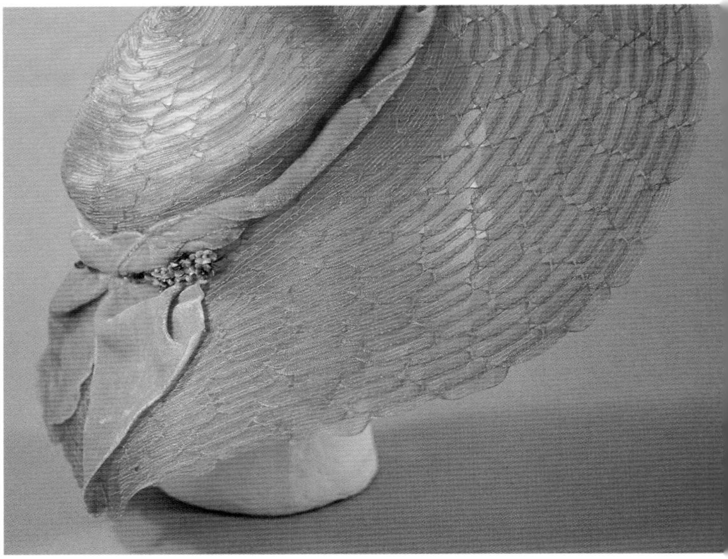

Horsehair Pamela banded with salmon-colored velvet and fitted with a satin extension at the inner crown. Label: American Hat Co. Ltd., Toronto. *Aline Banting Collection, Mobile Millinery Museum.* $250-300.

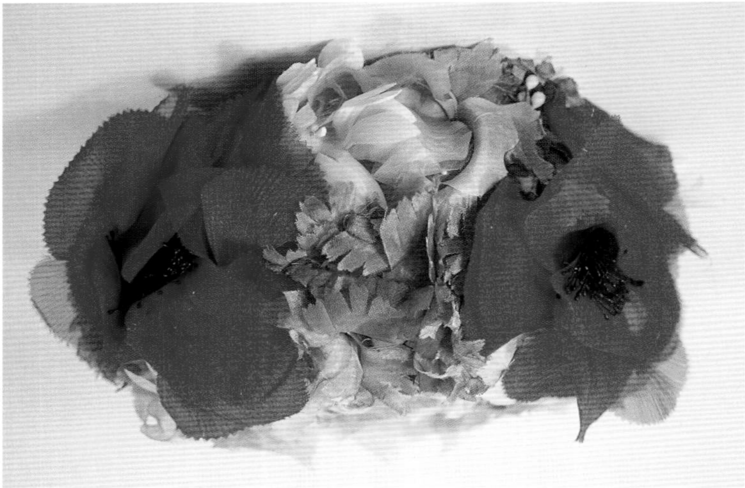

This multicolored floral on a buckram frame appears to have been homemade. *Aline Banting Collection, Mobile Millinery Museum*. $40-50.

A Milan straw cap of creamy beige is banded in rich, green velvet. Clusters of yellow velvet campanula anchor a small diamond-dot veil. Label: A Peggy Model. *Aline Banting Collection, Mobile Millinery Museum.* $125-175.

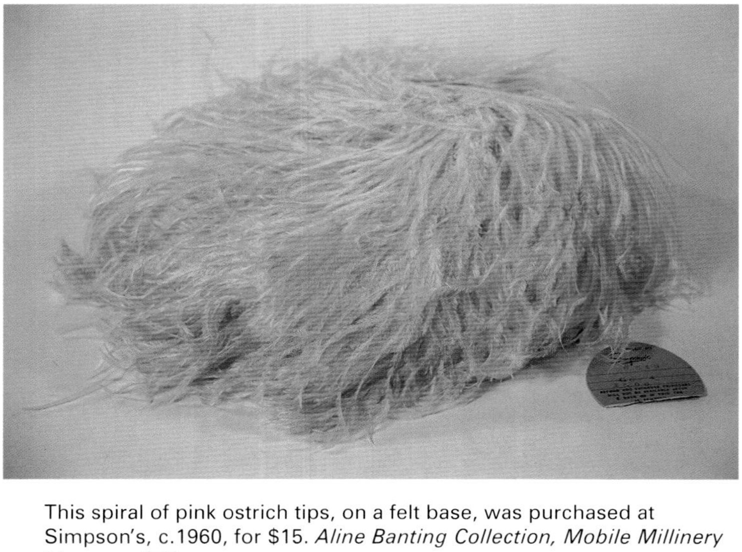

This spiral of pink ostrich tips, on a felt base, was purchased at Simpson's, c.1960, for $15. *Aline Banting Collection, Mobile Millinery Museum*. $80.

A skillfully crafted straw from the 1960s aligns a slanted brim, bow, and crown. The unusual color combination of caramel and squash is surprisingly pleasing to the eye. Label: Elizabeth Ford, New York. *Aline Banting Collection, Mobile Millinery Museum*. $150-250.

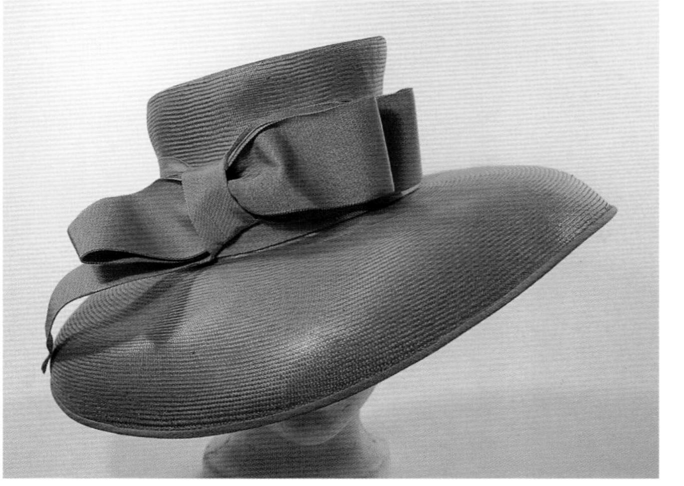

A black and white straw topper, light as air, is embroidered in a leaf pattern. A cascade of white blossoms nestles in a bed of crisp, black, leaves. Label: A Peggy Claire Original. Original price, $25. *Aline Banting Collection, Mobile Millinery Museum*. $150.

A pink straw saucer, edged in velvet, creates back interest with bigemminal orchids. Checkerboard veiling drops to the brow line. Label: an original by Dajon, New York. *Aline Banting Collection, Mobile Millinery Museum*. $150-180.

A Milan-straw topper, in slate and confederate gray, is banded with matching velvet ribbon, fitted with a chin-length veil, and finished with fabric roses in red, pink, yellow, and oyster. An occasional tiny rhinestone adds sparkle. Label: Original Leslie Monroe, Paris, New York. Purchased in the 1940s at Liberty Women's Wear, Hamilton for $3, reduced from $16.50. *Aline Banting Collection, Mobile Millinery Museum*. $150-175.

Olive-green ostrich fronds are layered on the brim of a 1950s picture hat to surround a crown of poultry feathers, dyed a yellowy-green. Matching silk stilettos by Rayne. Hat purchased at Eaton's for $11.25, reduced from $22.50. *Aline Banting Collection, Mobile Millinery Museum*. $250-350.

Close up showing fabric-covered under-brim.

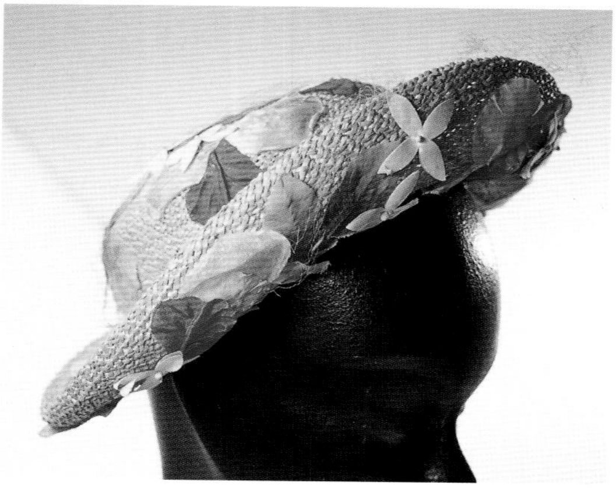

Left:
A flowered halo hat in summer straw by Schiaparelli. *Aline Banting Collection, Mobile Millinery Museum.* $225-250.

Right:
This 1960s toque of floral-print chiffon is almost weightless. Label: Duby, New York. *Aline Banting Collection, Mobile Millinery Museum.* $75-100.

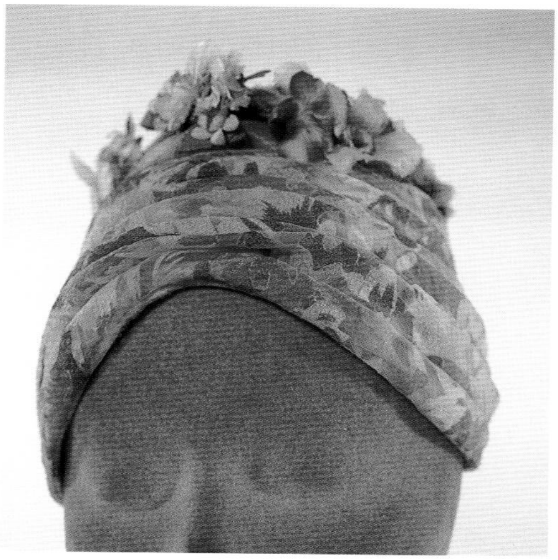

A 1960s floral bubble toque with green velvet pears. Label: Hudson's Bay Company. *Aline Banting, Collection, Mobile Millinery Museum*. $50-75.

Electric-green summer straw banded with grosgrain. Purchased on sale, c.1968. *Aline Banting Collection, Mobile Millinery Museum*. $80.

Velvet coins dangle from a deep 1960s pillbox of cerise satin; a throwback to the early, Eastern custom of covering a woman's hat with silver coins to display a family's wealth. Label: Mr. Phil. *Aline Banting Collection, Mobile Millinery Museum.* $125.

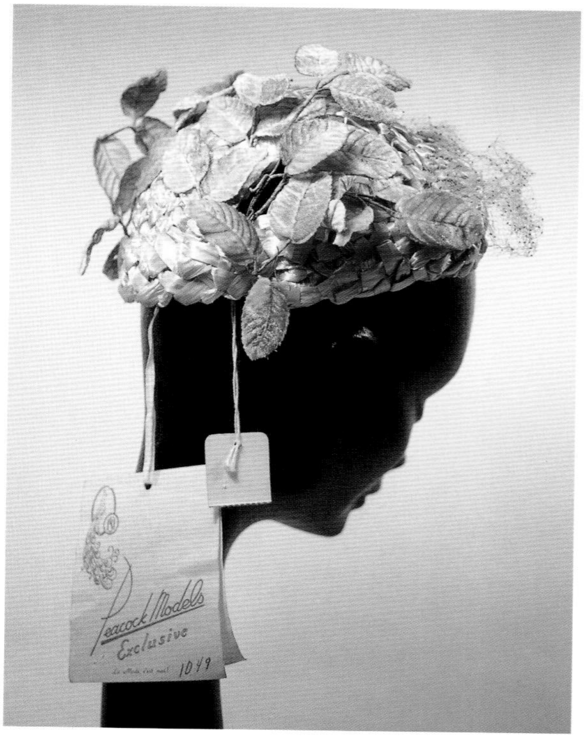

A woven cellophane straw sports nose-length green veiling with tiny seed-like dots. Variegated velvet leaves ascend from wiry vines. Label: Peacock Model Exclusive. *Aline Banting Collection, Mobile Millinery Museum*. $200-250.

Evening hat of paisley velvet, hand-beaded and adorned with a raspberry-colored pipe cleaner. Label: André. Snakeskin shoes by Vanity Fair. *Aline Banting Collection, Mobile Millinery Museum*. Hat: $125-150.

A schoolgirl Breton, woven of turquoise, cream, coffee, and chocolate cellophane straw. A chocolate velvet bow marks the center front. Purchased for $5 in the mid-sixties. *Aline Banting Collection, Mobile Millinery Museum*. $100-125.

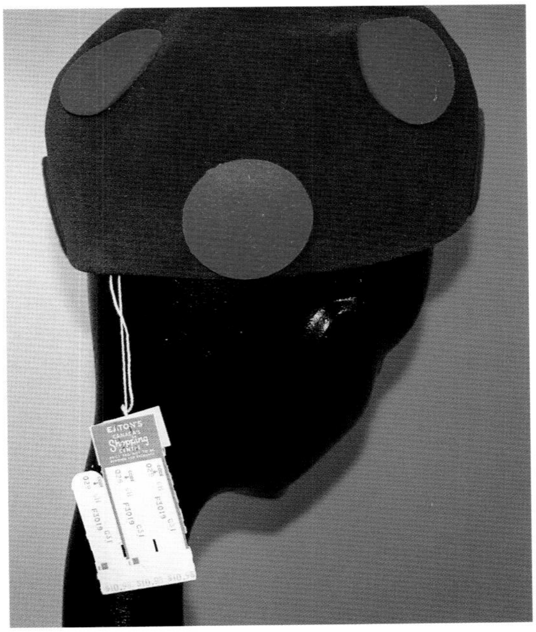

Giant felt polka-dots add cheer to a velour bubble toque. Purchased at Eaton's, c.1965, for $10.98. *Aline Banting Collection, Mobile Millinery Museum*. $75-100.

A frame of wired black chenille supports vines of variegated leaves in shades of pink, bronze, and raspberry. Pink, pearlized, papier-mâché buds are sprinkled throughout. *Aline Banting Collection, Mobile Millinery Museum*. $100-150.

A rhinestone ball on a grosgrain chevron adds punch to this simple woven straw, c.1940. Label: Piko, Paris, New York. Matching suede pumps are labeled "Gold Cross Shoes". *Aline Banting Collection, Mobile Millinery Museum*. $120-150.

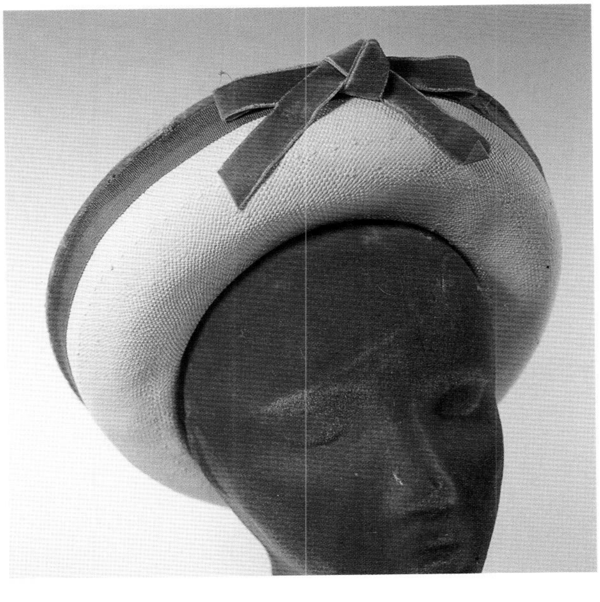

Velvet-trimmed halo Breton fashioned of Panama straw. Label: Jonquil Original. *Aline Banting Collection, Mobile Millinery Museum*. $125.

A dressy boater of lemon-yellow straw is banded with peach-colored rayon. Purchased in the mid-sixties @ 2 for $10. *Aline Banting Collection, Mobile Millinery Museum*. $125.

This early 1960s bouclé straw pillbox is draped with pleated ecru and taupe organdie. A rhinestone chevron, with two stones missing, ornaments the narrow brim, which has been turned back on the crown. *Aline Banting Collection, Mobile Millinery Museum*. $100-125.

Modified homburg, c.1965; double-banded in stiffened fabric. Label: Robin New York. *Aline Banting Collection, Mobile Millinery Museum*. $125.

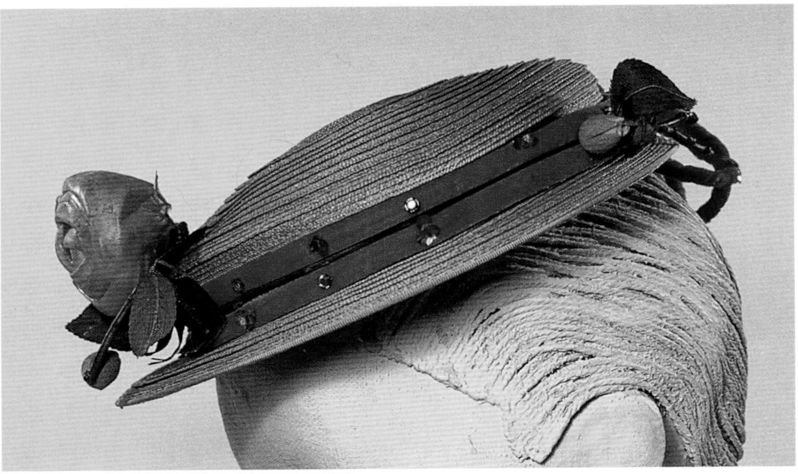

An exquisitely crafted, tan-colored straw boasts a lacquered-fabric rose bud and narrow double band of sequin and rhinestone-studded, cherry-colored velvet. Label: Designed and handmade for Raphael-Mack, Hamilton. *Aline Banting Collection, Mobile Millinery Museum*. $75-125.

Summer straw halo sombrero in beige and gray. Label: M'Sieu Léon, Paris, Roma, New York. *Aline Banting Collection, Mobile Millinery Museum*. $80-100.

A spiral-shaped, 1930s, Milan straw is edged in two-toned blue silk posies. Label: The Raphael-Mack, Hamilton. *Aline Banting Collection, Mobile Millinery Museum.* $120-150.

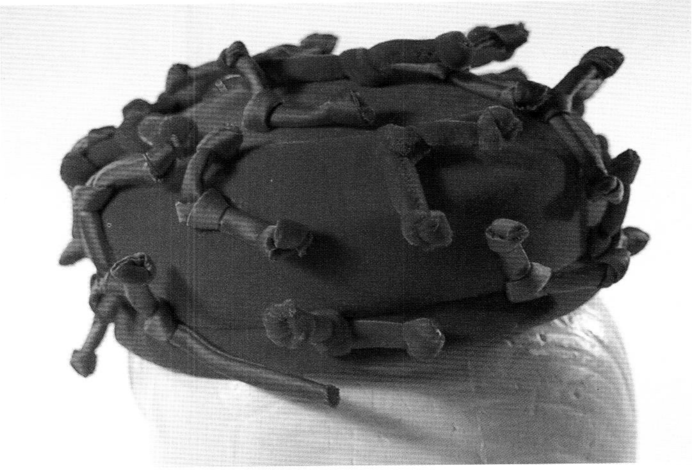

Cords of perfectly matched satin and velvet are *knotted to make an unusual trim for a 1960s pillbox*. Label: Bellini. *Aline Banting Collection, Mobile Millinery Museum.* $150.

Interior, showing Bellini Label.

Circa 1968: A cheerful straw topper by Maggy Plouffe is brimming with abstract roses and star flowers. *Aline Banting Collection, Mobile Millinery Museum*. $150-200.

This widebrim woven straw with narrow grosgrain band has great texture. Label: Boutique Kates, Canada. Original "Right House" price tag shows a sale price of $6.00, reduced from $12.00. *Aline Banting Collection, Mobile Millinery Museum*. $125-150.

Poor boy cap, c.1968, in three shades of green velvet. Trapunto stitching on visor. Original Eaton's tag shows $18. Label: Martine, Paris. *Aline Banting Collection, Mobile Millinery Museum.* $125-150.

Betty wears a peach-toned, 1950s, shade hat by Maggy Plouffe, purchased for $3.99, reduced from $14.00. *Aline Banting Collection, Mobile Millinery Museum.* $75-125.

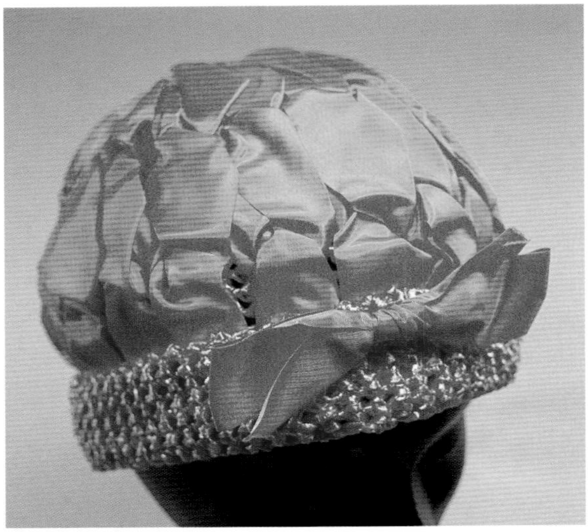

Satin ribbon is woven though the crown of a raffia straw skull cap. These were produced in several colors. *Aline Banting Collection, Mobile Millinery Museum.* $40-60.

The brim of this taupe-to-brown velvet and organza floral is cut away at the center back, allowing the hair to be curled into a roll. *Aline Banting Collection, Mobile Millinery Museum*. $60-80.

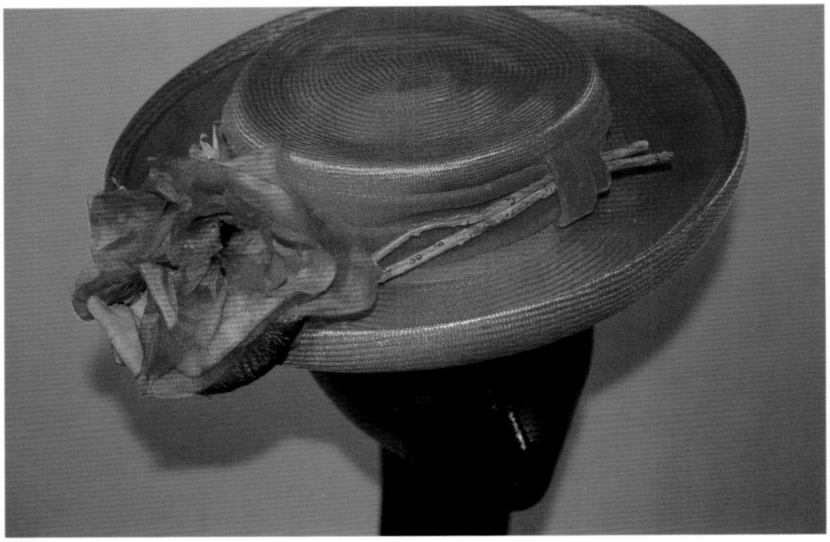

A 1940s, shallow-crowned, Christmas red, boater. The silk and chiffon rose is complete with realistic thorns. *Aline Banting Collection, Mobile Millinery Museum.* $150-200.

A navy straw picture hat from the late 1940s brims with red, yellow, white, and blue silk flowers. Label: Schiaparelli, Paris. Size 22. *Aline Banting Collection, Mobile Millinery Museum*. $250-300.

This draped turban by Simpson's is exquisitely trimmed with velvet fruit in rich jewel tones. *Aline Banting Collection, Mobile Millinery Museum*. $75-100.

A band of purple grosgrain separates a crown and brim of contrasting straw. Label: Mr. Fredericks Young Modes. *Aline Banting Collection, Mobile Millinery Museum*. $150.

Natural straw picture hat, ringed in red, white, yellow, and blue. *Aline Banting Collection, Mobile Millinery Museum.* $80-120.

A tailored, ribbon bow for a grass-green, factory straw. *Aline Banting Collection, Mobile Millinery Museum.* $75-100.

Ascot Hats

"Wagon wheels carry us into summer. Exclusive importations in our French Room are suitable for June horse shows, garden parties, luncheons, teas, and dinner dances."

— *Advertisement for Simpson's millinery dept, Mayfair Magazine, Spring 1935*

"We used to buy extravagant hats at *Eaton's* and wear them to the running of *Queen's Plate*. We'd check the papers the next day, and if we hadn't been photographed, we'd return the hats to *Eaton's*. They had a no-questions-asked return policy.

— *Anonymous*

Ascot, Belmont, the *Kentucky Derby*, and the *Queen's Plate* have always been associated with high fashion and millinery style. Traditionally, men were expected to attend in nothing short of a gray silk top hat and women would select a stylish chapeau that reflected the latest fashion trend.

During the Edwardian period, women's hats seen at Ascot were so extravagant that they developed their own identity. *Black Ascot*, held in 1910 following the death of King Edward VII, was the inspiration for the black and white costuming in the *My Fair Lady* Ascot scene. In the 1970s, designers took Ascot hats to the extreme as they competed for photo opportunities.

Costume Museum of Canada postcard depicting a straw hat, c.1909, worn to the horse races in Winnipeg, MB. *Photo by Doug Dealy*.

Barbie® dressed for *Black Ascot* as Eliza Dolittle. Her costume is a replica of that worn by Audrey Hepburn in *My Fair Lady*. The white satin hat with feathers, flowers, and striped ribbon is worn over a boudoir cap of a floral-trimmed, white lace, boudoir cap. *Private Collection.*

A millennium interpretation of the *Black Ascot* hat, designed by the author. This variation on the dish is completely covered with domestic poultry feathers in white, with a splash of black. The inner crown is edged in black velvet. *Private Collection*.

Cellophane strands, interspersed with black turkey feathers, catch the light and move with the slightest air current to produce a dazzling "special occasion" hat. Hat, and matching muff, designed by the author. *Private Collection*.

This tan straw shade hat is equipped with an inner crown of matching satin with a silk ribbon and navy drawstring. The removable, navy grosgrain, band and bow are secured with a large snap. The label, which reads "Tailored by Okun", pictures an equestrienne. *Mobile Millinery Museum*. $250.

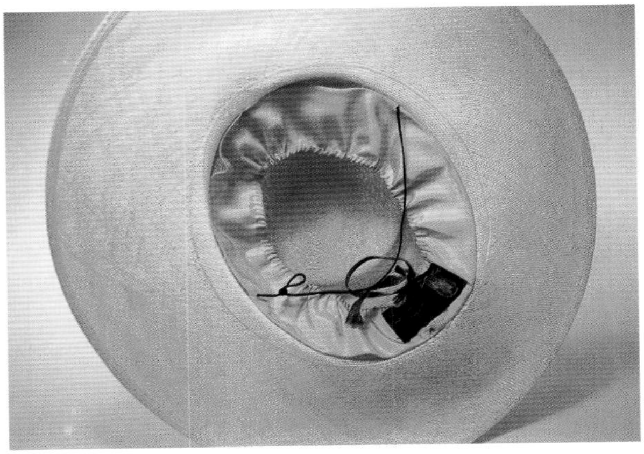

Interior.

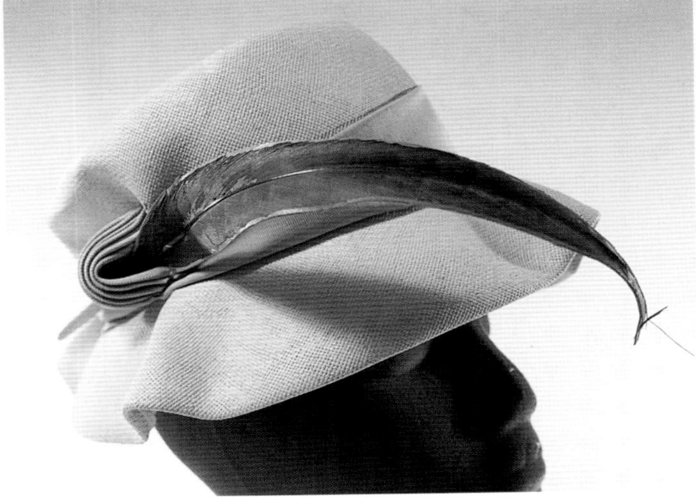

Circa 1930: A leghorn straw with pinch-pleated brim is banded in aqua grosgrain. Grosgrain chevrons are layered to provide support for a magnificent, bonded-to-suede, aqua quill. The silk label of this exquisite topper illustrates a young woman on horseback, carrying a hatbox. (Size 22). *Mobile Millinery Museum*. $125.

Today, the tradition continues, with many milliners focusing their design efforts on such special occasion hats alone. Australian milliner, Georgina Conheady, claims the majority of her clients are "race goers".

Men's hat makers each have their own interpretation of the Ascot hat. The Ascot hat by *Stetson*, a classic western style, appears on the *Stetson* website in tomato red while the *Harley-Davidson*® Ascot hat, in cotton or leather, resembles a jockey cap. Some manufacturers, however, more appropriately apply the name to a gray silk top hat.

A magnificent bicorn in yellow straw by Philip Warde. Green velvet ribbon loops through the crown/brim join and makes its way to the straw flowers that adorn each corner. Green velvet ribbon also trails from the center back. *Courtesy of Joy Drew*. $400-500.

Chicken coop veiling enhances the appeal of a brilliant, orange straw by Philip Warde. *Courtesy of Joy Drew*. $350-450.

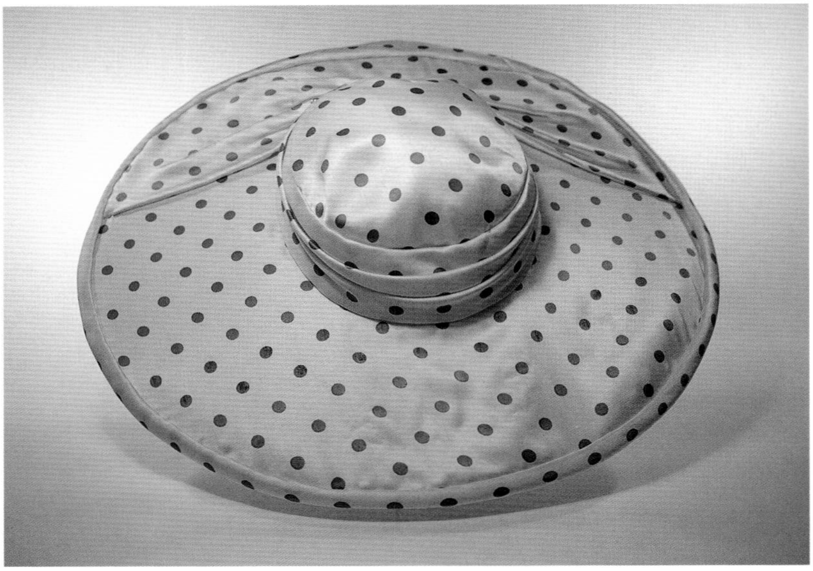

The crown of this stunning polka-dot silk picture hat is pleated and extended to form a self-fabric bow at the back. Label: Jo-Anne Designer, 1566 Yonge St., Toronto. *Eleanor Auld Collection, Mobile Millinery Museum*. $300-350.

Reverse view. A giant black velvet bow at the nape of the neck secures an upturned back brim.

Candy blossoms add whimsy to a serious black straw widebrim. *Mobile Millinery Museum.* $400-450.

A stunning combination of black and crimson on a widebrim straw. *Ascot Collection, Mobile Millinery Museum.* $450-550.

Christmas Hats

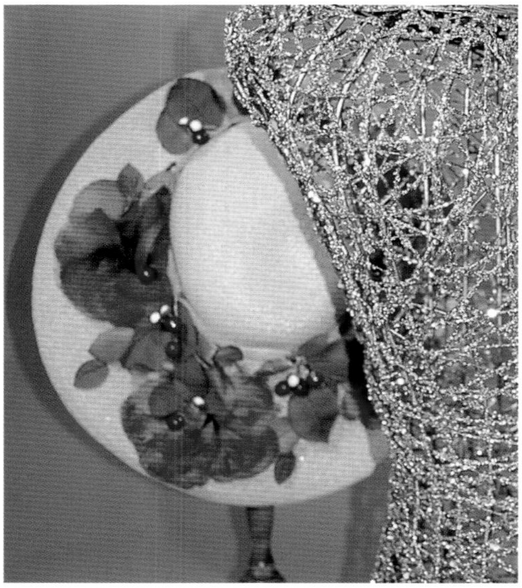

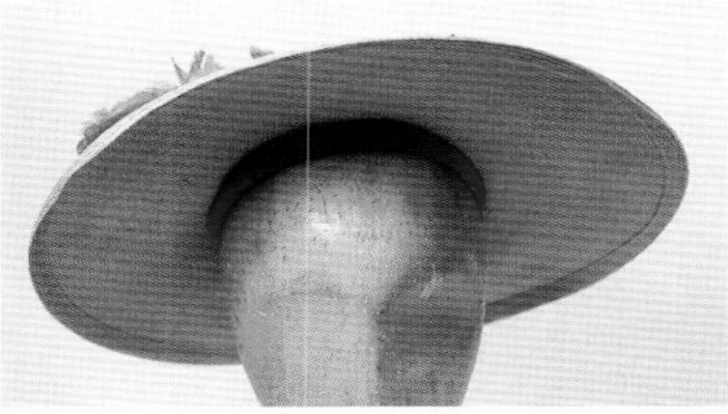

View of under-brim.

An inner band of crimson velvet supports a late 1940s sewn straw picture hat, decorated about the brim in red and green. Price tag: Northway's, $11.95 *Aline Banting Collection, Mobile Millinery Museum.*

Back view showing cranberries and silk roses.

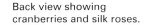

Winter berries and red velvet bows adorn a simple Christmas hat, c.1930. Matching gray suede open-toes were handmade for The Right House. *Aline Banting Collection, Mobile Millinery Museum*. Hat: $150.

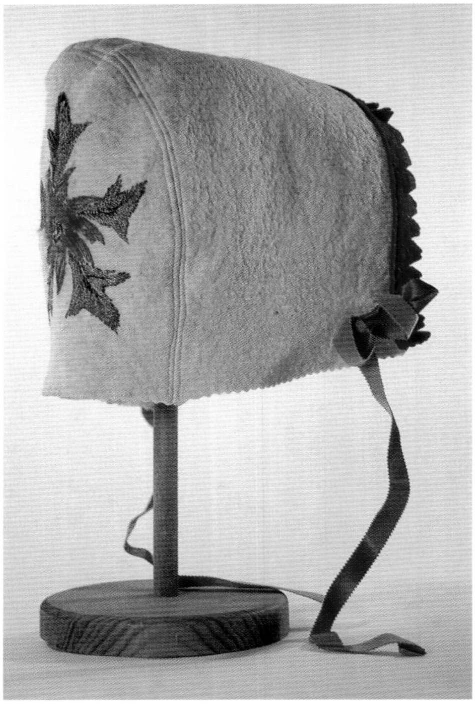

Wool felt Christmas bonnet for a Victorian child. Ribbon ties are of satin-backed velvet. Hand-embroidered poinsettia at center back. *Christmas Collection, Mobile Millinery Museum*. $250.

A cluster of cherries and an evergreen tree add whimsy to this red and green felt, Christmas hat. Grosgrain ribbon trim. *Christmas Collection, Mobile Millinery Museum*. $225.

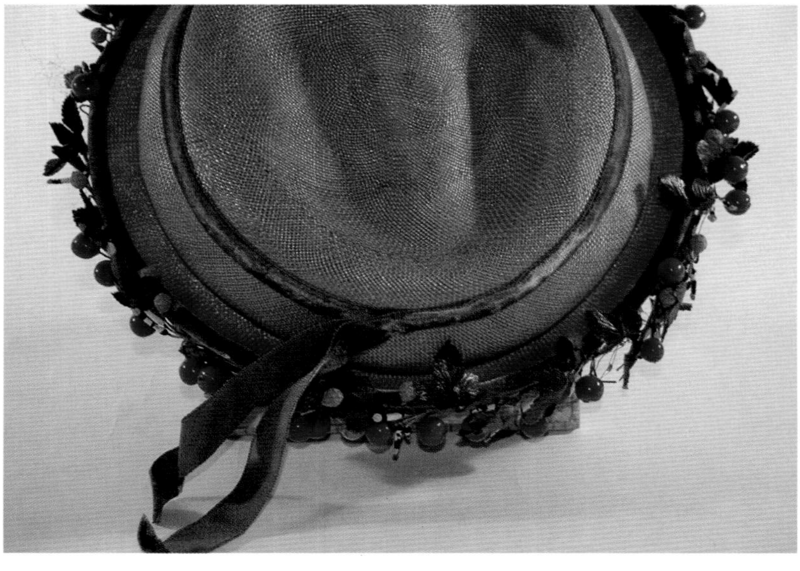

Holly bound, 1950s, Christmas straw. Label: Schiaparelli. *Aline Banting Collection, Mobile Millinery Museum*. $225.

Inner view showing Schiaparelli label.

An elegant Christmas straw by Shiaparelli is appliquéd with a machine-embroidered rose. Tiny velvet flowers and prickly thistles add texture. Label: Schiaparelli Paris. *Aline Banting Collection, Mobile Millinery Museum*. $250.

The felt base of this 1940s holly strewn charmer is shaped like a military service cap. *Christmas Collection, Mobile Millinery Museum*.

This pillbox/turban hybrid of gold tinsel fabric is a holiday head-turner. *Christmas Collection, Mobile Millinery Museum.* $100-150.

Silver lamé close hat and matching shoes. *Aline Banting Collection, Mobile Millinery Museum.* Hat: $100-150.

Miniature hats, enclosed in hat boxes such as this, were given as Christmas gifts during the mid-twentieth century. The recipient of such a gift could exchange the miniature hat for a full-size chapeau of their choosing. The boxes also served to protect small feathers of different colors, which could be placed in the band of a gentleman's homburg or fedora. Label: Knox Hats, New York. *Christmas Collection, Mobile Millinery Museum*. $250.

Daisies

Few collectors can resist the charm of daisies.

A schoolgirl Breton of stiffened net is banded in olive-green velvet and sprinkled with chenille-centered cotton daisies. Label: Brewster, New York. *Aline Banting Collection, Mobile Millinery Museum.* $100-150.

A pair of 1960s daisy trimmed turquoise hats. The first is a chip straw lampshade; the second, a beribboned whimsy. *Mobile Millinery Museum*. $150-200 each.

This all-over floral of pink and white daisies was made by a pair of home milliners over a bottle of wine. A pair of deep green leaves rest against a pink organza band. *Mobile Millinery Museum*. $150-200.

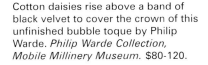

Cotton daisies rise above a band of black velvet to cover the crown of this unfinished bubble toque by Philip Warde. *Philip Warde Collection, Mobile Millinery Museum.* $80-120.

A 1960s pillbox of blush daisies with baby-pink chenille centers is rich with bright green foliage. A moss-green veil covers all but one fabric flower, which serves as a "button" for the center crown. *Mobile Millinery Museum*. $180-220.

Curler cap of brightly-colored daisies. *Mobile Millinery Museum*. $50-60.

This fully lined, straw cloth lampshade in cameo pink is strewn with raspberry-tipped, soft-pink daisies with banana-yellow chenille centers. *Mobile Millinery Museum*. $100-150.

A 1920s bronze lace daisy-motif cloche. Bronze silk lining. *Marg McGuire Collection, Mobile Millinery Museum*. $150-250.

Pink daisies add cheer to this depression-era navy opencrown. A faded satin bow presides over the center back. *Mobile Millinery Museum*. $150.

Feathered Hats

Postcard from New Zealand, c.1910, depicts Otago Maoris in ceremonial dress. The adults each wear a single feather in their hair. *Courtesy of Iris Hillyer.*

Feathered bumper pillbox, c.1960, shaded cranberry and deep grape. Label: Fleur de Lis Chapeau. *Mobile Millinery Museum*. $175.

Feathered ducktail cap. Label: Hamilton and Co., New Haven. *Mobile Millinery Museum*. $150-175.

Left:
A delicate opencrown of turquoise marabou and ostrich fronds. Original Simpson's price tag reads $11.98. *Aline Banting Collection, Mobile Millinery Museum*. $175-225.

Right:
Feathered close hat, c.1955. *Mobile Millinery Museum.* $100-150.

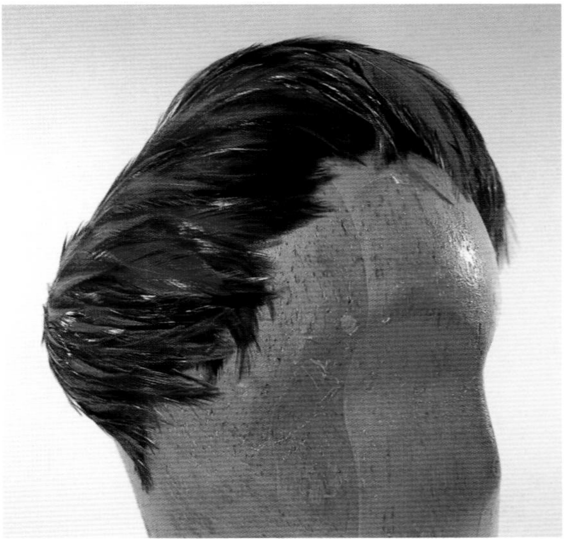

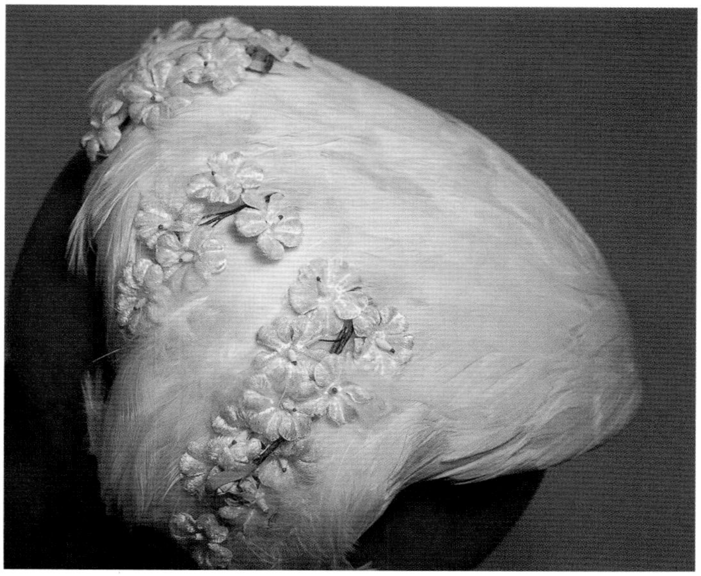

This mid-1950s cap demonstrates an unusual combination of feathers and flowers. Label: Made in U.S.A. *Mobile Millinery Museum*. $60-80.

Crimson feathered cap speckled with a touch of taupe, brown, and peach. *Mobile Millinery Museum*. $125-150.

A pliable green feather band to wrap a chignon. *Mobile Millinery Museum*. $125.

Felt-foundation pillbox of bottle-green marabou. *Mobile Millinery Museum*. $180-200.

Baby-pink marabou lampshade with matching velvet ribbon band. Traces of aged glue can be seen on the inside. *Mobile Millinery Museum*. $125-150.

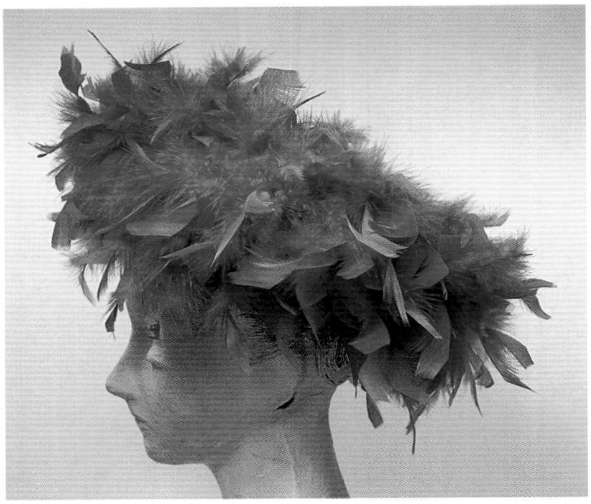

Millennium opencrown of turquoise poultry feathers. *Mobile Millinery Museum*. $250-350.

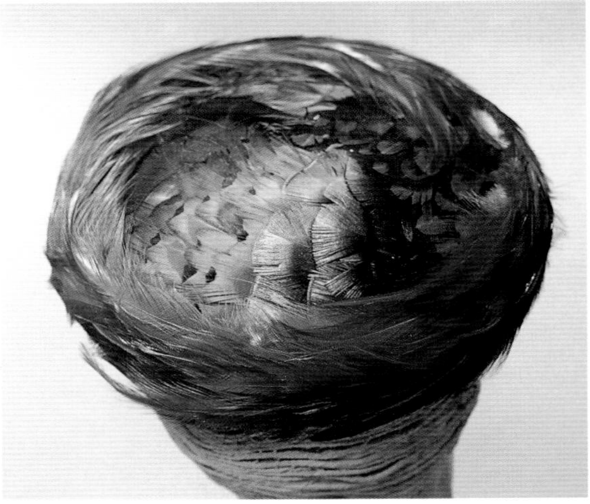

A 1960s pillbox bumpered in a swirl of pacific-blue feathers. *Mobile Millinery Museum.* $100-120.

Feather pads in shades of peacock-blue surround a deep 1960s pillbox. *Mobile Millinery Museum*. $80-120.

A velvet-banded pink flower pot sprouts a shower of clipped brown feathers. Label: Jacqueline Original. *Mobile Millinery Museum*. $120-150.

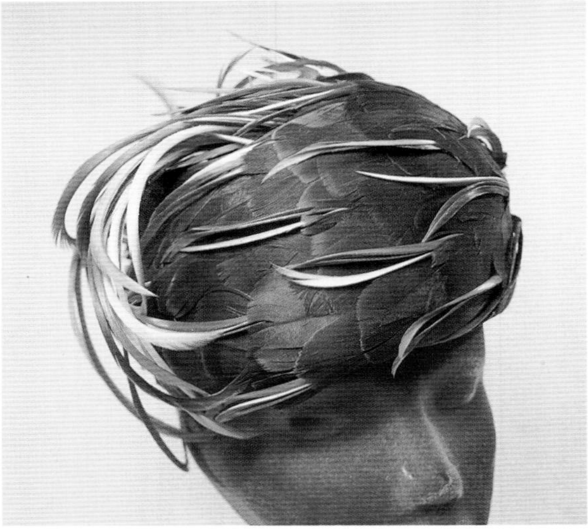

Orange and white feather tendrils satellite about a brown feather, 1960s, bubble toque. *Mobile Millinery Museum*. $120.

The feathers of this lullaby-pink bubble toque have been curled and individually secured to a buckram frame.

Furs, Hides, and Imitations

"I wore my furs to the office today and the girls were all admiring them."

— *Jane Christina Philip in a letter to her fiancée, Dec. 17, 1912*

"Four sisters in Las Vegas for four days and on this night we wore faux fur hats only the most fashionable pimp would think of putting on his head. ...So we walked the Vegas strip – a high school vice-principal, a doctor, a business executive, and a journalist – giggling at our own joke and accepting the occasional, 'now those are hats,' comment."

— *Michelle Shephard, crime reporter, Toronto Star*

Prior to the fifties, when issues of conservation were first raised, fashion furs of all descriptions were widely available, albeit for a price. Victorian and Edwardian ladies viewed fleece and fur as a status symbol and proudly wore Persian lamb, astrakhan, monkey, and muskrat on their hats, in both winter and summer. Badger, fox, raccoon, and other bulky furs trimmed hats and were slung over shoulders in the teens and twenties.

By the 1930s, when matched items were the rage, fur hats teamed with muffs or matching scarves and stoles. Of the non-endangered furs, mink and sable have always been the most expensive, while easy to trap and abundant rabbit, raccoon, squirrel, and skunk were less costly.

Photo postcard, c.1915, in which a trapper shows off his five-week catch of fifty-one fox, thirty-three mink, and five racoon pelts. A note on the back indicates he was robbed of an additional seven fox skins. *Courtesy of Iris Hillyer*.

Black rabbit skating cap, c.1890. *Mobile Millinery Museum*. $250-300.

Circa 1880: The author's great aunts Kate and Margaret, in fur caps to match their fur-trimmed Victorian garments. *Photo by L. E. Desmarais, Montreal*.

Late Victorian wool felt skating cap banded with muskrat. Matching muskrat muff. *Mobile Millinery Museum*. Ensemble: $200-250.

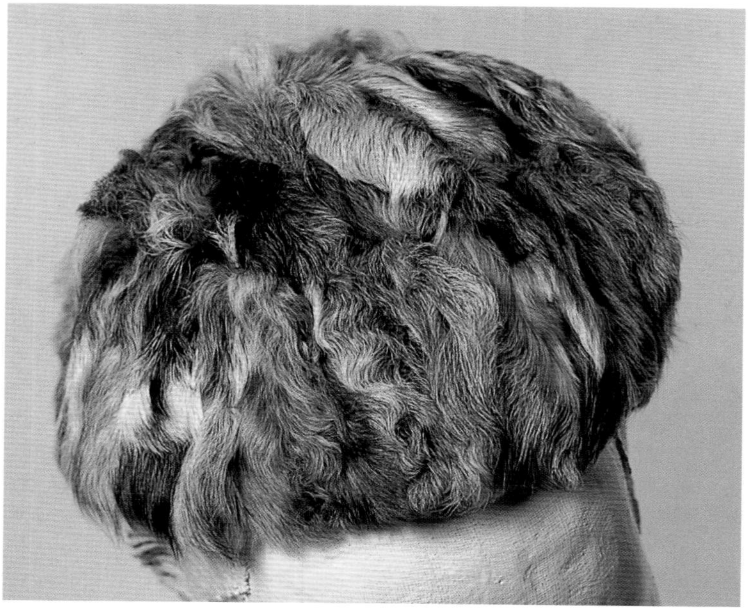

Gray astrakhan cap, c.1930. *Mobile Millinery Museum*. $225.

Following World War II, when government restrictions were lifted on the number of man-hours that could go into the making of garments, mink came into vogue and held firm in the hearts and closets of the fashion conscious for several decades. The species, considered to be one of the warmest furs for its weight, was so favoured that furriers often utilized entire pelts, leaving heads, feet, tails, and even claws intact. Designers turned skins and their remnants into a variety of hats: pillboxes, and whimsies in the fifties; fedoras and helmet styles in the sixties.

Mink, due to its size, was labor intensive and therefore expensive. A less costly option for consumers was kolinsky, or Russian squirrel.

Mink Ranching

"During fleshing season, Dad would remove his overalls before coming in the house to eat, but the mink odor clung to his clothes. I hated the smell of mink pelts and never missed an opportunity to say so. 'Ah, but you like the smell of the money they bring,' Dad would always say."

— *Iris Hillyer*, a mink rancher's daughter

A newsboy cap in rich, dark mink. A satin band separates the visor from the crown. *Mobile Millinery Museum*. $125-150.

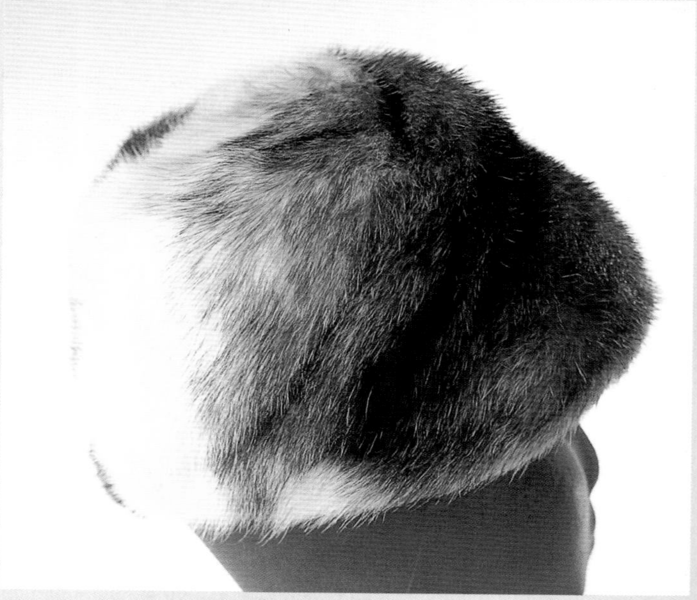

Circa 1960: A beautifully shaped hat of black-cross mink. Label: Holt Renfrew. *Mobile Millinery Museum.* $150-200.

Satin bows on a bandeau of dark mink-tail make for an elegant cocktail hat, c.1960. Brown sen sen veiling falls to nose level. *Mobile Millinery Museum.* $80-100.

A blonde-mink beret rests on a hat box from Holt Renfrew. *Mobile Millinery Museum*. Hat: $125.

A pair of mink tails team with satin bows to form a 1950s bandeau. Matching mink wrap. *Mobile Millinery Museum*. Ensemble: $250.

This deep (4 1/2 inches) mink Cossack is a 1960s creation of Toronto's Philip Warde. Shown with matching collared stole. *Philip Warde Collection, Mobile Millinery Museum.* Ensemble: $350-450.

Close-up showing how the pelt has been draped, leaving the legs, feet, and claws intact.

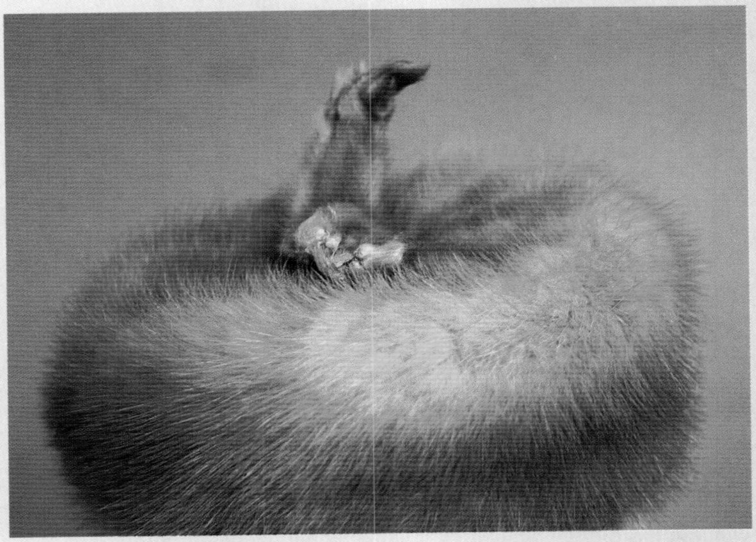

A pair of feet, complete with claws, form the button for this mink tambourine, c.1965. *Myra Krangle Collection, Mobile Millinery Museum*. $200-250.

The author's grandfather, Fred Thomas, makes the rounds with "Old Billy", a mink he managed, over time, to tame. *Photo courtesy of Iris Hillyer*.

A caged, dark (natural) mink. *Photo courtesy of Iris Hillyer*.

Rare white mink. *Photo courtesy of Iris Hillyer*.

For years a tall, steel fence, embedded deep into the ground, surrounded the mink yard beside Fred Thomas's home in rural Quebec. Should one of the vicious creatures he raised break loose from its individual wire cage and climb the enclosure, it would be unable to escape because of the V-shaped, metal ceiling of the pen.

Thomas oversaw every aspect of his ranching operation from building the separate cages, to purchasing animals from breeders, to hiring and training seasonal workers, who prepared the pelts in the fall, when the fur was prime. The animals were killed humanely (asphyxiated with carbon monoxide), fleshed, then stretched and dried on long, thin boards. Hundreds of these were cut and fashioned from trees that Thomas felled himself.

Circa 1940, a single common black or brown pelt fetched as much as one hundred dollars with rarer colors such as sapphire (blonde), white, or silver/blue, selling for considerably more. Culls, taken from mink that died naturally during the off-season, were sold as well, but at much lower prices.

Thomas sold a particularly lustrous and beautifully colored strain of mink, which was popular with furriers in Montreal and at the Hudson's Bay auctions. This he developed from wild mink, which he trapped after scouting tracks by the river. According to authorities, only the most highly skilled hunters are successful at trapping wild mink.

Thomas's daughter, Iris Hillyer, remembers having to check the traps on one occasion when her father was out of town. Instead of finding mink, she discovered a large raccoon had wedged himself in the box enclosure and forced his head through the air outlet at the top of the cage. "That fellow was heavy, and glad to get out of there," she recalls.

Hillyer also remembers horsemeat being delivered regularly to the ranch. The meat, which was kept in a large underground freezer, was ground and mixed with supplements, then loaded onto a stoneboat and dragged by horsepower to the mink yard. Thomas supervised the daily feeding ritual, personally pressing handfuls of the mixture into each cage. "Old Billy", a mink he had managed to tame, followed him on his rounds. When horsemeat became scarce, due to its popularity with fox breeders and other ranchers, whale protein was substituted.

During the Second World War, one of the mink harvests was lost due to army maneuvers. Thomas's acreage was a few miles from the Farnham Army base and one morning before dawn, military officials organized a practice attack. Troops, hiding in the woods surrounding the ranch, made an advance on the mink yard, under cover of a smoke screen. The animals, which had just produced litters, killed their offspring. The army settled with Thomas over his financial loss and the procedure was never repeated.

On another occasion, Thomas suffered a loss of two thousand dollars worth of mink, this time due to theft. The *R.C.M.P.* and Quebec provincial police were called in to investigate the break-in, which occurred one foggy night in the fall of 1963. A letter written by his daughter at the time records the incident:

> Apparently the thieves were scared off as there was close to $60,000.00 worth of furs on the property. As someone said, "If the thieves knew Dad at all, they probably thought he was sneaking up behind them with his high-powered Winchester!" We're thankful he didn't know what was going on, or he would have been doing just that and probably have gotten himself killed.

Eventually fur fashion excesses reached a saturation point. Fur had become so popular at mid-century that concern mounted over ecological and cruelty issues. Animal rights groups emerged, urging governments to enact protection legislation for live creatures. Many furs have disappeared from the market due to these strict conservation laws. Others are simply gone.

During the peak of its fashion popularity in the 1960s and 1970s, approximately 18,000 jaguars were killed annually. More of these beautiful animals were sacrificed each year than the total that remain: an estimated 15,000. Three subspecies of tigers (Caspian, Balinese, and Javan) suffered extinction in the past century.

As for cheetah, approximately 100,000 of these beautiful animals inhabited the planet c.1900. Only ten to fifteen thousand of them remained a century later.

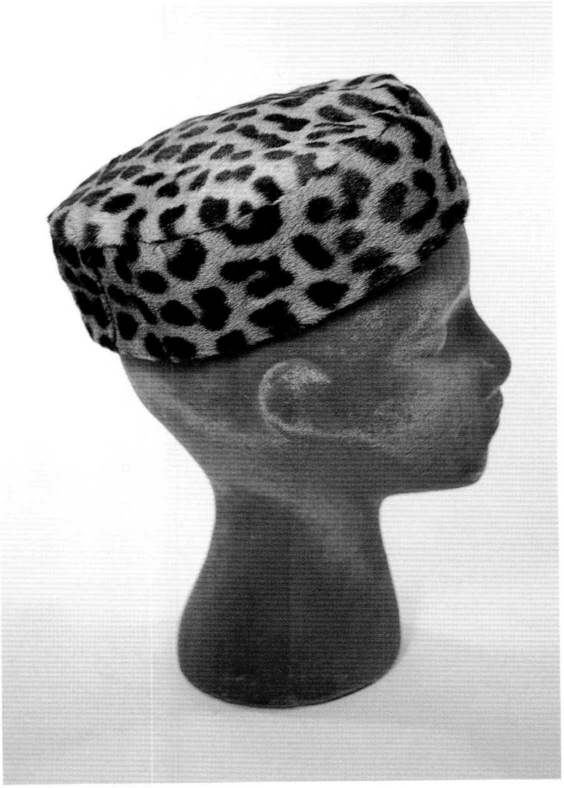

Egyptian tomb paintings depict human figures wearing the easily recognizable spotted cheetah pelt, which for centuries was considered a sign of wealth.

The *American Endangered Species Act* now prohibits the importation and sale of exotic pelts such as polar bear, jaguar, and tiger. Great cats like the snow leopard, prized by the fashion industry for its coloration and long, dense underfur, benefited from the efforts of protesters who raised eyebrows by hurling paint on fur-wearing patrons of *La Scala* in the 1960s. Public awareness was raised to such a degree by the end of the 1970s that it was socially unacceptable to wear fur of any type.

Now, after two decades of furless fashion, natural fur is experiencing the same comeback that hats themselves are enjoying. A new generation is valuing fur for its warmth and beauty.

Burgundy felt tilt hat, purchased in 1939, is banded with genuine snow leopard. The original owner says she felt "like a million dollars" when she wore this hat. *Catharine Snellings Collection, Mobile Millinery Museum*. $400-550.

Jaguar pillbox purchased in Africa, c.1970, as a gift for Karen Johnson, who later donated the hat to the *Mobile Millinery Museum*. Johnson's conscience would not allow her to wear the hat. *Mobile Millinery Museum*. $800-1000.

Reverse view demonstrates a strap, which secures the hat at the back of the head, and a self-fabric hatpin, used by Snellings to fasten the hat to a roll of upswept hair.

The fur for this peaked cap, c.1965, appears to have been taken from the face or neck area of a tiger species. Label: Creation by André. *Mobile Millinery Museum*. $1200-1500.

Fur garments are appearing in shops and on runways in exciting new forms. Designers have experimented with mingling several varieties of natural hide within the same ensemble. It is even correct to combine new fur with vintage.

Some animal rights activists have resumed their protests: raiding fur factories, spraying graffiti on shop storefronts, issuing death threats, cutting phone lines, etc. Stores in Australia that sell garments trimmed with rabbit and possum fur, for example, have had their locks damaged with superglue. In May of 1973, five shoppers were trapped for an hour inside an Auckland, New Zealand, fashion outlet when three women chained themselves to the front of the store. In the United States, handfuls of activists attempt to influence public opinion and disrupt business by demonstrating outside of design houses when new collections are presented. Such tactics are considered by authorities to be acts of eco-terrorism.

But while furs are back in the form of hats, gloves, scarves, and wraps, we can be certain that many of the exotic species found in fashion throughout the twentieth century will never appear in shops again. Conservation laws have increased the values of antique hats made from endangered and extinct species.

Fur hats fall into several distinct categories:

A 1930s cap and muff set, skillfully crafted of genuine ocelot. Label: Saks Fifth Avenue. *Mobile Millinery Museum*. This soft, plush set commands a high price due to its condition, composition, label, and enduring style. $1200-1500.

A 1960s leopard skin helmet. *Aline Banting Collection, Mobile Millinery Museum*. $600-800.

This 1950s eggshell makes an unusual cocktail hat. Through careful piecing, the milliner has made the most of the margay's longitudinal stripes and spots to create visual interest from every angle. Label: Créations Madeleine, Fait á la main (made by hand), 6096 Ouest Blvd. Gouin. *Mobile Millinery Museum*. $450-550.

A 1960s, genuine leopard skin, flower pot banded with velvet. *Mobile Millinery Museum*. $600-800.

- Natural furs: These closely resemble the animal from which they are made. These include rabbit, lynx, beaver, lamb, skunk, squirrel, monkey, leopard, jaguar, ocelot, mink, chinchilla, and other ranched and trapped animals.

An enormous, stiffened felt widebrim rimmed in luxurious mink. A custom design by Philip Warde. *Courtesy of Joy Drew*. $1000-1200.

Back view, showing black satin band and bow.

Side view.

A reversible Zhivago hat of Canadian lynx, faced with brown velvet, is the ultimate in warmth when the fur is worn next to the skin. *Aline Banting Collection, Mobile Millinery Museum*. $225.

Circa 1920: A man's coyote pelt hat, lined with patterned silk. *Mobile Millinery Museum*. $350-450.

This red fox is similar, but made without the chin strap. It rises high at the back of the crown and tapers to the nape of the neck. *Mobile Millinery Museum*. $250.

A warm and wonderful brown suede floppy features an under-brim of Canadian lynx. Label: André. *Mobile Millinery Museum*. $350-400.

Trapunto stitching on a champagne satin band matches the under-brim of this dressy, 1960s, kangaroo fur cap. *Mobile Millinery Museum*. $225.

This cozy cloche has a crown and under-brim of black karakurl. The band and trapunto-stitched brim are of black satin. Label: Stetson, Fifth Avenue. *Mobile Millinery Museum*. $175.

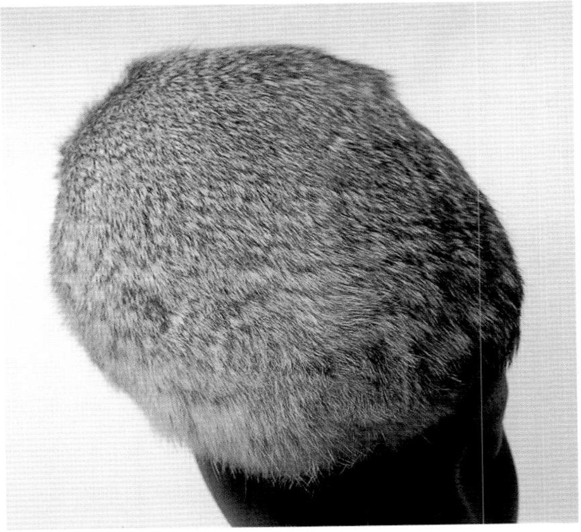

Late Victorian chinchilla cap. *Mobile Millinery Museum*. $175-225.

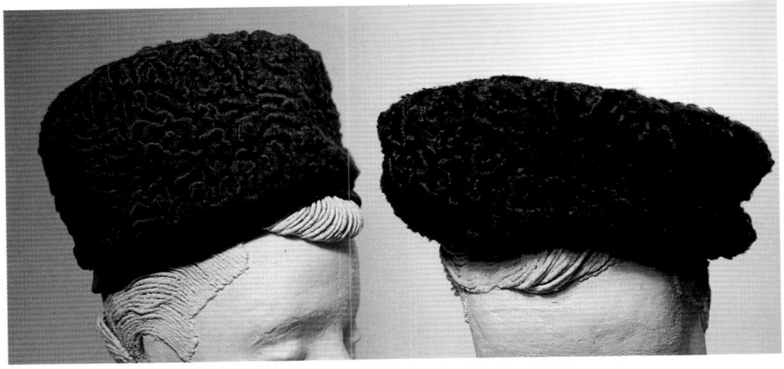

These brown Persian lamb hats were each made in the 1960s, but show a variation in style and tint. The tall pillbox rests on a velvet band. Label: Hand made hats by Elizabeth, Hamilton. The shallow-crowned, deep brown example is fitted with a tapered band. Label: M'sieu Léon. *Mobile Millinery Museum*. $225-275 each.

A pair of natural furs, perfect for skiing in the Laurentians. The first is of Russian wolf; the second, white fox. Labels: Jean Guy Haute Mode/ Holt Renfrew and Chapeaux Pierre Balmain, Paris. *Mobile Millinery Museum*. Value: $250-350 each.

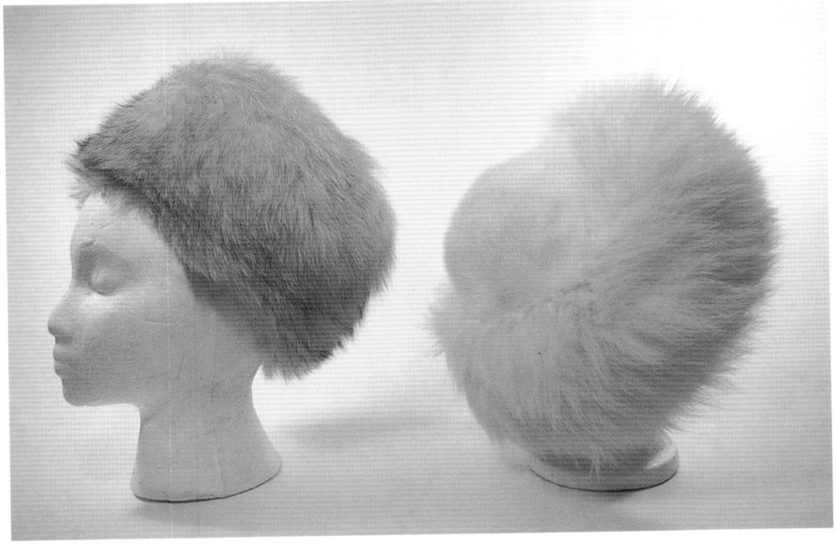

A majestic 1960s toque in sheared, natural brown, sable. Label: Stetson, Fifth Avenue. *Mobile Millinery Museum*. $400-450.

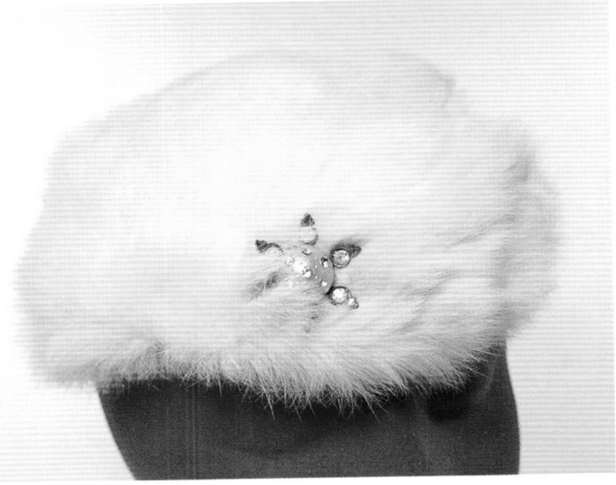

Circa 1900: White rabbit pelt dressed with a starburst pin. *Mobile Millinery Museum.* $225.

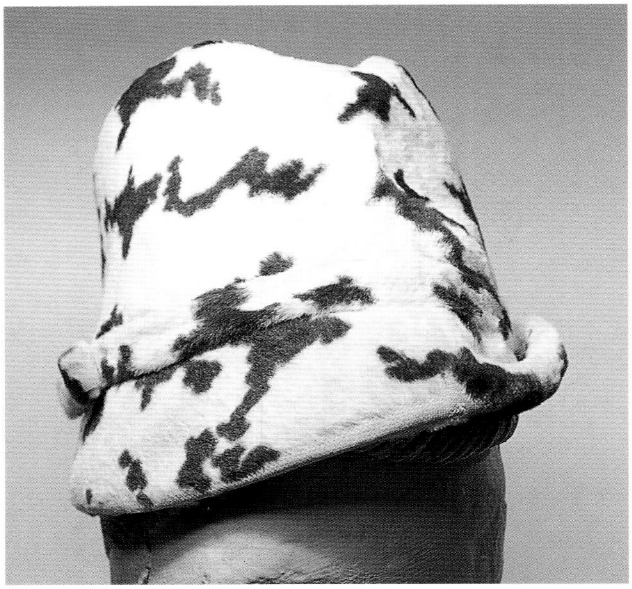

Alpine hat of brown and white ponyskin. *Mobile Millinery Museum*. $200-250.

This black muskrat winter cap, with wool ear flaps, was formerly owned by a female member of the Canadian military. An opening along the brim allows for the insertion of a badge. Label: Canadian Hat Manufacturing Corp. *Mobile Millinery Museum*. $200-250.

- Treated furs: Authentic pelts of various species that have been bleached, dyed, sheared or in some way altered. Often common, inexpensive pelts are dyed to look like exotic species (e.g. Rabbit fur, masquerading as leopard skin). Hat labels are unlikely to reveal information regarding the fibre content and origin of such a piece, unless the original sales tag is intact. In the United States, legislation was passed in the 1950s ensuring that manufacturers label every fur, selling for over five dollars, with the English name of the animal from which it was made, as well as any alternations performed (bleaching, dying, etc).

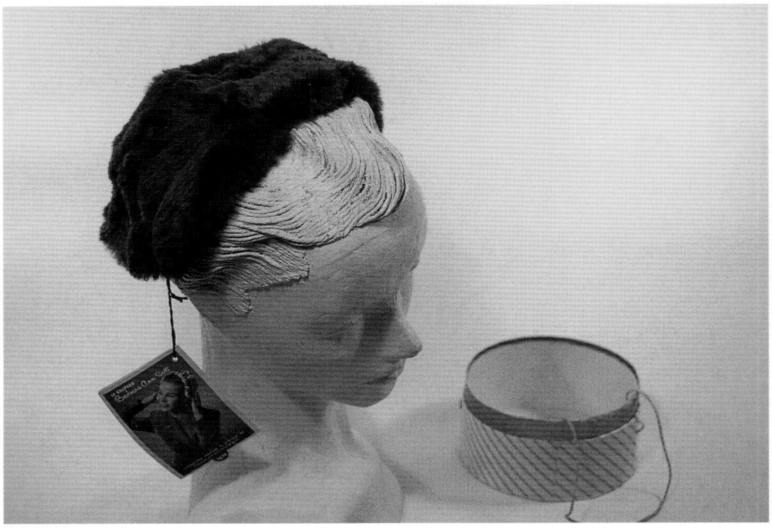

The Barbara Ann Scott hat, named for the Olympic skater, came in several colors. Shown with original hatbox and price tag of $4.98. Label: The Barbara Ann Scott Hat, Styled by Ivy of Montreal, Canada. *Mobile Millinery Museum*. $175-225.

Barbara Ann Scott Hat bilingual label (English on the cover and French on the reverse.

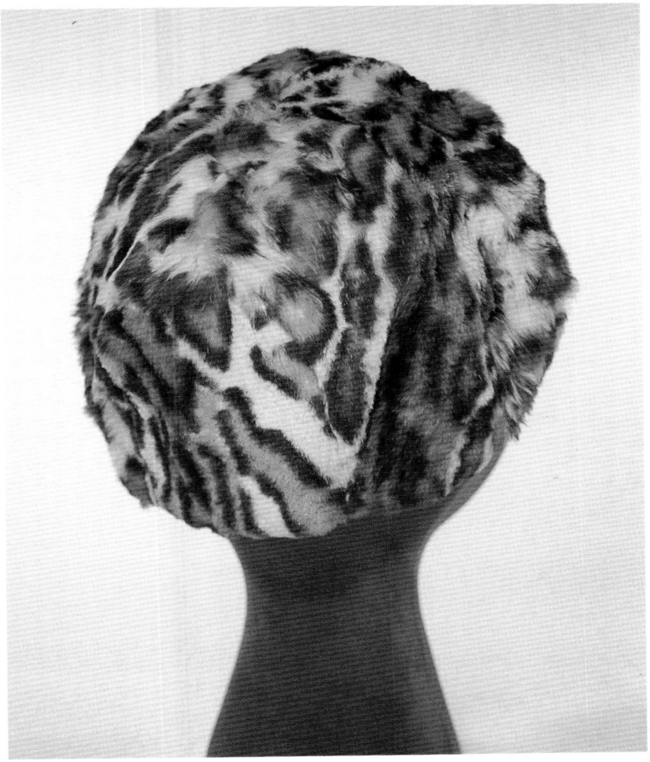

A similar Barbara Ann Scott hat, this one a faux leopard print. The two hats were worn by sisters in the 1940s. *Mobile Millinery Museum*. $175-225.

- Extreme furs: Dyes are used by the fashion industry to color fur vibrant colors, turning seal, rabbit, fox, and mink into luxurious fashion accents that bear minimal resemblance to their original form.

Purple seal lampshade, c.1968.

- Synthetic fur: Manufactured fur has been available since the 1960s and can appear to be the real thing or spring from the designer's imagination as fun fur. Imitation mink, Persian lamb, beaver, mouton, and seal will give themselves away by their cotton-like backing. These furs are really deep pile fabrics, woven on circular knitting machines.

HOW TO TAKE CARE OF YOUR

Barbara Ann Scott HAT

r Barabra Ann Scott Hat is made of ✻enuine ermine sheared lapin*. It should be replaced in the plastic box after each wearing. After many wearings hold hat over a steaming kettle to loosen nap, then brush with a clean brush and replace in box.

STYLED BY Ivy OF MONTREAL CANADA

MANUFACTURED BY I. VINEGOR FURS LTD.

*DYED RABBIT

Inside view of label, showing care instructions.

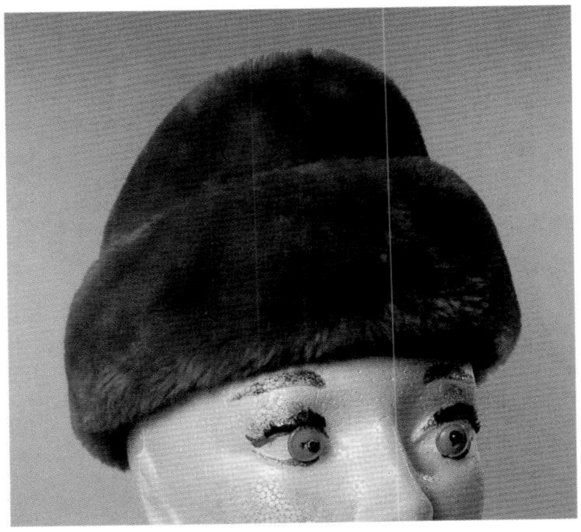

The Brezhnev, adapted for women in gorgeous turquoise Borg®. Label: Millinery Import, Made in England for Eaton's. *Mobile Millinery Museum*. $200-250.

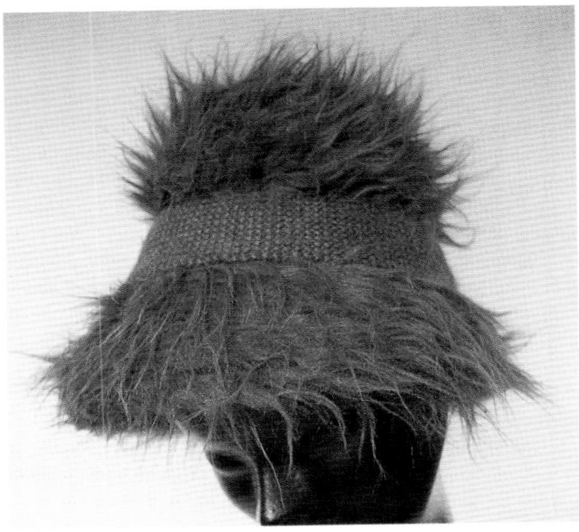

Late 1960s, Muppet®-like faux fur lampshade, banded with teal and lavender double knit wool. Label: Made in Western Germany. *Mobile Millinery Museum*. $250.

A child's winter cap of early faux fur shows wear and tear on the brim's edge and chin straps. A well-loved hat. *Mobile Millinery Museum*. $150-175.

The milliner's skill at stitching and blocking is shown in the swirls of this Kelly-green faux fur lampshade with olive-green bow. Label: made in USA. *Mobile Millinery Museum.* $200-250.

Winter white, machine-knitted, wool cap wrapped in a band of deep pile faux fur. *Mobile Millinery Museum*. $150.

Iris Hillyer warms up in an animal print faux fur cap and scarf.

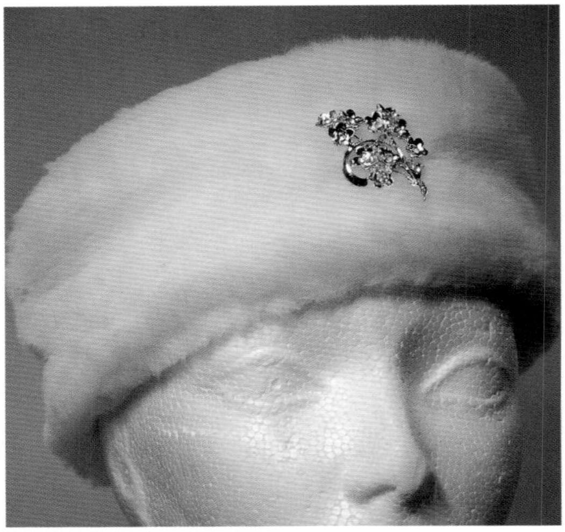

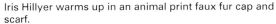

A silver-tone rhinestone pin sparkles against a winter white faux fur pillbox. *Marie Minaker Collection, Mobile Millinery Museum*. $150-200.

Left:
This brushed beaver high hat with stiffened crown imitates leopard skin. Band and button of genuine leather. *Philip Warde Collection, Mobile Millinery Museum*. $300-350.

Right:
This deep pile faux fur winter warmer was purchased new for $45.00 in 2003. *Private Collection*.

The Cat in the Hat; Recognizing Feline Furs

- Bobcat: Tawny fur with indistinct black spots and stripes.
- Cheetah: Coarse, golden or tawny fur, marked with solid black spots.
- Cougar: Short, lush, reddish-brown to gray-brown fur.
- Jaguar: Well-defined, geometrically shaped rosettes, often centered with a small dark spot. Base fur is brown to yellow.
- Leopard: The pelt is primarily golden yellow or reddish-brown with dark brown rosettes and open spots.
- Lynx: Thick cinnamon-brown underfur. Guard hairs are a mixture of black, gray, and tan.
- Margay: Margay fur is distinguished by ill-defined, black-ringed rosettes on a yellow or tan background that is lighter in color than the interior of the markings; similar in appearance to the ocelot.
- Ocelot: Pelts are marked with black-edged, irregular-shaped brown spots and stripes on a creamy yellow or yellow-brown base coat.
- Snow Leopard: The fur of this species is longer and woollier than that of the common leopard. Its white fur is marked by widely spaced brown on dark-brown rosettes with sporadic, creamy-yellow areas.
- Tiger: Generally a striped pattern of white, black, and orange, although several subspecies present a somewhat different coloration.

Nursing Caps

"As nursing students in the fifties, we used to hide our cigarettes up under our caps, and catch a smoke with a patient whenever we could."

— *Anonymous*

In the days of Florence Nightingale, nurses caps, many equipped with chin ties, resembled bonnets. These service caps evolved in the twentieth century to identify a nurse's rank and graduate school. By 1970, caps went the way of most millinery with nursing school "capping ceremonies" being gradually phased out.

An assortment of mid-twentieth century student and graduate nursing caps, representing various hospital affiliations.

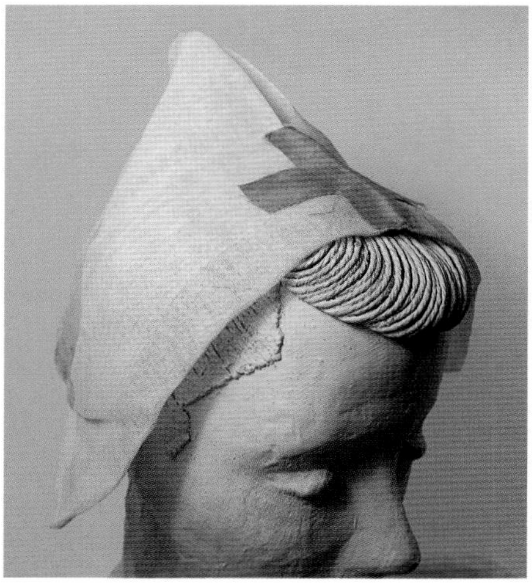

Muslin red cross cap, c.1918.

Philip Warde Collection

Three unidentified women from the seventies in enormously wide-brimmed Philip Warde hats. *Philip Warde Collection, Mobile Millinery Museum*.

Unlabelled 1940s open crown adorned with papier-mâché mirabelles. *Philip Warde Collection, Mobile Millinery Museum*. $150.

This stand-up beret in upholstery-weight white was custom designed for Lieutenant-Governor Pauline McGibbon. Label: Designed by Philip Warde, Toronto. *Mobile Millinery Museum*. $250.

Back view, showing pinwheel effect of trapunto stitching.

A deep mid-1960s pillbox woven from ribbons of pink straw. A silk cabbage rose in pink, shaded-to-raspberry, sits on a deep 1960s pillbox, woven from ribbons of pink straw. *Marjorie Wilson Collection, Mobile Millinery Museum.* $200-250.

Lieutenant-Governor Pauline McGibbon in the stand-up beret by Philip Warde.

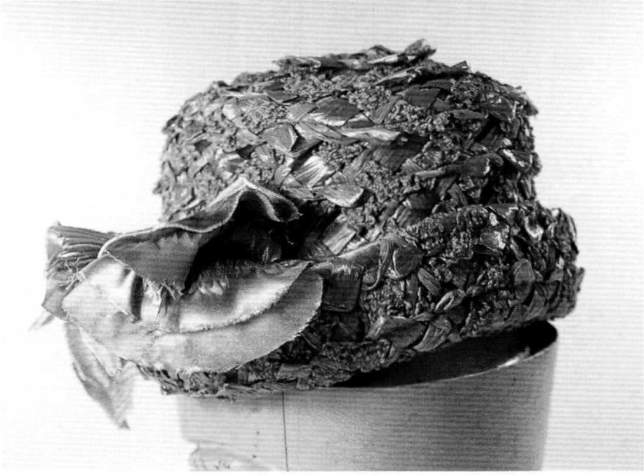

This 1960s straw cloche by Philip Warde is trimmed with satin and velvet leaves in woodland greens and browns. *Philip Warde Collection, Mobile Millinery Museum*. $125.

Constructed of a bonded white fabric, this designer beret is fitted with straps to secure the hair. A tuft of silk fringe tops the confection. *Philip Warde Collection, Mobile Millinery Museum*. $150-200.

An unfinished, blush-silk beret is pieced and stitched to stand tall. *Philip Warde Collection, Mobile Millinery Museum.* $150-200.

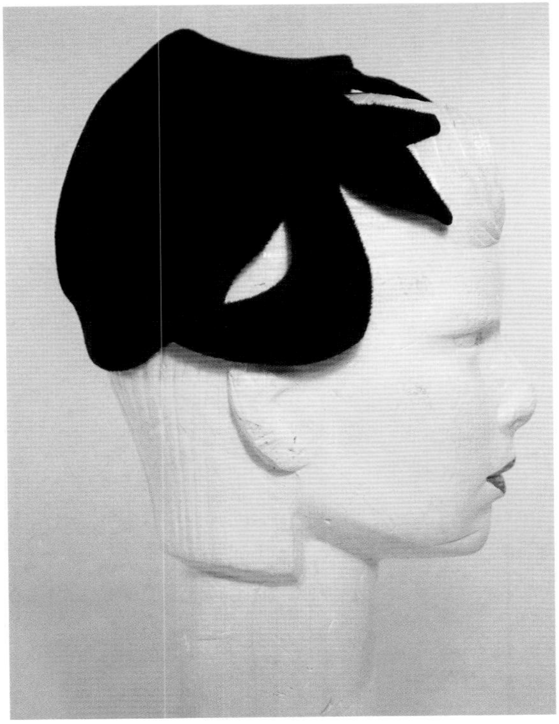

A skull-hugging brown felt cap with a fine velour finish. Self-fabric waves overlap along the crown. Label: Designed by Philip Warde, Toronto. *Philip Warde Collection, Mobile Millinery Museum*. $200-250.

This early 1950s, blue, jeweled beauty was designed to encircle upswept hair. Layers of tiny, ink-blue sequins form a bed for the stylized flowers that sparkle under evening lights. *Philip Warde Collection, Mobile Millinery Museum*. $250-350.

The sought-after Philip Warde label.

This designer original is an eye-catcher from every angle. Self-fabric bow and hatpin. Label: Philip Warde Boutique. *Philip Warde Collection, Mobile Millinery Museum.* $250-350.

A 1940s, feathered, Easter bonnet, lined with satin, proudly displays a Philip Warde label. *Philip Warde Collection, Mobile Millinery Museum*. $225.

An emerald-green turban/busby, á la Gloria Swanson, is stitched about the crown in a wave motif. *Philip Warde Collection, Mobile Millinery Museum*. $300-350.

Philip Warde shows his finesse with fabric in this 1940s draped indigo pillbox with larger-than-life, center-front bow. Pink satin lining. *Mobile Millinery Museum*. $300-350.

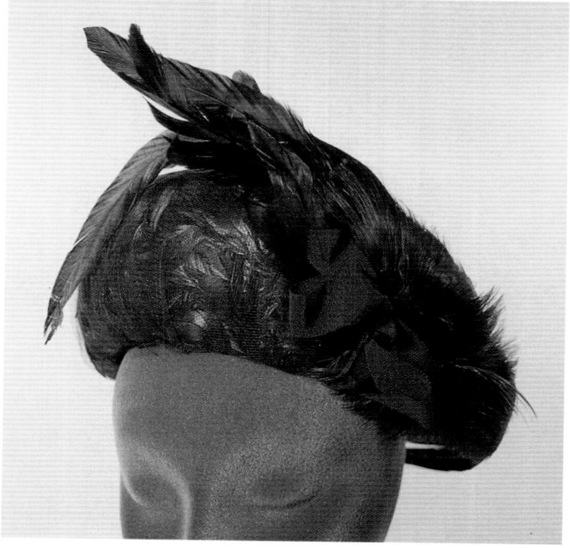

Coq of the Walk: A 1940s toque, iridescent rooster feathers. Label: Designed by Philip Warde, Toronto. *Philip Warde Collection, Mobile Millinery Museum*. $300-350.

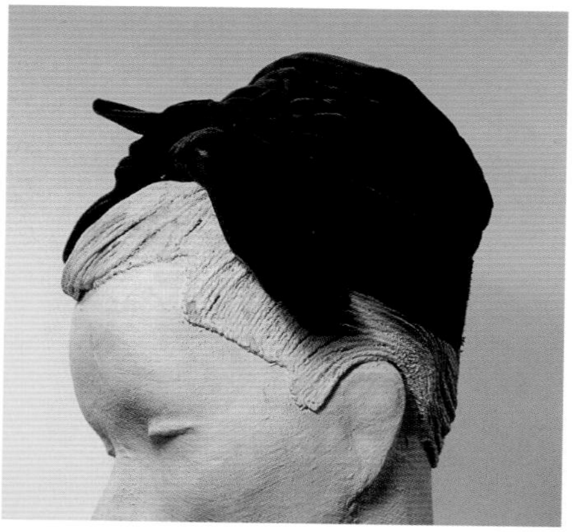

A smaller version of the draped pillbox, this time in brown velvet, is adorned at the front with twin bows. *Philip Warde Collection, Mobile Millinery Museum*. $300-350.

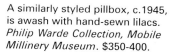

A similarly styled pillbox, c.1945, is awash with hand-sewn lilacs. *Philip Warde Collection, Mobile Millinery Museum*. $350-400.

A charming chouquette: Strips of cellophane straw have been formed into cylinders, then crocheted to form a beret. A trio of ribbons in hot pink, Kelly green, and purple is woven through the crown, then knotted. *Philip Warde Collection, Mobile Millinery Museum*. $250-300.

A stiff-brimmed variation on the boater. The high crown is worked with alternating rings of navy and white cellophane straw. A triple coil of navy straw descends from a strip at the center crown and rests on the brim, reminiscent of a snail. *Philip Warde Collection, Mobile Millinery Museum*. $300-350.

A Philip Warde showstopper in the Edwardian style. Hunter-green chip is wired at the brim's edge in matching grosgrain and casually banded with a braided, black silk cord. *Philip Warde Collection, Mobile Millinery Museum*. $450-550.

The scoop-shaped brim is the interesting feature of this goldenrod, long-nap felt. The crown is banded in black satin and adorned at the right temple with a trapunto-stitched, forward-facing bow. *Philip Warde Collection, Mobile Millinery Museum*. $350-450.

The tall, pointed crown of this celery plush-beaver cap rests on a narrow self-fabric visor. A green and tan feather emerges from under a self-fabric, half bow at the left ear. Shown with the block segment used to shape the center crown. *Philip Warde Collection, Mobile Millinery Museum*. $300-350.

A high-crowned cloche by Philip Warde is beautifully shaped from white-on-grape beaverette. The hat is banded with purple satin and finished with a feather flower. *Philip Warde Collection, Mobile Millinery Museum*. $250-300.

I didn't need to look at the label of this ink-black velour to know that it was a Philip Warde creation. His artistry can be seen in the twin pleats, which balance each other at the center-front crown and right brim. The hat is edged, banded, and finished with woven braid; a nod to the Zhivago craze of the mid-1960s. Label: Designed by Philip Warde, Toronto. *Philip Warde Collection, Mobile Millinery Museum*. $300-400.

The crown of this smoke-gray beavertail comes to a blunt point. The crown/brim join is marked with a ribbon of pewter-colored beads. *Philip Warde Collection, Mobile Millinery Museum*. $200-250.

Plastic-stemmed pink rosebuds climb a wall of blush straw. A band of black velvet and a scarf of dotted-net wrap the crown. A custom creation by Toronto designer Philip Warde. *Courtesy of Joy Drew*. $350-450.

This dramatic black felt by Philip Warde exhibits a Russian influence. *Courtesy of Joy Drew.* $350-450.

This Mad Hatter by Philip Warde was custom designed to be worn with a coat of the same wool fabric. The crown reaches a height of eight inches. *Courtesy of Joy Drew*. $400-450.

An eye-popper from Philip Warde in crisp, white, cellophane straw is wrapped in five brilliant colors of grosgrain ribbon. *Courtesy of Joy Drew*. $350-450.

A turquoise silk turban exhibits green highlights when struck by the light. A self-fabric rose follows the lines of this unfinished hat by Philip Warde. *Philip Warde Collection, Mobile Millinery Museum*. $300.

A blue carnation anchors an accordion-pleated scarf to band a perky brown straw by Philip Warde. *Mobile Millinery Museum*. $200-250.

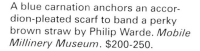

This pieced felt in beige, deep brown, and mulberry takes inspiration from the Cumberland, a high hat worn by men, c.1820. A wired brim folds up in slightly in back. Label: Designed by Phillip Warde, Toronto. *Mobile Millinery Museum*. $250-300.

This Philip Warde showstopper in raspberry straw speaks for itself. The special occasion piece with its giant, twin cabbage roses exemplifies the great designer's love of color and drama. *Mobile Millinery Museum*. $1200.

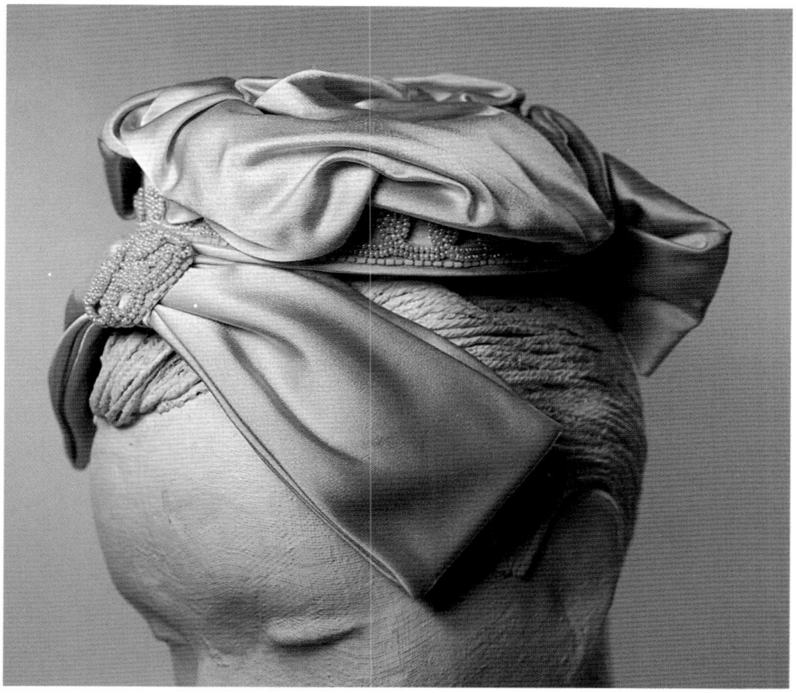

A 1950s beaded beauty, in powder-blue satin, features a stiffened, self-fabric bow at the brow line and a half bow at back. *Philip Warde Collection, Mobile Millinery Museum*. $350-450.

This unfinished summer-white confection shows just the right touch of green. *Philip Warde Collection, Mobile Millinery Museum.* $250-300.

Seashell-pink rosebuds rest in a bed of fox-brown velvet. Cocoa-colored tulle swaths the confection. *Philip Warde Collection, Mobile Millinery Museum*. $350-400.

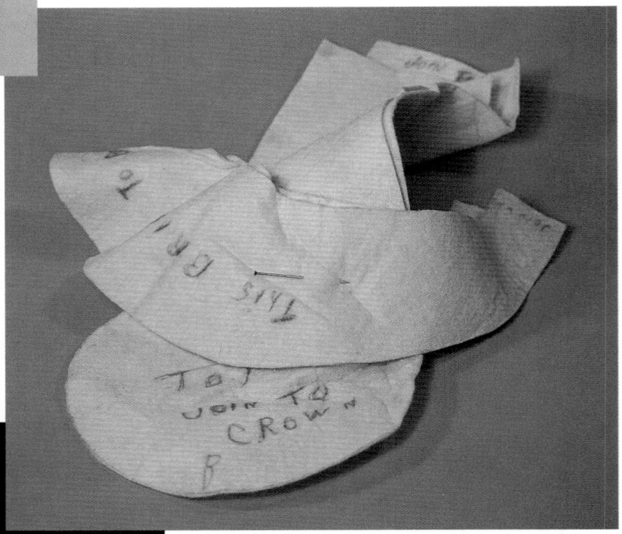

One of many felt hat patterns designed by Philip Warde. Labeled: This brim to be double fur. *Mobile Millinery Museum*.

Giant choux, tinted to match a lemon-yellow straw, exude drama when set against a black velvet band. *Philip Warde Collection, Mobile Millinery Museum*. $350-450.

Red Hats

Warning

When I am an old woman I shall wear purple
With a red hat, which doesn't go and doesn't suit me.

— *Jenny Joseph*

As hats make a comeback, it may seem that they are doing so one color at a time. In an effort to cater to Red Hatters, most hat shops now carry a healthy selection of chapeaux rouge. Red hats were not always plentiful however, due to the Victorian conviction that a red hat meant "no knickers."

Blue hats are also making a comeback. *The Women's Institute*, a well-established international organization, has recently adopted the practice of wearing blue hats at certain functions.

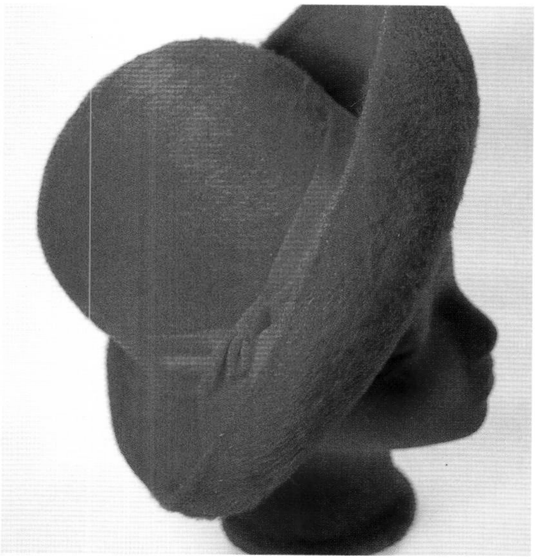

A 1960s halo hat in long-nap beaver. Label: Otto Lucas Junior, Made in England. *Mobile Millinery Museum*. $300-350.

Loops of Christmas-red form a 1950s topper. A red velvet bow is anchored with crystal stones. *Mobile Millinery Museum*. $225.

A modified bowler from the 1980s features black ostrich fronds and diamond-dot veiling. Label: Holt Renfrew. *Mobile Millinery Museum*. $80-100.

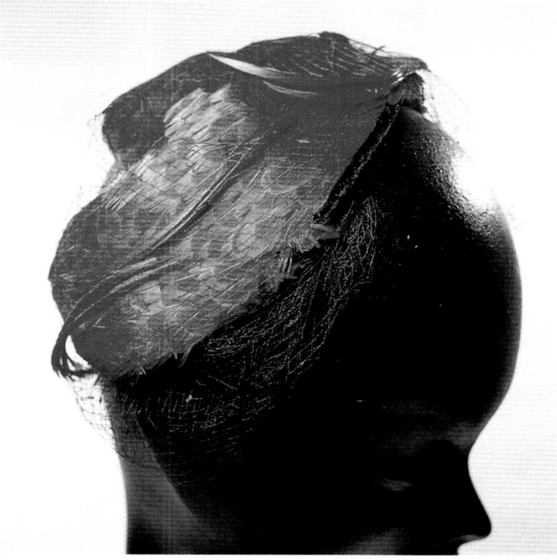

A 1940s woven cellophane straw edged with velvet ribbon and draped with diamond-dot veiling. *Mobile Millinery Museum*. $200-250.

A snappy black and red felt is made in England by Bermona. *Mobile Millinery Museum*. $80-100.

A stiff-brimmed straw in fire-engine red is softened with a pouf of red ruffles at the center back. Label: Designed by Jodi J. for Sylvia of St. Louis. *Mobile Millinery Museum*. $350-400.

A 1920s beaverette toque of deep, insignia red hints at a brim that sweeps upward to form a half-bow. Label: Genuine Imported Beaver. *Mobile Millinery Museum*. $150-200.

Circa 1935: Red straw harlequin. *Mobile Millinery Museum*. $250.

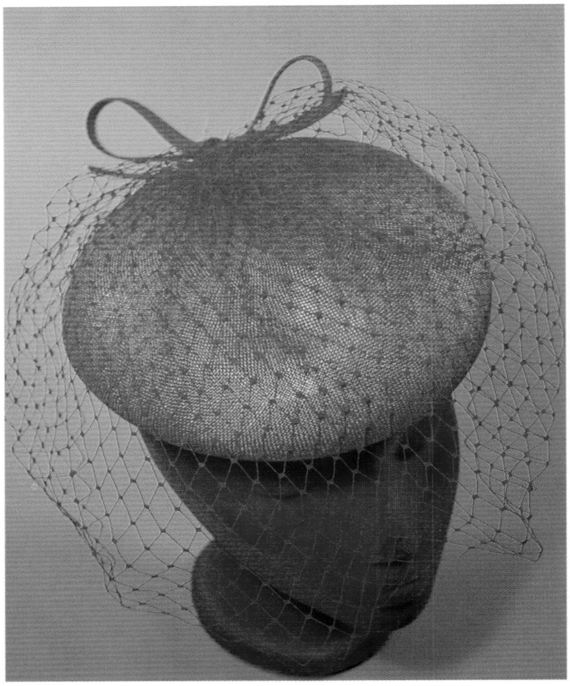

Veiled straw "Princess Diana hat. *Mobile Millinery Museum*. $120.

Circa 1955: Special occasion hat of cranberry velvet. Tapered, trapunto-stitched brim. Label: Hudson's Bay Company, incorporated May 1670. *Mobile Millinery Museum*. $150-200.

From the late 1940s: red and white straw are woven together to create a charming summer hat with face-enveloping veil. *Mobile Millinery Museum*. $125.

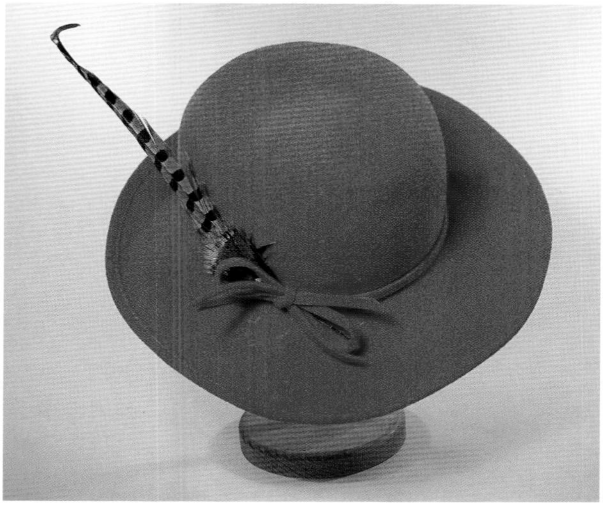

Afternoon hat of orange/red felt, c.1970. *Mobile Millinery Museum*. $80-100.

Female guests at a June wedding in rural Quebec, c.1943, wear or carry a variety of special occasion hats.

Wedding Hats

The horsehair Pamelas, worn by the bride and her attendant, help to date this wedding photo from the 1920s.

A World War II bride and her female guests brighten the day with shallow-crowned, brimmed confections.

Gladys Ernst "left it up to them" to create this straw confection, to match her wartime wedding suit, purchased at Simpson's in Toronto.

A similar hat from the same era, in baby-pink straw and in black satin. Black eyebrow veiling passes under a bunch of roses to tie at the center back. Elastic chignon strap. *Mobile Millinery Museum*. $200-250.

Gladys Ernst's fox-trimmed gray wedding suit, c.1943.

June 1943: Bride Iris Thomas, in a blue tulle "doll" hat, is attended by her cousin, Kathleen Baird, who sports a chic, flowered topper.

Bride Roberta Brooks in a 1960s bridal headpiece known as a miner's cap.

In 2001: Bride Corinne Shephard poses for her picture in the traditional, gift-bow, bridal shower bonnet.

A 1980s, pleated chiffon, bridal hat adorned with pearls and machine embroidery. Fine mesh veils the face and trails from a bow at the center back. *Wedding Collection, Mobile Millinery Museum*. $150.

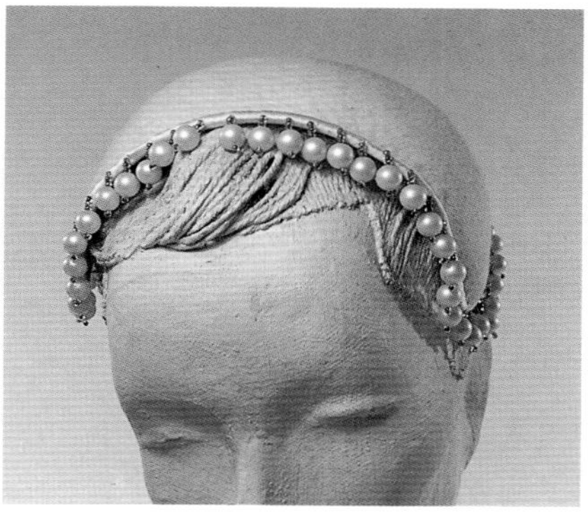

A Juliet cap of eggshell felt is rimmed with pearl drops. Label: Schiaparelli, Paris. *Aline Banting Collection, Mobile Millinery Museum*. $200-225.

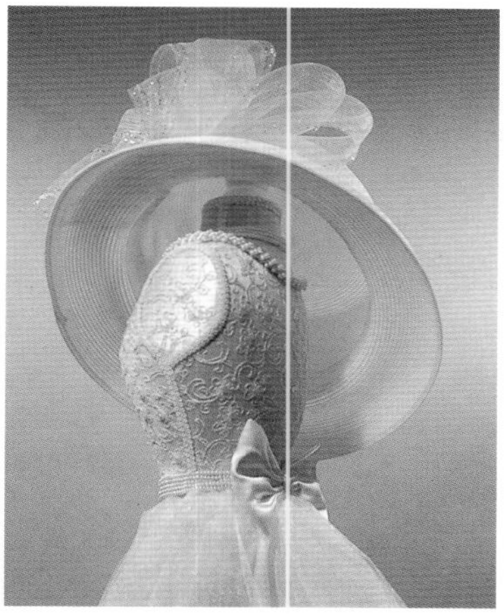

C. 2004: White, straw, mushroom brim with a silver-trimmed, horsehair bow. *Wedding Collection, Mobile Millinery Museum*. $175-200.

Front detail.

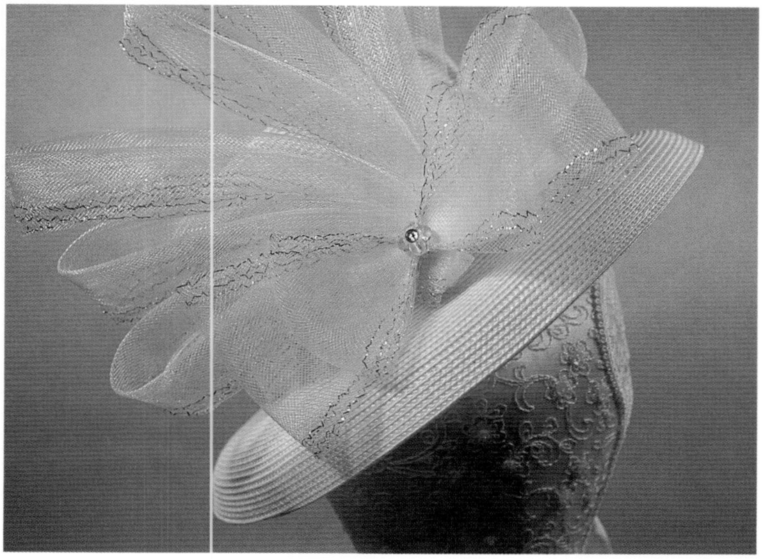

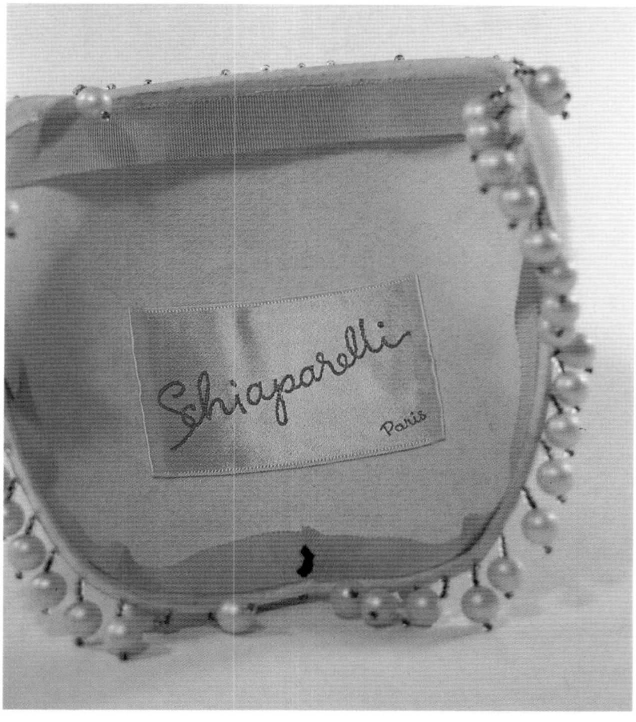

Inner view, showing the great designer's label.

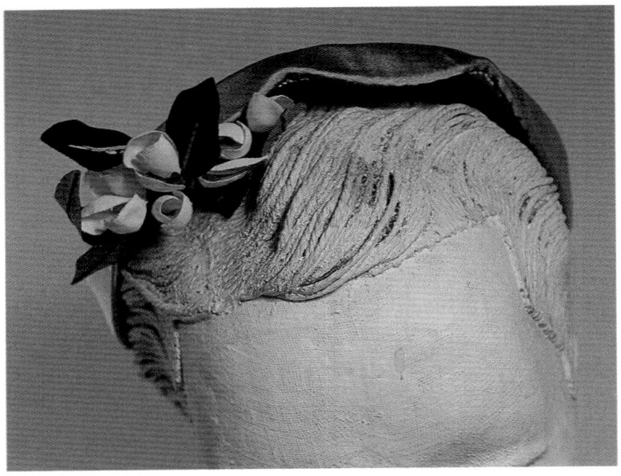

A cluster of crocus peeks from beneath the crown of a blue satin bridesmaid's cap, c.1955. *Wedding Collection, Mobile Millinery Museum*. $40.

Lime-green lampshade cinched with deep-green net. Velvet dots simulate confetti. A white rose adds the final bridal touch to this going-away hat, c.1965. *Wedding Collection, Mobile Millinery Museum*. $75-125.

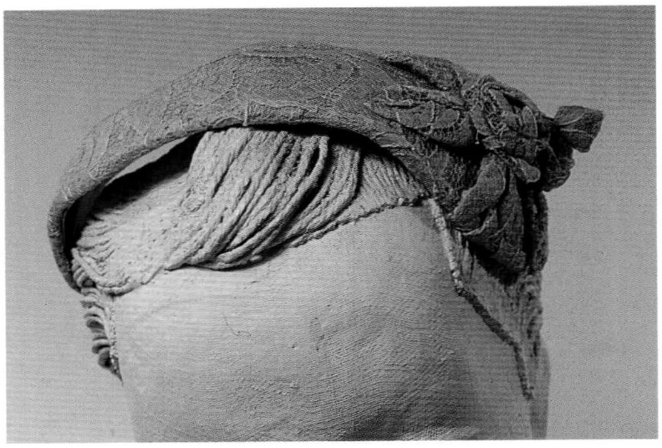

Lace rosettes and a self-fabric hatpin add charm to a simple Juliet cap of Wedgwood-blue lace. *Wedding Collection, Mobile Millinery Museum*. $80-100.

A 1960s tulle bridal veil depends from a diadem of floral braid. Clear plastic beads mark the center of each floret. *Wedding Collection, Mobile Millinery Museum*. $100-150.

A bride's going-away hat of periwinkle velvet is heart-shaped at the back. Pearls are strung from beaded loops along the crown and interspersed with rhinestones to dot the crown. Label: Robin, New York. *Wedding Collection, Mobile Millinery Museum*. $200-250.

A 1950s pink organdie going-away hat hides paper confetti in its woven crown. A pair of pearl-tipped hatpins flanks a sequined appliqué. Shown with machine-embroidered mesh gloves by Kayser. *Wedding Collection, Mobile Millinery Museum*. Hat: $75-100.

A feather and floral wreath, on a rope of silk and velvet ribbon, for a bridesmaid, c.1920. *Mobile Millinery Museum*. $225.

Going-away hat with net cap foundation. Orange blossoms are sprinkled throughout the predominantly pink and green blossoms. *Wedding Collection, Mobile Millinery Museum*. $225.

An eye-popper from the 1940s. Curled ostrich tips are fashioned on a buckram crown. Center front, powder-blue bow of bridal satin. Label: An Original by Dajon, New York. *Wedding Collection*, *Mobile Millinery Museum*. $300-350.

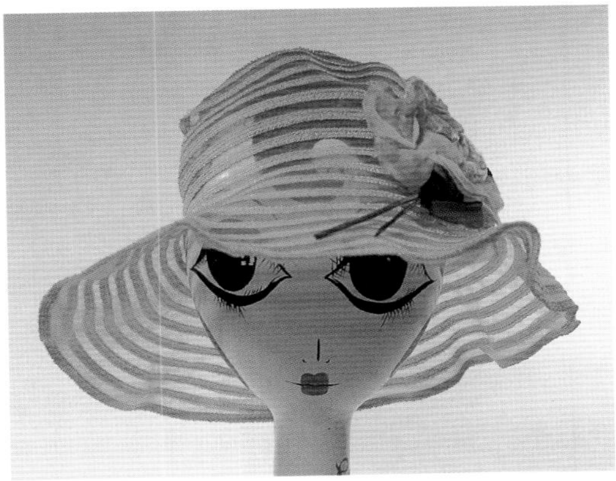

A 1920s banana-yellow bridal cloche. *Wedding Collection*, *Mobile Millinery Museum*. $200-250.

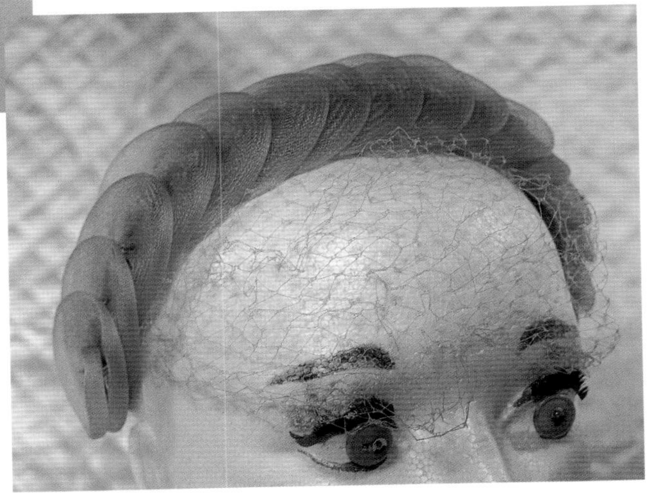

A bridesmaid's veiled hairband from the 1950s is constructed of horsehair medallions on a velvet-covered band. *Wedding Collection*, *Mobile Millinery Museum*. $60-80.

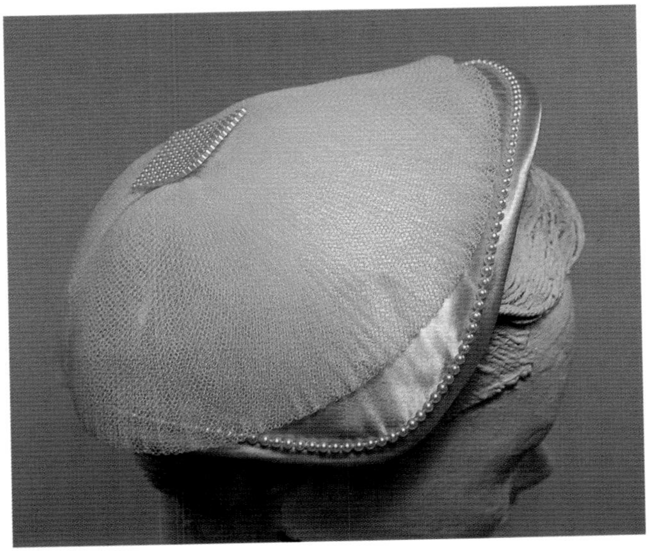

A champagne satin bridal cap, c.1950, is rimmed with pearls and crowned with accordion-pleated net. *Wedding Collection*, *Mobile Millinery Museum*. $75-125.

A 1940s ivory-satin Juliet cap encased in crystal-dotted veiling. *Mobile Millinery Museum*. $80-120.

This 1920s oyster-colored bridal cloche may have been fashioned from the same material as the original owner's wedding gown. The cap features a fashionable "angel's wing" bound with silver cord. *Wedding Collection, Mobile Millinery Museum*. $350-400.

Royal blue satin on a buckram frame forms a typical 1980s bridesmaid's hat. *Mobile Millinery Museum*. $60-80.

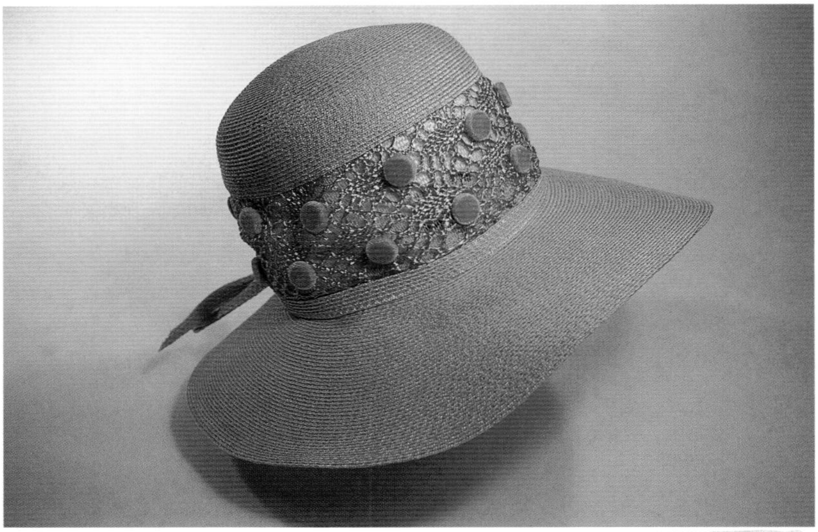

A picture hat of golden yellow straw with open-weave raffia is dressed up with velvet-covered buttons. Label: Henri Original. The hat was purchased in 1966 by bride Judy Saunders and worn as a going away hat. *Mobile Millinery Museum*. $160-180.

Henri Label.

A graceful peony rests on the brim of a horsehair Pamela, c.1928. *Mobile Millinery Museum*. $250-300.

This 1920s straw and chiffon wedding hat looks as new as the day it was made. *Private Collection*. NP **(No Price)**.

A chiffon scarf wraps the crown of a lavender horsehair Pamela, providing a background for a shaded-to-purple tea rose. *Mobile Millinery Museum*. $200-250.

Lavender straw wedding hat and leather handbag of Mrs. John Dakin, who was married August 4, 1914. *Courtesy of Kathryn Crowder*. Ensemble: $200-300.

Horsehair wedding Pamela, c.1973. Yellow stitching matches the ribbon band and lace trim. *Mobile Millinery Museum.* $120-150.

Interior view showing the paper label.

This 1960s wedding hat in delicate pink organza carries a hint of perfume. Shown with matching gloves and aurora crystal necklace. *Mobile Millinery Museum*. Hat: $250-300.

A 1970s bride, Denise Crockford, in a snow-white Pamela, made to match her lace-trimmed wedding gown.

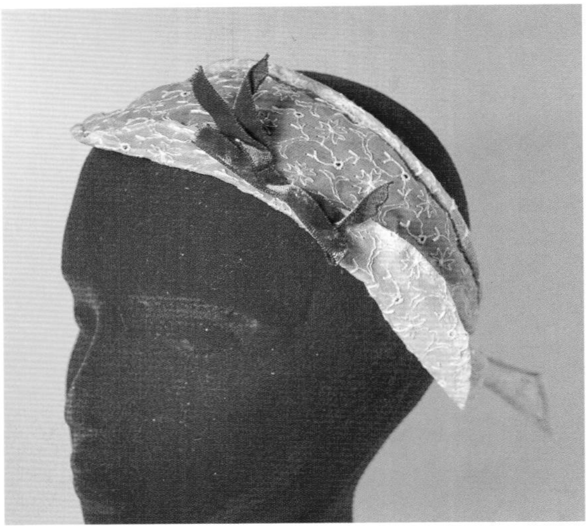

A 1930s open-crown slouch. This delicate bridesmaid's headpiece is fashioned on a wire frame. *Marg McGuire Collection, Mobile Millinery Museum*. $125-150. X

Mother-of-the-groom hat made by the owner of Star Millinery of Hamilton, Ontario, for the occasion of her son's wedding in the 1960s. *Mobile Millinery Museum*. $225.

A pyramid of ruffled tulle for a bride, c.1968. This style is reminiscent of the medieval hennin. *Mobile Millinery Museum*. $150-250.

Acknowledgements

This book would not have been possible without the assistance of many persons and organizations. Too numerous to mention, but highly appreciated, are all those individuals who donated hats, shared remembrances, or allowed me to photograph their treasures; those museums who offered assistance; and those in the media who made appeals and opened doors for the *Mobile Millinery Museum*.

I offer my heartfelt appreciation to all of my assistants over the years, starting with Linda Francis. Thanks especially to Suzanne Bourret, Patricia Boyle, Catherine DeLuca, Joy Drew, Marie Minaker, Kevin Neufeld, Ernie Paglietti, Corinne Shephard, the members of Quick Brown Fox, and, as always, my supportive mother, Iris, and my loving husband, Jim.

I am indebted to the Schiffer team for their expertise in transforming this project into a tangible reality. Finally, to those who find their own hat stories within these pages: Remember, I warned you that I don't keep secrets.

Bibliography

Academy of Millinery Design. *Professional Custom Millinery Course Book*. East Rutherford, New Jersey: Technical Home Study Schools Inc.

Augustyniak, J. Michael. *Collector's Encyclopedia of Barbie Doll Exclusives*. Paducah, Kentucky: Collector Books, 1997.

Baker, Lillian. *Baker's Encyclopedia of Hatpins and Hatpin Holders.* Atglen, Pennsylvania: Schiffer Publishing Ltd., 1998.

Ball, Joanne D. *Wedding Traditions, Here Comes The Bride*. Dubuque, Iowa: Antique Trader Books, 1997.

Bardey, Catherine. *Wearing Vintage*. New York, New York: Black Dog & Leventhal Publishers, 2002.

Biggar, Joan. *The Magic of Roses, Victorian Decorating and Lifestyle Magazine*. New York, New York: Goodman Media Group, July 2000.

Blum, Stella. *Victorian Fashions & Costumes From Harper's Bazar: 1867-1898.* New York, New York: Dover Publications, 1974.

Brome County Historical Society. *Yesterdays of Brome County.* Knowlton, Quebec: Brome County Historical Society, 1985.

Campione, Adele. *Women's Hats.* San Francisco, California: Chronicle Books, 1989.

Chambers, Captain Ernest J. *The Book of Montreal*. Montreal, Quebec: Book of Montreal Company, Publishers, 1903.

Chase, Deborah. *Terms of Adornment, the Ultimate Guide to Accessories*. New York, New York: HarperCollins Publishers, Inc., 1999.

Dubin, Tiffany. *Vintage Style*. New York, New York: HarperCollins Publishers Inc., 2000.

Eaton, Faith. *Dolls for the Princesses; the Story of France and Marianne.* London, United Kingdom: Royal Collection Enterprises Ltd., 2002.

Editors of *Victoria Magazine*. *The Romance of Hats*. New York, New York: Hearst Books, 1994.

Fraser, Sylvia. *A Woman's Place; Seventy Years in the Lives of Canadian Women.* Toronto, Ontario: Key Porter Books Ltd., 1997.

French, Viola. *How to Draw and Paint Fashions*. Tustin, California: Walter T. Foster Art Books #61.

Fukai, Akiko. *Fashion, a History from the 18th to the 20th Century*. Kōln, Germany: Taschen, 2002.

Godey's Ladies Book, January - April 1850. Philadelphia, Pennsylvania: 1850.

Hansen, Henny H. *Costume Cavalcade.* London, United Kingdom: Methuen and Co. Ltd., 1956.

Harris, Carol. *Miller's Collecting Fashion & Accessories.* London, United Kingdom: Octopus Publishing Group Ltd., 2000

Harris, Christina. *Good Sports, Victorian Decorating and Lifestyle Magazine*. New York, New York: Goodman Media Group, July 2000.

Hawkins, Joyce M. *The Oxford Paperback Dictionary*. Oxford, United Kingdom: Oxford University Press, 1988.

Langley, Susan. *Vintage Hats & Bonnets, 1770 - 1970*. Paducah, Kentucky: Collector Books, 1998.

Lansell, Avril. *History in Camera, Wedding Fashions 1860-1980.* Buckinghamshire, United Kingdom: Shire Publications Ltd.,1997.

Lipsett, Linda O. *To Love & To Cherish, Brides Remembered*. Lincolnwood, Illinois: The Quilt Digest Press, 1989.

Little, William. *The Oxford Universal Dictionary*. Oxford, United Kingdom: Clarendon Press, 1955.

MacLeod, Elizabeth. *Lucy Maud Montgomery; A Writer's Life*. Tonawanda, New York: Kids Can Press Ltd., 2001.

Malaher, Rosemary. *Dugald Costume Museum, the Story*. Dugald, Manitoba: Dugald Costume Museum, 1989.

McDowell, Colin. *Hats; Status, Style and Glamour*. London, United Kingdom: Thames and Hudson Ltd., 1992.

Milbank, Caroline R. *The Couture Accessory*. New York, New York: Harry N. Abrams, Inc., 2002.

Mulvey, Kate. *Decades of Beauty; The Changing Image of Women 1880s - 1990s.* New York, New York: Reed Consumer Books Ltd., 1998.

Palmer, Alexandra. *Couture & Commerce*. Vancouver, British Columbia: UBC Press, 2001.

Quilter, Harry. *What's What 1902*. London, United Kingdom: 1902.

Raymond, Louise. *Good Housekeeping's Book of Today's Etiquette*. New York, New York: Harper & Row Publishers, 1965.

Reilly, Maureen. *Women's Hats of the 20th Century*. Atglen, Pennsylvania: Schiffer Publishing Ltd., 1997.

Robinson, Ben. *Ballet Russe de Monte Carlo 1959-1960.* New York, New York: Playbill Magazine, 1959.

Rogers, Chester E. *A Brief History of the Pilgrims, A Continuous History*. Plymouth, Massachusetts: The Rogers Print, 1947.

Severn, Bill. *Here's Your Hat*. New York, New York: David McKay Company, Inc., 1963.

Shipstad, L. *Shipstads & Johnson Ice Follies of 1954, Official Program*. Minneapolis, Minnesota: Official Program Printing Inc., 1954.

Shipstad, L. *Shipstads & Johnson Ice Follies of 1962, Official Program*. Minneapolis, Minnesota: Official Program Printing Inc., 1962.

Shipstad, L. *Shipstads & Johnson Ice Follies of 1963, Official Program*. Minneapolis, Minnesota: Official Program Printing Inc., 1963.

Shipstad, L. *Shipstads & Johnson Ice Follies of 1969, Official Program*. San Francisco, California: Ice Follies, 1969.

Smith, Desire. *Hats, with Values*. Atglen, Pennsylvania: Schiffer Publishing Ltd., 1996.

Tober, Barbara. *The Bride, A Celebration*. New York, New York: Harry N. Abrams, Inc., 1984.

Tracanelli, Carine. *The Essential Guide to Embroidery*. London, United Kingdom: Murdock Books Ltd., 2002.

Trucco, Terry. *Style with Hattitude, Victoria Magazine*. New York, New York: Hearst Communications. June 2003.

Veksler, Bella. *Lace, the Poetry of Fashion.* Atglen, Pennsylvania: Schiffer Publishing Ltd., 1998.

Wilcox, R. Turner. *The Mode in Hats and Headdress*. New York, New York: Charles Scribner's Sons, 1959.

Original research includes, but is not limited to, conversations and interviews with the following persons: Arlene Allen, Kathleen Baird, Peter Banting, Bev Brown, Irene Burstyn, Peggy Claire, Valerie Denton, Frank Dorsen, Joy Drew, Edra Ferguson, Jenna Gibb, Iris Hillyer, Nancy Hooper, Jean Lemay, Lillian Lieberman, Laurabelle MacLean, Marie Minaker, Rita Minion, Kevin Neufeld, Ernie Paglietti, Eileen Punnett, Fran Richardson, Charlene Roberts, Catherine Sherlock, and Catherine Snellings.

Index

Adolpho, 15, 44, 52
Agnès, 86
Aigrette, 9, 51, 54, 59, 60, 69, 103, 107, 115, 128
Alsatian Bows, 9, 16, 44
American Endangered Species Act, 227
André, 82, 108, 111, 118, 126, 151, 152, 156, 158, 162, 170, 199, 202, 207, 227, 230
Ascot, 212-215
Audubon Plumage Law, 59

Balmain, 143, 231
Bandbox, 28
Banting, Aline, 40, 87, 92, 183-211
Barbara Ann Scott, 232, 233
Bavolet, 10, 19, 23, 30, 30, 31
Bellini, 209
Bes-Ben, 86
Bibi, 27, 28, 29
Biltmore, 71, 74, 86, 97
Bloomingdale's, 36, 150
Bonnet Board, 11, 24, 33, 71, 101
Bonwit Teller, 15, 101, 156, 169
Borsalino, 158
Boudoir Cap, 11, 26, 27, 212
Bourrelet, 11, 19
Bowler, 11, 13, 58, 66, 93, 94, 143, 149, 153, 155
Bowler, William, 11, 32
Brae Burn, 107, 202

Cadogan Bows, 11, 35, 36
Calash, 11, 22
Capeline, 12, 71, 77
Capote, 12, 22, 41, 51
Carnegie, Hattie, 193
Chanel, 77, 126
Chang, Simon, 174
Claire, Peggy, 106, 150, 198, 205
Claque, 17
Cloche, 12, 72, 77-86, 96, 117, 129, 138, 140, 145, 152, 163, 169, 219, 231, 236, 240, 251, 252
Cornet, 27

Desert Turban, 123
Daché, Lilly, 106, 126, 144, 145, 159
Darcel, 98, 160, 186, 188
Dior, 13, 126, 128, 143
Dobb's, 39, 62, 77
Doll, 13, 22, 86, 92, 105, 109, 112, 115, 248
Drawn Bonnet, 13, 22, 30, 31

Eaton's, 5, 17, 41, 67, 72, 77, 82, 98, 185, 190, 191, 194, 196, 197, 199, 203, 205, 207, 209, 212, 233
Eleanor-Mack, 95
Empress Eugenie, 13, 86
En marmotte, 24
Evelyn, 42, 93, 101, 123, 125
Evelyn Varon, 125
Eve-Marie, 200, 210
Extinct, 8, 55, 226, 228

Fanchon, 13, 32
Ferronieres, 22
Flirtation Ribbons, 32, 33
Flo-Raye, 7, 186, 194
Fly-away, 27
Ford, Elizabeth, 138, 194, 195, 204
Fox, Frederick, 167

Gainsborough, 14, 42, 59, 67
Garbo, 18, 86
Garnell, Helene, 86
Georgette, 90, 126, 128, 138, 157, 158, 163, 165, 172, 184
Glen Mawr, 34, 63
Gondolier, 15, 68
Gondolier Net, 35
Guy, Maria, 86

Hatpin, 12, 15, 25, 30, 36, 51, 59, 67, 77, 85, 91, 92, 97, 99, 105, 110, 113, 118, 122, 140, 171, 203, 227, 237, 250
Henri, 126, 185, 252
Henry Morgan & Co., 134
Hudson's Bay, 132, 192, 206, 226, 246
Hutterite, 51

Irene of Montreal, 127, 159
Irene of New York, 162

Jo-Anne, 120, 133, 146, 214
John-Frederics, 126

Klein's, 125
Knox Hats, 217

Lachance, Madame, 129
Lady's Home Journal, 104, 108, 126
Lappets, 13, 26, 28, 32, 35
Leopold Original, 136, 164
Lord and Taylor, 36, 125
Lily's Hat Shop, 107, 152, 163
Lilliput, 175
Lucas, Otto, 143, 245

Macy's, 36, 89
Marcel Wave, 59, 73
Margo's, 178
Mayfair Magazine, 77, 86, 179, 212
McConnell, Jack, 157
Mennonite, 12, 51
Mephisto Feathers, 16, 69
Merry Widow, 16, 72, 76
Milkmaid, 16, 49
Mourning, 16, 20, 35, 72, 86
Mr. Arnold Jr., 192
Mr. Charles, 161
Mr. Fredericks, 155, 160, 162, 211
Mr. John Jr., 144, 149, 161, 164, 196
M'Sieu Léon, 132, 143, 148, 163, 208, 231

Northridge, Laddie, 115

Olive, Frank, 152, 156, 169, 171
Opera Hood, 29
Otto Lucas, 43

Palmer, 36, 74, 149, 150
Patou, 86
Paulette, 65
Paulvin, Norman, 111
Pennington, Gwenn, 151
Piko, 83, 96, 109, 163, 207
Plouffe, Maggie, 136, 153, 209, 210
Poke, 18, 23, 24, 27, 32, 86
Pompadour, 18, 55, 56, 57, 73
Pork pie, 18, 132
Postillion, 18, 144, 156, 162
Princess Anne, 145
Princess Diana, 13, 175, 246

Quaker bonnet, 51
Queen Anne, 65
Queen Elizabeth, 150, 167
Queen Mary, 55
Queen Mother, 145, 172
Queen Victoria, 51

Raphael-Mack, 184, 185, 196, 203, 208
Reboux, Caroline, 77, 179
Robichaud, Michel, 201

Saks, 228
Scarlet O'Hara, 49, 123
Schiaparelli, 5, 86, 126, 128, 131, 138, 150, 183, 190, 192, 206, 210, 216, 217, 249
Simpson's, 5, 63, 77, 82, 109, 114, 134, 137, 140, 158, 186, 192, 193, 204, 211, 212, 220, 248
Simpson's, Sears, 173, 191, 193
Skimmer, 48, 49, 57, 65
Slouch, 18, 86, 89-91, 93, 96, 97, 100, 102, 254
Snood, 10, 13, 18, 101, 104
Spoon bonnet, 27, 32, 33
Stetson, 18, 86, 105, 214, 231
Straw Cloth, 24, 33, 38, 47, 64, 81, 85, 102, 107, 165, 219
Studio of American Design, 99
Suffragette, 51
Sylvia, 176, 246

Tall Round, 64, 70, 74
Tambourine, 19, 143, 144, 225
Tam o-shanter, 19, 38
The Right House, 186, 209, 216
Trotteau, 19, 34, 35
Tyrolean, 19, 36, 86, 103

Underwood, Patricia, 183

Variety Hat Co., 95, 125, 126, 161
Veiling, 12, 18, 24, 28, 29, 34, 35, 37, 38, 40, 41, 44-46, 58, 66, 68, 69, 72, 85-95, 100, 102, 103, 105, 106, 108-115, 118, 119, 122, 126, 129, 131-133, 137, 138, 140, 142-144, 154, 160, 163-164, 169, 178, 184, 189-192, 197, 199-200, 202, 204-206, 214, 219, 224-246, 248-252
Vera Anne Millinery, 158
Victoria Magazine, 182
Vogue, 129, 142, 143
Voilette, 20, 34, 94, 101, 151

Warde, Philip, 7, 15, 51, 85, 145, 172, 214, 218, 225, 229, 234, 235-244
Wimbledon Hats, 107
Woodhouse, Sohia, 24